THE LIMERICK

THE LIMERICK

1700 EXAMPLES, WITH NOTES
VARIANTS AND INDEX

EDITED BY
G. LEGMAN

BELL PUBLISHING COMPANY · NEW YORK

Copyright © MCMLXIV, MCMLXIX by G. Legman
Library of Congress Catalog Card Number: 74-78758
All rights reserved.
This edition is published by Bell Publishing Company,
by arrangement with Brandywine Press.
Manufactured in the United States of America
ISBN: 0-517-139111
z y x w

CONTENTS

	PAGE
INTRODUCTION	vii
I LITTLE ROMANCES	1
II ORGANS	27
III STRANGE INTERCOURSE	55
IV ORAL IRREGULARITY	78
V BUGGERY	92
VI ABUSES OF THE CLERGY	109
VII ZOOPHILY	118
VIII EXCREMENT	137
IX GOURMANDS	157
X VIRGINITY	165
XI MOTHERHOOD	187
XII PROSTITUTION	203
XIII DISEASES	220
XIV LOSSES	232
XV SEX SUBSTITUTES	254
XVI ASSORTED ECCENTRICITIES	281
XVII WEAK SISTERS	323
XVIII CHAMBER OF HORRORS	329
XIX ADDENDA	334
BIBLIOGRAPHY	359
NOTES & VARIANTS	369
INDEX OF RHYMES	467
INDEX OF NAMES	479

INTRODUCTION
TO THE LIMERICK

KNOWN to everyone, but its paternity admitted by very few, the bawdy limerick has held its place now, for exactly a century, as the chosen vehicle of cultivated, if unrepressed, sexual humor in the English language. As almost nothing that has been written about the limerick can be taken seriously — which is perhaps only fitting — a few words may not be out of place here, as to its real history, it origins, and its century of triumph, by way of celebrating the centenary of that triumph.

The limerick is, and was originally, an indecent verse-form. The "clean" sort of limerick is an obviously palliation, its content insipid, it rhyming artificially ingenious, its whole pervaded with a frustrated nonsense that vents itself typically in explosive and aggressive violence. There are, certainly, aggressive bawdy limericks too, but they are not in the majority. Except as the maidenly delight and silly delectation of a few elderly gentlemen, such as the late Langford Reed, and several still living who might as well remain nameless, the clean limerick has never been of the slightest real interest to anyone, since the end of its brief fad in the 1860's. Nor has this fad ever been successfully revived by the periodic advertising contests, exciting amateur versifiers to hack together clean limericks by the tens of thousands. It should be observed in this connection, and despite the continuous devaluation of any monetary sum over the sixty years past, that were a prize to be offered here of £3 a week *for life,* as has been given for a limerick last line, in a British cigarette contest in 1907, the present writer could seriously demand and safely expect that thousands of unpoetic amateurs in Great Britain and the United States would slap themselves silly for the next six months or two years, trying to compose seven-line stanzas in spondaic hexameter — alternating with amphibrachs and amphimacers, if I felt like being cruel — all seven lines to rhyme solely with the words *silver, swollen, spoilt,* and *sylph* (none of which have rhymes). Needless to say, the winning entry and all seventeen thousand losing entries would immediately and forever be forgotten, except by their authors, the moment the winner would be announced. Viable folk-poetry, and folk-poetic forms, cannot be created by any such cash-on-the barrelhead methods.

The original limerick fad was accidentally created by the reprinting in London, in 1863, of Edward Lear's *Book of Nonsense,* a volume of very tepidly humorous limericks, illustrated by the author, that had first appeared nearly twenty years before, in 1846, without any extraordinary success. Inspired by the reprint however, *Punch,* the humorous English magazine, seized upon the form. The same was done in America by a minor writer and sedulous-ape, Charles Godfrey Leland, who later also embarrassingly imitated Lewis Carroll's *Alice in Wonderland* — illustrations, typography and all — in *Johnnykin and the Goblins* (1877). Leland's anonymous imitation of Lear was called *Ye Book of Copperheads,* and was published by Leypoldt in Philadelphia in 1863. It is entirely satirical, all its limericks being directed against the Northern "copperhead" defeatists, and the anti-Lincoln agitations during the Civil War. In the same year there had also appeared a set of "Nursery Rhymes for the Army," in Wilkes' *Spirit of the Times,* in New York; twenty-three limericks signed L.L.D., initials that may possibly represent Leland's name with the vowels omitted. A British imitation of Lear, which had perhaps sparked Leland's, was *Ye Book of Sense* (Torquay & London, 1863).

Almost immediately after, a much more widely circulated

INTRODUCTION ix

imitation appeared, this time acknowledging Lear's inspiration in the title, *The New Book of Nonsense*, and issued in Philadelphia in 1864 to be sold for the profit of the Sanitary Commission, the Red Cross of the Civil War. With that, the limerick fad was launched in America, though always under the name of "nonsense rhymes" or "nursery rhymes" until the 1880's, when, for the first time, the name *limerick* seems to have been applied to the form. The name is of unknown origin, having been appropriated from that of the town in Ireland for reasons never really explained, possibly from a now-forgotten chorus, "Won't you come up to Limerick?"

The limerick metre was, in fact, very commonly used in songs in the Irish language, usually dedicated to liquor, love, or patriotism throughout the eighteenth century, as any collection of these will show. See, for numerous examples, Kathleen Hoagland's *1000 Years of Irish Poetry*. The form also appears in English in the Irish songs of Thomas Moore in the early nineteenth century, such as "The Time I've Lost in Wooing", "A Lottery," and "The Young May Moon" (Quiller-Couch's *Oxford Book of English Verse*, No. 582), this last clearly inspired by Herrick's exquisite "The Night-piece: To Julia," two centuries before, as will be seen. The Irish limericks are, in any case, very late in the history of the metrical form.

Other imitations came thick and fast after the American Sanitary Commission volume of 1864: *Ye Book of Bubbles* (which took even the "Ye" of its title from Leland), *Inklings for Thinklings*, and at least one other proposed *Nonsense Book* to be illustrated by the children's artist, Susan Hale. The fatuousness into which the form immediately fell, without the excitements of the Civil War to get its teeth into, is pathetically betrayed in a letter from Miss Hale, as to her final volume of the sort, remarking: "Mrs. Billy Weld ... provides, collects and invents the rhymes, and I draw the pictures right off into a nice long-shaped blank book. I have got 22 done, and they go off very fast, much quicker than the Nursery Rhymes for the fair, for the rhymes are only fool stuff ..."

Punch was similarly running "fool stuff" in the 1860's, and might have gone on forever except that the fad of the clean limerick was suddenly brought to an end — owing to a disconcerting number of bawdy and sacrilegious limericks being submitted anonymously, among the entries to *Punch*'s first big geographical-limerick contest. According to a tradition, the leaders of this anti-fad, and authors of all the best early dirty limericks, which immediately began to circulate orally, of course, were a group of college wits and clubmen, notably the poet Swinburne; an army officer, Capt. Edward Sellon, and the war-correspondent, George Augustus Sala, all three of whom are known to have written much other sub-rosa poetry and erotic prose, mostly flagellational. *Punch* closed down its geographical contest with a slam, and the clean-limerick fad fell dead. It had lasted hardly five years, a great deal longer than most fads. Since that time, the clean limerick has lived on fitfully only as the last resource of newspaper poets (especially about the 1900's) hard-up for witty fillers, as a useful framework for humorous artists to hang their drawings on, and, as aforesaid, as advertising-contest pap from time to time. As for the public at large — that is to say, the authentic folklore-transmitting group — the only real popularity of the limerick during the entire century of its modern existence, since the end of the Civil War, has been wholly and solely in the bawdy form.

A few assessments other than my own might perhaps not be out of place here. Langford Reed, who led with his chin in writing to all the literary panjandrums of the 1920's asking what they thought of his project of publishing a thoroughly expurgated *Complete Limerick Book* (London, 1924), was almost crushed under a chorus of plain statements like these: From Arnold Bennett: "In reply to your letter, all I have to say about Limericks is that the best ones are entirely unprintable." (The one about the Young Plumber of Leigh, No. 60 in the present collection, was also nominated by Bennett as "The best limerick of all.") From George Bernard Shaw: "There are several personal limericks by D. G. Rossetti, and some by Swinburne, which became known in their generation, but like the large number of geographical limericks which preceded them they are mostly unfit for publication. They must be left for oral tradition..." Arthur Wimperis used fewer words to say a great deal more: "The only limericks in my experience of any literary merit are distinctly Rabelaisian. Beside these, the more polite and printable examples fade away into the dim haze of mediocrity."

On the other side of the Atlantic, the consensus of opinion has been the same. Don Marquis is reported to have divided limericks into three kinds (sometimes in rising order of price): "Limericks to be told when ladies are present; limericks to be told when ladies are absent but clergymen are present — and LIMERICKS." Prof. Morris Bishop, the unquestionable modern master in the clean limerick line, has put the essence of his art into verse, as half — and not really the better half — of his "The Sonnet and the Limerick":

> The limerick is furtive and mean;
> You must keep her in close quarantine,
> Or she sneaks to the slums
> And promptly becomes
> Disorderly, drunk and obscene.

Finally, in William S. Baring-Gould's *The Lure of the Limerick* (New York: Clarkson N. Potter, Inc., 1967), the first publicly issued collection to combine both clean and bawdy examples, a mildly scatological limerick on tea-&-pee sent in to the Salada Tea contest in recent years is cited, p. 186 — it did not win! — with the observation: "Mike Nichols, once asked to judge a limerick contest, is reported to have said: 'It was easy. We just threw out the dirty limericks and gave the prize to the one that was left'."

Before continuing with the further history of the limerick which looks as though it will continue for quite a while yet, what about its pre-history? It has been tiresomely repeated, and is even partly true, that Lear took the form of his "nonsense rhymes" from several illustrated children's books of the early 1820's: *Anecdotes and Adventures of Fifteen Gentlemen*, attributed to one R. S. Sharpe, and *The History of Sixteen Wonderful Old Women* of a competing publisher. (There was also a *Fifteen Young Ladies* collection too.) Actually, these 1820's limericks are far better than Lear's, and the drawings — probably by Robert Cruikshank — incomparably better. The specific rhyme known to have inspired Lear is the following, reproduced with its amusing illustration in Iona & Peter Opie's *Oxford Dictionary of Nursery Rhymes*, at "Tobago:"

> There was a sick man of Tobago
> Liv'd long on rice-gruel and sago;
>   But at last, to his bliss,
>   The physician said this —
> "To a roast leg of mutton you may go."

The illustration shows him attacking the leg of mutton, which looks more like a ham, with a carving-fork and knife and a blissful expression. This poor chap evidently had gout, in the bad old days before Allo-purinol came to cut its suffering and its cruelly restricted diet.

Two other limericks from Sharpe's *Fifteen Gentlemen*, with their spirited illustrations, are reproduced in Philip James' & C. G. Holme's *Children's Books of Yesterday* (London: The Studio, 1933). These colored books of the 1820's, which appeared when Lear was eight or ten years old, and whose jolly illustrations are so much better than the overrated whimsy of his own feeble scratchings, are generally in the pure limerick form of the example cited above. Occasionally, as in one on a young man of St. Kitts, the last line repeats and commiserates with the hero of the opening line: "Alas! poor young man of St. Kitts." This repeated or unrhyming line is actually one of the oldest forms of the limerick stanza, and was already several centuries out of date by the 1820's.

Lear's imitation of this form, as is well known, invariably drops back, from the simple but dramatic resolution of the action in the final line, to the namby-pamby repetition of the first line — very weak, even for nonsense verse — made to do double duty as the last line as well, possibly with some tremendously unimportant change in the adjective rung in by way of climax. Lear also curiously betrayed, in many of his limericks, an unsurmountable private fear of public disgrace (the only passions of his life being, unfortunately, for cats and handsome Greek boys), in the continuous importation into his couplets of the Mrs. Grundy of public opinion, in the horrendous and ever-present *They:* "When they said, 'Why is that?' he fell in his hat, That frightened old man of Corfu," and so on. The whole thing, and most particularly the invariable echoic last line, represents a clear failure of nerve, an inability to take the obvious and final jump, and to resolve even the stated nursery situation in some satisfactory way. This is the neurotic problem at the root of all "nonsense," and is — as much with Lewis Carroll as with Lear — the secret or Sense of Nonsense.

II

THE PRE-HISTORY of the limerick is remarkably easy to trace. It is necessary only to recognize, as modern developments not really essential to the limerick pattern, the anapestic form or foot (two short syllables and a long) in which it has become familiar, as well as the falsely stressed "There *was* . . ." in the opening line, which is two centuries older than Lear in any case. The earliest limericks will be found in nursery rhymes, or something very much like them, as far back as the fourteenth century. To avoid controversy, I do not insist that "Sumer is i-cumen in" (about 1300), the oldest popular song in the English language, is in the limerick form, but a rather good case can be made for its stanzaic portion at least, and the possibility ought not be overlooked. In modernized spelling:

> Ewè bleateth after lamb,
> Low'th after calvè coo;
> Bullock starteth,
> Buckè farteth —
> Merry sing cuck*oo*!

With all that has been written about "Sumer is i-cumen in"— and it has taken almost a library of learned annotation to vindicate even the simple barnyard humor of the buck's crepitation at the highest note and melodic climax of the song — no suggestion has ever yet been made as to just what its prosodic form may be; and where, and when, and whether any verses similar to it may be found, in any language.

In their excellent manual of the poet's craft, *The Making of Verse* (1934) p. 102, Robert Swann and Frank Sidgwick have discovered another early animal limerick (and that it is a limerick they clearly state) in the British Museum's Harleian Manuscript 7322, dating from the fourteenth century:

> The lion is wondirliche strong,
> & ful of wiles of wo;
> & wether he pleye
> other take his preye
> he can not do bot slo (*slay*).

This is followed in the manuscript by similar warning rhymes, as to dragons and bears, but not in the limerick metre. A century and a half then pass without any record of this engaging form, except perhaps in the "Poulter's measure" or "short metre" of Elizabethan hymnology, to be discussed below. The limerick form itself, still partly in iambic metre, reappears suddenly in the late sixteenth century, in the mad-songs of the half-naked wandering beggars, turned out to mump their livelihood after 1536, at the dissolution of the religious almonries under Henry VIII. Where it had lain in the meanwhile, and whether the madmen learned it from the musician-monks, or the monks from the madmen, there is now no way of knowing.

The mad "Bedlams," as they were called, were still wandering and singing two hundred years later, in both England and Ireland, as recorded by the Irish poet and physician, Oliver Goldsmith (who is also believed to have been the first editor of the *Mother Goose* rhymes in English), in his play *The Good Natur'd Man* in 1768, III.ii.4–9, where Honeywood asks his servant for his brown and silver suit of clothes, only to be told: "That, your honour gave away to the begging gentleman that makes verses, because it was as good as new." The greatest of the mumpers' songs is "Mad Tom," or "Tom o' Bedlam," first recorded in Giles Earle's manuscript music-book about 1615, though probably decades old by then, and in the limerick metre throughout, to a tune as haunting as the words:

>From the hagg & hungry Goblin,
>That into raggs would rend yee,
>   & the spirit that stand's
>   by the naked man,
>in the booke of moones defend yee...

>Of thirty bare years have I
>twice twenty bin enragèd,
>   & of forty bin
>   three tymes fifteene
>in durance soundlie cagèd,

> On the lordlie loftes of Bedlam
> with stubble softe & dainty,
>   brave braceletts strong,
>   sweet whips ding dong
> with wholsome hunger plenty...

That is nonsense too, but of a different kind than Lear's. This superb poem of "Tom o' Bedlam," of which hardly more than the beginning is given above, has been made the subject of an entire quarto monograph, in the impeccable scholarship of Jack Lindsay, under the title *Loving Mad Tom*, published at the author's own Fanfrolico Press in 1927 (which is getting to be the only way to do things anymore), and giving samples of the endless variants rung, in the same metre, throughout the seventeenth century, in praise of tobacco, in dispraise of women, in mockery of the Puritans, and for the benefit of other "wandering professions" besides that of madman: tinkers, blind beggars, jovial peddlers, oakermen, and simple drunkards — a whole anthology of superlative balladry, all in the limerick metre of "Tom o' Bedlam."

Later, in its turn, "Tom o' Bedlam" also inspired the one greatest mad-song of the English language, "Halloo my fancy," written in part (at the age of eighteen) by Col. William Cleland, uncle of the author of *Fanny Hill*. "Halloo my fancy" is given complete, along with "Tom o' Bedlam," in Charles Williams' & Lord David Cecil's *New Book of English Verse* (1935) pp. 419–24 and 249–51, where both will well repay the trouble of looking them up. The original text of "Halloo my fancy" is in the *Percy Folio Manuscript*, about 1620 (edited by Hales & Furnivall, 1868); and, as revised by Cleland, at the end of the first part of James Watson's *Choice Collection of Comic and Serious Scots Poems* (Edinburgh, 1706–11, repr. Glasgow 1869. A humorous imitation, called "The Shiftless Student," has not formerly been noted: it appears in Sir John Mennis' & Dr. James Smith's *Wit and Drollery*, 1661, p. 223–26.)

INTRODUCTION xvii

The one subject other than madness and rascalry for which the limerick metre was at first found utterly fitting was the praise of the much-censured tobacco, as first in the moralizing "A Religious Use of taking Tobacco," or "The Indian Weed," usually but erroneously attributed to Thomas Jenner or to George Wither, whose attack on smoking in *Abuses Stript and Whipt* (1613) seems — but only seems — to be recollected in its opening line:

> The Indian weed, witherèd quite,
> Green at morn, cut down at night,
> Shows thy decay,
> All flesh is hay:
> Thus think, then drink Tobacco.

(The full text will be found in Quiller-Couch's *Golden Pomp*, 1896, and his *Oxford Book of English Verse*, 1900, No. 390-i; also in William S. Braithwaite's very valuable *Book of Elizabethan Verse*, 1908, No. 522, noting its real author. It is printed exactly from MS. 877, Trinity College, Dublin, in Norman Ault's *Elizabethan Lyrics*, 2nd ed. 1928, pp. 53, 506.) The real author of this four-stanza moralization in the limerick metre was Robert Wisdome, a Protestant divine who died in 1568, having been a fugitive in Germany during the reign of Bloody Mary. "The Indian Weed" was first printed without author's name as the last of the "thirtie and one spirituall emblems" in Thomas Jenner's *The Soules Solace* (1626) f. G3v, and was much revised by a Scottish dissenting minister, Ralph Erskine over a century later — he died in 1752 — as "Tobacco Spiritualised," beginning: "Tobacco is an Indian weed," the form still sung today.

Inspired by Wisdome's "Indian Weed," or perhaps its own folk source, is a solitary surviving limerick stanza, also in the iambic foot, "O Metaphysical Tobacco," in *A Book of Madrigales for Viols and Voices* (1606):

> O metaphysical Tobacco,
> Fetched as far as from Morocco,
> Thy searching fume
> Exhales the rheum,
> O metaphysical Tobacco.

(Reprinted by Dr. Edmund H. Fellowes, *English Madrigal Verse*, 1920, p. 81, and first recognized as a limerick [by Richard Linn Edsall] in the *Atlantic Monthly*, Boston, 1924, vol. 134: p. 135.)

Still in transition toward the anapestic foot — here in the couplet only — and evidently drawing from "Tom o' Bedlam" in its echoic chorus, the limerick form appears in print full-fledged in Barten Holyday's university comedy, *Technogamia, or The Marriages of the Arts* (1618) II. iii, but again either the first line does not rhyme, or the last is still a repeat:

> Tobacco's a Musician
> And in a Pipe delighteth:
> It descends in a Close
> Through the Organ of the nose
> With a Rellish that inviteth.
>
> *This makes me sing, So ho, hó —*
> *So ho hó, boyes!*
> *Ho boyes, sound I loudly:*
> *Earth ne're did breed*
> *Such a Joviall weed*
> *Whereof to boast so proudly.*

In the same play, Act III, scene v, Holyday uses the limerick form in a love-song, humorously of course, as the impish but false "beginna-a" rhyme shows:

> Come kisse, come kisse, my Corinna
> And still that sport wee'l beginn-a

INTRODUCTION

    That our soules so may meet
    In our lippes, while they greet,
  Come kisse, come kisse, my Corinna.

A love-song in limerick — the first, I believe — had already been attempted at least a decade before, in Robert Jones' *The Muses Gardin for Delights, or The Fift Booke of Ayres* (1610; the modern reprint, Oxford, 1901, is expurgated of song No. 13, "As I lay lately in a dreame"). This is the first song in the book, the simple and naïve "Love is a pretty frenzy":

  Love is a pretty pedlar
Whose pack is fraught with sorrows,
    With doubts and fears
    With sighs and tears,
Some joys — but those he borrows.

Even the use of the limerick as a chorus in drinking-songs was seen in England about the 1610's, antedating by almost a century the presumed use of such choruses in Limerick, Ireland. The round-song, "Now that the Spring hath filled our veins," by William Browne (*fl.* 1614), a university poet of the school of Spenser and Ben Jonson, not only has the rhyming couplet actually marked in stanza 2, "Sing we a song with merry glee," but ends in a limerick stanza — with anapestic couplet and conclusion — sung in chorus by "All." (Printed in William S. Braithwaite's *Book of Elizabethan Verse*, 1908, No. 36.) Note that the first line still does not rhyme:

  Shear sheep that have them, cry we still,
    But see that nó man 'scape
    To drink of the sherry,
    That makes us so merry,
  And plump as the lusty grape.

The necessary rhyming word at the end of the opening line of the true limerick, calling forth all the matching rhymes, was also achieved by the 1610's, as in Holyday's "Corinna" song, and later became standard at the popular or folk level of the broadside ballads. For example, in "The Two Yorkshire Lovers, A Pleasant Northerne Song, To the tune of *Willy*" (before 1633; in *Roxburghe Ballads*, ed. William Chappell, 1873, II. 228; the tune being identical with that of "Tom o' Bedlam"):

> Of nuts Ile give thee plenty
> And red-side apples twenty:
>   My butter Ile lease
>   To make thee summer cheese,
> And creame to make egge-pies dainty.

Despite the charm and simplicity of the images and rhymes, the difficulty of being altogether serious in so rollicking a rhythm was clear almost from its beginning. Also, always in the background, was the sinister echo, the warning clack-dish or bell, of the original madmen and rascals whose song it was. Perhaps this explains why, as Jack Lindsay has wondered (*Loving Mad Tom*, page 67), "the possibilities of this insinuating stanza as a wooing poem were not much followed up."

One last ghost to lay, or snake to scotch, before closing this consideration of the early proto-limericks of the Elizabethan age: Robert Swann and Frank Sidgwick, in *The Making of Verse* (1934) p. 101, first drew attention to the formal if somewhat tenuous relation between the limerick form and the "short metre" or "Poulter's measure" of Elizabethan hymnology. This is composed of two long lines, alternating twelve and fourteen syllables, and rhyming with each other in couplet form. It is usually divided, by pauses, into four lines of six, six, eight, and six syllables respectively, as in Shakespeare's *A Midsummer Night's Dream*, III.i.22, where Quince wants the Prologue to be "written in eight and six." There is no inner rhyme in the eight-syllable line, as would be necessary to make it into a short couplet, and thus approach the limerick form in a recognizable

INTRODUCTION   xxi

way. Swann & Sidgwick note several Elizabethan poets who used this "short metre," p. 63, and give a stanza of this kind attributed to Queen Elizabeth:

> The Daughter of debate
> That eke discord doth sow,
> Shall reap no gain where former rule
> Hath taught still peace to grow.

Despite the long third line, of eight syllables, this is obviously not a limerick. Very curiously, however, a variant form of this stanza is quoted in Baring-Gould's *The Lure of the Limerick* (1967) p. 15–16, on the authority of the modern poet Leonard Bacon, who maintains that Queen Elizabeth has here closely approached the limerick form "by introducing the interior rhyme in the fourteen-syllable line." Unfortunately, there is something very wrong with Queen Elizabeth's poem, as Mr. Bacon gives it. An interior rhyme has indeed been introduced, with numerous other changes, the second and third lines above now reading as follows:

> Who discord aye doth sow,
> Hath reaped no gain
> Where former *reign* ...

What is most singular, perhaps, about this quotation, is that only and precisely this sixth stanza (of eight) is given, in changed form, that is quoted in its original form by Swann & Sidgwick. Nor is even the pretense made, concerning this brief poem by Queen Elizabeth, "The Doubt" (given complete in William S. Braithwaite's *Book of Elizabethan Verse*, London, 1908, preceding No. 1), that any of the *other* seven stanzas, all in the same "short metre," contain any internal rhyme at all! One wonders about the source of Mr. Bacon's text.

There is no authority whatever for this unavowed change of the non-rhyming "rule" to the rhyming *reign*, on which the whole case for this, as a limerick, rests. It will be observed that the second line has also been grossly modernized: "That" is changed to *Who*; also "eke" to *aye*, and "Shall" to *Hath* (changing the tense of the poem entirely). Worst of all, the changed position of the word "*dis*cord" seems intended to give it the modern pronunciation, with the accent on the first syllable, though it was pronounced by the Elizabethans — as the original text, above, makes clear — with the accent always on the last, as "dis*cord*." Verdict: the so-called limerick of Queen Elizabeth must be dismissed as a clumsy modern fake, by hand or hands unknown. In the same way, an accidental — or perhaps purposeful — inner rhyme in a similar Latin hymn attributed to St. Thomas Aquinas (*Thanksgiving after Mass*) has led eager searchers, of the type who write of their discoveries to the Sunday papers, to credit the Italian monk, Aquinas, with the creation of the English limerick. Again, to say the least, an error. (On this presumed discovery see the review by the English limerick-poet, Father Ronald Knox, in *English Life*, February 1925, of Langford's Reed's *The Complete Limerick Book*. Also *New York Times*, August 1st, 1944, page 14/7.)

III

FORMAL poets have never scorned the possibilities of the madmen's song and its limerick metre. On this pattern, Edgar, in Shakespeare's *King Lear*, III.iv.120, disguised as the mad beggar, "poore Tom," chants his spell to the rhythm of "Tom o' Bedlam," and here there is no mistake about the couplet:

> Swithold footed thrice the old,
> He met the night mare and her nine fold,
>   Bid her alight
>   And her troth plight,
> And aroint thee, witch, aroint thee!

INTRODUCTION   xxiii

At least three other songs by Shakespeare are also in the limerick form: Iago's drinking-song in *Othello*, II.iii.70, which he states he "learned... in England, where indeed they are most potent in potting," beginning: "And let me the cannakin clinke, clinke;" and Ophelia's touching mad-song in *Hamlet*, IV.v.190, "And will he not come again?" especially the second stanza, "His beard was white as snow." Also first seen in Shakespeare is the modern rising anapestic metre of the limerick, replacing the older iambics, as in Stephano's sea-song in *The Tempest* (MS. 1612) II.ii.52:

> For she had a tongue with a tang,
>   Would cry to a sailor, Goe hang!
> She lov'd not the savour of Tar nor of Pitch
> Yet a Tailor might scratch her where ere she did itch:
>   Then to Sea, Boyes, and let her goe hang!

This innovation of a double-length couplet was never followed up, and is seldom used in modern limericks, Shakespeare himself remarking: "This is a scurvy tune too..."

As will be observed, two of Shakespeare's songs in the limerick form are mad-songs, and two are drinking-songs; implying that he felt the form was too "popular" or too simple to be used seriously. Yet the possibilities of the same metre, for "pure" or lyric poetry, were brilliantly explored by the rival school of Ben Jonson, first in Jonson's own "Wheel of Fortune" song, "The Faery beame uppon you," in his *Masque of The Gypsies Metamorphos'd* (MS. 1621; *Works*, ed. Herford & Simpson, 1941, VII. 573–5, lines 262–306).

There is a clear connection between Jonson's *Masque of The Gypsies Metamorphos'd* and Barten Holyday's play *Technogamia*, three years before. The limerick song in Holyday's play, in praise of tobacco, "Tobacco's a Musician," quoted above, had offended tobacco-hating King James when the play was given before him late in August 1621. (See John Nichols, *Progresses... of King James I*, 1828, vol. IV (IIIb): p. 714; and Anthony à Wood, *Athenae Oxonienses*, 1692, II. 170.) At the third presentation of Jonson's masque before James, early in September of the same year at Windsor, lines were specially added by Jonson at the end of the "Divells Arse-a-Peake" song (*causâ modestiae*, "Cock-Lorell song") and elsewhere, obviously intended to contradict Holyday's encomium, and declaring tobacco to be the Devil's clyster-pipe and its odor his farting. (*Works*, ed. 1941, VII. 603, 610–11; lines 1126–37 and 1349–60.) Here is the opening of Jonson's "Wheel of Fortune" song, in the "Tom o' Bedlam" metre already used by Holyday, but with an extra inner rhyme in the couplet:

> The faery beame uppon you,
> The starres to glister on you,
>   A Moone of light
>   In the Noone of night
> Till the firedrake hath ore'gone you.

Unquestionably through Jonson, whose protégé he was, great ugly Robert Herrick was led to attempt a love-song in the limerick stanza, the exquisite "Night-piece: To Julia," first published in his *Hesperides* in 1648, though undoubtedly written long before. That the very images here are improved from Jonson's gypsy "Wheel of Fortune," just quoted, is remarked upon by Jack Lindsay (*Loving Mad Tom*, 1927, p. 66), and in Norman Ault's *Seventeenth Century Lyrics* (1928) p. 483. Herrick's "Night-piece" begins superbly:

> Her eyes the Glow-worme lend thee,
> The Shooting starres attend thee,
>   And the Elves alsó
>   Whose little eyes glow
> Like the sparks of fire, befriend thee.

INTRODUCTION

No *Will-o'-th'-Wispe* mis-light thee,
Nor Snake, or Slow-worme bite thee:
  But on, on thy way
  Not making a stay,
Since Ghost there's none to affright thee.

The rest is not given here, to leave the pleasure and the discovery of this jewel, to whoever does not know it, who will look it up. (*Oxford Book of English Verse*, No. 262; and the original text in Herrick's *Poetical Works*, ed. F. W. Moorman, Oxford, 1915, p. 217.) It should be mentioned that the relation of both Jonson's "Wheel of Fortune" and Herrick's "Night-piece" to "Tom o' Bedlam" was first noted by Miss Ethel Seaton in the *London Mercury* (1923) VIII. 79, to which journal is owed all the modern interest in Mad Tom's song, already in danger of being forgotten again, despite its rediscovery and reprinting, almost complete, at the article "Tom o' Bedlams," in Isaac D'Israeli's *Curiosities of Literature* (ed. 1849, II. 343–9).

Very typical and personal in Herrick's poetry is his sado-masochistic alternation of character. On the one hand are his sweetly beautiful food-&-breast-oriented love songs, not forgetting, however, the foot-&-underwear fetichism of the masochist ("Shew me thy feet", "When as in silks my Julia goes," and "The Description of a Woman," ed. Moorman, p. 404–6), the concentration on the woman's body odors ("Love perfumes all parts" and "Upon Julia's unlacing her self"), the frank references to cunnilinctus as a submissive act ("Pardon my trespasse, Sylvia," and "Blisse, last night drunk"), and even to bondage and flagellation ("Bind me but to thee with thine haire" and "Sufferance;" also throughout his religious *Noble Numbers*).

On the other hand are Herrick's endlessly bitter and sardonic epigrams, mixed in; modelled on those of Martial, and, like their model, revelling in sexual and scatological insult.

Most of these are addressed to men — in sado-masochistic alternation or structuring referred to above — but the most violent of all, on the stalking horse or Turk's-head victim, the ugly old woman or frightful witch, is "The Hagg," of which Herrick wrote two versions, one more ugly and scatological than the other. (*Poetical Works,* ed. Moorman, pp. 225 and 333–4.) See further, on the tradition of this anti-gallant alternation in the earlier French satirical poets, the "Blasons" and "Contreblasons" of the fabliaux period, and especially Robert Angot de l'Eperonnière in his *Euterpe, ou La Muse épineuse* (1637), in my *Rationale of the Dirty Joke: Second Series,* 14.1.4, the chapter "Dysphemism, Cursing & Insults." Shakespeare's alternating gallant and anti-gallant *Sonnets,* Nos. 127 and 130, "My mistress' eyes are nothing like the sun," are also very much in this tradition — though comparatively mild. Predictably enough, the limerick rhythm of the lovely "Night-piece: To Julia" is also adapted by Herrick to the crude anti-woman doggerel of his "Upon Jone and Jane" (ed. Moorman, p. 229):

Jone is a wench that's painted,
Jone is a Girle that's tainted;
   Yet *Jone* she goes
   Like one of those
Whom purity had Sainted.

Jane is a Girle that's prittie,
Jane is a wench that's wittie;
   Yet, who wo*ul*d think
   Her breath do's stinke,
As so it doth? that's pittie.

Eventually, another friend of Ben Jonson's and member of his poetic school, Bishop Richard Corbet, removed the limerick rhythm almost completely from the use of madmen, lovers, and tobacco-addicts, to personal satire, as in Herrick's

"Upon Jone and Jane," somewhere in the early seventeenth century. Here, in satire, the limerick has principally remained. The surviving element of "Tom o' Bedlam's" insanity is perhaps the concentration, still today, upon "nonsense" in the clean limerick, of which Prof. Morris Bishop observes frankly (in the *New York Times Book Review*, January 3, 1965): "The structure should be a rise from the commonplace reality of line one to logical madness in line five." In other words, "Tom o' Bedlam" rationalized but still in chains.

Bishop Corbet's famous limerick ballad, "The Distracted Puritan," which was probably the most popular song of the English Revolution — on the Royalist side — was written before 1636, but could only first be printed after the Restoration, at the end of the drollery-book *Le Prince d'Amour, or The Prince of Love* (1660), also in *The Rump* (ed. 1662) I. 237-9, as "The Mad Zealot." The Apocalyptic "beast" referred to is, of course, Roman Catholicism:

> Of the beast's ten hornes (God bless us)
> I have knockt off three already:
>   If they let me alone
>   I will leave him none,
> But they say I am too heady.
>
> *Boldly I preach, Hate a Cross —*
>   *hate a Surplese!*
> *Miters, Copes and Rochets!*
>   *Come hear me pray*
>   *Nine times aday,*
> *And fill your heads with Crotchets.*

Corbet is adding here, to the galloping anapests of his stanzas, "Tom o' Bedlam's" old refrain, with its strange pausing echo after the first line, to fit its melancholy tune, thus making melodically clear — as well as in words — the intended satirizing of the Puritan ranter as insane. Even the purported response to Corbet, "The Zealous Puritan," written about 1639 but only first allowed to be printed in *Merry Drollery* (1661), replies in the identical metre. Corbet thus set the tone for all the later anti-Puritan and Restoration satire in limerick form, much of which is also insistently scatological in its humor.

All the drolleries, in fact, through to the last and largest of these, John Playford & Thomas Durfey's *Wit and Mirth, or Pills to Purge Melancholy*, in six volumes (1699–1720, and modern reprints), are absolute encyclopaedias of bawdy songs in the limerick metre, along with many other metres of course. Some continue the format of "Tom o' Bedlam," but as to other trades, with the unmistakable pause-line in the whining refrain; others are simply in the satirical style of Herrick and Bishop Corbet (without refrains); and some curiously hark back to Holyday's "Corinna," half a century earlier or more, which either had created a rhyming-style or had itself been set to a folk-tune ("*John Dory*") with unaccented *-a* ending one or more lines. Even the briefest examination of the drolleries will show that the concentration on verbal obscenity and scatology, imagined by many to be a modern addition to or perversion of the limerick form, is already in very florid cultivation in the seventeenth-century drollery limericks, as for example in "Joane Easie," printed in *Wit and Drollery* (1661) with an extra couplet and conclusion:

> Joane Easie got her a Nag and a Sledge
> To the Privy-house for to slide, a:
>   The hole was beshit
>   That she could not sit,
> But did cack as she lay on her side, a:
>
>   She was not wind [?]
>   For she sent forth a sound
> Did stretch her fundament wide, a.

INTRODUCTION   xxix

So many examples of these evident predecessors of the modern limerick, mostly in anapests mixed with the iambic foot, could be quoted from the great outpouring of English humorous and folk poetry in the seventeenth century, especially in the satirical drollery collections of the Restoration, that one despairs of trying, short of having the space of a whole book to quote them in. For a very full, but by no means complete, selection, the reader is referred again to Jack Lindsay's elegant monograph, *Loving Mad Tom* (1927), with which one can disagree only as to the accustomed balderdash of Mr. Robert Graves, in his Foreword; and the excessive caution of Lindsay's inquiry (p. 75) whether it be not "fanciful to see something of a lingering memory or a chance re-invention of the stanzaic effect in the limerick of our contemporary coversation, in which is crystallised so much brilliant obscenity."

IV

A PARTICULAR element, which entered these early limericks at some time during the seventeenth century, was the obviously satirical use of proper names — of persons, later places — to set the opening rhyme, or in other rhyming positions. To us, at least, these seem intentionally burlesque, yet they were by no means always so intended in that century. Herrick uses name-rhymes often in his humorous and sardonic epigrams, sometimes in the closing couplet: always a prime doggerel position, as at the ends of the Acts in Shakespeare's plays and those of his contemporaries. In Herrick's "Upon Jack and Jill" (ed. Moorman, p. 186), Jack feeds Jill on kisses, telling her that these are the "food of Poets," to which she replies, obviously wanting something more solid:

> Let Poets feed on aire, or what they will;
> Let me feed full, till that I fart, says *Jill*.

In his "The *Peter*-penny" (ed. Moorman, p. 256), in the two-couplet metre of which the limerick form itself may be a worn-down survival, Herrick end-rhymes not only on the Paternoster ("No pennie, no Pater Noster": an old proverb), but also boldly rhymes "St. Peter" with "sweeter"! Even more outrageous to modern ideas of formal poetry is the opening of Herrick's "To God," in his very serious *Noble Numbers* (1647; *Works*, ed. Moorman, p. 343), involving not only a double rhyme on proper names to open the poem, as will be seen, but even the diddley-dumpty syllable-ing out of *Revela-ti-on* to make the needed five syllables:

> Do with me, God! as Thou didst deal with *John*,
>   (Who writ that heavenly *Revelation*).

Perfectly acceptable then, in the gravest kind of apostrophe to God, a rhyme like that can be used today only in the most burlesque type of humorous poetry and song, for example the college-girls' song about the tubercular prostitute: "Lil, she was a beauty; She lived in a house of ill repute-y," who finally has to drink "Scott's Emul-si-on." Altogether anti-clerical and anti-godlin, this song is probably parodying an American survival of syllable-ing out in singing hyms.

Barten Holyday's false-rhyme or added syllable, to rhyme with the name, "Come kisse, come kisse, my Corinna," in his play *Technogamia* (1618) III. v, has already been quoted. By the time of the English Revolution and Restoration, with their satirical drollery-collections in verse, the use of proper names to open the song or poem had become essential to the personal satire that was the drolleries' stock-in-trade, even when a rhyme could not be found. For example, in an anti-Puritan, anti-Cromwell song to the old tune of "Tom o' Bedlam," appearing in *The Rump, or Collection of Songs and Ballads, made upon those who would be a* Parliament, *and were but the* Rump *of an House of Commons, five times dissolv'd* (1660: a hoked-up scatological title for a drollery-book first issued in the same

INTRODUCTION   xxxi

year as *Ratts Rhimed to Death, or The Rump-Parliament Hang'd up in the Shambles*). This is Sir John Denham's "News from Colchester, or A Proper new Ballad of certain Carnal passages betwixt a Quaker and a Colt," demonstrating "that a Mare's as good as a Madam," (ed. 1662) I. 354 *ff*.:

> Help, Woodcock, Fox, and Naylor,
> For Brother Green's a Stallion:
>   Now alas what hope
>   Of converting the Pope
> When a Quaker turns *Italian!* . . .

(The Italians have always had a bad reputation, since Roman times, for sexual perversion, especially anal intercourse. This is nowadays usually assimilated to the even older Greeks.)

Two songs earlier in the same work — skipping over "The four Legg'd Elder; or a Relation of a Horrible Dog and an Elder's Maid"—"The Bloody Bed-roll, or Treason displayed in its Colours" (ed. 1662, I. 343—50) entirely in double-limerick stanzas and entirely of named personal satire, beginning: "Old Oliver's gone to the Dogs . . ."

> Here cómes Sir HENRY MARTYN
> As good as ever pist,
>   This wenching beast
>   Had Whores at least
> A thousand on his list.

Even the falsely stressed iambic opening, "There *was* . . ." so typical of modern limericks, was not uncommon in early seventeenth-century humorous verse, if not earlier, as in:

> There was a Lady lov'd a hogge, hony quoth shee,
> Woo't thou lie with me tonight? ogh, quoth he, *&c.*

Given thus, with the "*&c.*" implying a long folk-history preceding, in an unpublished Twelfth Night revel, *Grobiana's Nuptialls*, about 1620 (Bodley MS. 30). By July 1st, 1626, a similar folk-opening for a humorous poem or nursery rhyme was recorded: "There was a Crow sate on a stone, He flew away & then there was none"— the ancestor of the modern "Ten Little Injuns"— in a satirical parody on the failure of the piratical expedition of the party of Buckingham against Cadiz, in Spain, in 1625, of which the failure left England bankrupt and the Revolution a certainty. (The song is quoted in a letter dated 1626, by the Rev. Joseph Mead of Cambridge; Harleian MS. 390. See further, on both the above, Iona & Peter Opie, *The Oxford Dictionary of Nursery Rhymes*, 1951, notes 294 and 355.) By the end of the seventeenth century, when the imitations by Samuel Butler and others in England of Scarron's travesties of the classics in France had made even anti-godlin and anti-Biblical "mocks" and parodies a possibility, one had even such rhyme-openings as that in the invocation "To the Reader," f. A7, in Samuel Colville's *Mock-Poem, or Whiggs Supplication* (1681): "There was a Man called Job... He had a good gift of the Gob." All of which leaves very little for modern limerick poets to invent.

Let me end this very brief survey, with one of the most technically unexceptionable seventeenth-century limericks, the first in which all the modern peculiarities of the form (with the exception of "There *was*") appear: "Mondayes Work... To the tune of *I owe my hostesse money*," in the *Roxburghe Ballads* (ed. William Chappell, 1871–2) I. 514–20; II. 148–53. Published in broadside ballad form before 1640, this is a perfect modern limerick — anapestic metre (here and there), proper names setting the rhyme of the stanzas, and all:

> Good morow, neighbour Gamble,
> Come let you and I goe ramble:
>   Last night I was shot
>   Through the braines with a pot
> And now my stomacke doth wamble...

> Gramarcy, neighbour Jinkin
> I see thou lovest no shrinking,
>   And I, for my part
>   From thee will not start:
> Come fill us a little more drinke in.

The rhyme here, as a matter of fact, is rather close to that of the modern bawdy limerick about the fellow named Perkin, whose gherkin was sherkin' his ferkin'; not to mention Skinner and Tupper, who took the young lady to supper. A parallel inspiration or "chance re-invention," to be sure.

Before another century had passed, the limerick form, now fully achieved in all its particulars, had so often been turned to the uses and abuses of satire, in poems and songs of drinking, wenching, and other "low professions," that no one, not even Herrick, could have saved it as a lyric form, and Shakespeare's refusal to take it seriously was vindicated. Eventually the rhythm "fell"— probably still carried by the wandering bedlam beggars, the ancestors of our own hoboes and tramps — to the dialect songs of Scotland and Ireland, as in "Katy's Answer" to the young Laird, in Ramsay's *Tea-Table Miscellany* of 1724 (ed. 1871, I. 63):

> My mither's ay glowran o'er me,
> Tho' she did the same before me:
>   I canna get leave
>   To look to my loove,
> Or else she'll be like to devour me...

Certain of the peculiarities, picked up along the way, turned even the dialect form to dialect satire, particularly the use of a proper name (improperly, of course, according to the rules of all modern poetry but humorous) in calling forth the rhyme. "Neighbour Jinkin," just noted, seems to deserve some part of the blame here, as the commonest tune used for the dialect satire songs in the limerick rhythm mentions him (in the anti-Welsh form of his name) in the opening line: "Of noble race was Shenkin." The same rhythm and tune are later used in a violently erotic piece, "The Pious Parson," in all editions of *The Merry Muses* after 1830, still surviving in Britain as "The Hero Alexander," referring not to the Macedonian emperor but to Alexander, Great Steward of Scotland, renowned for his heroism in the victory over King Haakon the Old of Norway, at the Battle of Largs in 1263. The surviving song is an adaptation of some of the anti-Puritan rhymes in "The Bloody Bedroll," quoted above, now directed against either Protestant or Catholics clerics, depending on the singer's prejudices. Latest version, almost unexpurgated, in Harry Morgan's *Why Was He Born So Beautiful, and Other Rugby Songs* (London: Sphere Books – Nelson, 1967) p. 33, beginning: "There was a priest, the dirty beast, Whose name was Alexander..." The hero of the Battle of Largs has been forgotten.

Finally, the limerick metre was abandoned altogether to the uses of nonsense and nursery rhymes — the classic decay and descent of much folklore, of which the last traces often survive only in children's rhymes and games. It is among the nursery rhymes, since the early eighteenth century at least, that the limerick form will mainly be found, as in "Hickory dickory dock", "Dance a baby, diddy," and many others that he who seeks will find. (See *passim* in Iona & Peter Opie's *Oxford Dictionary of Nursery Rhymes*, 1951, and William & Ceil Baring-Gould's *The Annotated Mother Goose,* New York: Clarkson N. Potter, Inc., 1962.) Quite in addition to those many eighteenth-century English nursery rhymes in classic limerick form, beginning "There *was*..."

So typical of the nursery was the limerick with its rhyming on proper names eventually felt to be, that its form was used by mid-century in a mock-critical piece, "To the Critics and Poets," reprinted in *The New Boghouse Miscellany, or A Companion for the Close-Stool* in 1761, p. 207, and burlesquing the pompous flatulence of the learned commentators of the day. This particular vein of satire had first been mined in Swift's *Tale of a Tub,* and Dr William Wagstaffe's *Comment upon the History of Tom Thumb* in 1711, and by Hyacinthe Cordonnier, in his *Chef d'Oeuvre d'un Inconnu* (1714) and its many imitations, which one would have thought had finished off the commentators and their excesses forever; but are, instead, themselves forgotten, while the commentators go endlessly on.

The poem of the anonymous Boghouse poet is entitled —

On Jollity: An Ode, or Song, or both.

I.

There was a jovial butcher,
He liv'd at Northern-fall-gate,
   He kept a stall
   At Leadenhall,
And got drunk at the boy at Aldgate.

II.

He ran down Hounsditch reeling,
At Bedlam he was frighted,
   He in Moorfields
   Besh–t his heels
And at Hoxton he was wipèd.

The commentary that follows (by Oliver Goldsmith?) precisely in the mock-serious style later used by Norman Douglas in handling bawdy limericks, notes carefully, for example, how, in the second stanza, "The geography of the places where the action happened is strictly observed." This is almost identical with Douglas' note, as to the logical order of events in the equally scatological misadventure of the lady named Skinner (or Pinner), "who dreamt that her lover was in her." (Quoted at p. 418 below, Note 729.) It is also worth observing that, though proper names had already been set as rhymes in the limerick form, in "Mondayes Work" — concerning neighbors Gamble and Jinkin — the present example, "On Jollity," from the *New Boghouse Miscellany* of 1761, is the earliest "geographical" limerick yet discovered (first appearing in *The Midwife, or Old Woman's Magazine*, about 1750, as reprinted also in *The Non-pareil*, 1757, p. 165-70), and has certainly enough place-names, false rhymes, and even an opening "There was ..." to satisfy any historian.

V

So MUCH for the history of the limerick before Lear, which has here obviously been only briefly sketched. Sufficient has been shown, however, to justify the opening statement that the limerick is, and was originally, an indecent verse-form. For anyone who cares to trace it further back than the unrepressed buckè of "Sumer is i-cumen in," the field is wide open. But history, as everyone knows, is only half the story. The other half, and the harder part, is what is nowadays called the psychological element: earlier the "soul," or spirit of the thing. Fortunately for any such profound study, all the materials are still in existence for the examination of the erotic content of the limerick, since its revival as a popular art form, and its elevation from the nursery, owing to the efforts of *Punch*, Lear, Leland, and the nameless poets of the 1860's.

All the materials, or perhaps lacking only one early document, chastely entitled *A New Book of Nonsense* (London, 1868), and extending to only twelve pages. This is the earliest collection of erotic limericks known to have existed, though no sure trace of this brochure has survived except a bare reference to its title, in the important Campbell-Reddie manuscript bibliography of nineteenth-century erotica (in the British Museum, II. 175). Almost immediately after, however, there appeared the much larger collection of bawdy and sacrilegious verse, *Cythera's Hymnal,* with the mock imprint 'Oxford: Printed at the University Press, for the Society for Promoting Useful Knowledge,' 1870; which collection gives at the end a group of fifty-one erotic limericks, headed "Nursery Rhymes," which, since they cover almost exactly an equivalent dozen pages, lead one to believe that the lost *New Book of Nonsense* of 1868 was perhaps only a preprint of these pages.

Cythera's Hymnal is known, through the revelations of the bibliographer of erotica, H. Spencer Ashbee ('Pisanus Fraxi'), to have been the joint production of Capt. Edward Sellon, author of numerous erotic novels, and a study of Hindu eroticism, who died a suicide in 1866 (note the date); and the journalist, George Augustus Sala, assisted by several other Oxford men. The same authors also paid their respects to the classic erotic and satirical poet, Martial — their obvious inspiration, as he had been for Herrick — in an *Index Expurgatorius Martialis,* published at about the same time, and translating *only* those bawdy epigrams of Martial usually omitted from college pony-translations. Most of the poems of *Cythera's Hymnal* are howling and even revolting parodies, Sellon's "Chordee" (a parody of "Excelsior") being the least objectionable. From the viewpoint of the social critic, the most interesting piece is a satire on the noble do-gooders of the nineteenth century, out preaching a hypocritical gospel of sexual repression among the children of the poor. This is set to the infectious rhythm of the nursery rhyme or song, "There was a little man, And he wooed a little maid, And he said, Little maid, will you wed, wed, wed?" printed for Walpole at the Strawberry Hill Press in 1764 as the work of Sir Charles Sedley, the Restoration wit.

This particular parody is reprinted, with a new group of sixty-five bawdy limericks spread through the eighteen consecutive issues, in the extraordinary erotic magazine, *The Pearl*, published secretly in London from July 1879 to December 1880 (with matching "Christmas Annuals," which are very rare) by a mysterious individual of the real name of Lazenby — according to H. Spencer Ashbee's manuscript notes in the copies of his own bibliographies in the British Museum — using the obvious pseudonym of 'D. Cameron.' *The Pearl* has been reprinted complete at least four times, most recently — and for the first time openly — in New York by the Grove Press (1968) in one fat pocket-book. The parody referred to, entitled "The Good Nobleman," is in the issue for August 1880 (Grove Press reprint, p. 489–90), where it is perhaps worth looking up, as it is the funniest piece in the entire run of *The Pearl,* especially the penultimate stanza in which the disabused little children turn upon their hypocritical benefactor, and tear down his breeches to check on the purity he is preaching.

On the poetry side, and except for limericks, *The Pearl* is largely composed, like *Cythera's Hymnal*, of long narrative poems on flagellation, a type of sub-poetic doggerel excruciating for anyone to try to read who does not share this typically Anglo-Saxon and German perversion. Most of these poems may be suspected of coming from the pen of the journalist and war-correspondent, G. A. Sala, a man whose secret biography is waiting to be written. The hundred and twenty limericks included, in all, in these two sources, and in the continuations of *The Pearl* (and its "Christmas Annuals") as *The Boudoir* and *The Cremorne,* falsely dated '1851,' also include a large proportion of the bawdy limericks still in oral circulation in both England and America, and these must be considered the classics or old favorites of the genre. Evidently their main circulation, in both their own century and this, was by word-of-mouth, in the classic folklore fashion, and certainly not via the very rare secret publications, of limited circulation, in which they were committed to print.

INTRODUCTION

I would not care to fall into the modern mania of counting and measuring the themes and motifs of the hundred and twenty limericks here cited, and the perhaps hundred and fifty more that make up the total "float" or repertoire of orally-circulated modern limericks — the only ones that can be agreed to be socially indicative and significant. Much less would I care to try sliding them through the sucking-&-blowing apertures of a calculating machine, in order to discover the leading "traits" or themes with which they are concerned, even assuming that anything meaningful could be learned in any such way. As the card-punching and sampling system has, so far, guessed wrong in all the political elections on which it has been tried; I do not think any serious folklorist would care to trust it with the significance of bawdy limericks.

Even without too much measuring, and Hollerith hole-punching machine entertainments, it is clear that, in a preponderant way, most bawdy limericks are concerned with the unconscious or unwilling *humor* of the sexual impulse: its organ-inferiorities, its attitudes, and misadventures. The form being unrepressed, by definition, no holds seem to be barred as to the naked hostility expressed. The same is also true of clean limericks and of the even more sadistic "Little Willies" proposed at the turn of the present century by Harry Graham ('Col. D. Streamer') in *Ruthless Rhymes for Heartless Homes,* first published in 1899, in a gleefully gruesome and anti-family style carried on for years afterward — also in an attempted feminist version — by the murder-mystery writer, and clean limerick and whimsy-poesy fancier, Miss Carolyn Wells. All in all, a study of the quite unrepressed aggressions of the type of humor thought of as "clean."

The most gruesomely sadistic clean limericks are, of set purpose, those published as *The Listing Attic* (New York & Boston, 1954) and sequels, by a writer significantly named 'Edward Gorey.' Of 'Gorey's' productions, the by-no-means fainthearted critic, Clifton Fadiman, in his essay on limericks, "There Was an Old Man of Tobago," in *Any Number Can Play* (Cleveland, 1957), remarks flatly: "These are so appalling that I prefer not to quote them here. They are evidence of the bounds to which the Limerick may be pushed by an imagination at once febrile and cynical. Mr. Gorey thinks nothing of wrapping up such material as infanticide, simple murder, algolagnia, human vivisection, and the lynching of sexual deviants in a verse form traditionally consecrated to the innocent enjoyments of the nursery."

It is curious how much of this sexual hostility, in the frankly bawdy limericks, is turned against the poet or protagonist himself, the hapless hero with whose disasters and phallic insufficiencies the limerick poet so clearly identifies. There can be no question that this is a sort of neurotic whistling in the dark, for the people who make up the bawdy limericks and who nowadays also sing them; attempting, as it were, to laugh away their sexual fears and impotencies — real and imaginary — in short satirical efforts of elaborate rhyme, in which, be it said once and for all, *woman* is the usual butt of the satire, as is true of almost all drinking songs.

The death of the limerick as a harmless if satirical verse form, in the early eighteenth century, was only a minor casualty in the broad campaign of moral repression, as well in literature as in ostensible life, operated in England at the level of printed matter by its early literary dictators, Alexander Pope, Joseph Addison, and the pachydermatous Dr. Samuel Johnson, the biggest literary bluff of his century. (There have been bigger since.) Quite aside from Johnson's English dictionary of 1755, expurgated into shape on the basis of Nathanael Bailey's earlier and *un*expurgated folio dictionary of the 1730's, under the flatulent Della Cruscan pretext of "purifying" the English language — as though language depended upon dictionaries for its vocabulary! — it should not be overlooked that Alexander

INTRODUCTION

Pope had already opened the battle with an expurgated edition of Shakespeare in 1725, though poor Dr. Bowdler, a century later, invariably gets the ridicule and the discredit. The bathetic depths of mock prudery to which the English-speaking world descended for two full centuries from the 1740's to the 1940's are too well known to discuss here, though there is little recognition of the hidden intention of shoring up economic privilege by these means against the advancing revolutionary spirit. This became extremely clear in the "New Freedom" for both unrepressed speech and sexuality in the 1960's. (For an excellent introduction to the whole subject, see Victor F. Calverton's *Sex Expression in Literature,* 1926, a Marxist approach; Maurice Quinlan's *Victorian Prelude,* 1941; and Gordon Rattray Taylor's *The Angel-Makers,* 1958; as well as two excellent popular works, both entitled *Mrs. Grundy,* the first by Leo Markun, the second by Peter Fryer, 1963.)

As, in such campaigns for purity, sobriety, industriousness (note well!) and so forth, children and the working-class are the invariable first targets, the folksongs of the folk and the nursery rhymes of the nursery had immediately to go through the moral wringer. By the 1790's, with the "clear and present danger" of the French Revolution escalating the moral war, even the outlying British territories, such as Scotland and Ireland — and, of course, America, by the usual cultural osmosis — were obliged to expurgate their folklore and folk-literature. This naturally led to the immediate creation of a subterranean erotic lore and literature, already begun in England under the moral suasions of the 1740's which had resulted at once in the overblown Cytherean prose of John Cleland's *Fanny Hill* (1749).

That is how, and essentially that is why the limerick died, or rather was killed off in the mid-eighteenth century. Already fallen away to the nursery and dialect level, it was laundered out of existence and disappeared. Thus, as was only to be expected, at its revival just a century later, in the 1860's — taking off from the vapid innocuousness by then standard in the nursery forms, and in the imitations of these by Sharpe (1822), Lear, and *Punch* — the limerick, as revived, was somehow transmogrified by the poetry-loving nineteenth century, from mere "nonsensical" bawdy and satire, into a gruelling combination of sick sex and sadistic scatology. And that is what the limerick now is. There are exceptions, of course: the healthy specimens or "Little Romances from Real Life" with which the collection here presented begins; but, as their numbers show, they form only a very small minority. The limerick — the limerick really popular among adults — became a century ago, and still remains, the underground showcase and receptacle of all the most repellent erotic imaginings, the most scatological satire and aggression, and the sickest sexual fears and fantasies of the nineteenth and twentieth centuries, passed off always as *wit,* among the better-educated and presumably more cultivated classes. It is this record which is laid naked before the reader, at full length, in the collection which follows.

Far from being some victory for folk-poetry and unexpurgaiety, what had really happened was the inevitable and unhealthy result of the century-long censorship that both preceded and has run concurrently with the century of the bawdy limerick. The sexual censorship of the eighteenth century, and since, has operated always on a most significant principle or system of balances: the forbidding and removing of the sexual parts of literature and of life, no matter how normal; which assumes and involves that the necessary "action" or excitement will then be supplied by the substitution of a permitted concentration on the most repulsive details of violence and death. As I have already published a hundred-page monograph on this cultural paradox or blind-spot that would make sex worse than murder, *Love & Death: A Study in Censorship* (New York: Breaking Point, 1949) — and the subject was in any case masterfully handled half a century before in France, on the inspiration of a passage by Montaigne, in the eloquent diatribe, *The Pornography of Murder*, by Maurice Le Blond, the son-in-law of Zola — I will only touch upon it here.

One thing is certain: the Anglo-Saxon culture is now, and will long be harvesting the poisoned fruit of its demanded substitution of an allowed sadism for a prohibited sexual normality, despite the recent relative collapse of the censorship since 1960, first in the Scandinavian countries and now in America and England. The "New Freedom" achieved is invariably accepted first, not as the long-awaited freedom from the censorship of sexual normality — which is its true purpose — but rather as an open social acceptance or shooting-permit for all the old degeneracies, such as sadism, sexual perversion, hallucinatory drugs, and the like, that every rational person was hoping to get rid of. The evil residue of the censorship is exactly this: that the new and partial literary freedom is immediately seized upon and exploited by the Gangsters of the New Freedom strictly as the freedom to print, propagandize for, and gloat over all the most nauseating details of the sadistic and other sex-linked abnormalities, which originally had appeared in literature and probably in life as an "escape" from that censorship and its sexual repression.

The real point is not that the sex-substituted sadisms of modern literature, motion pictures, television, *and life* leap to any critical eye, but that the same substitution of an allowed sadism for the still-prohibited sexuality in the folk-literature and electrically-promulgated "entertainment arts" of mass circulation in our time, can only result in the most dangerous and most sinister abnormalization of the whole psychic structure of future generations. That is the *real* message of the limericks of which the present collection is in major part composed, as it must be of any collection of authentic erotic folklore in the English language, sampled up out of the depths at the present time. As to the most recent social and human, rather than merely literary aspects of the same problem, see my pamphlet *The Fake Revolt, or Gangsters of the New Freedom* (1967), with its supplement, *Models of Madness*, specifically on the new drug "scene" being peddled to adolescents. And if you can't read, look around and bear witness, brother!

VI

IN THE ONLY serious psychological study ever made of limericks, by Prof. Weston LaBarre, in the journal *Psychiatry* (Washington, May 1939) II. 203-12, entitled "The Psychopathology of Drinking Songs" but not quoting a single one, the important point is made that limericks are written and retailed only by the educated group, a group apparently perfectly attuned to the special impropriety of the limerick, both prosodic and moral. As the *Journal of American Folklore* was so kind as to allow me to remark a few years ago, in its epochal "Symposium on Obscenity in Folklore" (July 1962, vol. 75: p. 187-265), under the title "Misconceptions in Erotic Folklore," an article reprinted in my volume of essays, *The Horn Book* (1964), without the expurgations demanded for the *Journal* symposium by a Dr. John Greenway — which came to half the total length of the piece! — bawdy limericks apparently represent for the educated group a sort of private revolt against the rules of prosody and propriety, at one and the same time, owing to the false accent with which most limericks begin, the improper geographical rhyme, and the gruellingly obscene subject matter, which is usually of a far more alembicated nastiness than any other kind of folksong ever is.

This is a type of literary revolt that almost no other social class cares to share. Few persons of non-college background know, or want to know, any limericks at all, whether clean or bawdy, or perhaps only one or two used infrequently as toasts.

INTRODUCTION   xlv

Limericks are the folk-expression almost solely of the college group, particularly the professors, concentrating specifically on the bawdy limerick. The bawdy limerick remains thereafter the special delectation of college-educated men (and a few disoriented women nowadays), especially those in the quasi-intellectual professions, such as journalism, publishing, advertising, stock-jobbing, law and politics, and the entertainment arts. Limericks are not only the folklore almost solely of the educated, but are almost their *only* folklore, with the exception of jokes and tales — including a large number credulously believed to be true — and a limited repertoire of bawdy and sentimental songs remembered from college days.

Limericks are not liked by, nor commonly to be collected among, workingmen, farm-hands, cowboys, sailors, and other classic oral sources — "as yodelling tipplers are called by philologists" (Sydney Goodsir Smith). Many non-college and non-white-collar people who have no objection to bawdry, will neither recite limericks nor listen to them unless they are sung. Except for the basic subject-matter, non-college people simply do not find it easy to understand where the humor is supposed to reside, in all the trick geographical rhyming and other purely formal and intellectual ornamentation of the limerick. It seems transpicuously clear that the daring prosodic revolt of the falsely stressed "There *was*..." and the even falser geographical rhyme of the typical limerick, do titillate persons who have been educated to believe that these are poetically "wrong," but no one else. The epigrammatic quality of the limerick, which it shares with its formal ancestors of the *Greek Anthology* and the *Priapeia,* and among the Roman satirists such as Martial, also makes it unsuitable for non-college folk, who far prefer the larger developmental and adventurous possibilities of the longer ballad form.

Since World War I and a bit earlier, an attempted democratization has been taking place, in the possibility of *singing* the limerick, in the eighteenth-century Irish style which apparently gave the name of "Limerick" to this verse-form. In Rudyard Kipling's *Stalky & Co.* (1899), the story "The Propagation of Knowledge" tells of singing-fests like this, with the chorus between stanzas, "Won't you come up to Limerick?" among British schoolboys as far back as about 1880. This tradition of singing the limericks is obviously much more vital than declaiming or reciting them, or simply collecting and trading examples in manuscript or typewritten form (now also on tape-recordings). Limericks can now often be heard sung in the convivial company of college fraternities (and sometimes sororities), the drinking-clubs of army and air officers, and so forth; but even there the groups involved are usually drawn from the educated classes. Quite a number of limerick collections have in recent years been mimeographed and privately circulated by such college and armed-service groups, nothing "new" ever appearing in these mimeographica except the science-fiction limericks of recent vintage. The pages of limericks given are now clearly thought of as a single object or song, with a chorus indicated.

As sung, the limericks are chanted *seriatim* by various members of the group, to the tune, usually, of the venereal-disease song, "The Spanish Nobilio" or "Gay Caballero" (much worn down musically in the transmission), each singer electing himself or herself to come forward with a remembered or presumably extemporarily invented limerick, which thus becomes part of the "song" being communally improvised by the group in classic folksong fashion, and never twice the same. The stanzas are separated, and the singers allowed to catch breath, take a drink, or furbish up their inspiration, by a chorus or challenge sung by the whole audience:

> That...was...a very nice song,
> Sing us another one —
> Just like the other one —
> Sing us another one, do!

INTRODUCTION xlvii

In America, the chorus or connective verse has become more recently, to the tune of "Cielito lindo":

> Aye, yi, yi-yi! –
> In China they never eat chili;
> So sing me (here's to) the next verse,
> Much worse than the last verse,
> And waltz me around again, Willie!

In the courageous and competent *Annotated Field Collection of Songs from the American College Student Oral Tradition* — I guess that delimits the field very exactly — by Richard A. Reuss (Indiana University, Department of Folklore, master's dissertation, 1965) f. 220–22, various burlesque versions or replies to the usual "In China they never eat chili" line are cited, making a further possibility of extemporaneous elaboration between stanzas. Reuss cites: "Freshmen never eat pussy..." and "Your mother swims after troop ships..." also "Your father licks toilet seats," which fails of the correct metre and is obviously only a catch-phrase of insult; with an even more elaborate form collected at Indiana in 1964:

> Aye, yi, yi, yi —
> I'd rather get laid than get eaten.
> So sing me a chorus
> While I eat your clitóris,
> So waltz me around again, Willie.

These have evidently come a long way from County Limerick. The intention here is openly to encourage the next singer to an even "worse verse" — no longer merely "another one, just like the other one" — as everyone becomes slightly more intoxicated, in part by the singing, and a great deal less repressed. The British connecting chorus is the most interesting of all:

> Now hear, all ye dukes and ye duchesses,
> Take heed of my warning, I say,

> Be sure that you owns all you touches-es,
> Or I'll land you in Botany Bay!

These choruses are naturally sung in as many different ways as there are different singers, so it will be of no use writing to me in care of the publisher to say that the above wordings of the chorus are "wrong," a word which has, after all, no real meaning folkloristically. One man's wit is another man's poison. Of course, additional *verses* in the limerick form would be far from unwelcome — as also songs and poems — but should perhaps be transmitted by homing-pigeon, St. Bernard dog, or some other uncommon carrier, as they might very well turn out to be illegal in the mails.

The note struck in the British limerick chorus, of absurd and out-of-place resistance to non-existent authority figures, such as the "dukes and duchesses" who are boldly warned off the (sexual) property of the singer, is the crucial element in the psychological structure of all limericks, as in most erotic and satirical poetry whatever its metrical pattern may be. Authority figures can be almost anything or anyone, depending on the background of the poet or singer: some people hate royalty, some people hate bishops, monks and ministers, Englishmen or policemen. There are people who write books against the law of gravity (which they hate simply because it's referred to as a "law"), or to prove that Einstein was wrong, or that Shakespeare was written *by another man of the same name,* as Mark Twain put it. I knew a man once who would become furious over printed signs in public places that did not begin with the word "Please...." Few people can admit that they are fighting non-existent authority figures, as they seldom fought the parents who are the real authority figures that they are still seething about, and who, in the present case, appear in the limericks they write or quote disguised as kings, dukes, and bishops.

The main focus of resistance and hostility in limericks tends to circulate in this way about perfectly mythical figures of royalty and nobility, such as the petrified image of poor mad George III hidden in American folklore since 1776 under the stereotyped heading of the hated Englishman or superior snob. See the entire section, "Bloody Englishmen," in the chapter on Fools in my *Rationale of the Dirty Joke: First Series* (1968) p. 167-71, which takes the whole matter a good deal further.

Resistance to the clergy comes only second in limericks, and would probably long since have faded, along with the now utterly uninteresting religious controversies stirred up a century ago by Darwin on evolution and Bishop Colenso's "Higher Criticism" of the Bible, demonstrating that it is largely a forgery and could not possibly have been written by Moses. However, the geographical necessities of the limerick rhyme have perpetuated in certain favorite limericks such otherwise unknown and irrelevant dignitaries as the Bishops of Twickenham, Woking, and Chichester, of whom the last is practically dragged in by the seat of his britches only in order to get another part of that garment somehow involved in a florid rhyming scheme concerning a young lady whose charms had already "made all the saints in their niches stir." It is obvious that the ordinary cowboy, miner, field-hand or workingman will not go for effete and over-intellectual stuff like that.

The average workingman, in such a mood, much prefers singing "The One-Eyed Riley" or " 'Twas on the Good Ship *Venus*" or "The Bastard King of England" or "The Crab Fish," when he does any singing at all, or is *allowed* to sing — even polite songs — in his public bar (where the juke-box or television machine suffers from no such restriction). Whatever he may sing in the way of bawdy, the uneducated singer inevitably prefers the more active and adventurous ballad form, giving room for a more phallic, and less pettily linguistic, sexuality.

Probably the pettiest of all revolts in the limerick is its intense concentration on the personal or geographical name setting the rhyme in the opening line. This is a leftover nursery-rhyme or satirical form of the early seventeenth century, as has already been shown. At best, it is a type of trick-rhyming — often triple: rhyming three full syllables in improbable fashion — splendidly done by certain nineteenth-century humorous poets like R. H. Barham in his *Ingoldsby Legends* (1837), Thackeray, Sydney Smith, and W. S. Gilbert; also in many limericks of the Golden Period, such as No. 1 in the present collection, usually attributed to Swinburne. It is a trick that palls rapidly unless very well done indeed, as implied in W. S. Gilbert's totally *non*-rhyming reply to Lear, on the old man of St. Bees, "Who was stung in the arm by a Wasp." (He thought it was a hornet.)

Another type of resistance is expressed in the infrequent mock-limericks in which, like the Young Man of Japan, "You try to get as many words into the last line as you possibly can!" Langford Reed's *Complete Limerick Book* (2nd ed. 1926, p. 47) gives a more logical form of this, under the "Clerical Limerick," supplied by Dean William Inge, with the last line — to rhyme with "lamb" and "jam"—"We all heard our Vicar say, 'Stand up please, while I say grace'." In Martin Gardner's edition of C. C. Bombaugh's *Oddities and Curiosities of Words* (New York: Dover, 1961) p. 362, the opposite is tried, concerning the Young Poet in China: "His limericks tend, To come to an end — Quite suddenly." As can be seen, all these new niceties are simply forms of revolt against the prosodic revolt that the limerick itself is supposed to be!

The principal attractiveness of personal or geographical rhyme in run-of-the-mill limericks, which often have not even the necessary excuse of personal satire, seems to operate solely on over-educated people, titillated by the idea that such rhymes are prosodically "wrong," and therefore an expression of some private poetic revolt. Actually, in the seventeenth century, when the limerick assumed its modern form in all essentials, such rhyming was not only not considered wrong, but was even taken calmly to such lengths as the example already quoted from Herrick's apostrophe "To God," in his *Noble Numbers, or Pious Pieces* (1647), which opens flatly with the absolutely howling rhyme of the name "John" (the Evangelist) with *Revela-ti-on*! The total rejection of this concern with silly nominal rhymes in the limerick, by the author of some of the best modern erotic limericks, the late Carlyle Ferren MacIntyre, beginning with the famous "While Titian was mixing rose-madder..." (No. 1473 below), which demotes the name-rhyme to the couplet, will be discussed further at the end of this essay.

VII

CONSCIOUS of being without real audience over the last long century, practitioners of the "clean" limerick have tried desperately for interesting minor innovations in the limerick form itself. Most of these presumed innovations are, however, mere petty peculiarities, amusing only to the most infantile and word-oriented minds. It should be observed, of course, that such infantile minds are particularly common in the principal haunts of the limerick: the faculties of language-study and mathematics in the university world, and the shady edges of intellectual pursuit, such as journalism, where what is dealt with is always strictly the external *form* or vehicle of ideas, never the true matter or *subject*, this being falsified or forbidden — like that crime against the Holy Ghost: expressing VALUE JUDGMENTS! — by the rules of these delayed-adolescent professions themselves.

Among the worst limerick innovations attempted have been, certainly, the hypothetically amusing re-spelling of the end words of the lines to match curiously pronounced English place-names, a type of vaudeville-stage humor dating from the 1900's in *Punch* and principally amusing to big-city hicks. All the whimsical humor of the resultant limerick-objects — which plainly admit that they aspire to no other humor — is presumed to rise from such kittenishness as bringing onstage a hero named Cholmondeley, pronounced "Chumly," to rhyme with "bumly" (spelled *bolmondeley*, of course); or Salisbury, pronounced "Sarum," to rhyme with *halisbury-scalisbury*; or Featherstonehaugh, pronounced "Fanshaw," to rhyme with "handsaw" (spelled *handerstonehaugh*!); or perhaps Hampshire, pronounced "Hants," to rhyme with *pampshire* for "pants." Very naughty, that. Out of mercy for the reader, I omit further examples.

Also purely verbal or literal in nature is the intended humor of the heavily assonant or alliterative style afflicted in Conrad Aiken's *A Seizure of Limericks* (1964):

> The limerick's, admitted, a verse form:
> A terse form: a curse form: a hearse form.
>   It may not be lyric
>   And at best it's Satyric,
> And a whale of a tail in perverse form.

So extreme a reliance on inner-rhyme or alliteration is typical of much ancient poetry, written during the infancy of any language, and is best seen in early English and Scottish alliterative verse. I have quoted one fine example of this in *The Horn Book*, p. 147, noting also its use in Urquhart's translation of Rabelais, and in the great Scottish "Flyting" in insults — so similar to the modern Negro "playing the Dozens" — between Polwart and Montgomery. The original, which is extremely long and obscene, will be found in James Watson's *Choice Collection of Comic & Serious Scots Poems* (Edinburgh, 1706-11; repr. Glasgow, 1869, III. 1–32), running to hundreds of alliterative lines.

Mr. Aiken's *Seizure of Limericks* is not derived from this type of authentic folk-source, but is apparently in imitation of similar verbal tricks and the semi-insane — or perhaps entirely

INTRODUCTION

insane — echolalic traits in James Joyce's *Finnegans Wake* and *Ulysses* (1922), earlier imitated *in toto* in Aiken's *Blue Voyage* (1927). Prof. Morris Bishop, who is himself a notable limerick poet in both the clean and semi-bawdy forms — I will not say more: these last in his murder-mystery *The Widening Stain* (1942), under the pseudonym, 'W. Bolingbroke Johnson'— has reviewed Aiken's *Seizure* slashingly in what is one of the most penetrating articles written "On the Limerick" (in the *New York Times Book Review*, January 3rd, 1965), remarking icily on Aiken's title: "*Seizure* is good; a mild taste for limericks can lead to seizures, addiction, septic logorrhea and compulsive recitation neuroses."

Other pathetically uninteresting peculiarities in modern limericks are evident attempts to jazz up the creaking machinery of the "clean" variety and give it a new lease on life: attempts which have invariably failed. In particular, there is the omission of the last line, in puzzle style, which the reader is then challenged to invent. (*Line-lost Limericks*, 1915, by Fred E. Woodward.) This is the format of practically all the advertising contests based on limericks, in which, of course, as the present essay began by maintaining, the real and entire interest to everyone concerned is never the tons of worthless limericks fomented by these means, but the monetary prize or bait. Also attempting to import a bit of puzzle or mystery — replacing, unquestionably, the primitive sexual mystery being evaded in the clean limerick: "*Where do babies come from?*"— are the self-styled "Glimericks, or Mystifying Limericks" proposed in the volume, *The Glimerick Book* (New York, 1925), credited to one 'Shaemas J. A. Witherspoon,' believed to be the journalist Herbert Bayard Swope, editor of the *New York World*. In the mystery line there are even *Fifty Original Cryptogram Limericks* (1929) by George W. Wilson. But why go on? The real danger is that some machine-tending geek will realize that computing machines could easily be programmed to produce clean or bawdy limericks by the mile or until turned off, at which point we had all better leave for the Moon. (Compare "The Sorcerer's Apprentice," and "The Quern, or Salt-Grinding Mill": Aarne-Thompson folktale types Nos. 325* and 565.)

More interesting, certainly, is the double-couplet limerick, in which the couplet is extended to double length. As noted, this was invented — and immediately dropped — by Shakespeare, in *The Tempest* (MS. 1612) II.ii.52, in the song "For she had a tongue with a tang," quoted above. Only the modern poet and stylist, Walter de la Mare, whose little-known short story, "The Tree," is perhaps the most perfect gem of modern lapidary style, has attempted anything in the double-couplet line. These he calls "Twiners," and presents two batches of them in his volume of humorous verse, *Stuff and Nonsense* (London, 1927). De la Mare's "Twiners" invariably involve a sort of sub-sexual marriage arranged between two theoretically separate limericks, each with its own personal or geographical rhyme, one about a man and one about a woman. Their marriage is then consummated in verse, by alternating or intertwining line with line, including a couplet of double length or longer, as in his "The Eel" (p. 54), of which the symbolic element is only too obvious:

> There was an old person of Dover
> Who called on his sister in Deal,
> With a sack hanging over his shoulder
> In which was a whopping great eel.
> It leapt down the area, scuttled upstairs,
> It golloped up bolsters and wash-jugs and chairs,
> Her boots, shoes, and slippers, in singles and pairs...

It ends, of course, with the ogresome Eel eating up the sister completely. Though both Shakespeare's and De la Mare's doubled anapests do make a rollicking rhyme, most limerick poets would probably find the "Twiner" just as unsatisfactory a verse-form as it is patently a repressed sexual act or intermingling.

Only Ambrose Bierce, the best of the American turn-of-the-century "black humorists," was able to infuse any real life into the doubled limerick form, but, in the form he proposed, it is precisely the couplet that remains — like its author-hero — irresolutely single. I quote the only example of Bierce's double-line limericks known to me, "The Owl," from Wilson Follett's *Modern American Usage*, edited by Jacques Barzun (New York, 1966) p. 360, where it is intended to illustrate the boldly colloquial ungrammaticality of saying "who," where petty grammarians and phoneme-grinders would demand "whom":

Sitting singly in the gloaming and no longer two and two,
As unwilling to be wedded as unpracticed how to woo;
    With regard to being mated
    Asking still with aggravated
Ungrammatical acerbity: "To who? To who?"

This compares well with the rapid pace of some of the best of W. S. Gilbert's patter-songs in the Gilbert & Sullivan operettas, several of which songs are purposely in limericks, as quoted by William Baring-Gould, *The Lure of the Limerick* (1967) p. 55. Baring-Gould does not correctly distinguish, however, pp. 15 and 54, between true modern limericks in the anapestic metre, and those longer ballads in the more rapid beat called the *paeonic* measure, an ancient Greek metre used for songs of joy or triumph (paeans), in a foot of four syllables — three short, and one long — in which, for example, "The Story of Prince Agib," in Gilbert's *Bab Ballads* (1869) is cast. H. I. Brock's *Little Book of Limericks* (1947) also quotes as a limerick a stanza in this metre, from the well-known lying-song of the 1900's, "I Was Born About Ten Thousand Years Ago," of which there is also a recent political version called "Passing Through" and a picketing parody, "Pass 'em By!" It should be recognized that these are all developed from the "Pratie Song" of the Irish potato-famine of the mid-nineteenth century, which resulted in the Irish immigration to North America. Entitled

"The Wonderful Song of 'Over There' " (four stanzas, with music), this was first published by Atwill in New York in 1844. But compare the more honest yearning for Ireland — and to hell with "North Ameri-kee"! — in the well-known parody of Allan Cunningham's "Home, Boys, Home."

Three further parodies or developments of the "Pratie Song" are given in the present collection, p. 320-22, Nos. 1561 *ff.*: "Up at Yale", "Over There," and "In Mobile" (or "On the Teal"), with a single-stanza song or recitation in the same metre, at No. 368, "It's Only Human Nature, After All," in which the couplet is purposely spun out to double length — or *ad lib.—* all in rhymes on "-tion," to increase the mounting tension and orgasmic impact of the final mock-moralizing title line. These *paeonic* ballads are probably not really limericks at all, but are included in the present collection owing to their related erotic themes, and their use of so close a variant of the form. Again, it is curious that the line of descent leads back to Ireland, as with the intermediate limericks of the eighteenth century.

As a number of writings on the limerick, for example the introduction to the erotic collection by 'John Falmouth,' *Ninety-five Limericks* (Suffern, N.Y., 1932), erroneously state that the limerick is in the dactylic metre, it is perhaps worth insisting here that the limerick is *not* dactylic, but anapestic. As these two different prosodic feet, which are the exact reverse of each other, both contain one long and two short syllables, the difference may seem unimportant, but it is actually of the very essence. The feel or *movement* of any song or poem in triple-metre is almost entirely determined by whether it RISES from its short syllables to an accented long syllable, or FALLS from its long syllable to the unaccented short. (On this very important point, see further Swann & Sidgwick, p. 29-31.) The limerick, technically described, is in *anapestic trimeter.*

It is the anapestic short syllables that open the limerick line — one short syllable usually being dropped at the very beginning — and not the dactylic reverse. It is this that makes all the liveliness and bounce of the limerick form. A line of dactyls, to the contrary, almost invariably sinks continuously in dirge-like solemnity, striking hammer-hard at every foot. One has only to compare the joyous, rising gallop of that greatest of all anapestic passages, Rossini's *William Tell Overture* ("Titty-RUMP, titty-RUMP, titty-rump-rump-RUMP!") with the ever-descending gloom of the only long poem in English entirely in unrelieved dactyls, Thomas Hood's "The Bridge of Sighs," so lugubrious that it is funny, beginning: "One more Unfortunate, weary of breath, Rashly importunate, gone to her death;" and sinking to lines of such utter dactylic bathos as: "Ere her limbs frigidly, Stiffen too rigidly..." (Oh, come *on!*)

> WHAT is the LIMerick's TRUE physiOGnomy?
> DACtyl or ANapest, WHICH can it BE? —
> MErciful GOD how the DACtyl treads HEAVily...
> While the ANapest GALlops with GLEE!

VIII

ONE OF THE elements in the limerick that has tended to further its formalized presentation in private drinking-clubs, in the colleges and elsewhere, is the greater ease of its recollection, in quintain form, than that of the long ballads preferred by folksingers. This epigrammatic or witty quality is common, as well, to the similar form popular among German students, the "Frau Wirtin" quintains, and the erotic quatrains or "Vierzeiler" of even wider popularity in the German-speaking countries. (See the collections in E. K. Blümml's *Futilitates, Erotische Volkslieder*, and *Der Spittelberg*, Vienna, 1907-8, 5 vols., and 1924.) The historical original of this formalized presentation is the erotic toast, about which little if anything has ever been written. This type of toast —"Gentlemen, I give you (*or*, Here's to)..." followed by some prose or rhymed typification of the person or institution to be drunk to by all — had its greatest development in the mug-house clubs of Great Britain throughout the eighteenth century. Various collections of these toasts will be found printed in the erotic songsters and jestbooks of the time, continuing well into the nineteenth century in all the editions (except the first) of *The Merry Muses.* The toast is now almost extinct in England, being reduced to the mere muttered formula, "Cheers!" to the fractured-English "Chin-chin!" in France, and the curious "Mud in your eye!" in America, a scatological or equestrian survival. Much more will be found as to erotic toasts, as survivals of earlier sexual *ordeals,* such as those of mad lovers, in the draft of the present essay appearing in my *The Horn Book* (1964) p. 441-5, and, at quite a different level of interpretation, in the section "Cunnilinctus & Masochism," in *Rationale of the Dirty Joke: First Series* (1968) p. 573-5, to which the interested reader is referred.

One of the clearest deficiencies of the limerick, preventing it from ever achieving broad folk-acceptance, and keeping it class-linked to the basically non-singing educated group, is the lack of a really good limerick tune. Almost anything is acceptable in the way of words, to both singers and audiences alike — though obviously not to poets — if the tune makes some basic appeal. If proof were required of this, one need only consider the unconscionable drivel set as words nowadays to so-called "popular" songs, whose popularity is shorter-lived than a sick pup, in part because the tunes are so awful too.

The limerick has nothing to compare with the folksongs, as to music, and simply cannot compete. The "Gay Caballero" tune, generally used, is hopelessly weak, and melodically very circumscribed. It takes quite a deal of alcohol to be able to listen to twenty limericks in succession sung to its tune, no matter how loud the audience shouts out the connecting chorus, and begs for "another one." The few efforts that have been made to work up a new limerick tune have never been followed, mostly because they are not worth following; for instance that attempted in W. R. Titterton's over-manly *Drinking Songs* (1928), which is also outfitted with a *tooralooloo* refrain, and an echoic repeat of the final line ("Please don't shoot the pianist — he is doing his best.")

By far the best limerick tunes are those of Sir Arthur Sullivan, who — for a change! — dropped his cynical plagiarizing of Mozart and Offenbach (even his setting of the Rev. Baring-Gould's hymn, "Onward Christian Soldiers" is nothing but the opening of Beethoven's *Violin Concerto*), and belted out at least three splendid limerick tunes: "A man who would woo a fair maid," in *The Yeomen of the Guard* (1888) "A plague on this vagary," in *Iolanthe*; also, in *Patience*, "I shall, with cultured taste;" and especially that in *The Sorcerer* (1877), for the sorcerer's limerick song, beginning, "My name is John Wellington Wells." But this too has never been used, outside the Gilbert & Sullivan operetta. Its only influence seems to have been on the late Aleister Crowley, who luxuriated in the reputation of being "the worst man in the world" — an undeserved distinction which he did his best to keep going by writing obscene and insulting limericks against all his friends, among other entertainments. Among the last that Crowley ever wrote is this poetic "signature," parodied directly from Gilbert, but given here because it indicates the correct pronunciation of Crowley's own name, which people usually get wrong, while claiming nevertheless to have gone on Black Masses with him (in their youth):

> My name it is Aleister Crowley,
> I'm a master of Magick unholy,
>   Of philtres and pentacles,
>   Covens, conventicles;
> Of basil, nepenthe, and moly.

A few of Crowley's bawdy limericks are given in his very rare volume of horrible parodies and pornographica, *Snowdrops from a Curate's Garden* ('Cosmopoli, 1881' [actually

Paris, about 1904], copy: B.N. *Enfer*), at the end of the section, "The Bromo Book," p. 129–31. At least fifty others are extant, though still unprinted. Among them, another group of seventeen horrendous limericks by Crowley, almost all about intercourse with birds, is noted frankly at the end: "Above all written straight off under the influence of cocaine in the early hours of the morning on 11 Oct. 1920, at the Villa Santa Barbara, Cefalu, Sicily," with the penultimate note: "6.15 a.m. I'll shave." They say that narcissistic details like this show the inner workings of a poet's mind, but I wonder.

The final question as to the limerick is that implied in Crowley's signed example: who are the authors of bawdy limericks? It is understood that most limericks entertain only their authors, and, whatever attempts may be made to circulate them, never achieve folklore status at all. But what of the others, that everyone knows — who writes them? Some of the original authors, when the form was new, and classics were being cast in the hot mould of Victorian anti-clericalism, have been mentioned above, in particular Swinburne, to whom what must be Limerick No. 1 in any collection has always been ascribed, the charmingly normal idyll, in extravagant rhyme, as to the young couple of Aberystwyth, "who united the organs they kissed with," moving on finally — in lay-analytic terms — from the oral to the genital stage at last. Other known limerick authors of Swinburne's time and circle were Dante Gabriel Rossetti (who obviously had to write them, if only to get the "languid love for lilies" of his published poetry out of his system), and the university humorist, A. C. Hilton, whose parody of Swinburne, "The Octopus," is the funniest and most lethal example of the parodist's art in English. Of course, *which* limericks were written by which poets is the part most difficult to discover.

On the other hand, one is wise not to be taken in by the facile attributions of everything bawdy to everyone temporarily

INTRODUCTION lxi

in the news. Nothing is sadder than to see the hoary attributions of bawdy folksongs to poets who never in the world wrote them, especially Lord Byron, changing faithlessly to new and equally positive attributions, as new writers come into vogue; these also soon to be replaced in their turn by others as the "secret authors." Thus one has recently seen Sala's bawdy farce, *Harlequin Prince Cherrytop* attributed in print to Gilbert & Sullivan (!) under the title *The Sod's Opera*, by the irrepressible Mr. Ralph Ginzburg, on the authority of a British barrister, Mr. St.John-Stevas, who should have known better (see the horrible details in my *The Horn Book*, p. 95–6); and "The Bastard King of England," which once used to be fathered off on Kipling — never forgetting to add, "Yes, and it cost 'im the poet-lariatship too!"— later attributed to Robert W. Service, the sourdough poet of the Alaska gold-rush; then to A. P. Herbert, Member of Parliament; and, most recently — perish the thought! — to Noël Coward. It is the same with attributions of bawdy limericks to Tennyson, Woodrow Wilson, and whonot: one must ask to see the documentary proofs, or to speak to the person who is supposed to have heard the putative poet recite his verse. Or else, as with the great Sea Monster of Loch Ness, the case must be left "unproved."

Occasionally the matter is entirely reversed. *Everybody* wants to be the father, and instead of being unable to discover the author, one is embarrassed with an excessive richness of rival claimants. Of one particular item, probably of the 1930's,

> Have you heard about Magda Lupescu,
> Who came to Rumania's rescue?
> It's a wonderful thing
> To be under a king —
> Is democracy better, I esk you?

it is necessary sadly to admit that the present writer has personally encountered not one, but three separate and distinct "authors" of this rhyme, one of whom — of Teutonic origin and fresh off the boat — could hardly pronounce any further words of the English language than this one limerick and his claim to authorship.

The bawdy limerick has now quieted down a good deal, from the days when it was an outcast thing, as evidenced in the remarkable letter on the mystery of its *name*, written by Dr. Murray, editor of the *Oxford English Dictionary*, to *Notes & Queries* in 1898, strongly objecting to its use in referring to innocent nonsense rhymes. It may be observed, as to the name "limerick," that the bawdy examples in *Cythera's Hymnal* and *The Pearl*, in the 1870's, and finally in *The Cremorne* ('1851,' really 1882), are invariably given under the rubric of "Nursery Rhymes." This pinpoints the coinage or acceptance of the name "limerick" as at some time between 1882 and 1898, possibly in the columns of the sporting newspaper, *The Pink 'Un* (a sort of British *Police Gazette*; both being imitations of earlier French risqué journals on colored pulp, such as *Le Piron*), to which Murray's indignant letter seems to allude, if not to *Pick-Me-Up*, or *Judy*. A retrospective volume of *Purple Plums Picked from the "Pink 'Un"* — of which the true title was actually *The Sporting Times,* founded in 1865 — was privately issued on the demise of this lively rag in 1931, on pink paper of course. Unfortunately, the "Plums" reprinted cover only the period beginning with World War I. Among these are indeed included many slightly off-color limericks, which is probably about as naughty as *The Pink 'Un* ever got.

IX

THE SHELVING away of the bawdy limerick now, almost as classic, is largely due to the collection published in Florence in 1928 by the Scottish antiquarian and novelist, Norman Douglas, who is the only person ever to have had the courage to sign a wholly bawdy limerick collection with his real name. *Some Limericks*, as Douglas' volume is modestly called, is not particularly large, containing only sixty-eight limericks, of which few can have been original with him, though one may suspect his improving hand in many. In his introduction, which is a masterpiece of dry humor, Douglas seems seriously to imply that he had also made a collection of Florentine swear words — and had "caught the old ones in the nick of time" — at the period when he was also compiling the "breathless catalogue" of his classic study (which he had to publish himself) of *London Street Games*, in 1913-16, with their titles so reminiscent of the similar list of old dances in the rediscovered manuscript fragments of Rabelais' *Pantagruel*, Bk. v, ch. xxxiii (translated by W. F. Smith, and Samuel Putnam). If the collection of swear words was not just one of Douglas' leg-pulls, which it does not seem to have been, it is a great pity it has not survived. Julian Sharman's perfectly titled *Cursory History of Swearing* (1884) does exist, and a more recent study by Prof. Burges Johnson, along with a curious manuscript collection on the subject, preserved at Princeton; and, for French, Robert Edouard's *Dictionnaire des Injures* (Paris: Tchou, 1967), with a similar work in Italian about ten years before; but these are not worth what a study at the hands of a master like Douglas would have been, as evidenced by the brief sample of his intended introduction, printed in that of *Some Limericks*.

If sheer size were any criterion, Douglas' work might be far overshadowed — which it most certainly is not — by the present collection, *The Limerick*, first published anonymously in Paris, 1953, giving nearly eighteen hundred bawdy limericks, good, bad, and indifferent, without critical evaluation or psychological study, but with a certain amount of historical annotation and folklore parallels. This reprints all formerly published bawdy limericks, and more than double that number of unpublished examples, arriving at the largest collection of limericks ever published, erotic or otherwise. An Addenda of nearly the same number of further examples has been accumulated since that time, in part from the private mimeographica of college students in the United States, and other privately printed works, and this should eventually be published. Meanwhile, a pamphlet plagiarism — if folklore can ever be said to be plagiarized — was issued by Maurice Girodias-Kahane's Olympia Press in Paris in 1955, edited by 'Count Palmiro Vicarrion,' magnanimously offering the tourist public a selection of two hundred limericks, taken and ruthlessly "improved" from *The Limerick*. A similar *'Bagman's'* volume — a title intended, of course, to twit the present writer — was also issued by the largest foreign-language bookstore in Paris, under the false imprint 'Milan.' The pseudonymous 'Vicarrion' is identified, in recent catalogues of the British bookseller Bernard Stone, as the internationally famous Liverpudlian poet, Mr. Christopher Logue, whose own signed volumes of Angry Young Man (British beatnik) poetry have been compared by *Time* magazine to the *Song of Songs*. I would not go quite so far.

Douglas' collection is nothing so pedestrian. His annotations, which have made the fame of his book, and are in part responsible for the continued popularity of the limerick, are strictly in the mock-serious style of Dr. Wagstaffe on *Tom Thumb*, Oliver Goldsmith's annotations to *Mother Goose*, and "To the Critics and Poets," earlier mentioned, as well as many similar *jeux d'esprit* in the eighteenth century. There is even a Geographical Index, similar to that of Cordonnier's *Chef d'Oeuvre d'un Inconnu*, tabulating with great seriousness all the sexual and scatological minutiae of the limerick adventures described. Since the original publication of *Some Limericks*, privately in Florence in 1928, there have been many piratical reprints (all listed below, in *The Limerick*, Bibliography, pp. 361–69). One in particular is disguised under the title, *From Bed to Worse*, printed secretly in Wiesbaden, in 1945, by "some members of the Army of Occupation in Germany," as its title-page states; forgetting, however, to mention Douglas at all. (Copy: Yale.)

A number of slavish imitations, not of Douglas' collection but of his manner of annotation in mock-serious style, have also been laboriously assembled and constructed, in manuscript and in print, most of them infinitely lacking in the wit of Douglas. The most glaring example is the preface to the 'Vicarrion' collection, mentioned above, which is almost difficult to credit, in its flat imitation and grovelling unhumorousness, confusing the mere use of dirty words and surréalist non-sequiturs with the art of bawdy humor. An equally bathetic plagiarism of Douglas was issued in Switzerland in 1944, under the title *A Collection of Limericks*, by one 'Nosti,' a would-be humorist somewhat imperfectly acquainted with the English language, and having the temerity not only to steal most of Douglas' text and notes, but to attempt to improve on and paraphrase the latter in broken English. The book is fortunately very rare. (Copy: Collection A. Plesch.)

One very striking lack, in the literature of the limerick, is that of almost any serious critical writing on the subject, despite the plethora of mock-pedantic — or do I mean very pedantic? — discussion of the sexual content of specific bawdy limericks, in the style of Douglas. The introductions to the usual clean collections, such as Louis Untermeyer's *Lots of Limericks: Light, Lusty, and Lasting* (New York, 1961), Bennett Cerf's *Out On a Limerick* (1960), and Langford Reed's *Complete Limerick Book* (2nd ed., London, 1926), which is one of the largest, are mostly twaddle. On the historical side, they are particularly hopeless, usually beginning — if not with Lear — with a wholly erroneous genealogy starting in France in the early eighteenth century, and arriving in Britain via Ireland. As against the century-long development of the limerick form in England from late medieval times, through the sixteenth-century song of the wandering madmen, "Tom o' Bedlam," exposed in the preceding pages, I do not think the French-Irish genealogical theory will bear scrutiny. As to the general psychology of the limerick, limerick-poets and limerick-fanciers, the two best early articles are that in the *Encyclopaedia Britannica* (14th ed., 1929) XIV. 130, by Edmund G. V. Knox, later editor of *Punch*; and especially "The Cult of the Limerick" by C. L. Graves, in the *Cornhill Magazine* (February 1918, vol. 44: No. 260). Valuable information is also brought together, in popular form, in William S. Baring-Gould's *The Lure of the Limerick* (New York, 1967), which is the first publicly-issued limerick collection courageously to include any bawdy examples without expurgation. The erotic newspaper, *Screw*, the most astonishing product — so far — of the New Freedom in America, also ran a page of bawdy limericks in its No. 22 (New York, July 31, 1969).

The American critic, Clifton Fadiman, writing on the limerick in "There Was an Old Man of Tobago," in his collection of essays, *Any Number Can Play* (Cleveland, 1957), goes so far as to deny that even Norman Douglas' own notes have any wit about them, and states coldly that "the book on the whole is a bore that makes its strongest appeal to the phoney Bohemian temperament." This sounds like treason in the ranks, but the true explanation is probably that Mr. Fadiman likes — and I suspect writes — those god-awful "clerihews," which are some kind of poetico-prosaic morphodites that only their inventors could love; so perhaps his testimony should be written off as biassed. All clerihews being perfervidly clean, they are all signed and of known authorship, something on the style of the epigraphs one observes in public lavatories: "I came, I seen, I SAW!!" as found by Dr. Allen Walker Read (*Lexical Evidence from Folk Epigraphy*, Paris, 1935, p. 18) in Timpanogos Cave, northern Utah. This sort of thing is vowed to the swift forgetfulness of a coat of paint, and is folklore only by courtesy. Far different are the anonymous gems of real folk-poetry and epigraphy, scrawled in diamond on the glasses and windows of old English taverns, as recorded in *The Merry-Thought, or The Glass-Window and Bog-House Miscellany* of 1731, in four parts. (Copies: Oxford, and Harding Collection, Chicago; with incomplete copies at Harvard, and British Museum, P.C.) The recent publicly-issued "Graffiti" volumes are all expurgated.

Since World War II, whole clubs have been organized for the perpetuation of bawdy limericks (never of clean ones), and their public annotation — inevitably in the style of Dr. Wagstaffe and Norman Douglas. An amusing phonograph recording has also been issued, under the title *Limerix,* about 1962, by a small American company (Cook), purportedly a .tape-recorded transcript of the proceedings of such a limerick club or society, with a harried president trying to run the meeting, and members of both sexes doing the singing and reciting, amid all the usual drinking, fighting, and ego-boost. The tone is, in fact, rather similar to that of the real meetings of such clubs, except for the omitted touch of self-satisfied whimsy in the Annual Norman Douglas Lecture; but the limericks presented — on the recording, at least — are of the mildest possible naughtiness, with all the impact of wet gingersnaps.

The real clubs of this kind have flourished mostly in the American west and midwest, in particular the American Limerick Society (which met in the home of Dr. MacIntyre in Berkeley, California, during the 1940's), and the Fifth Line Society of Chicago. The last-named, known in full as The Society for the Preservation of the Fifth Line, is the subject of a long explanatory letter or manifesto by one of its members, Mr. Merlin Bowen, in *Evergreen Review* (New York, August 1966) No. 42: pp. 16 and 93, announcing the Society's intention of bringing to public attention in the "strict iambic pentameter" [?!] of "action limericks ... the human side of sadism, the enlarging effects of pederasty, the genetic advantages of lesbianism, and the dietary benefits of fellatio. Most of us, let me say, are ashamed of our callous normality in the past and hope to do better in the future." If this was not, in fact, the peroration of the Annual Norman Douglas Lecture for 1967, the tone is close enough to serve as an exact sample. Aside from the mock-serious format, all this is of course an outgrowth of the similar college fraternity and army and air-force officers' bawdy-song societies and informal "beer busts," with their manuscript or mimeographed collections, few of which are ever seen by "outsiders" or are preserved. One wishes one could somehow convince the college professors, businessmen, advertising photographers, librarians, and science-fiction enthusiasts, who seem to make up most of the membership of these limerick clubs, that Norman Douglas has now had enough adulation and imitation, and please to lay off.

The only really interesting continuation of Douglas' little jest so far—and even there the notes are the least successful part of the imitation—is *That Immoral Garland*, an original manuscript by the American poet and translator (worth any twenty others today), the late Carlyle Ferren MacIntyre. This manuscript, dated 1942, includes over a hundred of this poet's original bawdy limericks, of which he was justly proud, in particular the one beginning "While Titian was mixing rose-madder" (No. 1473 in the present collection), which has already entered authentic oral circulation as folklore—something that very few new limericks ever do—and is probably the best known and most appreciated modern bawdy limerick.

As can be seen in the "Titian" prototype, not one of Dr. MacIntyre's limericks begins with the inactive "There *was*..." but leaps incontinently into the action of the piece from the very first line on. This attempt to free the limerick from the trammels of its wasted line—still generally thrown away on the meaningless affectation of an "improper" geographical rhyme, as Lear threw away *both* the first and last lines on the

INTRODUCTION lxix

same — is the only real improvement in the limerick form in over two centuries. Were it to be continued successfully, this might give the limerick a new lease on life. As it stands, the only other new element in modern limericks is purely one of content, imported by an enthusiast group utterly collegiate in background, which is now also concerning itself with the concoction of bawdy limericks: the science-fiction fan club kids, both adolescent and superannuated. Of their output it can only be said that if the organ-deficiencies and melancholy accidents of normally bawdy limericks sometimes make depressing reading, the same *in mathematical symbols*, and involving complicated quasi-sexual intercourse with mechanical contraptions and with the blue gleeps and green bleeps of the planets Mars and Venus, is truly too sad to endure.

Certain rich gifte-booke publishers, such as the late Peter Beilenson of the over-modestly titled "Peter Pauper Press," and most of the theoretically terribly virile "men's magazines" in America and Britain, such as *Playboy, Penthouse*, and their mutually incestuous imitations, all of which are expurgated to the hilt, have also been featuring, since the mid-1950's, volumelets or a page per issue of mildly bawdy jokes and limericks, more or less on the Naughty-Naughts style of *The Pink 'Un* in the 1890's, and all running pretty $tinking $cared, if the truth is to be told. The best part of these publications is usually the art-work, when this does not descend to low cartoon-humor, high camp and *kitsch*. In this line, an extended series of newly-written though not very off-color limericks appeared in the more than twenty issues of the bawdy joke-&-cartoon magazine, *Sex to Sexty* (Arlington, Texas: John Newbern Co.) during the 1960's. Most of these were written by a San Francisco advertising man, the late John Coulthard (pronounced: Cole-th'rd), who believed, probably correctly, that he had written the largest number of limericks ever produced by one person, thus barely getting in ahead of the IBM machine. — "Ten thousand raunchy limericks, and another ten thousand clean!" his publisher announces proudly, in volume 4 of *Sex to Sexty* (December 1965), which is cover-titled *Grand Prix Limerix*, and is devoted entirely to one thousand and one of Coulthard's "semi-dirty" anonymous originals — meaning dirty, but without any four-letter words! As an act of dying contrition, Coulthard then issued privately a large, folding sheet of some of his unexpurgated examples, with erotic cartoon illustrations by himself. Very few copies of this erotic supplement were printed, nor did it accompany the *Sex to Sexty* issue, which it makes look very weak.

Driving hard for the world's record, a new SUPER *Sex to Sexty* No. 7 was issued in 1969, containing three hundred original off-color limericks, "every one illustrated," edited and in part written by a woman, Peggy "Goose" Rodebaugh. (The Los Angeles left-wing collection, *Unexpurgated*, in 1943, had earlier also been co-edited by a woman.) A 448-page illustrated paperback volume, reprinting all the limericks that had appeared to date in *Sex to Sexty* — including John Coulthard's "semi-dirty" thousand — was also announced, to include 2,200 examples. This is still, of course, far from Coulthard's total, or even from that of the present collection and its Addenda.

The neurotic compulsiveness or gigantism implied in the brag about writing twenty thousand limericks (in only one lifetime) is unfortunately no longer the private folly of one limerick poet. In Baring-Gould's *The Lure of the Limerick*, p. 109-10, mention is made of a current New York luncheon club, apparently called The Poets Club, "composed entirely of highly literate business and professional men," whose purpose, aside from a very creditable concern about Shakespeare's reputation as a playwright — every little bit helps — is "to collect and card-file in their archives every erotic limerick known to English-speaking man." Perhaps they should begin with John Coulthard's unpublished limericks, which he wrote into large scrapbooks sent to a friend, often in the margins of pages torn from medical works and the like, showing genital diseases and malformations, which the limerick celebrates or reproves. These scrapbooks are now in the possession of his publisher, but nothing seems to have been printed from them. A transcript of the best thousand of these limericks was entrusted to me by Coulthard just before his death, for use in the proposed Addenda volume to the present work. One good limerick out of every ten written is a better average than most poets hit. The best recent unexpurgated limericks I have seen are those of Mr. Jay Thompson, formerly of South Carolina, none of which have as yet been published.

What remains to be said? The future. Have limericks a future? Yes, certainly they have a future, and a livelier present than those damn clerihews! Only in English, of course, though imitations and even translations of both the clean and bawdy forms do exist abroad, oddly enough only in the proto-English languages, Dutch and German. These are definitely imitations and do not date earlier than the present century, being now at the level of a minor newspaper fad. All limericks in French are actually in "fractured French," by English-speaking poets, and are usually terrible. The worst are those in 'Gorey's' *The Listing Attic*; the best are by George du Maurier, reprinted in Langford Reed's *The Complete Limerick Book*, p. 68–69, and they are a mark to shoot at for poets who consider this type of ungrammatical language-parody funny. As Prof. Brander Matthews long ago observed, in *A Study of Versification* (1911) p. 145: "The humble limerick has the distinction of being the only fixed [poetic] form which is actually indigenous to English." It apparently also intends to stay that way.

It should be clearly understood that rhymed poetry of any kind other than limericks is seldom written today in English, the rhymeless poetry of Walt Whitman's spasmodic school having swept the board. The principal exceptions are the would-be "popular songs," composed and copyrighted by the tens of thousands (specifically, sixty thousand per year in the U.S.A. alone!) in the delusory hope of monetary gain. These songs no one but their composers ever sings — if them — and the long-suffering public is never even exposed to 99% of them. With this signal exception, the limerick — specifically the bawdy limerick — represents today the principal type and amount of traditionally rhymed poetry being written in the English language, and with any audience. It is also the only newly-composed poetry in English with any chance whatever of oral circulation at the popular level, in traditional folklore fashion, something available to even the most popular of "popular songs" only for a brief few months or weeks. Meanwhile, dozens of bawdy limericks now anywhere up to a century old are today still being endlessly sung or recited, as old favorites, and their popularity shows no sign of diminishing.

It must of course be admitted that, what with the New Freedom on the one hand making the bawdy limerick's themes and defied repressions somewhat old-hat, and the New Passivity of the media-feedback culture on the other hand making *any* kind of poetry almost too much of an effort for the colorless and unvirile people ("unisex") multiplying like skinned rabbits all around us, the limerick may fall dead and disappear tomorrow. In that case, perhaps this will be the record of its only really popular form in the century of its popularity. For, not to put too fine a point to it, the limerick is not only the only fixed poetic form original to the English language, but the bawdy limerick in particular is today the *only* kind of newly-composed poetry in English, or song, which has the slightest chance whatever of survival.

All in all, one suspects that the limerick of the future will be hopelessly similar to the limerick of the past, and will change merely externally, in the technology and terminology of the horrible castratory accidents over which it all too often gloats. Even so, it would be manifestly unfair to deny to any class, even the educated class, the right to create and circulate whatever folklore and folksong it is capable of, however weakly verbal and uselessly formal the more virile classes might find this folklore to be. The egghead is getting it from all sides: I do not feel his limerick should be taken away from him, or that he should be forced to sing it — just to prove he's one of "the Boyes," which he isn't — when, really, he would much prefer to be sitting placidly in the library annotating his limericks with parallel texts from Martial, the *Priapeia,* and the *Greek Anthology*; and never get out and *do* any of the boldly bawdy things mentioned in these limerick fantasies at all.

To avoid the accusation of having cravenly evaded giving any real limericks, in all the dusty library-annotation that has gone before, let me end this essay and open the brawl — as to my errors, "tone," and so on — by quoting at least one limerick, which is not only authentically erotic, in its mild way, and does not begin with the false and wasted accent of "There *was*..." but has also the remarkable peculiarity of being the favorite limerick of quite a few women, most of whom otherwise loathe limericks (in which they generally figure both as villain and victim), for the same reason that calves hate cookbooks:

> For the tenth time, dull Daphnis, said Chloë,
> You have told me my bosom is snowy;
>   You've made much fine verse on
>   Each part of my person,
> Now *do* something — there's a good boy!

La Clé des Champs
Valbonne (Alpes-Maritimes)
FRANCE

SOURCES

This is the largest collection of limericks ever published, erotic or otherwise. The seventeen hundred examples gathered here stem, about one-third, from some twenty printed sources dating from 1870 to 1952, most of which duplicate each other to a great extent. The rest are principally from three oral collections, made in Ann Arbor, Michigan (MS. 1938-1941), in Berkeley, California (1942-1947), and in New York (1941-1952). Almost no British materials after 1928 have been available. The chapter-titles are those of *Lapses in Limerick,* the Michigan collection. A chronological list of the sources used follows. Fuller details, and a few minor sources, will be found in the bibliography preceding the notes.

Variant lines, couplets and conclusions are given at the end of the text, with varia in geographical and personal names (in rhyming positions) cited and indexed. Minor variations in phrasing and vocabulary have not seemed worth reporting here. A full Index, of names and rhymes, will be found at the end of the volume, and should make convenient the locating of any desired limerick in spite of the division of the text into chapters. A few folklore parallels are made and explanations given, but humorous and didactic excursi on the style of Norman Douglas' *Some Limericks* (1928) have not been attempted.

Sources are given for each limerick by means of the date. Dates and sources are listed together facing the next page. Where two dates follow a limerick, the second is the actual source of the text; the first is the earliest known variant printing or collecting of it.

These dates have other uses as well, such as turning up all the new limericks in any listed source, or the complete contents of the three known collections of original limericks: *Cythera's Hymnal* (1870), *The Pearl* (1879-1880), and *That Immoral Garland* (MS. 1942A). Chronological changes in the dominant limerick themes over the last eighty years in England and America may also easily be traced, and will provide an unparalleled key to the socio-sexual anxieties of the period.

No improvement has been made upon orally transmitted or printed materials. The limericks are given as found in the sources credited. (Exceptions: punctuation and the spelling of geographical names have been made uniform, expurgations have been spelled out, and the first names of real private persons have been dropped.) The text is eclectic only to the degree of choosing one form — not necessarily the oldest — on which to base all variants. The prejudices, cruelty, and humorless quality of many of the limericks included are deeply regretted. However, no falsification of the material has been made.

THE EDITOR.

SOURCES

1870. *Cythera's Hymnal, or Flakes from the Foreskin.*
1879 to 1880. *The Pearl* ('Oxford').
1882. *The Cremorne* ('March 1851').
1910 to 1911. Dr. SUSRUTA, in *Anthropophyteia.*
1927. *Immortalia* (Philadelphia).
1927A. *Anecdota Americana* ('Boston').
1928. Norman DOUGLAS: *Some Limericks.*
1928A. 'O. U. SCHWEINICKLE': *The Book of 1000 Laughs.*
1928B. *Poems, Ballads and Parodies* ('Paris, 1923').
1928C. 'Dave E. JONES': *A Collection of Sea Songs.*
1932. 'John FALMOUTH': *Ninety-five Limericks.*
1934. *Anecdota Americana, Second Series* ('Boston').
1938 to 1941. *Lapses in Limerick* (MS.)
1939A. Weston LA BARRE, in *Psychiatry* (May 1939).
1941A. *Pornographia Literaria* (mimeo).
1942 to 1947. *Index Limericus* (MS.)
1942A. *That Immoral Garland* (MS.)
1943A. *Unexpurgated* (Los Angeles).
1943B. [Clement WOOD] *The Facts of Life in Limericks.*
1943C. *An Investigation into... Limericks* (mimeo).
1944A to 1948A. New York (oral collection).
1945C. *Farmer Gray* (mimeo).
1946B. [DAVIS] *The International Set.*
1947B. [HARRISON MS.]
1948. [MORSE] *The Limerick: A Facet of Our Culture.*
1949. [DRAKE] *A Book of Anglo-Saxon Verse.*
1950 to 1952. New York (oral collection).

THE LIMERICK

I

LITTLE ROMANCES

1

There was a young girl of Aberystwyth
Who took grain to the mill to get grist with.
    The miller's son, Jack,
      Laid her flat on her back,
And united the organs they pissed with.
                      1927-1941.

2

There was a young lady of Arden,
The tool of whose swain wouldn't harden.
    Said she with a frown,
    " I've been sadly let down
By the tool of a fool in a garden."
                      1941.

3

There once was a yokel of Beaconsfield
Engaged to look after the deacon's field,
    But he lurked in the ditches
    And diddled the bitches
Who happened to cross that antique 'un's field.
                      1941.

4

There's a charming young lady named Beaulieu
Who's often been screwed by yours truly,
    But now—it's appallin'—
    My balls always fall in!
I fear that I've fucked her unduly.
                      1941.

LITTLE ROMANCES

5

There was a young girl in Berlin
Who was fucked by an elderly Finn.
  Though he diddled his best,
  And fucked her with zest,
She kept asking, " Hey, Pop, is it in ? "
1927-1941.

6

I wooed a stewed nude in Bermuda,
I was lewd, but my God! she was lewder.
  She said it was crude
  To be wooed in the nude—
I pursued her, subdued her, and screwed her!
1941-1952.

7

There was a young lady of Bicester
Who was nicer by far than her sister:
  The sister would giggle
  And wiggle and jiggle,
But this one would come if you kissed her.
1941-1952.

8

There once was a son-of-a-bitch,
Neither clever, nor handsome, nor rich,
  Yet the girls he would dazzle,
  And fuck to a frazzle,
And then *ditch* them, the son-of-a-bitch!
1941.

9

There was a young fellow named Blaine,
And he screwed some disgusting old jane.
  She was ugly and smelly,
  With an awful pot-belly,
But... well, they were caught in the rain.
1941.

10

There was a young sailor from Brighton
Who remarked to his girl, " You're a tight one. "
    She replied, " 'Pon my soul,
    You're in the wrong hole;
There's plenty of room in the right one. "
                        1882-1943C.

11

A lacklustre lady of Brougham
Weaveth all night at her loom.
    Anon she doth blench
    When her lord and his wench
Pull a chain in the neighbouring room.
                        1942.

12

A middle-aged codger named Bruin
Found his love life completely a-ruin,
    For he flirted with flirts
    Wearing pants and no skirts,
And he never got in for no screwin'.
                        1946A.

13

There was a young fellow of Burma
Whose betrothed had good reason to murmur.
    But now that he's married he's
    Been using cantharides
And the root of their love is much firmer.
                        1939A.

14

There was a young fellow from Cal.,
In bed with a passionate gal.
    He leapt from the bed,
    To the toilet he sped;
Said the gal, " What about *me*, old pal ? "
                        1952.

15

There was a young man from Calcutta
Who was heard in his beard to mutter,
    "If her Bartholin glands
    Don't respond to my hands,
I'm afraid I shall have to use butter."

              1947B.

16

There once was a kiddie named Carr
Caught a man on top of his mar.
    As he saw him stick 'er,
    He said with a snicker,
"You do it much faster than par."

              1927.

17

There was a young fellow named Charteris
Put his hand where his young lady's garter is.
    Said she, "I don't mind,
    And up higher you'll find
The place where my fucker and farter is."

              1927-1941.

18

A young woman got married at Chester,
Her mother she kissed and she blessed her.
    Says she, "You're in luck,
    He's a stunning good fuck,
For I've had him myself down in Leicester."

              1870.

19

"For the tenth time, dull Daphnis," said Chloe,
"You have told me my bosom is snowy;
    You have made much fine verse on
    Each part of my person,
Now *do* something—there's a good boy!"

              1942.

20

A maiden who wrote of big cities
Some songs full of love, fun and pities,
    Sold her stuff at the shop
    Of a musical wop
Who played with her soft little titties.
*1935**

21

There once was a gouty old colonel
Who grew glum when the weather grew vernal,
    And he cried in his tiffin
    For his prick wouldn't stiffen,
And the *size* of the thing was infernal.
1941.

22

A lady while dining at Crewe
Found an elephant's whang in her stew.
    Said the waiter, "Don't shout,
    And don't wave it about,
Or the others will all want one too."
1941.

23

There was a young lady of Dee
Who went down to the river to pee.
    A man in a punt
    Put his hand on her cunt,
And God! how I wish it was me.
1870-1941.

24

I never have had Miss Defauw,
But it wouldn't have been quite so raw
    If she'd only said "No"
    When I wanted her so;
But she didn't—she laughed and said "Naw!"
1941.

25

A beautiful belle of Del Norte
Is reckoned disdainful and haughrty
   Because during the day
   She says : " Boys, keep away! "
But she fucks in the gloaming like forty.
1946A.

26

A young man by a girl was desired
To give her the thrills she required,
   But he died of old age
   Ere his cock could assuage
The volcanic desire it inspired.
1941.

27

There was a young lady of Dover
Whose passion was such that it drove her
   To cry, when you came,
   " Oh dear! What a shame!
Well, now we shall have to start over. "
1941.

28

There was a young man of Dumfries
Who said to his girl, " If you please,
   It would give me great bliss
   If, while playing with this,
You would pay some attention to these! "
1941.

29

There was a young lady of Ealing
And her lover before her was kneeling.
   Said she, " Dearest Jim,
   Take your hand off my quim;
I much prefer fucking to feeling. "
1870.

30

A lonely young lad of Eton
Used always to sleep with the heat on,
    Till he ran into a lass
    Who showed him her ass—
Now they sleep with only a sheet on.
                      1943.

31

There was a young lady of Exeter,
So pretty, that men craned their necks at her.
    One was even so brave
    As to take out and wave
The distinguishing mark of his sex at her.
                     1927-1941.

32

There was a young lady of fashion
Who had oodles and oodles of passion.
    To her lover she said,
    As they climbed into bed,
" Here's *one* thing the bastards can't ration! "
                      1942.

33

There was a young girl in Dakota
Had a letter from Ickes; he wrote her:
    " In addition to gas
    We are rationing ass,
And you've greatly exceeded your quota. "
                      1942.

34

There was a young lady named Flynn
Who thought fornication a sin,
    But when she was tight
    It seemed quite all right,
So everyone filled her with gin.
                     1927-1941.

35

A reckless young lady of France
Had no qualms about taking a chance,
    But she thought it was crude
    To get screwed in the nude,
So she always went home with damp pants.

1941.

36

A nervous young fellow named Fred
Took a charming young widow to bed.
    When he'd diddled a while
    She remarked with a smile,
" You've got it all in but the head. "

1941.

37

There was a young fellow named Fyfe
Whose marriage was ruined for life,
    For he had an aversion
    To every perversion,
And only liked fucking his wife.

Well, one year the poor woman struck,
And she wept, and she cursed at her luck,
    And said, " Where have you gotten us
    With your goddamn monotonous
Fuck after fuck after fuck?

" I once knew a harlot named Lou—
And a versatile girl she was, too.
    After ten years of whoredom
    She perished of boredom
When she married a jackass like you! "

1938.

40

There was a young lady of Gloucester,
Met a passionate fellow who tossed her.
    She wasn't much hurt,
    But he dirtied her skirt,
So think of the anguish it cost her.

                    1927-1941.

41

There was a young lady of Gloucester
Whose friends they thought they had lost her,
    Till they found on the grass
    The marks of her arse,
And the knees of the man who had crossed her.

                    1870.

42

There was a young fellow named Goody
Who claimed that he wouldn't, but would he?
    If he found himself nude
    With a gal in the mood,
The question's not woody but could he?

                    1944A.

43

In my sweet little Alice Blue gown
Was the first time I ever laid down,
    I was both proud and shy
    As he opened his fly
And the moment I saw it I thought I would die.

Oh it hung almost down to the ground,
As it went in I made not a sound,
    The more that he shoved it
    The more that I loved it,
As he came on my Alice Blue gown.

                    1944A.

45

In my sweet little night gown of blue,
On the first night that I slept with you,
    I was both shy and scared
    As the bed was prepared,
And you played peekaboo with my ribbons of blue.

As we both watched the break of the day,
And in peaceful submission I lay,
    You said you adored it
    But dammit, you tore it,
My sweet little night gown of blue.

                      1944*

47

Winter is here with his grouch,
The time when you sneeze and slouch.
    You can't take your women
    Canoein' or swimmin',
But a lot can be done on a couch.

                      1927.

48

It always delights me at Hanks
To walk up the old river banks.
    One time in the grass
    I stepped on an ass,
And heard a young girl murmur, " Thanks. "

                      1946A.

49

There was a young girl from Hong Kong
Who said, " You are utterly wrong
    To say my vagina
    's the largest in China,
Just because of your mean little dong. "

                      1944.

50

There was once a sad Maître d'hôtel
Who said, " They can all go to hell !
    What they do to my wife—
    Why it ruins my life;
And the worst is, they all do it well. "

1943A.

51

There was a young man named Hughes
Who swore off all kinds of booze.
    He said, " When I'm muddled
    My senses get fuddled,
And I pass up too many screws. "

1927.

52

There were three ladies of Huxham,
And whenever we meets 'em we fucks 'em,
    And when that game grows stale
    We sits on a rail,
And pulls out our pricks and they sucks 'em.

1870.

53

There was a young lady named Inge
Who went on a binge with a dinge.
    Now I won't breathe a word
    Of what really occurred—
But her cunt has a chocolate fringe.

1943B.

54

An octogenarian Jew
To his wife remained steadfastly true.
    This was not from compunction,
    But due to dysfunction
Of his spermatic glands—nuts to you.

1941.

55

"Snyder's got a stiff ticket," said Kay,
"Come on, take it out, and let's play."
   He pulled it on out,
   But she started to pout,
His ticket was only a quarter-inch stout.
                             1943.

56

A pansy who lived in Khartoum
Took a lesbian up to his room,
   And they argued all night
   Over who had the right
To do what, and with which, and to whom.
                         1941-1952.

57

There was an old lady who lay
With her legs wide apart in the hay,
   Then, calling the ploughman,
   She said, "Do it now, man!
Don't wait till your hair has turned gray."
                         1928-1941.

58

There was a young lady of Lee
Who scrambled up into a tree,
   When she got there
   Her arsehole was bare,
And so was her K U N T.
                             1870.

59

A worn-out young husband named Lehr
Heard daily his wife's plaintive prayer:
   "Slip on a sheath, quick,
   Then slip your big dick
Between these lips covered with hair."
                           1945A.

60

There was a young plumber of Leigh
Who was plumbing a girl by the sea.
   She said, " Stop your plumbing,
   There's somebody coming! "
Said the plumber, still plumbing, " It's me. "
                     1927-1928.

61

Il y avait un plombier, François,
Qui plombait sa femme dans le Bois.
   Dit-elle, " Arrêtez!
   J'entends quelqu'un venait. "
Dit le plombier, en plombant, " C'est moi. "
                     1941.

62

Es giebt ein Arbeiter von Tinz,
Er schläft mit ein Mädel von Linz.
   Sie sagt, " Halt sein' plummen,
   Ich höre Mann kommen. "
" Jacht, jacht, " sagt der Plummer, " Ich binz. "
                     1952.

63

Prope mare erat tubulator
Qui virginem ingrediebatur.
   Dessine ingressus
   Audivi progressus :
Est mihi inquit tubulator.
                     1941.

64

Have you heard of knock-kneed Samuel McGuzzum
Who married Samantha, his bow-legged cousin ?
   Some people say
   Love finds a way,
But for Sam and Samantha it doesn'.
                     1947B.

65

In bed Dr. Oscar McPugh
Spoke of Spengler—and ate crackers too.
    His wife said, " Oh, stuff
    That philosophy guff
Up your ass, dear, and throw me a screw! "

                          1941.

66

There was a young lady named Maud
A terrible society fraud :
    In company, I'm told
    She was awfully cold.
But if you got her alone, Oh God!

                          1927.

67

There was a young lady named May
Who strolled in a park by the way,
    And she met a young man
    Who fucked her and ran—
Now she goes to the park every day.

                          1941.

68

There once was a Swede in Minneapolis,
Discovered his sex life was hapless :
    The more he would screw
    The more he'd want *to,*
And he feared he would soon be quite sapless.

                         1946A.

69

There was a young dolly named Molly
Who thought that to frig was folly.
    Said she, " Your pee-pee
    Means nothing to me,
But I'll do it just to be jolly. "

                          1927.

70

Of his face she thought *not* very much,
But then, at the very first touch,
    Her attitude shifted—
    He was terribly gifted
At frigging and fucking and such.

                  1948A.

71

The King plugged the Queen's ass with mustard
To make her fuck hot, but got flustered,
    And he cried, " Oh, my dear,
    I am coming, I fear,
But the mustard will make you come *plus tard!* "

                  1941.

72

There was a young lad from Nahant
Who was made like the Sensitive Plant.
    When asked, " Do you fuck ? "
    He replied, " No such luck.
I would if I could but I can't. "

                1928-1932.

73

There was a young man of Natal
Who was fucking a Hottentot gal.
    Said she, " You're a sluggard! "
    Said he, " You be buggered!
I like to fuck slow, and I shall. "

                1879-1941.

74

There was a young man of Natal
And Sue was the name of his gal.
    One day, north of Aden,
    He got his hard rod in,
And came clear up Suez Canal.

                1928-1943B.

75

There was a gay dog from Ontario
Who fancied himself a Lothario.
    At a wench's glance
    He'd snatch off his pants
And make for her Mons Venerio.

1946A.

76

There was a young man of Ostend
Who let a girl play with his end.
    She took hold of Rover,
    And felt it all over,
And it did what she didn't intend.

1927-1941.

77

There was a young man of Ostend
Whose wife caught him fucking her friend.
    " It's no use, my duck,
    Interrupting our fuck,
For I'm damned if I draw till I spend. "

1879.

78

There was a young fellow from Parma
Who was solemnly screwing his charmer.
    Said the damsel, demure,
    " You'll excuse me, I'm sure,
But I *must* say you fuck like a farmer. "

1941.

79

A newly-wed man of Peru
Found himself in a terrible stew :
    His wife was in bed
    Much deader than dead,
And so he had no one to screw.

1946A.

80

There was a young girl of Pitlochry
Who was had by a man in a rockery.
    She said, " Oh! You've come
      All over my bum;
This isn't a fuck—it's a mockery."
                                            1928.

81

There was a young lady named Prentice
Who had an affair with a dentist.
    To make the thing easier
      He used anesthesia,
And diddled her, *non compos mentis*.
                                            1941.

82

There was a young man with a prick
Which into his wife he would stick
    Every morning and night
    If it stood up all right—
Not a very remarkable trick.

His wife had a nice little cunt:
It was hairy, and soft, and in front,
    And with this she would fuck him,
    Though sometimes she'd suck him—
A charming, if commonplace, stunt.
                                           1941.

84

There was a young man from Purdue
Who was only just learning to screw,
    But he hadn't the knack,
    And he got too far back—
In the right church, but in the wrong pew.
                                            1941.

85

A young lady sat on a quay,
Just as proper as proper could be.
   A young fellow goosed her,
   And roughly seduced her,
So she thanked him and went home to tea.

1941.

86

I once was annoyed by a queer
Who made his intentions quite clear.
   Said I, " I'm no prude,
   So don't think me rude,
But I'm already stewed, screwed, and tattooed."

1944-1952.

87

A young wife in the outskirts of Reims
Preferred frigging to going to mass.
   Said her husband, " Take Jacques,
   Or any young cock,
For I cannot live up to your ass."

1942A.

88

The king named Œdipus Rex
Who started this fuss about sex
   Put the world to great pains
   By the spots and the stains
Which he made on his mother's pubex.

1946A.

89

Now hear this fair lass from Rhode Isle
Who said with a wink and a smile,
   " Sure, please stick it in,
   Be it thick be it thin,
But if's rough I won't do as a file."

1952.

90

There was a young lady of Rhyll
In an omnibus was taken ill,
    So she called the conductor,
    Who got in and fucked her,
Which did her more good than a pill.
              1870.

91

There was a young German named Ringer
Who was screwing an opera singer.
    Said he with a grin,
    " Well, I've sure got it in! "
Said she, " You mean that ain't your finger? "
              1941.

92

A young violinist from Rio
Was seducing a lady named Cleo.
    As she took down her panties
    She said, " No *andantes*;
I want this *allegro con brio!* "
              1941.

93

A young Juliet of St. Louis
On a balcony stood, acting screwy.
    Her Romeo climbed,
    But he wasn't well timed,
And half-way up, off he went—blooey!
             1927-1941.

94

Said a lecherous fellow named Shea,
When his prick wouldn't rise for a lay,
    " You must seize it, and squeeze it,
    And tease it, and please it,
For Rome wasn't built in a day. "
              1941.

95
There was a young man from Siam
Who said, " I go in with a wham,
    But I soon lose my starch
    Like the mad month of March,
And the lion comes out like a lamb. "
                                 1947.

96
Prince Absalom lay with his sister
And bundled and nibbled and kissed her,
    But the kid was so tight,
    And it was deep night—
Though he shot at the target, he missed her.
                               1942A.

97
There was a young fellow named Skinner
Who took a young lady to dinner.
    At a quarter to nine
    They sat down to dine;
At twenty to ten it was in her.
    The dinner, not Skinner—
Skinner was in her before dinner.

There was a young fellow named Tupper
Who took a young lady to supper.
    At a quarter to nine
    They sat down to dine,
And at twenty to ten it was up her.
    Not the supper—not Tupper—
It was some son-of-a-bitch named Skinner!
                             1911-1948A.

99
" My back aches. My penis is sore.
I simply can't fuck any more.
    I'm dripping with sweat,
    And you haven't come yet;
And, my God! it's a quarter to four! "
                                 1941.

LITTLE ROMANCES

100

There was a young lady of Spain
Who took down her pants on a train.
    There was a young porter
    Saw more than he orter,
And asked her to do it again.
                    1939A.

101

There was a young man of high station
Who was found by a pious relation
    Making love in a ditch
    To—I won't say a bitch—
But a woman of *no* reputation.
                    1938.

102

There once was a dentist named Stone
Who saw all his patients alone.
    In a fit of depravity
    He filled the wrong cavity,
And my, how his practice has grown!
                    1945-1947B.

103

A sailor who slept in the sun
Woke to find his fly-buttons undone.
    He remarked with a smile,
    " Jesus Christ, a sundial!
And it's now a quarter past one. "
                    1948A.

104

A plumber whose name was Ten Brink
Plumbed the cook as she bent o'er the sink.
    Her resistance was stout,
    And Ten Brink petered out
With his pipe-wrench all limber and pink.
                    1942A.

105

The spouse of a pretty young thing
Came home from the wars in the spring.
    He was lame but he came
    With his dame like a flame—
A discharge is a wonderful thing.

1947B.

106

I wonder what my wife will want tonight;
Wonder if the wife will fuss and fight?
    I wonder can she tell
    That I've been raising hell;
Wonder if she'll know that I've been tight?

My wife is just as nice as nice can be,
I hope she doesn't feel too nice toward me,
    For an afternoon of joy
    Is hell on the old boy.
I wonder what the wife will want tonight!

1927.

108

There's an unbroken babe from Toronto,
Exceedingly hard to get onto,
    But when you get there,
    And have parted the hair,
You can fuck her as much as you want to.

1941.

109

Une jolie épousette à Tours
Voulait de gig-gig tous les jours.
    Mais le mari disait, " Non!
    De trop n'est pas bon!
Mon derrière exige du secours! "

1942A.

110

A pretty wife living in Tours
Demanded her daily amour.
    But the husband said, "No!
    It's too much. Let it go!
My backsides are dragging the floor."

1942A

111

In the shade of the old apple tree
Where between her fat legs I could see
    A little brown spot
    With the hair in a knot,
And it certainly looked good to me.

I asked as I tickled her tit
If she thought that my big thing would fit.
    She said it would do
    So we had a good screw
In the shade of the old apple tree.

In the shade of the old apple tree
I got all that was coming to me.
    In the soft dewy grass
    I had a fine piece of ass
From a maiden that was fine to see.

I could hear the dull buzz of the bee
As he sunk his grub hooks into me.
    Her ass it was fine
    But you should have seen mine
In the shade of the old apple tree.

1928B.

115

A lad from far-off Transvaal
Was lustful, but tactful withal.
    He'd say, just for luck,
    " Mam'selle, do you fuck ? "
But he'd bow till he almost would crawl.

                      1939A.

116

There was a young lady of Twickenham
Who thought men had not enough prick in 'em.
    On her knees every day
    To God she would pray
To lengthen and strengthen and thicken 'em.

                      1927–1932.

117

There was a young lady named Twiss
Who said she thought fucking a bliss,
    For it tickled her bum
    And caused her to come
While comfortably lying like this.

                      1948A.

118

There once was a husky young Viking
Whose sexual prowess was striking.
    Every time he got hot
    He would scour the twat
Of some girl that might be to his liking.

                      1947.

119

At the moment Japan declared war
A sailor was fucking a whore.
    He said, " After this poke
    'Long and hard' ain't no joke;
This means *months* till I get back ashore. "

                      1942–1951.

120

There was a young lady of Wheeling
Said to her beau, " I've a feeling
   My little brown jug
   Has need of a plug "—
And straightway she started to peeling.

                             1927.

121

Two anglers were fishing off Wight
And his bobber was dipping all night.
   Murmured she, with a laugh,
 " It is ready to gaff,
But don't break your rod, which is light. "

A couple was fishing near Clombe
When the maid began looking quite glum,
   And said, " Bother the fish!
   I'd rather coish! "
Which they did—which was why they had come.

As two consular clerks in Madras
Fished, hidden in deep shore-grass,
   " What a marvelous pole, "
   Said she, " but control
Your sinkers—they're banging my ass. "

                            1942A.

124

Love letters no longer they write us,
To their homes they so seldom invite us.
   It grieves me to say,
   They have learned with dismay,
We can't cure their *vulva pruritus*.

                             1927.

125

There was a young student from Yale
Who was getting his first piece of tail.
   He shoved in his pole,
   But in the wrong hole,
And a voice from beneath yelled : " No sale! "
1941.

II

ORGANS

126

In the Garden of Eden lay Adam,
Complacently stroking his madam,
    And loud was his mirth
    For on all of the earth
There were only two balls—and he had 'em.
                              1941.

127

There was a young bride of Antigua
Whose husband said, " Dear me, how big you are! "
    Said the girl, " What damn'd rot!
    Why, you've often felt my twot,
My legs and my arse and my figua! "
                              1880.

128

There was a young damsel named Baker
Who was poked in a pew by a Quaker.
    He yelled, " My God! what
    Do you call this—a twat?
Why, the entrance is more than an acre! "
                              1943B.

129

There was once a mechanic named Bench
Whose best tool was a sturdy gut-wrench.
    With this vibrant device
    He could reach, in a trice,
The innermost parts of a wench.
                              1943A.

130

There was a young man of Bengal
Who swore he had only one ball,
    But two little bitches
    Unbuttoned his britches,
And found he had *no* balls at all.

                        1870-1941.

131

A chippy who worked in Black Bluff
Had a pussy as large as a muff.
    It had room for both hands
    And some intimate glands,
And was soft as a little duck's fluff.

                        1942A.

132

There was a young lady named Blount
Who had a rectangular cunt.
    She learned for diversion
    Posterior perversion,
Since no one could fit her in front.

                        1943A.

133

There was a young fellow named Bowen
Whose pecker kept growin' and growin'.
    It grew so tremendous,
    So long and so pendulous,
'Twas no good for fuckin'—just showin'.

                        1945C.

134

There was a young lady named Brent
With a cunt of enormous extent,
    And so deep and so wide,
    The acoustics inside
Were so good you could hear when you spent

                        1941.

135

There was a young girl from the Bronix
Who had a vagina of onyx.
    She had so much *tsoris*
    With her clitoris,
She traded it in for a Packard.

                           1943C.

136

There was a young lady from Brussels
Who was proud of her vaginal muscles.
    She could easily plex them
    And so interflex them
As to whistle love songs through her bustles.

                       1941A-1942.

137

There was a young lady of Bude
Who walked down the street in the nude.
    A bobby said, " Whattum
    Magnificent bottom! "
And slapped it as hard as he could.

                             1938.

138

There once was a Queen of Bulgaria
Whose bush had grown hairier and hairier,
    Till a Prince from Peru
    Who came up for a screw
Had to hunt for her cunt with a terrier.

                             1938.

139

There was a young girl of Cah'lina,
Had a very capricious vagina :
    To the shock of the fucker
    'Twould suddenly pucker,
And whistle the chorus of " Dinah ."

                             1941.

140

A lady with features cherubic
Was famed for her area pubic.
    When they asked her its size
    She replied in surprise,
" Are you speaking of square feet, or cubic ? "
1941.

141

There was a fat lady of China
Who'd a really enormous vagina,
    And when she was dead
    They painted it red,
And used it for docking a liner.
1941.

142

I met a young man in Chungking
Who had a very long thing—
    But you'll guess my surprise
    When I found that its size
Just measured a third-finger ring!
1945.

143

There was a young man of Coblenz
Whose ballocks were simply immense :
    It took forty-four draymen,
    A priest and three laymen
To carry them thither and thence.
1941.

144

There was an old man of Connaught
Whose prick was remarkably short.
    When he got into bed
    The old woman said,
" This isn't a prick, it's a wart. "
1879.

145

There once was a girl from Cornell
Whose teats were shaped like a bell.
    When you touched them they shrunk,
    Except when she was drunk,
And then they got bigger than hell.

               1939A.

146

There once was a lady of Crete
So enormously broad in the beam
    That one day in the ocean
    She caused such commotion
That Admiral Byrd claimed her for America.

               1946A.

147

There was a young fellow named Cribbs
Whose cock was so big it had ribs.
    They were inches apart,
    And to suck it took art,
While to fuck it took forty-two trips.

               1944-1951.

148

There was a young lady whose cunt
Could accomodate a small punt.
    Her mother said, " Annie,
    It matches your fanny,
Which never was that of a runt."

               1941*

149

There's a young Yiddish slut with two cunts,
Whose pleasure in life is to pruntz.
    When one pireg is shot,
    There's that alternate twat,
But the ausgefuckt male merely grunts.

               1941.

150

There was a young man from Dallas
Who had an exceptional phallus.
  He couldn't find room
  In any girl's womb
Without rubbing it first with Vitalis.
         1946A.

151

There was a young girl of Des Moines
Whose cunt could be fitted with coins,
  Till a guy from Hoboken
  Went and dropped in a token,
And now she rides free on the ferry.
         1948A.

152

To his bride said the keen-eyed detective,
" Can it be that my eyesight's defective?
  Has the east tit the least bit
  The best of the west tit,
Or is it the faulty perspective? "
         1941-1942.

153

There was a young girl of Detroit
Who at fucking was very adroit:
  She could squeeze her vagina
  To a pin-point, or finer,
Or open it out like a quoit.
         1926*

And she had a friend named Durand
Whose cock could contract or expand.
  He could diddle a midge
  Or the arch of a bridge—
Their performance together was grand!
         1938.

155

There was a young man of Devizes
Whose balls were of different sizes.
    His tool, when at ease,
    Hung down to his knees,
Oh, what must it be when it rises!
                    1927-1941.

156

Visas erat : huic geminarum
Dispar modus testicularum :
    Minor haec nihili,
    Palma triplici,
Jam fecerat altera clarum.
                    1941.

157

There was a young fellow whose dong
Was prodigiously massive and long.
    On each side of this whang
    Two testes did hang
That attracted a curious throng.
                    1942.

158

There was a young man from East Wubley
Whose cock was bifurcated doubly.
    Each quadruplicate shaft
    Had two balls hanging aft,
And the general effect was quite lovely.
                    1947-1951.

159

While I, with my usual enthusiasm,
Was exploring in Ermintrude's busiasm,
    She explained, " They are flat,
    But think nothing of that—
You will find that my sweet sister Susiasm."
                    1943.

160

There was a young fellow from Florida
Who liked a friend's wife, so he borrowed her.
    When they got into bed
    He cried, " God strike me dead!
This ain't a cunt—it's a corridor! "

                       1927-1941.

161

An old man at the Folies Bergère
Had a jock, a most wondrous affair :
    It snipped off a twat-curl
    From each new chorus girl,
And he had a wig made of the hair.

                       1942A.

162

There was a young man with one foot
Who had a very long root.
    If he used this peg
    As an extra leg
Is a question exceedingly moot.

                       1939*

163

In the case of a lady named Frost,
Whose cunt's a good two feet acrost,
    It's the best part of valor
    To bugger the gal, or
You're apt to fall in and get lost.

                       1941.

164

A certain young person of Ghent,
Uncertain if lady or gent,
    Shows his organs at large
    For a small handling charge
To assist him in paying the rent.

                       1944A.

165

There was an old woman of Ghent
Who swore that her cunt had no scent.
    She got fucked so often
    At last she got rotten,
And didn't she stink when she spent.

1870.

166

There was a young man from Glengozzle
Who found a remarkable fossil.
    He knew by the bend
    And the wart on the end,
'Twas the peter of Paul the Apostle.

1938.

167

There was a young fellow of Greenwich
Whose balls were all covered with spinach.
    He had such a tool
    It was wound on a spool,
And he reeled it out inich by inich.

But this tale has an unhappy finich,
For due to the sand in the spinach
    His ballocks grew rough
    And wrecked his wife's muff,
And scratched up her thatch in the scrimmage.

1927-1941.

169

A mathematician named Hall
Had a hexahedronical ball,
    And the cube of its weight
    Times his pecker, plus eight,
Was four fifths of five eighths of fuck-all.

1941.

170

There was a young fellow of Harrow
Whose john was the size of a marrow.
    He said to his tart,
    " How's this for a start ?
My balls are outside in a barrow. "

                    1941.

171

There was a young fellow named Harry,
Had a joint that was long, huge and scary.
    He pressed it on a virgin
    Who, without any urgin',
Immediately spread like a fairy.

                    1943.

172

There was a young girl named Heather
Whose twitcher was made out of leather.
    She made a queer noise,
    Which attracted the boys,
By flapping the edges together.

                   1945C.

173

There was an old curate of Hestion
Who'd erect at the slightest suggestion.
    But so small was his tool
    He could scarce screw a spool,
And a cunt was quite out of the question.

                    1941.

174

There was a young man from Hong Kong
Who had a trifurcated prong :
    A small one for sucking,
    A large one for fucking,
And a *honey* for beating a gong.

                    1942.

175

A fellow whose surname was Hunt
Trained his cock to perform a slick stunt:
    This versatile spout
    Could be turned inside out,
Like a glove, and be used as a cunt.
                             1942.

176

Alas for the Countess d'Isère,
Whose muff wasn't furnished with hair.
    Said the Count, " Quelle surprise! "
    When he parted her thighs;
" Magnifique! Pourtant pas de la guerre. "
                             1941.

177

A highly aesthetic young Jew
Had eyes of a heavenly blue;
    The end of his dillie
    Was shaped like a lily,
And his balls were too utterly *two*!
                             1941.

178

There once was a lady from Kansas
Whose cunt was as big as Bonanzas.
    It was nine inches deep
    And the sides were quite steep—
It had whiskers like General Carranza's.
                           1927-1932.

179

Oh, pity the Duchess of Kent!
Her cunt is so dreadfully bent,
    The poor wench doth stammer,
    " I need a sledgehammer
To pound a man into my vent. "
                             1939A.

180

There was an old gent from Kentuck
Who boasted a filigreed schmuck,
   But he put it away
   For fear that one day
He might put it in and get stuck.

                                    1952.

181

There was an old lady of Kewry
Whose cunt was a *lusus naturæ* :
   The *introitus vaginæ*
   Was unnaturally tiny,
And the thought of it filled her with fury.

                                    1941.

182

There was a young fellow named Kimble
Whose prick was exceedingly nimble,
   But fragile and slender,
   And dainty and tender,
So he kept it encased in a thimble.

                                    1941.

183

There was a young man of Lahore
Whose prick was one inch and no more.
   It was all right for key-holes
   And little girls' pee-holes,
But not worth a damn with a whore.

                                1927-1941.

184

There once was a horse named Lily
Whose dingus was really a dilly.
   It was vaginoid duply,
   And labial quadruply—
In fact, he was really a filly.

                                  1942-1952.

185

There was a young fellow from Leeds
Who swallowed a package of seeds.
    Great tufts of grass
    Sprouted out of his ass
And his balls were all covered with weeds.

                    1938-1952.

186

The wife of young Richard of Limerick
Complained to her husband, " My quim, Rick,
    Still grows in diameter
    Each time that you ram at her;
How can your poor tool stay so slim, Rick ? "

                    1944.

187

There was a young lady of Lincoln
Who said that her cunt was a pink'un,
    So she had a prick lent her
    Which turned it magenta,
This artful old lady of Lincoln.

                    1870.

188

There was a young girl of Llewellyn
Whose breasts were as big as a melon.
    They were big, it is true,
    But her cunt was big too,
Like a bifocal, full-color, aerial view
Of Cape Horn and the Straits of Magellan.

                    1941.

189

A contortionist hailing from Lynch
Used to rent out his tool by the inch.
    A foot cost a quid—
    He could and he did
Stretch it to three in a pinch.

                    1942A.

190

There was a young man from Lynn
Whose cock was the size of a pin.
   Said his girl with a laugh
   As she felt his staff,
" This won't be much of a sin. "

1927.

191

There was a young girl named McCall
Whose cunt was exceedingly small,
   But the size of her anus
   Was something quite heinous—
It could hold seven pricks and one ball.

1941.

192

There was an old satyr named Mack
Whose prick had a left-handed tack.
   If the ladies he loves
   Don't spin when he shoves,
Their cervixes frequently crack.

1950.

193

An envious girl named McMeanus
Was jealous of her lover's big penis.
   It was small consolation
   That the rest of the nation
Of women were with her in weeness.

1942-1952.

194

There was a young man named McNamiter
With a tool of prodigious diameter.
   But it wasn't the size
   Gave the girls a surprise,
But his rhythm—iambic pentameter.

1946A.

195

There was a young man of Madras
Whose balls were constructed of brass.
    When jangled together
      They played " Stormy Weather, "
And lightning shot out of his ass.
                      1938.

196

A bad little girl in Madrid,
A most reprehensible kid,
    Told her Tante Louise
      That her cunt smelled like cheese,
And the worst of it was that it did!
                      1941.

197

There was a young man from Maine
Whose prick was as strong as a cane;
    It was almost as long,
      So he strolled with his dong
Extended in sunshine and rain.
                      1952.

198

There was a young girl from Medina
Who could completely control her vagina.
    She could twist it around
      Like the cunts that are found
In Japan, Manchukuo and China.
                      1948.

199

There was a young fellow named Morgan
Who possessed an unusual organ :
    The end of his dong,
      Which was nine inches long,
Was tipped with the head of a gorgon.
                      1943A.

200

There was a young soldier from Munich
Whose penis hung down past his tunic,
   And their chops girls would lick
   When they thought of his prick,
But alas! he was only a eunuch.

1941.

201

There was a young lady of Natchez
Who chanced to be born with two snatches,
   And she often said, " Shit!
   Why, I'd give either tit
For a man with equipment that matches. "

There was a young fellow named Locke
Who was born with a two-headed cock.
   When he'd fondle the thing
   It would rise up and sing
An antiphonal chorus by Bach.

But whether these two ever met
Has not been recorded as yet,
   Still, it would be diverting
   To see him inserting
His whang while it sang a duet.

1939*-1941.

204

A girl of uncertain nativity
Had an ass of extreme sensitivity
   When she sat on the lap
   Of a German or Jap,
She could sense Fifth Column activity.

1943B-1946A.

205

There was a gay parson of Norton
Whose prick, although thick, was a short 'un.
    To make up for this loss,
    He had balls like a horse,
And never spent less than a quartern.

1879.

206

A farmer I know named O'Doole
Has a long and incredible tool.
    He can use it to plow,
    Or to diddle a cow,
Or just as a cue-stick at pool.

1946A.

207

A chap down in Oklahoma
Had a cock that could sing La Paloma,
    But the sweetness of pitch
    Couldn't put off the hitch
Of impotence, size and aroma.

1952.

208

There was a young girl named O'Malley
Who wanted to dance in the ballet.
    She got roars of applause
    When she kicked off her drawers,
But her hair and her bush didn't tally.

1941.

209

There was a young maiden from Osset
Whose quim was nine inches across it.
    Said a young man named Tong,
    With tool nine inches long,
" I'll put bugger-in if I loss it. "

1942.

210

"The testes are cooler outside,"
Said the doc to the curious bride,
  "For the semen must not
    Get too fucking hot,
And the bag fans your bum on the ride."
                              1942A.

211

There was a young fellow named Paul
Who confessed, "I have only one ball.
  But the size of my prick
    Is God's dirtiest trick,
For my girls always ask, 'Is that all?'"
                            1943A-1952.

212

There was a young girl of Pawtucket
Whose box was as big as a bucket.
  Her boy-friend said, "Toots,
    I'll have to wear boots,
For I see I must muck it, not fuck it."
                                  1941.

213

When I was a baby, my penis
Was as white as the buttocks of Venus.
  But now 'tis as red
    As her nipples instead—
All because of the feminine genus!
                                   1939A.

214

Two roosters in one of our pens
Found their pricks were no larger than wens.
  As they looked at their foreskins
    And wished they had more skins,
They discovered they'd both become hens.
                                    1941*

215

There was a young fellow of Perth
Whose balls were the finest on earth.
    They grew to such size
    That one won a prize,
And goodness knows what they were worth.

1941.

216

To his bride a young bridegroom said, " Pish!
Your cunt is as big as a dish! "
    She replied, " Why, you fool,
    With your limp little tool
It's like driving a nail with a fish! "

1941.

217

A very odd pair are the Pitts :
His balls are as large as her tits,
    Her tits are as large
    As an invasion barge—
Neither knows how the other cohabits.

1944-1951.

218

A young man from the banks of the Po
Found his cock had elongated so,
    That when he'd pee
    It was not he
But only his neighbors who'd know.

1944.

219

There was a young fellow named Prynne
Whose prick was so short and so thin,
    His wife found she needed
    A Fuckoscope—she did—
To see if he'd gotten it in.

1941.

220

A beautiful lady named Psyche
Is loved by a fellow named Ikey.
    One thing about Ike
    The lady can't like
Is his prick, which is dreadfully spikey.

                                  1946A.

221

There was a fat man from Rangoon
Whose prick was much like a balloon.
    He tried hard to ride her
    And when finally inside her
She thought she was pregnant too soon.

                                  1942.

222

There was a young fellow called Rex
With diminutive organs of sex.
    When charged with exposure
    He said with composure,
" *De minimis non curat lex!* "

                               1948-1952.

223

There was a young lady named Riddle
Who had an untouchable middle.
    She had many friends
    Because of her ends,
Since it isn't the middle you diddle.

                                  1943A.

224

There was a young man from Salinas
Who had an extremely long penis:
    Believe it or not,
    When he lay on his cot
It reached from Marín to Martinez.

                                  1942.

225

There was a young harlot named Schwartz
Whose cock-pit was studded with warts,
   And they tickled so nice
   She drew a high price
From the studs at the summer resorts.

Her pimp, a young fellow named Biddle,
Was seldom hard up for a diddle,
   For according to rumor
   His tool had a tumor
And a fine row of warts down the middle.

Her brother, a bastard named Ben,
Could rotate his pecker, and then
   He would shoot through his rear
   Which made him the dear
Of the girls, and the envy of men.

Her other young brother, named Saul,
Was able to bounce either ball,
   He could stretch them and snap them,
   And juggle and clap them,
Which earned him the plaudits of all.

1941.

229

The skater, Barbara Ann Scott
Is so fuckingly " winsome " a snot,
   That when posed on her toes
   She elaborately shows
Teeth, fat ass, titties and twat.

1952.

230

A cowhand way out in Seattle
Had a dooflicker flat as a paddle.
    He said, " No, I can't fuck
    A lamb or a duck,
But golly! it just fits the cattle. "

1941.

231

There was a young man from Seattle
Whose testicles tended to rattle.
    He said as he fuckèd
    Some stones in a bucket,
" If Stravinsky won't deafen you—that'll. "

1939A.

232

There's a lovely young lady named Shittlecock
Who loves to play diddle and fiddle-cock,
    But her cunt's got a pucker
    That's best not to fuck, or
When least you expect it to, it'll lock.

1952.

233

There was an old fellow named Skinner
Whose prick, his wife said, had grown thinner.
    But still, by and large,
    It would always discharge
Once he could just get it in her.

1941-1948.

234

An ingenious young man in South Bend
Made a synthetic arse for a friend,
    But the friend shortly found
    Its construction unsound,
It was simply a bother—no end.

1944A.

235

An aesthete from South Carolina
Had a cock that tinkled like china,
    But while shooting his load
    It cracked like old Spode,
So he's bought him a Steuben vagina.

                        1952.

236

There was a young blade from South Greece
Whose bush did so greatly increase
    That before he could shack
    He must hunt needle in stack.
'Twas as bad as being obese.

                        1944-1951.

237

There was a young lady from Spain
Whose face was exceedingly plain,
    But her cunt had a pucker
    That made the men fuck her,
Again, and again, and again.

                        1927A.

238

Il y avait une madame de Lahore
Dont la figure n'était la meilleure,
    Mais la vagine très forte,
    Toujours ouverte la porte,
Encore, et encore, et encore.

                        1941.

239

De Hispanice puella verumque
Simplex oris verborumque
    Tulit potens vagina
    Hominum agmina
Iterum iterum iterumque.

                        1941.

240

There once was a girl from Spokane
Went to bed with a one-legged man.
    She said, " I know you—
    You've really got two!
Why didn't you say so when we began? "

                      1942.

241

There was a young man from Stamboul
Who boasted so torrid a tool
    That each female crater
    Explored by this satyr
Seemed almost unpleasantly cool.

                      1939A.

242

There was a young fellow of Strensall
Whose prick was as sharp as a pencil.
    On the night of his wedding
    It went through the bedding,
And shattered the chamber utensil.

So here was this fellow of Strensall
Whose pecker was shaped like a pencil,
    Anemic, 'tis true,
    But an interesting screw,
Inasmuch as the tip was prehensile.

                      1938-1952.

244

A wonderful tribe are the Sweenies,
Renowned for the length of their peenies.
    The hair on their balls
    Sweeps the floors of their halls,
But they don't look at women, the meanies.

                      1943A.

245

There was an old man of Tagore
Whose tool was a yard long or more,
    So he wore the damn thing
    In a surgical sling
To keep it from wiping the floor.
                      1941.

246

There was a young lady whose thighs,
When spread showed a slit of such size,
    And so deep and so wide,
    You could play cards inside—
Much to her bridegroom's surprise.
                      1941.

247

There was a young hayseed from Tiffan
Whose cock would constantly stiffen.
    This knob out in front
    Attracted foul cunt
Which he greatly delighted in sniffin'.
                      1941*

248

There's a charming young girl in Tobruk
Who refers to her quiff as a nook.
    It's deep and it's wide,
    —You can curl up inside
With a nice easy chair and a book.
                      1946B.

249

There was a gay parson of Tooting
Whose roe he was frequently shooting,
    Till he married a lass
    With a face like my arse,
And a cunt you could put a top-boot in.
                      1879.

250

There was a young man of Toulouse
Who had a deficient prepuce,
    But the foreskin he lacked
    He made up in his sac;
The result was, his balls were too loose.

                              1943.

251

A wide-bottomed girl named Trasket
Had a hole as big as a basket.
    A spot, as a bride,
    In it now, you could hide,
And include with your luggage your mascot.

                              1946A.

252

A young man maintained that his trigger
Was so big that there weren't any bigger.
    But this long and thick pud
    Was so heavy it could
Scarcely lift up its head. It lacked vigor.

                              1941*

253

A cautious young fellow named Tunney
Had a whang that was worth any money.
    When eased in half-way,
    The girl's sigh made him say,
" Why the sigh? " " For the rest of it, honey. "

                              1942.

254

There was an old man who said, " Tush!
My balls always hang in the brush,
    And I fumble about,
    Half in and half out,
With a pecker as limber as mush. "

                              1941.

255

A pious old woman named Tweak
Had taught her vagina to speak.
    It was frequently liable
    To quote from the Bible,
But when fucking—not even a squeak!
                            1941.

256

There once was a newspaper vendor,
A person of dubious gender.
    He would charge one-and-two
    For permission to view
His remarkable double pudenda.
                             1941.

257

A maiden who lived in Virginny
Had a cunt that could bark, neigh and whinny.
    The horsey set rushed her,
    But success finally crushed her
For her tone soon became harsh and tinny.
                             1952.

258

There was a young fellow of Warwick
Who had reason for feeling euphoric,
    For he could by election
    Have triune erection:
Ionic, Corinthian, Doric.
                         1945-1949.

259

When he tried to inject his huge whanger
A young man aroused his girl's anger.
    As they strove in the dark
    She was heard to remark,
" What you need is a zeppelin hangar. "
                             1942.

260

There was a young squaw of Wohunt
Who possessed a collapsible cunt.
    It had many odd uses,
    Produced no papooses,
And fitted both giant and runt.

1944A.

261

There was a young laundress named Wrangle
Whose tits tilted up at an angle.
    " They may tickle my chin, "
    She said with a grin,
" But at least they keep out of the mangle. "

1945.

262

An organist playing in York
Had a prick that could hold a small fork,
    And between obbligatos
    He'd munch at tomatoes,
And keep up his strength while at work.

1942A.

263

There was a young man named Zerubbabel
Who had only one real, and one rubber ball.
    When they asked if his pleasure
    Was only half measure,
He replied, " That is highly improbable. "

1941.

264

There was a young man named Zerubbabub
Who belonged to the Block, Fuck & Bugger Club,
    But the pride of his life
    Were the tits of his wife—
One real, and one India-rubber bub.

1941.

III

STRANGE INTERCOURSE

265

Thus spake I AM THAT I AM:
"For the Virgin I don't give a damn.
   What pleases Me most
   Is to bugger the Ghost,
And then be sucked off by the Lamb."

                       1928.

266

Así dije YO SOY QUE YO SOY:
"Por La Vírgen un carajo no doy.
   Lo que debe gustar
   Es Jesús caporar—
Y para hacerlo Yo voy."

                       1941.

267

Dame Catherine of Ashton-on-Lynches
Got on with her grooms and her wenches:
   She went down on the gents,
   And pronged the girls' vents
With a clitoris reaching six inches.

                       1942A.

268

There was a young lady named Astor
Who never let any get past her.
   She finally got plenty
   By stopping twenty,
Which certainly ought to last her.

                       1942.

269

Oden the bardling averred
His muse was the bum of a bird,
    And his Lesbian wife
    Would finger his fife
While Fisherwood waited as third.

          1942A.

270

There was a young fellow named Babbitt
Who could screw nine times like a rabbit,
    But a girl from Johore
    Could do it twice more,
Which was just enough extra to crab it.

          1942.

271

A young polo-player of Berkeley
Made love to his sweetheart berserkly.
    In the midst of each chukker
    He would break off and fuck her
Horizontally, laterally, and verkeley.

          1943.

272

There once was a jolly old bloke
Who picked up a girl for a poke.
    He took down her pants,
    Fucked her into a trance,
And then shit in her shoe for a joke.

          1941.

273

There was a young idler named Blood,
Made a fortune performing at stud,
    With a fifteen-inch peter,
    A double-beat metre,
And a load like the Biblical Flood.

          1941.

274
Though the invalid Saint of Brac
Lay all of his life on his back,
    His wife got her share,
    And the pilgrims now stare
At the scene, in his shrine, on a plaque.
                    1943.

275
There was an old man of Brienz
The length of whose cock was immense:
    With one swerve he could plug
    A boy's bottom in Zug,
And a kitchen-maid's cunt in Coblenz.
                    1928.

276
There once was a Duchess of Bruges
Whose cunt was incredibly huge.
    Said the King to this dame
    As he thunderously came:
" Mon Dieu! Après moi, le déluge! "
                    1941.

277
There was an old man of Cajon
Who never could get a good bone.
    With the aid of a gland
    It grew simply grand;
Now his wife cannot leave it alone.
                    1941*

278
There was a young girl of Cape Cod
Who dreamt she'd been buggered by God.
    But it wasn't Jehovah
    That turned the girl over,
'Twas Roger the lodger, the dirty old codger,
The bugger, the bastard, the sod!
                1938-1952.

279

There once was a lady named Carter,
Fell in love with a virile young Tartar.
   She stripped off his pants,
   At his prick quickly glanced,
And cried: " For that I'll be a martyr! "

1946A.

280

A talented fuckstress, Miss Chisholm,
Was renowned for her fine paroxysm.
   While the man detumesced
   She still spent on with zest,
Her rapture sheer anachronism.

1941.

281

There was a young man in the choir
Whose penis rose higher and higher,
   Till it reached such a height
   It was quite out of sight—
But of course you know I'm a liar.

1946A.

282

There was a young man from the Coast
Who had an affair with a ghost.
   At the height of orgasm
   Said the pallid phantasm,
" I think I can feel it—almost! "

1942.

283

Have you heard of the lady named Cox
Who had a capacious old box?
   When her lover was in place
   She said, " Please turn your face.
I look like a gal, but I screw like a fox. "

1942.

284

A team playing baseball in Dallas
Called the umpire a shit out of malice.
    While this worthy had fits
    The team made eight hits
And a girl in the bleachers named Alice.
                              1946A.

285

There was a young girl of Darjeeling
Who could dance with such exquisite feeling
    There was never a sound
    For miles around
Save of fly-buttons hitting the ceiling.
                        1943A-1949.

286

There was a young woman in Dee
Who stayed with each man she did see.
    When it came to a test
    She wished to be best,
And practice makes perfect, you see.
                                  1927.

287

There was a family named Doe,
An ideal family to know.
    As father screwed mother,
    She said, " You're heavier than brother."
And he said, " Yes, Sis told me so! "
                                  1948.

288

A lady, by passion deluded,
Found an African drunk and denuded,
    And—fit as a fiddle,
    And hot for a diddle—
She tied splints to his penis and screwed it.
                                  1941.

289

There was a strong man of Drumrig
Who one day did seven times frig.
    He buggered three sailors,
      Four Jews and two tailors,
And ended by fucking a pig.

                      1879.

290

There was an old man of Duluth
Whose cock was shot off in his youth.
    He fucked with his nose
      And with fingers and toes,
And he came through a hole in his tooth.

                      1941.

291

There was an old man of Dundee
Who came home as drunk as could be.
    He wound up the clock
      With the end of his cock,
And buggered his wife with the key.

                      1927-1928.

292

A rapturous young fellatrix
One day was at work on five pricks.
    With an unholy cry
      She whipped out her glass eye:
" Tell the boys I can now take on six. "

                      1942-1952.

293

There was a young man with a fiddle
Who asked of his girl, " Do you diddle? "
    She replied, " Yes, I do,
      But prefer to with two—
It's twice as much fun in the middle. "

                      1943A.

294

I dined with Lord Hughing Fitz-Bluing
Who said, "Do you squirm when you're screwing?"
    I replied, " Simple shagging
    Without any wagging
Is only for screwing canoeing. "
                                   1947.

295

There was a young fellow named Fletcher,
Was reputed an infamous lecher.
    When he'd take on a whore
    She'd need a rebore,
And they'd carry him out on a stretcher.
                                   1943A.

296

A young fellow discovered through Freud
That although of a penis devoid,
    He could practice coitus
    By eating a fœtus,
And his parents were quite overjoyed.
                                   1941.

297

There was a young man from Jodhpur
Who found he could easily cure
    His dread diabetes
    By eating a fœtus
Served up in a sauce of manure.
                                   1945.

298

There once was a sailor named Gasted,
A swell guy, as long as he lasted,
    He could jerk himself off
    In a basket, aloft,
Or a breeches-buoy swung from the masthead.
                                   1941.

299

There was a young girl of Gibraltar
Who was raped as she knelt at the altar.
    It really seems odd
    That a virtuous God
Should answer her prayers and assault her.

                  1943A.

300

A young man with passions quite gingery
Tore a hole in his sister's best lingerie.
    He slapped her behind
    And made up his mind
To add incest to insult and injury.

                1941*-1947B.

301

A passionate red-headed girl,
When you kissed her, her senses would whirl,
    And her twat would get wet
    And would wiggle and fret,
And her cunt-lips would curl and unfurl.

                    1941.

302

There was a young lady named Gloria
Who was had by Sir Gerald Du Maurier,
    And then by six men,
    Sir Gerald again,
And the band at the Waldorf-Astoria.

                    1943.

303

Thank God for the Duchess of Gloucester,
She obliges all who accost her.
    She welcomes the prick
    Of Tom, Harry or Dick,
Or Baldwin, or even Lord Astor.

                    1939A.

304

The latest reports from Good Hope
State that apes there have pricks thick as rope,
   And fuck high, wide, and free,
     From the top of one tree
To the top of the next—what a scope!
                         1941.

305

A newlywed couple from Goshen
Spent their honeymoon sailing the ocean.
   In twenty-eight days
    They got laid eighty ways—
Imagine such fucking devotion!
                         1941.

306

There was a young fellow named Grimes
Who fucked his girl seventeen times
   In the course of a week—
    And this isn't to speak
Of assorted venereal crimes.
                         1947.

307

There was a young lady named Hatch
Who would always come through in a scratch.
   If a guy wouldn't neck her,
    She'd grab up his pecker
And shove the damn thing up her snatch.
                         1945.

308

There was a young lady named Hilda
Who went for a walk with a builder.
   He knew that he could,
    And he should, and he would—
And he did—and he goddam near killed her!
                     1928A-1941.

309

Cum Hilde autem ambulabat
Homo qui ædificabat.
    Dixit volebat. Debet et potebat.
    Sic ille ducebat. Statim faciebat.
Sed virginem pine necebat.

                              1941.

310

I know of a fortunate Hindu
Who is sought in the towns that he's been to
    By the ladies he knows,
    Who are thrilled to the toes
By the tricks he can make his foreskín do.

                              1948A.

311

If you're speaking of actions immoral
Then how about giving the laurel
    To doughty Queen Esther,
    No three men could best her—
One fore, and one aft, and one oral.

                         1941-1952.

312

There was a young miss from Johore
Who'd lie on a mat on the floor;
    In a manner uncanny
    She'd wobble her fanny,
And drain your nuts dry to the core.

                                 1942.

313

There was a young fellow of Kent
Whose prick was so long that it bent,
    So to save himself trouble
    He put it in double,
And instead of coming he went.

                         1927-1941.

314

There was a young man of Kildare
Who was fucking a girl on the stair.
   The bannister broke,
   But he doubled his stroke
And finished her off in mid-air.
                                1927-1952.

315

A young man of Llanfairpwllgwyngyll
While bent over plucking a dingle
   Had the whole Eisteddfod
   Taking turns at his pod
While they sang some impossible jingle.
                                1952.

316

There once were two brothers named Luntz
Who buggered each other at once.
   When asked to account
   For this intricate mount,
They said, " Ass-holes are tighter than cunts."
                                1941.

317

There was a young lady named Mable
Who liked to sprawl out on the table,
   Then cry to her man,
   " Stuff in all you can—
Get your ballocks in, too, if you're able."
                                1943.

318

An impotent Scot named MacDougall
Had to husband his sperm and be frugal.
   He was gathering semen
   To gender a he-man,
By screwing his wife through a bugle.
                                1941.

319

There once was a girl named McGoffin
Who was diddled amazingly often.
    She was rogered by scores
    Who'd been turned down by whores,
And was finally screwed in her coffin.

1941.

320

A stout Gaelic warrior, McPherson,
Was having a captive, a person
    Who was not averse
    Though she had the curse,
And he'd breeches of bristling furs on.

1942A.

321

There was a young Scot in Madrid
Who got fifty-five fucks for a quid.
    When they said, " Are you faint? "
    He replied, " No, I ain't,
But I *don't* feel as good as I did. "

1941.

322

There was a young fellow of Mayence
Who fucked his own arse, in defiance
    Not only of custom
    And morals, dad-bust him,
But most of the known laws of science.

1949.

323

The woman who lives on the moon
Is still cherishing the balloon
    Of an earthling who'd come
    And given her some,
But had dribbled away all too soon.

1942A.

324

There is a young faggot named Mose
Who insists that you fuck his long nose.
    And you'll double the joy
    Of this lecherous boy
If you'll tickle his balls with your toes.
                       1946A.

325

There was an Old Man of the Mountain
Who frigged himself into a fountain
    Fifteen times had he spent,
    Still he wasn't content,
He simply got tired of the counting.
                       1879.

326

There was a young lady named Nance
Who learned about fucking in France,
    And when you'd insert it
    She'd squeeze till she hurt it,
And shoved it right back in your pants.
                       1951.

327

A studious professor named Nestor
Bet a whore all his books he could best her.
    But she drained out his balls
    And skipped up the walls,
Beseeching poor Nestor to rest her.
                       1941A.

328

The late Brigham Young was no neuter—
No faggot, no fairy, no fruiter.
    Where ten thousand virgins
    Succumbed to his urgin's
There now stands the great State of Utah.
                       1941.

329

There was a young girl of Newcastle
Whose charms were declared universal.
   While one man in front
   Wired into her cunt,
Another was engaged at her arsehole.

1879.

330

There was a young girl from New York
Who plugged up her cunt with a cork.
   A woodpecker or two
   Made the grade, it is true,
But it totally baffled the stork.

Till along came a man who presented
A tool that was strangely indented.
   With a dizzying twirl
   He punctured that girl,
And thus was the cork-screw invented.

1938.

332

There was a young girl named O'Clare
Whose body was covered with hair.
   It was really quite fun
   To probe with one's gun,
For her quimmy might be anywhere.

1947.

333

There once was a gay young Parisian
Who screwed an appendix incision,
   And the girl of his choice
   Could hardly rejoice
At this horrible lack of precision.

1941.

334

While spending the winter at Pau
Lady Pamela forgot to say " No. "
   So the head-porter made her
   The second-cook laid her;
The waiters were all hanging low.
                    1942A.

335

There was a young girl of Penzance
Who boarded a bus in a trance.
   The passengers fucked her,
   Likewise the conductor.
The driver shot off in his pants.
                  1927-1928.

336

The Shah of the Empire of Persia
Lay for days in a sexual merger.
   When the nautch asked the Shah,
   " Won't you ever withdraw ? "
He replied with a yawn, " It's inertia. "
                  1938-1941.

337

A remarkable race are the Persians,
They have such peculiar diversions.
   They screw the whole day
   In the regular way,
And save up the nights for perversions.
                  1941.

338

There was a young girl of Rangoon
Who was blocked by the Man in the Moon.
   " Well, it *has* been great fun, "
   She remarked when he'd done,
" But I'm sorry you came quite so soon. "
                  1928-1941.

339

There was a young lady named Ransom
Who was rogered three times in a hansom.
    When she cried out for more
    A voice from the floor
Said, " My name is Simpson, not Samson. "
                  1938-1941.

340

A maestro directing in Rome
Had a quaint way of driving it home.
    Whoever he climbed
    Had to keep her tail timed
To the beat of his old metronome.
                  1942A.

341

" Last night, " said a lassie named Ruth,
" In a long-distance telephone booth,
    I enjoyed the perfection
    Of an ideal connection—
I was screwed, if you must know the truth."
                  1943A.

342

Said a Lesbian lady, " It's sad;
Of all of the girls that I've had,
    None gave me the thrill
    Of real rapture until
I learned how to be a tribade. "
                  1952.

343

There once was a handsome young seaman
Who with ladies was really a demon.
    In peace or in war,
    At sea or on shore,
He could certainly dish out the semen.
                  1942.

344

Said a girl being had in a shanty,
" My dear, you have got it in slanty. "
    He replied, " I can use
    Any angle I choose.
I ride as I please—I'm Duranty! "

1939A.

345

An old couple just at Shrovetide
Were having a piece—when he died.
    The wife for a week
    Sat tight on his peak,
And bounced up and down as she cried.

1942A.

346

My wife is an amorous soul
On fire for an African's pole.
    She told a coon chauffeur
    That he was her gopher—
And, say, did he go for her hole!

As he creamed my wife's cunt, the coon said,
" I could fuck this until she was dead! "
    As he plugged up her trough,
    I jerked myself off;
" If *that's* how you feel, go ahead! "

1943B.

348

There was a young lady of Spain
Who was fucked by a monk in a drain.
    They did it again,
    And again and again,
And again and again and again.

1943A.

349
Mr. Galsworthy rented a suite
In a building devoid of all heat.
    So he fucked for three months,
    Sucked thirty-nine cunts,
Which solved his problem quite neat.
                        1946A.

350
There was a young lady from Sydney
Who could take it right up to her kidney.
    But a man from Quebec
    Shoved it up to her neck.
He had a long one, now didn' he?
                       1943B-1952.

351
There was a young man of Tibet,
And this is the strangest one yet—
    His prick was so long,
    And so pointed and strong,
He could bugger six Greeks *en brochette*.
                           1941.

352
'Tis said that the Emperor Titius
Had a penchant for pleasantries vicious.
    He took two of his nieces
    And fucked them to pieces,
And said it was simply delicious.
                           1941.

353
There was a young man from Toledo
Who was cursed with excessive libido.
    To fuck and to screw,
    And to fornicate too,
Were the three major points of his credo.
                         1939A.

354

A virile young man of Touraine
Had vesicles no one could drain.
    With an unbroken flow
    Thrice the course he would go,
Then roll over and start in again.

                                1943A.

355

" Far dearer to me than my treasure, "
The heiress declared, " is my leisure.
    For then I can screw
    The whole Harvard crew—
They're slow, but that lengthens the pleasure. "

                                1941.

356

A certain old harpy from Umsk
Who was wholly unable to cumsk
    Would ecstatically shout
    When a samovar spout
Was shoved up her Muscovite rumpsk.

                                1945.

357

A young man with a passion quite vast
Used to talk about making it last,
    Till one day he discovered
    His sister uncovered,
And now he fucks often—and fast.

                                1948A.

358

A galactic patrolman from Venus
Had a hyper-extensible penis.
    Of all forms of life
    Which he'd taken to wife
He preferred a mere woman, from meanness.

                                1944.

359

The sex of the asteroid vermin
Is exceedingly hard to determine.
    The galactic patrol
    Simply fucks any hole
That will possibly let all the sperm in.
                              1944.

360

There was a young fellow from Wark
Who, when he screws, has to bark.
    His wife is a bitch
    With a terrible itch,
So the town never sleeps after dark.
                              1946A.

361

There was a debauched little wench
Whom nothing could ever make blench.
    She admitted men's poles
    At all possible holes,
And she'd bugger, fuck, jerk off, and french.
                              1943.

362

There's an over-sexed lady named Whyte
Who insists on a dozen a night.
    A fellow named Cheddar
    Had the brashness to wed her—
His chance of survival is slight.
                              1941.

363

There was a Hell's Kitchen Y.T.
Who said to two boyfriends, " Aw, gee,
    I don't think that coitus
    Could possibly hoit us! "
So they did it together, all three.
                            1943B-1944A.

364

A versatile lady of Zaandam
Made appointments completely at random,
    Since if two dates got mixed
    It was easily fixed
By letting them screw her in tandem.

                                1949.

365

While fucking one night, Dr. Zuck
His wife's nipples in his ears stuck.
    Then, his thumb up her bum,
    He could hear himself come,
Thus inventing the Radio Fuck.

Then on further experiment bent,
An improvement he thought he'd invent :
    With his prick as conductor,
    Combed her bush while he fucked her,
And his balls shot off sparks when she spent.

                                1941.

367

Here's to it, and through it, and to it again,
To suck it, and screw it, and screw it again!
    So in with it, out with it,
    Lord work his will with it!
Never a day we don't do it again!

                              1880-1941*

368

It's only human nature after all
If a fellow puts a girl against the wall
    And puts his inclination
    Into her accomodation
    To increase the population
    Of the rising generation—
Why, it's only human nature after all.

                            1943-1946A.

369. THEY A' DO'T

The grit folk an' the puir do't,
The blyte folk an' the sour do't,
   The black, the white,
   Rude an' polite,
Baith autocrat an' boor do't.

For they a' do't—they a' do't,
The beggars an' the braw do't,
   Folk that ance were,
   An' folk that are—
The folk that come will a' do't.

   The auld folk try't
   The young ane's spy't,
An' straightway kiss an' fa' to't,*
   The blind, the lame,
   The wild, the tame,
In warm climes an' in cauld do't.

The licensed by the law do't,
Forbidden folk an' a' do't,
   An' priest an' nun
   Enjoy the fun,
An' never ance say na' to't.

The goulocks an' the snails do't,
The cushie-doos an' quails do't,
   The dogs, the cats,
   The mice, the rats,
E'en elephants an' whales do't.

The weebit cocks an' hens do't,
The robins an' the wrens do't,
   The grizzly bears,
   The toads an' hares,
The puddocks in the fens do't.

The boars an' kangaroos do't,
The titlins an' cuckoos do't,
   While sparrows sma'
   An' rabbits a'
In countless swarms an' crews do't.

The midges, fleas, an' bees do't,
The mawkes an' mites in cheese do't,
   An' cauld earthworms
   Crawl up in swarms,
An' underneath the trees do't.

The kings an' queens an' a' do't,
The Sultan an' Pacha do't,
   An' Spanish dons
   Loup off their thrones
Pu' doon their breeks, an' fa' to't.

For they a' do't—they a' do't,
The grit as weel's the sma' do't,
   Frae crowned king
   To creeping thing,
'Tis just the same—they a' do't!

                        1832*-1880.

IV

ORAL IRREGULARITY

379
There once was a lady from Arden
Who sucked off a man in a garden.
    He said, " My dear Flo,
    Where does all that stuff go ? "
And she said, " (*swallow hard*)—I beg pardon ? "
                                   1932.

380
Said a man to a maid of Ashanti,
"Can one sniff of your twitchet, or can't he ? "
    Said she with a grin,
    " Sure, shove your nose in!
But *presto,* please—not too *andante.*"
                                   1941.

381
There was a young fairy named Bates
Who took out young fellows on dates.
    With his hands on their hips
    He applied his hot lips
To their phalluses, testes, and nates.
                                1947-1951.

382
There was a young girl in Berlin
Who eked out a living through sin.
    She didn't mind fucking,
    But much preferred sucking,
And she'd wipe off the pricks on her chin.
                                   1941.

383

A fastidious young fop of Bhogat
Would suck a girl's cunt, just like that,
    But he'd wipe off her jib,
    And then slip on a bib,
To make sure not to soil his cravat.

                        1941.

384

There was a young lass of Blackheath
Who frigged an old man with her teeth.
    She complained that he stunk
    Not so much from the spunk,
But his arsehole was just underneath.

                        1870.

385

An explorer whose habits were blunt
Once flavored some cannibal cunt.
    The asshole was shitty,
    And—more was the pity—
It oozed from the rear to the front.

                        1946A.

386

In his youth our old friend Boccaccio
Was having a girl in a patio.
    When it came to the twat
    She wasn't so hot,
But, boy, was she good at fellatio!

                 1939A-1948A.

387

There was an old fellow of Brest
Who sucked off his wife with a zest.
    Despite her great howls
    He sucked out her bowels,
And spat them all over her chest.

                   1927-1928.

388

There was a young fellow of Buckingham,
Wrote a treatise on cunts and on sucking them,
   But later this work
   Was eclipsed by a Turk
Whose topic was ass-holes and fucking them.
                                    1879-1941.

389

There was a young bride, a Canuck,
Told her husband, " Let's do more than suck.
   You say that I, maybe,
   Can have my first baby—
Let's give up this Frenching, and fuck! "
                               1943B-1944A.

390

King Louis gave a lesson in Class,
One time he was sexing a lass.
   When she used the word " Damn "
   He rebuked her: " Please ma'am,
Keep a more civil tongue in my ass. "
                                          1950.

391

There was an old bugger of Como
Who suddenly cried: " Ecce homo! "
   He tracked his man down
   To the heart of the town,
And gobbled him off in the duomo.
                                          1928.

392

A fellatrix' healthful condition
Proved the value of spunk as nutrition.
   Her remarkable diet
   (I suggest that you try it)
Was only her clients' emission.
                                       1952.

ORAL IRREGULARITY

393

A pert miss named Mary Contrary
Was attacked by a man on a ferry.
    When he'd done he said, " Come
    On now, swallow my scum! "
" I won't—but I want to, " said Mary.
                              1944A.

394

There was a young man named Isaac Cox
Who took as his motto, " I suck cocks. "
    This frank declaration
    Brought him such reputation
That he spent twenty years sucking cocks on the docks.
                             1942-1951.

395

A girl with a sebaceous cyst
Always came when her ass-hole was kissed.
    Her lover was gratified
    That she was so satisfied,
But regretted the fun that he missed.
                             1948A.

396

The nephew of one of the czars
Used to suck off Rasputin at Yars,
    Till the peasants revolted,
    The royal family bolted—
Now they're under the sickle and stars.
                             1952.

397

There once was a cuntlapper's daughter
Who, despite all her father had taught her,
    Would become so unstrung
    At the touch of a tongue
That she'd deluge her beau with her water.
                             1941.

398

There was an old man of Decatur,
Took out his red-hot pertater.
    He tried at her dent
    But when his thing bent,
He got down on his knees and he ate 'er.

                                        1927.

399

There once was a maid in Duluth,
A striver and seeker of truth.
    This pretty wench
    Was adept at French,
And said all else was uncouth.

                                        1927.

400

A progressive and young Eskimo
Grew tired of his squaw, and so
    Slipped out of his hut
    To look for a slut
Who knew the very fine art of Blow.

                                        1946A.

401

There was a young lady named Grace
Who took all she could in her face,
    But an adequate lad
    Gave her all that he had,
And blew tonsils all over the place.

                                        1943A.

402

That naughty old Sappho of Greece
Said, " What I prefer to a piece
    Is to have my pudenda
    Rubbed hard by the enda
The little pink nose of my niece."

                                      1928-1932.

403

There was a young Jewess named Hannah
Who sucked off her lover's banana.
    She swore that the cream
    That shot out in a stream
Tasted better than Biblical manna.
                  1942.

404

There was a young lady named Hix
Who was fond of sucking big pricks.
    One fellow she took
    Was a doctor named Snook,
Now *he's* in a hell of a fix.
                  1952*

405

A Roman of old named Horatio
Was fond of a form of fellatio.
    He kept accurate track
    Of the boys he'd attack,
And called it his cock-sucking ratio.
                  1943.

406

The priests at the temple of Isis
Used to offer up amber and spices,
    Then back of the shrine
    They would play 69
And other unmentionable vices.
                  1942A.

407

There was an old man from Keith
Who never could get any pieth
    By asking young men
    If they hadn't the yen
To get sucked off by one without teeth.
                1942-1952.

408

There was a young bounder named Link
Who possessed a very tart dink.
    To sweeten it some
    He steeped it in rum,
And he's driven the ladies to drink.
1946A.

409

There lived in French Louisiana
A quaint and deceived old duenna
    Who naively thought
    That a penis was wrought
To be et like a thick ripe banana.
1952.

410

There was an old maid from Luck
Who took it into her head to fuck.
    She was about to resign
    Till she hung out a sign :
" Come in, I've decided to suck. "
1943.

411

Aren't you a trifle atavistic, Mac,
With that little supernumerary nipple on your sac ?
    When I go down to eat
    My purpose I defeat
When my lips slip from meat to teat and back.
1942.

412

A canny Scotch lass named McFargle,
Without coaxing and such argy-bargle,
    Would suck a man's pud
    Just as hard as she could,
And she saved up the sperm for a gargle.
1941.

413

Said the priest to Miss Bridget McLennin,
" Sure, a kiss of your twat isn't sinnin'."
    And he stuck to this story
    Till he tasted the gory
And menstruous state she was then in.
                            1941.

414

A Lesbian lady named Maud
Got into the Wacs by a fraud.
    With a tongue long and knobby
    She raped Col. Hobby,
And now she's a major, by god!
                           1944A.

415

There was a young fellow named Meek
Who invented a lingual technique.
    It drove women frantic
    And made them romantic,
And wore all the hair off his cheek.
                            1945.

416

" It's dull in Duluth, Minnesota,
Of spirit there's not an iota— "
    Complained Alice to Joe,
    Who tried not to show
That he yawned in her snatch as he blowed her.
                            1952.

417

There was a young man of Nantucket
Whose prick was so long he could suck it.
    He said with a grin,
    As he wiped off his chin,
" If my ear were a cunt I could fuck it. "
                          1927-1928.

418

Nantucketensis ridebat
Penem longiorem sugebat:
   Si auris machina
   Aut potens vagina
Libenter ingredi potebat.

                              1941.

419

A socialite out on Nantucket
Had a twat that was wide as a bucket.
   She proclaimed, "If it's clean
   I will take it between—
If it's rotten I'd far better suck it."

                              1942A.

420

There once was an Anglican pastor
Whose maid didn't let much get past her.
   She said, "When you muff-dive on
   The living-room divan.
Please use an anti-macassar."

                              1948A.

421

There was a young fellow named Pell
Who didn't like cunt very well.
   He would finger and fuck one,
   But never would suck one—
He just couldn't get used to the smell.

                              1941.

422

There once was a brilliant young poet
Who loved it—wouldn't you know it?
   When you'd want to six nine
   His penis would pine.
"I just can't," it said; "I can't go it."

                              1942.

423

"At a séance," said a young man named Post,
"I was being sucked off by a ghost;
    Someone switched on the lights
    And there in gauze tights,
On his knees, was Tobias mine host."

1948A.

424

There was a young dancer, Priscilla,
Who flavored her cunt with vanilla.
    The taste was so fine,
    Men and beasts stood in line,
Including a stud armadilla.

1943B.

425

An old doctor who lacked protoplasm
Tried to give his young wife an orgasm,
    But his tongue jumped the track
    'Twixt the front and the back.
And got pinched in a bad anal spasm.

1947.

426

There once was a man of Sag Harbor
Who used to go *with* a fag barber.
    He gave some auditions
    In many positions,
And now he plays flute with Jan Garber.

1947B.

427

There was a young man of Saint Kitts
Who was very much troubled with fits.
    After chewing a gal's cunt
    He'd give a loud grunt
And try to bite off her two teats.

1946A.

ORAL IRREGULARITY

428

A young bride was once heard to say,
" Oh dear, I am wearing away!
　　The insides of my thighs
　　Look just like mince pies,
For my husband won't shave every day."

1943A.

429

There was a young man of Soho
Whose tastes were exceedingly low.
　　He said to his mother,
　　" Let us suck one another,
And swallow the seminal flow."

1882.

430

An Indian squaw up at Spruce
Was unable to have a papoose.
　　She said to her pater,
　　When he asked, " What's the matter?"
" I can't swallow the foul, slimy juice."

1946A-1952.

431

A worried young man from Stamboul
Discovered red spots on his tool.
　　Said the doctor, a cynic,
　　" Get out of my clinic!
Just wipe off the lipstick, you fool."

1944A-1952.

432

A tidy young lady of Streator
Dearly loved to nibble a peter.
　　She always would say,
　　" I prefer it this way.
I think it is very much neater."

1927-1941.

433
Old Louis Quatorze was hot stuff.
He tired of that game, blindman's buff,
    Up-ended his mistress,
    Kissed hers while she kissed his,
And thus taught the world *soixante-neuf*.

                              1943B.

434
There's a dowager near Sweden Landing
Whose manners are odd and demanding.
    It's one of her jests
    To suck off her guests—
She hates to keep gentlemen standing.

                              1952.

435
There was a young girl, very sweet,
Who thought sailors' meat quite a treat.
    When she sat on their lap
    She unbuttoned their flap,
And always had plenty to eat.

                              1944-1952.

436
There was a young fellow named Taylor
Who seduced a respectable sailor.
    When they put him in jail
    He worked out the bail
By licking the parts of the jailer.

                              1941A.

437
There was a young lady, and what do you think?
She said, " I care nought for a prick that don't stink,
    And I think that a fuck
    Ain't so good as a suck
When you've pulled back the foreskin and uncovered the pink. "

                              1870.

438

Have you heard of young Franchot Tone,
Who felt of his own peculiar bone?
    It was long and quite narrow
    And filled full of marrow,
And less edible than stale corn pone.
                                1942.

439

A caddy named Tommy the Tough
Had an heiress way out in the rough.
    He said, " What a swell fuck!
    Now let's you and me suck—
Or as you uppercrust say, 'Soixante-neuf'. "
                                1948A.

440

There was an old lady of Troy
Who invented a new kind of joy:
    She sugared her quim,
    And frosted the rim,
And then had it sucked by a boy.
                              1879-1941.

441

There was a young lady called Tucker,
And the parson he tried hard to fuck her.
    She said, " You gay sinner,
    Instead of your dinner,
At my cunt you shall have a good suck, ah. "
                                1870.

442

There was a young fellow named Tucker
Who, instructing a novice cock-sucker,
    Said, " Don't bow out your lips
    Like an elephant's hips,
The boys like it best when they pucker. "
                                1934.

443

There was an old Warden of Wadham, he
Was very much given to sodomy,
    But he shyly confessed,
    " I like tongue-fucking best,
God bless my soul, isn't it odd of me? "
                         1870.

444

There was an old party of Wokingham,
And his whores said he always was poking 'em,
    But all he could do
    Was to tongue-fuck a few,
And sniff at his fingers while roking 'em.
                         1870.

445

There is a new Baron of Wokingham,
The girls say he don't care for poking 'em,
    Preferring " Minette, "
    Which is pleasant, but yet,
There is one disadvantage, his choking 'em.
                         1879.

V

BUGGERY

446

A whimsical Arab from Aden,
His masculine member well laden,
    Cried : " Nuptial joy,
    When shared with a boy,
Is better than melon or maiden! "

1946B.

447

A pederast living in Arles
Used to bugger the bung of a barrel,
    But was heard to lament,
    " In the old days I went
Up the blue-blooded bum of an earl! "

1942A.

448

There was a young man of Arras
Who stretched himself out on the grass,
    And with no little trouble
    He bent himself double
And stuck his prick well up his ass.

1941.

449

A convict once, out in Australia,
Said unto his turnkey, " I'll tail yer. "
    But he said, " You be buggered,
    You filthy old sluggard,
You're forgetting as I am your gaoler. "

1870.

450

There was a young man from Axminster
Whose designs were quite base and quite sinister.
   His lifelong ambition
   Was anal coition
With the wife of the French foreign minister.

                              1950.

451

A young man who lived in Balbriggan
Went to sea to recover from frigging,
   But after a week
   As they climbed the fore-peak
He buggered the mate in the rigging.

                              1942A.

452

Berries, berries, all kinds of berries,
Chancres on her ass like California cherries.
   The first time I hit her
   I nearly broke her shitter,
Down where the Hasiampa flows.

                              1927.

453

There was a young party of Bicester
Who wanted to bugger his sister,
   But not liking dirt,
   He bought him a squirt,
And cleaned out her arse with a clyster.

                              1879.

454

Some night when you're drunk on Dutch Bols
Try changing the usual rôles.
   The backward position
   Is nice for coition
And it offers the choice of two holes.

                              1947B.

455
There was a young belle from Bombay
Who never had thought herself gay,
    Till a quean from Siam
      Said, "My dear, you're not jam!"
And brought that one out right away.

                                       1942.

456
There was a brave damsel of Brighton
Whom nothing could possibly frighten.
    She plunged in the sea
    And, with infinite glee,
Was fucked in the ass by a Triton.

                                       1952.

457
As he lay in his bath, mused Lord Byng,
"Oh Vimy! What memories you bring!
    That gorgeous young trooper...
    No! No! Gladys Cooper!
By Gad, sir! That was a near thing."

                                       1945A.

458
Coitus upon a cadaver
Is the ultimate way you can have 'er.
    Her inanimate state
    Means a man needn't wait,
And eliminates all the palaver.

                             1940*-1947B.

459
There was a young man of Calcutta
    Who thought he would do a smart trick,
So anointed his arsehole with butter,
    And in it inserted his prick.
    It was not for greed after gold,
    It was not for thirst after pelf;
    Twas simply because he'd been told
    To bloody well bugger himself.

                                       1879.

460

A Phi Delt known as Carruthers
Will never make little girls mothers.
    Around the old brown
    He is covered with down
To wipe off the dongs of his brothers.
                               1942.

461

There was a young man from Chubut
Who had a remarkable root:
    When hard it would bend
    With a curve at the end,
So he fucked himself in the petoot.
                               1942.

462

A parson who lived near Cremorne
Looked down on all women with scorn.
    E'en a boy's white, fat bum
    Could not make him come,
But an old man's piles gave him the horn.
                               1879.

463

There was a young fellow named Dave
Who kept a dead whore in a cave.
    He said, " I admit
    I'm a bit of a shit,
But think of the money I save! "
                             1927-1939A.

464

There was a young Jew of Delray
Who buggered his father one day.
    He said, " I like rather
    To stuff it up Father;
He's clean, and there's nothing to pay. "
                             1879-1928.

465

A depraved old Jew from Estretto
Buggered every young man in the ghetto.
    He once had his hose in
    A musician, composing,
Who said : " Not so slow—allegretto! "

                               1946B.

466

A mortician who practised in Fife
Made love to the corpse of his wife.
    " How could I know, Judge?
    She was cold, did not budge—
Just the same as she'd acted in life. "

                               1942A.

467

A glutted debauchee from Frome
Lured beauteous maids to his room,
    Where, after he'd strip 'em,
    He'd generally whip 'em
With a bundle of twigs or a broom.

                               1945.

468

When she wanted a new way to futter
He greased her behind with butter;
    Then, with a sock,
    In went his jock,
And they carried her home on a shutter.

                               1927.

469

There was a young pansy named Gene
Who cruised a sadistic Marine.
    Said the man with a smirk
    As they got down to work,
" In this game the Jack beats the Queen. "

                               1943A.

470

There was a young lady of Glasgow,
And fondly her lover did ask, " Oh,
    Pray allow me a fuck,"
    But she said, " No, my duck,
But you may, if you please, up my arse go."
                                        1879.

471

At the *Iphigenia* of Gluck
Two ushers attempted to fuck.
    At the blare of the brass
    One contracted his ass,
And they carted him off in a truck.
                                       1947B.

472

There was an old man named Grasty
Whose favorite sport was ass-ty.
    He'd bugger with joy
    Any innocent boy,
But thought fornication was nasty.
                                       1927.

473

A native of Havre de Grace
Once tired of Cunt, said, " I'll try arse."
    He unfolded his plan
    To another young man,
Who said, " Most decidedly, my arse!"
                                       1879.

474

There was a young fellow named Howell
Who buggered himself with a trowel.
    The triangular shape
    Was conducive to rape,
And was easily cleaned with a towel.
                                       1941A.

475

A prisoner in Château d'If
Ran around on all fours for a sniff
    Of his comrade's posterior,
    And said, " It's inferior,
But it somehow reminds me of quiff."

                      1942A.

476

A Sultan of old Istamboul
Had a varicose vein in his tool.
    This evoked joyous grunts
    From his harem of cunts,
But his boys suffered pain at the stool.

                      1928-1949.

477

Said an airy young fairy named Jess,
" The oral requires some finesse,
    While in method the anal
    Is terribly banal,
And the trousers will get out of press."

                      1943A.

478

A psychiatrist fellow, quite Jung,
Asked his wife, " May I bugger your bung?"
    And was so much annoyed
    When he found her a-Freud,
He went out in the yard and ate dung.

                      1941.

479

There was a young reb from Kadoches
Who had a hospitable toches.
    His friends had no fear
    To attack from the rear,
For he'd make it quite kosher with broches.

                      1943C.

480

An embalmer in ancient Karnak
Oozed it into a fresh corpse's crack.
    Rigor mortis set in
    And clamped off what had been
His pride, nor did he get it back.

1942A.

481

There was a young fellow named Kelly
Who preferred his wife's ass to her belly.
    He shrieked with delight
    As he ploughed through the shite,
And filled up her hole with his jelly.

1942.

482

There was an old man of Kentucky,
Said to his old woman, " Oi'll fuck ye."
    She replied, " Now you wunt
    Come anigh my old cunt,
For your prick is all stinking and mucky."

1870.

483

There was an old phoney named Kinsey
Whose ideas of fucking were flimsy.
    He knew how to measure
    A penis for pleasure,
But he came much too quick in a quim, see?

1952.

484

There was a young man from Liberia
Who was forced to flee to the interior.
    He'd buggered a brother,
    His father and mother—
He considered his sisters inferior.

1947B-1952.

485

A youth who seduced a poor lighterman,
Said, " I'd much sooner fuck than I'd fight a man,
    And although, Sir, I find
    You a very good grind,
I must say I've had a much tighter man. "
                      1870.

486

A young nigger boxer, Joe Louis,
Who buggered a bastardly Jewess,
    He said with a sigh
    As his engine went dry,
" I wonder where all of my goo is. "
                      1939A.

487

There was a young mate of a lugger
Who took out a girl just to hug her.
    " I've my monthlies, " she said,
    " And a cold in the head,
But my bowels work well... Do you bugger ? "
                      1928.

488

There was a young man of Madras
Who was having a boy in the grass.
    Then a cobra-capello
    Said, " Hello, young fellow! "
And bit a piece out of his arse.
                      1928.

489

There was a young priest from Madrid
Who looked with lewd eyes on a kid.
    He said, " With great joy
    I could bugger that boy.
I'll be damned if I don't! "— And he did.
                      1927A-1939A.

490

There was a hermaphrodite kid,
Made a pass at a man from Madrid.
" Why, you son of a maggot,
   Do you think *I'm* a faggot?
Just go fuck yourself! "— So he did.

                      1943B.

491

There was a young lady whose mind
Was never especially refined.
   She got on her knees,
   Her lover to please,
Who stuck in his prick from behind.

                      1939*

492

There once was a well-groomed young nance
Who responded to every advance,
   But rather than strip
   He let anything slip
Through a hole in the seat of his pants.

                      1942.

493

There was a young man from Nantasket
Who screwed a dead whore in a casket.
   He allowed 'twas no vice,
   But thought it was nice,
For she needed no money, nor'd ask it.

                      1947B.

494

There was a young man from Nantucket
Who had such a big cock he could suck it.
   He looked in the glass
   And saw his own ass,
And broke his neck trying to fuck it.

                      1939A-1946A.

495

Should a fellow discover some night
A girl's body in bed, it's all right.
   He should think it good luck,
   And accept the free fuck—
He will bugger her too, if he's bright.

                                      1941.

496

There was a Captain of MAG 94
More easily had than a two-bit whore.
   He wanted to drink
   And fondle your dink,
But he's not around any more.

                                      1945C.

497

There once was a doughty Norwegian
Who enlivened the French Foreign Legion,
   But his brothers-in-arms
   Who succumbed to his charms
All got clap in their hindermost region.

                                      1941.

498

There was a young fellow named Oakum
Whose brags about fucking were hokum,
   For he really preferred
   To suck cocks and stir turd—
He was Queen of the Flits in Hoboken.

                                      1941.

499

Said Oscar McDingle O'Figgle,
With an almost hysterical giggle,
   " Last night I was sick
   With delight when my prick
Felt dear Alfred's delicious arse wriggle! "

                                      1941.

500

There was a young man of Oswego,
Whose friends said, " Be off now, to sea go. "
    He there learned the trick
    Of skinning his prick,
And up arses thrusting his pego.

1870.

501

A young queer who was much oversexed
Was easily fretted and vexed.
    When out on a date
    He hardly could wait
To say, " Turn over, bud; my turn next. "

1942-1952.

502

There was a young man of Peru
Who dreamt he was had by a Jew.
    He woke up at night
    In a hell of a fright,
And found it was perfectly true.

1928.

503

There were three young men in Peru :
A German, a bugger, a Jew.
    The German he buggered
    The bugger, the bugger!
The bugger, he buggered the Jew.

1941.

504

There was an old man from Pinole
Who always got in the wrong hole,
    And when he withdrew,
    All covered with goo,
His temper was out of control.

1942.

505

A phenomenal fellow named Preston
Has a hair-padded lower intestine.
    Though exceedingly fine
    In the buggery line,
It isn't much good for digestin'.

1952.

506

A man who is lacking in pride
Attends funerals far, near, and wide.
    When asked about this
    His reply is, "It's bliss
To bugger a piece of dead hide."

1946A.

507

"I'll do it for Art—I'm no prude!"
He said, as he posed in the nude.
    But on viewing his ass
    The whole fairy class
Decided it ought to be screwed.

1946A-1952.

508

There was an old man of Ramnugger
Who drove a rare trade as a bugger,
    Till a fair young Circassian
    Brought fucking in fashion,
And spoilt all the trade in Ramnugger.

1870.

509

There once was an apple-cheeked runt
Who was welcomed with joy at the Front.
    This God's gift to he-men
    Prevented spilled semen,
For his ass was tattooed like a cunt.

1947B.

510. ROYAL SPASM IN FIVE FITS

Thus spake the King of Siam:
"For women I don't care a damn.
    But a fat-bottomed boy
    Is my pride and my joy—
They call me a bugger: I am."

"Indeed," quoth the King of Siam,
"For cunts I just don't give a damn.
    They haven't the grip,
    Nor the velvety tip,
Nor the scope of the ass-hole of man."

Then up spake the Bey of Algiers
And said to his harem, "My dears,
    You may think it odd o' me
    But I've given up sodomy—
Tonight there'll be fucking!" (*Loud cheers.*)

Then up spake the young King of Spain:
"To fuck and to bugger is pain.
    But it's not *infra dig*
    On occasion to frig,
And I do it again and again."

Then up spoke a Hindu mahout,
And said, "What's all this blithering about?
    Why, I shoot my spunk
    Up an elephant's trunk—"
(*Cries of* "Shame! He's a shit! Throw him out!")

                      1910-1938*

515

There was a young lady named Spruce
Whose favorite thrill was a goose.
    Just the sight of a thumb
    Made her tokus all numb,
And her bowels got excited—and loose.

1941.

516

In Glasgow a tender tapeworm
Was so starved that he barely could squirm,
    Until his host finally
    Was buggered divinely,
And Jimmie had vaseline and sperm.

1942A.

517

Meet Elmer, young son of the Thorpes,
Afflicted with psychotic warps.
    His idea of fun
    Is to bugger a nun,
And then vomit all over the corpse.

1946A.

518

An earnest young woman in Thrace
Said, " Darling, that's not the right place! "
    So he gave her a thwack,
    And did on her back
What he couldn't have done face to face.

1942A.

519

Close to 'long ass b'long coconut tree,
One fellow mary come up 'long me,
    Si' down long grass,
    Igot big fellow ass,
Italk ilike push-push 'long me.

1946.

520

There was a young colonel from Trent
Who lived in a lavender tent.
    He said that some sessions
    With interesting Hessians
Had taught him what war really meant.
                                        1942.

521. WHO'LL BUGGER THE TURK?

" I, " said Gladstone, " as Chief of the Nation,
And Premier of England, to gain reputation.
    I'll bugger the Turk,
    And ne'er let him shirk
My prick's Grand Demonstration! "
                                        1880.

522

Said Senator David I. Walsh,
" These charges against me are falsh.
    Though I did go to Brooklyn
    For sooklyn and fooklyn,
Not a gob laid his hands on my balsh. "
                                        1947B.

523. THE GOOD SHIP VENUS

The good ship's name was Venus,
Her mast a towering penis,
    Her figure-head
    A whore in bed—
A pretty sight, by Jesus!

The first mate's name was Andy,
By God, he was a dandy,
    They broke his cock
    With chunks of rock
For conking in the brandy.

The second mate was Morgan,
By God, he was a Gorgon,
   Nine times a day
   Fine tunes he'd play
On his reproductive organ.

The captain's daughter Mabel
They screwed when they were able,
   They nailed her tits,
   Those lousy shits,
Right to the captain's table.

The captain's other daughter,
They threw her in the water,
   You could tell by the squeals
   That some of the eels
Had found her reproductive quarter.

   The cabin-boy*
   Was the captain's joy,
A cunning little nipper,
   They filled his ass
   With broken glass
And circumcized the skipper.

Then in search of new sensation
In the forms of recreation,
   The ship was sunk
   In a wave of gunk
From mutual masturbation.

1946A.

VI

ABUSES OF THE CLERGY

530

There was a young lady named Alice
Who peed in a Catholic chalice.
    She said, " I do this
    From a great need to piss,
And not from sectarian malice."

                 1941.

531

There was a young girl in Alsace
Who was having her first piece of ass.
    " Oh, darling, you'll kill me!
    Oh, dearest, you thrill me
Like Father John's thumb after mass!"

                 1947.

532

A modern monk nicknamed Augustin,
His penis a boy's bottom thrust in.
    Then said Father Ignatius,
    " Now really! Good gracious!
Your conduct is really disgusting."

                 1870.

533

There was a young pansy named Birch
Who developed a taste for the church,
    And monks, priests, and preachers,
    And such mouthy creatures,
Were the uplifted ends of his search.

                 1941.

534

There were three young ladies of Birmingham,
And this is the scandal concerning 'em.
    They lifted the frock
    And tickled the cock
Of the Bishop engaged in confirming 'em.

Now, the Bishop was nobody's fool,
He'd been to a good public school,
    So he took down their britches
    And buggered those bitches
With his ten-inch episcopal tool.

Then up spoke a lady from Kew,
And said, as the Bishop withdrew,
    " The vicar is quicker
    And thicker and slicker,
And longer and stronger than you. "

1927A-1941*

537

There was a young Bishop from Brest
Who openly practiced incest.
    " My sisters and nieces
    Are all dandy pieces,
And they don't cost a cent, " he confessed.

1945.

538

There was a young curate of Buckingham
Who was blamed by the girls for not fucking 'em.
    He said, " Though my cock
    Is as hard as a rock,
Your cunts are too slack. Put a tuck in 'em. "

1928.

539

There was a young lady of Cheyne
Who crept into the vestry unseen.
    She pulled down her knickers,
      And also the vicar's,
And said, " How about it, old bean ? "

                                  1941.

540

There was a young lady of Chichester
Who made all the saints in their niches stir.
    One morning at matins
      Her breasts in white satins
Made the Bishop of Chichester's britches stir.

                              1939A-1941.

541

A young curate, just new to the cloth,
At sex was surely no sloth.
    He preached masturbation
      To his whole congregation,
And was washed down the aisle on the froth.

                                  1946B.

542

I once had the wife of a Dean
Seven times while the Dean was out ski'in'.
    She remarked with some gaiety,
     " Not bad for the laity,
Though the Bishop once managed thirteen. "

                                    1947B.

543

There was a young choir-boy from Devon
Who was raped in a hay-stack by seven
    High Anglican priests—
    (Lascivious beasts)—
For of such is the kingdom of heaven.

                              1941-1943A.

544

There was a young monk from Dundee
Who hung a nun's cunt on a tree.
    He grabbed her fair ass
    And performed a high mass
That even the Pope came to see.

1947A.

545

There was a young curate of Eltham
Who wouldn't fuck girls, but he felt 'em.
    In lanes he would linger
    And play at stink-finger,
And *scream* with delight when he smelt 'em.

1879-1935*

546

A Big Catholic Layman named Fox
Makes his living by sucking off cocks.
    In spells of depression
    He goes to confession,
And jacks off the priest in his box.

The priest, a cocksucker named Sheen,
Is delighted their sins aren't seen.
    "Though God sees through walls,"
    Says Monsignor, " — Oh, balls!
This God stuff is simply a screen."

1945-1951.

548

There was an archbishop in France
Who saw a nude woman by chance.
    The result, I affirm,
    Was emission of sperm
In the archiepiscopal pants.

1941.

549

There once was a priest of Gibraltar
Who wrote dirty jokes in his psalter.
    An inhibited nun
    Who had read every one
Made a vow to be laid on his altar.

                           1938.

550

There was a young lady named Jessary
Got deflowered while in a confessary.
    The priest who thus wrecked her
    Would scorn a protector,
While she'd never heard of a pessary!

                           1943B.

551

There was an old Abbot of Khief
Who thought the Impenitent Thief
    Had bollocks of brass
    And an amethyst arse.
He died in this awful belief.

                           1928.

552

There was a young monk of Kilkyre,
Was smitten with carnal desire.
    The immediate cause
    Was the abbess' drawers,
Which were hung up to dry by the fire.

                           1941.

553

There was a young rector of Kings
Whose mind was on heavenly things,
    But his heart was on fire
    For a boy in the choir
Whose ass was like jelly on springs.

                           1941.

554

Apud Rege tutor veteramus
Puellaria odit profanus
    Semper optandus
    Pueri sperandus
Gellifactus in siliis anus.

                            1941.

555

When a lecherous curate at Leeds
Was discovered, one day, in the weeds
    Astride a young nun,
    He said, " Christ, this is fun!
Far better than telling one's beads! "

                            1946B.

556

A Sunday-School student in Mass.
Soon rose to the head of the class,
    By reciting quite bright
    And by sleeping at night
With his tongue up the minister's ass.

                            1941.

557

In Kansas there lived a young monk
Who often was in a blue funk,
    For his come always froze
    On the sisters' thick hose,
And they never would part with a chunk.

                            1952.

558

A lecherous Bishop of Peoria,
In a state of constant euphoria,
    Enjoyed having fun
    With a whore or a nun
While chanting the Sanctus and Gloria.

                         1944-1945.

559

There was a gay rector of Poole
Most deservedly proud of his tool.
    With some trifling aid
    From the curate, 'tis said,
He rogered the National School.
                      1870.

560

A hoary old monk of Regina
Once said, " There is nothing diviner
    Than to sit in one's cell
    And let one's mind dwell
On the charms of the Virgin's vagina."
                    1941-1947B.

561

There was a young man of St. Giles
Who'd walked thousands and thousands of miles,
    From the Cape of Good Hope,
    Just to bugger the Pope,
But he couldn't — the pontiff had piles.
                      1941.

562

There was an old abbess quite shocked
To find nuns where the candles were locked.
    Said the abbess, " You nuns
    Should behave more like guns,
And never go off till you're cocked."
                      1941.

563

There was a young monk of Siberia
Who of frigging grew weary and wearier.
    At last, with a yell,
    He burst from his cell,
And buggered the Father Superior.
                    1879-1928.

564

There was a young monk from Siberia
Whose morals were very inferior.
    He did to a nun
    What he shouldn't have done,
And now she's a Mother Superior.

                      1933*-1941.

565

Three lustful young ladies of Simms
Were blessed with such over-size quims,
    The bishop of their diocese
    Got elephantiasis,
For his life wasn't all singing hymns.

                      1941.

566

A mediaeval recluse named Sissions
Was alarmed by his nightly emissions.
    His cell-mate, a sod,
    Said, "Leave it to God."
And taught him some nifty positions.

                      1941.

567

There once was a Bishop of Treet
Who decided to be indiscreet,
    But after one round
    To his horror he found
You repeat, and repeat, and repeat.

                      1944.

568

A Bishop whose See was Vermont
Used to jerk himself off in the font.
    The baptistry stank
    With an odor most rank,
And no one would sit up in front.

                      1952.

569

Said a Palestine pilgrim named Wadham,
"For religion I don't give a goddem!
   I've frequently peed in
   The Garden of Eden,
And buggered my guide when in Sodom."

                1952.

570

The bishop of Winchester Junction
Found his phallus would no longer function.
   So in black crêpe he wound it,
   Tied a lily around it,
And solemnly gave it last unction.

                1941.

571

A handsome young monk in a wood
Told a girl she should cling to the good.
   She obeyed him, and gladly;
   He repulsed her, but sadly:
"My dear, you have misunderstood."

                1943A.

572

   The Dean undressed
   With heaving breast,
The bishop's wife to lie on.
   He thought it lewd
   To do it nude,
So he kept his old school tie on.

                1941–1942.

573

The Book of God's beneath you,
The Man of God's above you.
   Salvation pole
   Is in your hole—
Now wiggle your ass to save your soul.

                1928A–1939*

VII

ZOOPHILY

574

There was a young man of Adair
Who thought he would diddle a mare.
   He climbed up a ladder
   And jolly well had her,
With his backside a-wave in the air.

                      1941.

575

There was a young man of Australia
Who went on a wild bacchanalia.
   He buggered a frog,
   Two mice and a dog,
And a bishop in fullest regalia.

                      1941.

576

There once was a sacred baboon
That lived by the river Rangoon,
   And all of the women
   That came to go swimmin'
He'd bang by the light of the moon.

                      1941.

577

There was a young man from Bangore
Who was tired and said to his whore,
   " If you'll only roll over
   I'll get my dog Rover,
And you can have six inches more."

                      1939A.

578

There once was a man of Belfast
Whose balls out of iron were cast.
    He'd managed somehow
    To bugger a sow,
Thus you get pig-iron, at last.

                      1947B.

579

There was a young man of Bengal
Who went to a fancy dress ball.
    Just for a stunt
    He dressed up as a cunt
And was fucked by a dog in the hall.

                      1928-1932.

580

A habit obscene and bizarre
Has taken a-hold of papa:
    He brings home young camels
    And other odd mammals,
And gives them a go at mama.

                      1946*-1947.

581

The Communist Party's Earl Browder
Was fucking a girl in a howda.
    The elephant's trunk
    Somehow got in her cunt
Which, they felt, made it terribly crowded.

                      1948A.

582

There was a young gaucho named Bruno
Who said, " Screwing is one thing I *do* know.
    A woman is fine,
    And a sheep is divine,
But a llama is Numero Uno. "

                      1942A-1944A.

583

Said an old taxidermist in Burrell,
As he skilfully mounted a squirrel,
    "This excess of tail is
    Obstructive to phallus;
One's much better off with a girl."

                            1942A.

584

There was an old man of the Cape
Who buggered a Barbary ape.
    The ape said, "You fool!
    You've got a square tool;
You've buggered my arse out of shape."

                          1879-1928.

585

A fisherman off of Cape Cod
Said, "I'll bugger that tuna, by God!"
    But the high-minded fish
    Resented his wish,
And nimbly swam off with his rod.

                            1942A.

586

There once was a man of Cape Nod
Who attempted to bugger a cod,
    When up came some scallops
    And nibbled his bollops,
And now he's a eunuch, by God.

                        1930*-1951.

587

Minnehaha was washing her clothes,
Unexpectant of sorrows or woes.
    A snake, a side-winder,
    Crawled in her behinder,
Wiggled 'round and came out of her nose.

                            1946A.

588

A sailor indulged in coitus
With a cow of the genus of Cetus.
    Piscatologists thundered,
    Biologists wondered,
At the anchor tattooed on the fœtus.

1942A.

589

A man who was richer than Croesus
Enjoyed being sucked off by feices,
    Till a vicious old hound
    Thought his stake was ground round,
And chewed it completely to pieces.

1942.

590

There once was a fairy named Cyril
Who was had in a wood by a squirrel,
    And he liked it so good
    That he stayed in the wood
Just as long as the squirrel was virile.

1941.

591

There once was a clergyman's daughter
Who detested the pony he bought her
    Till she found that its dong
    Was as hard and as long
As the prayers her father had taught her.

She married a fellow named Tony
Who soon found her fucking the pony.
    Said he, " What's it got,
    My dear, that I've not? "
Sighed she, " Just a yard-long bologna. "

1941.

593

That Harvard don down at El Djim—
Oh, wasn't it nasty of him,
    With the whole hareem randy,
    The sheik himself handy,
To muss up a young camel's quim?

1942A.

594

The eminent Mrs. DeVue
Was born in a cage at the zoo,
    And the curious rape
    Which made her an ape
Is highly fantastic, if true.

1945A.

595

There was a young girl of Dundee
Who was raped by an ape in a tree.
    The result was most horrid—
    All ass and no forehead,
Three balls and a purple goatee.

1938.

596

Pine insulensis inevit
Rectum simioli quem scivit
    Proles infrontata
    Horrida glandata
Et semper violare cupivit.

1941.

597

The prior of Dunstan St. Just,
Consumed with erotical lust,
    Raped the bishop's prize fowls,
    Buggered four startled owls
And a little green lizard, that bust.

1948A.

598

There was a young girl of Eau Claire
Who once was attacked by a bear.
    While chased in a field
    She tripped and revealed
Some meat to the bear that was rare.

1944A.

599

There was a young man of Eau Claire
Who had an affair with a bear,
    But the surly old brute
    With a snap of her snoot
Left him only one ball and some hair.

1927-1947B.

600

When Theocritus guarded his flock
He piped in the shade of a rock.
    It is said that his Muse
    Was one of the ewes
With a bum like a pink hollyhock.

1942A.

601

There was a young lady named Florence
Who for fucking professed an abhorrence,
    But they found her in bed
    With her cunt flaming red,
And her poodle-dog spending in torrents.

1941.

602

There once was a fellow named Fogg
Who attempted to bugger a hog.
    While engaged in his frolics
    The hog ate his bollix,
And now he's a eunuch, by God.

1930*-1946A.

603

One morning Mahatma Gandhi
Had a hard-on, and it was a dandy.
   So he said to his aide,
   " Please bring me a maid,
Or a goat, or whatever is handy."

                                  1941.

604

There once was a man of Geneva
Who buggered a black bitch retriever.
   The result was a sow,
   Two horses, a cow,
Three lambs and a London coal-heaver.

                               1930*-1952.

605

There was a young peasant named Gorse
Who fell madly in love with his horse.
   Said his wife, " You rapscallion,
   That horse is a stallion—
This constitutes grounds for divorce."

                               1941-1951.

606

There was an old man from near here,
Got awfully drunk upon beer.
   He fell in a ditch
   And a son of a bitch
Of a bull dog fucked him in the ear.

                                  1928B.

607

The Mahatma on Mt. Himavat
Opined as he diddled a cat:
   " She's a far better piece
   Than the Viceroy's niece,
Who has also more fur on her prat."

                                  1942A.

608

A fox-hound retired from the hunt
For he found that his lobes had grown blunt
    To the scent of the fox,
    But he still would sniff rocks
For the mystical fragrance of cunt.

                        1942A.

609

There was a young man with the itch
Who, because he was not at all rich,
    Had to harbor his tail
    In any female—
A duck or a sow or a bitch.

                        1941.

610

There was a young fellow named Jim
Whose wife kept a worm in her quim.
    It was silly and smelly,
    And tickled her belly,
And what the hell was it to *him*?

                        1944A.

611

A spinster in Kalamazoo
Once strolled after dark by the zoo.
    She was seized by the nape,
    And raped by an ape,
And she murmured, " A wonderful screw. "

And she added, " You're rough, yes, and hairy,
But I hope—yes I do—that I marry
    A man with a prick
    Half as stiff and as thick
As the kind that you zoo-keepers carry. "

                        1941.

613

All the lady-apes ran from King Kong
For his dong was unspeakably long.
    But a friendly giraffe
    Quaffed his yard and a half,
And ecstatically burst into song.

                                1941.

614

Said a lovely young lady named Lake,
Pervertedly fond of a snake,
    " If my good friend, the boa,
    Shoots spermatozoa,
What offspring we'll leave in our wake! "

Another young lady would make
Advances to snake after snake.
    Though men she had met
    Got her diaphragm wet,
She wanted her glottis to shake.

                           1928-1941.

616

In a meadow a man named Llewellyn
Had a dream he was bundling with Helen.
    When he woke he discovered
    A bull had him covered
With ballocks as big as a melon.

                             1942A.

617

There was an old Scot named McTavish
Who attempted an anthropoid ravish.
    The object of rape
    Was the wrong sex of ape,
And the anthropoid ravished McTavish.

                             1948A.

618

There was a young man, a Maltese,
Who could even screw horses with ease.
    He'd flout natural laws
    In this manner because
Of his dong, which hung down to his knees.
                              1943A.

619

Thus spake an old Chinese mandarin,
" There's a subject I'd like to use candor in :
    The geese of Pekin
    Are so steepèd in sin
They'd as soon let a man as a gander in. "
                              1941.

620

Here's to old King Montezuma,
For fun he would bugger a puma.
    The puma in play
    Clawed both balls away—
How's that for animal humor?
                              1948-1950.

621

There was a young lady of Mott
Who inserted a fly up her twat
    And pretended the buzz
    Was not what it was
But something she knew it was not.
                              1943-1949.

622

There was a young lady named Myrtle
Who had an affair with a turtle.
    She had crabs, so they say,
    In a year and a day,
Which proves that the turtle was fertile.
                              1927-1941.

623

There was a young man from Nantucket
Took a pig in a thicket to fuck it.
    Said the pig, " Oh, I'm queer,
    Get away from my rear...
Come around to the front and I'll suck it."

                                      1941.

624

There once was a laddie of Neep
Who demanded everything cheap.
    When he wanted to screw
    There was nothing to do
But take out his passion on sheep.

                                         1951.

625

There was a young man from New Haven
Who had an affair with a raven.
    He said with a grin
    As he wiped off his chin,
" Nevermore! "

                                       1943C.

626

There was a young man of Newminster Court
Bugger'd a pig, but his prick was too short.
    Said the hog, " It's not nice,
    But pray take my advice :
Make tracks, or by the police you'll be caught."

                                         1879.

627

An elderly pervert in Nice
Who was long past desire for a piece
    Would jack-off his hogs,
    His cows and his dogs,
But his parrot called in the police.

                                       1942A.

628

There was a young man named O'Rourke,
Heard babies were brought by the stork,
    So he went to the zoo
    And attempted to screw
One old bird—end-result: didn't work.
                        1951.

629

The notorious Duchess of Peels
Saw a fisherman fishing for eels.
    Said she, " Would you mind?—
    Shove one up my behind.
I am anxious to know how it feels."
                        1944A.

630

There was a young man in Peru
Who had nothing whatever to do,
    So he flew to the garret
    And buggered the parrot,
And sent the result to the zoo.
                        1879-1941.

631

A gruff anthropoid of Piltdown
Had a strange way of going to town:
    With maniacal howls
    He would bugger young owls,
And polish his balls on their down.
                        1942.

632

There was a young Nubian prince
Whose cock would make elephants wince.
    Once, while socking the sperm
    To a large pachyderm,
He slipped, and he's not been seen since.
                        1943A.

633

There was an old hostler named Rains,
Possessed of more ballocks than brains.
    He stood on a stool
    To bugger a mule,
And got kicked in the balls for his pains.

          1941.

634

There once was a girl named Miss Randall
Who kept a young bear cub to dandle.
    She said, " In a pinch
    This bear cub's six-inch
Is almost as good as a candle. "

          1944.

635

There was a young lady of Rhodes
Who sinned in unusual modes.
    At the height of her fame
    She abruptly became
The mother of four dozen toads.

          1943A.

636

A nigger in fair St. Domingo
Being blasé and worn, said, " By Jingo,
    Blast all women and boys,
    I'll try some new joys. "
So he went out and fucked a Flamingo.

          1880.

637

There was a young man of St. John's
Who wanted to bugger the swans.
    But the loyal hall-porter
    Said, " Pray take my daughter!
Them birds are reserved for the dons. "

          1928-1941.

638

There was a young man of St. Paul
Whose prick was exceedingly small.
    He could bugger a bug
    At the edge of a rug,
And the bug hardly felt it at all.

1927-1941.

639

A hermit who lived on St. Roque
Had a lily perfected to poke.
    He diddled the donkeys
    And meddled with monkeys,
And would have done worse, but it broke.

1942A.

640

There was an old man of Santander
Who attempted to bugger a gander.
    But that virtuous bird
    Plugged its ass with a turd,
And refused to such low tastes to pander.

There was a young man from Toulouse
Who thought he would diddle a goose.
    He hunted and bunted
    To get the thing cunted,
But decided it wasn't no use.

1879-1941.

642

There was an old person of Sark
Who buggered a pig in the dark.
    The swine, in surprise,
    Murmured, " God blast your eyes,
Do you take me for Boulton or Park ? "

1879.

643

There once was a sergeant named Schmitt
Who wanted a crime to commit.
    He thought raping women
    Was a little too common,
So he buggered an aged tomtit.

                                    1944.

644

There was a young lady named Schneider
Who often kept trysts with a spider.
    She found a strange bliss
    In the hiss of her piss,
As it strained through the cobwebs inside her.

                                    1941.

645

When Brother John wanted a screw
He would stuff a fat cat in a shoe,
    Pull up his cassock
    And kneel on a hassock,
Trying his damnedest to mew.

                                    1942A.

646

There was a young man of Seattle
Who bested a bull in a battle.
    With fire and gumption
    He assumed the bull's function,
And deflowered a whole herd of cattle.

                                    1945.

647

There was a young girl from Seattle
Whose hobby was sucking off cattle.
    But a bull from the South
    Left a wad in her mouth
That made both her ovaries rattle.

                              1941*-1946B.

648

If Gracie Allen were the last of her sex,
And I were the last of mine,
    I'd ease my tool
    By fucking a mule
Or even a porcupine.
                    1939A.

649

A rooster residing in Spain
Used to diddle his hens in the rain.
    " I give them a bloody
    Good time when it's muddy :
Which keeps them from getting too vain."
                    1942A.

650

There once was a Dutchman named Spiegle
Who slept with an elegant beagle.
    As they crawled into bed
    He wistfully said,
" It'll be much better if you wiggle."
                    1942.

651

Said the famous composer, R. Strauss
When asked why he buggered a mouse :
    " Though its cunt is quite tiny
    On occasion its heiny
Will stretch quite as big as a house."
                    1948A.

652

There was a young lady named Sutton
Who said, as she carved up the mutton,
    " My father preferred
    The last sheep in the herd—
This is one of his children I'm cuttin'."
                    1948A.

653

When Jupiter hid in a swan
And laid Leda low on the lawn,
    Pled she, "Stick your neck in,
    But please do not peck in
My box, for the lining is gone."

                        1942A.

654

There was a young lady from Teal
Who was raped in the lake by an eel.
    One morning at dawn
    She gave birth to a prawn,
Two crabs, and a small baby seal.

                    1939A-1941.

655

As the rabbi was cutting the throat
Of the annual tribal scape-goat,
    Said the beast, "I will cite you
    As a sodomite! You
Forget what we did on the boat."

                        1942A.

656

A novelist from Tortilla Flats
Repeatedly buggered stray cats.
    The alley-fence howls
    As he stirred up their bowels
Enormously pleased the town rats.

                        1940*

657

A broken-down harlot named Tupps
Was heard to confess in her cups:
    "The height of my folly
    Was fucking a collie—
But I got a nice price for the pups."

                        1941.

658

A vice both obscene and unsavory
Holds the Mayor of Southampton in slavery.
   With bloodcurdling howls
   He deflowers young owls
Which he keeps in an underground aviary.

1939*

659

A sheep-herder out in Van Buren
Lost half of his flock with the murrain.
   Quoth the state veterinary,
   " You ought not to carry
Them live spirochetes of your'n! "

1942A.

660

There was a young artist named Victor
Who purchased a boa constrictor.
   He intended to sketch her,
   But decided (the lecher!)
To fuck her instead of depict her.

1943A.

661

A promiscuous person named Willie
Had a dong that was simply a dilly.
   He would take on all mammals
   And was partial to camels,
But they never could tolerate Willie.

1942-1952.

662

There was a young lady of Wohl's Hill
Who sat herself down on a mole's hill.
   The resident mole
   Stuck his head up her hole—
The lady's all right, but the mole's ill.

1951.

663

There was a young man in Woods Hole
Who had an affair with a mole.
    Though a bit of a nancy
    He *did* like to fancy
Himself in a dominant role.
1951.

664

You've heard of the Duchess of York,
She's twice been blessed by the stork.
    The Duke will fuck
    Naught else but a duck,
While the Duchess she frequents the park.
1939A.

665

A keeper in Hamburg's great zoo
Tried to have a young girl kangaroo.
    But she zipped up her pouch,
    And the rascal said, " Ouch!
You've got a half peter in you."
1942A.

VIII

EXCREMENT

666

The Rajah of Afghanistan
Imported a Birmingham can,
    Which he set as a throne
    On a great Buddha stone—
But he crapped out-of-doors like a man.

1942A.

667

There was a young lady named Ames
Who would play at the jolliest games.
    She was great fun to lay
    For her rectum would play
Obbligatos, and call you bad names.

1941.

668

A young lady who lived in Astoria
Took a fancy to Fletcher's Castoria.
    She partook of this drink
    With her ass in the sink—
Now I ask you : ain't that foresight for ya?

1948A.

669

When a woman in strapless attire
Found her breasts working higher and higher,
    A guest, with great feeling,
    Exclaimed, "How appealing!
Do you mind if I piss in the fire?"

1945.

670

Sir Reginald Barrington, Bart.
Went to the masked ball as a fart.
    He had painted his face
    Like a more private place,
And his voice made the dowagers start.
                                1942A.

671

There was a young fellow named Bart
Who strained every shit through a fart.
    Each tip-tapered turd
    Was the very last word
In this deft and most intricate art.
                                1941.

672

There was a young man of Bhogat,
The cheeks of whose ass were so fat
    That they had to be parted
    Whenever he farted,
And propped wide apart when he shat.
                              1879-1941.

673

A cabman who drove in Biarritz
Once frightened a fare into fits.
    When reprov'd for a fart,
    He said, " God bless my heart,
When I break wind I usually shits. "
                                  1879.

674

There was a young fellow named Brewster
Who said to his wife as he goosed her,
    " It used to be grand
    But just look at my hand;
You ain't wiping as clean as you used to. "
                                  1942.

675

A nasty young joker named Bruce
Used to greet all his friends with a goose,
   Till it came to a stop
   In a handful of flop
From some bowels that were terribly loose.

                                1948A.

676

There was a fat lady of Bryde
Whose shoelaces once came untied.
   She didn't dare stoop
   For fear she would poop,
And she cried and she cried and she cried.

                           1927-1941.

677

There was a young man of Bulgaria
Who once went to piss down an area.
   Said Mary to cook,
   " Oh, do come and look,
Did you ever see anything hairier? "

                                   1880.

678

There was a young friar of Byhill
Who went up to shit on a high hill.
   When the abbot asked, " Was it
   A goodly deposit? "
He said, " *Vox et praeterea nihil.* "

                                   1941.

679

There was an old Bey of Calcutta
Who greased up his asshole with butter.
   Instead of the roar
   Which came there before,
Came a soft, oleaginous mutter.

                                 1946B.

680

There once was a horse from Cape Verdes
Who produced most unusual turds,
    By the simplest means
    He'd eat corn and beans
And make succotash for the birds.

                                1947B.

681

A tourist who stopped at Capri
Was had by an old maid for tea.
    When she wiggled he said,
    As he patted her head,
" Ah, you're changing the 't' to a 'p'! "

                                1942A.

682

There was a young man named Cattell
Who knew psychophysics so well,
    That each time he shit
    He'd stop, measure it—
Its length, and its breadth, and its smell.

                                1939A.

683

An efficient young fellow named Cave
Said, " Think of the time that I save
    By avoiding vacations
    And sexy relations,
And taking a crap while I shave. "

                                1945.

684

There was a young fellow named Charted
Who rubbed soap on his bung when it smarted,
    And to his surprise
    He received a grand prize,
For the bubbles he blew when he farted.

                                1941.

685

A nasty old bugger of Cheltenham
Once shit in his bags as he knelt in 'em.
    So he sold 'em at Ware
    To a gentleman there
Who didn't much like what he smelt in 'em.

1870.

686

There was a young fellow of Chiselhurst
Who never could piss till he'd whistle first.
    One evening in June
    He lost track of the tune—
Dum-da-de-dee... and his bladder burst!

1941.

687

There was a young fellow named Chivy
Who, whenever he went to the privy,
    First solaced his mind,
    And then wiped his behind,
With some well-chosen pages of Livy.

1946B.

688

Said the Duke to the Duchess of Chypre,
"Now, can-paper's grand for a wiper,
    But I don't give a damn for
    This new-fangled camphor-
and-menthol impregnated paper."

Said the Duchess, "Well yes, I daresay
Plain bum-wad's all right in its way,
    But there's nothing so grand
    As some leaves, or your hand,
When you're out in the woods for a day."

1941.

EXCREMENT

690

A young bio-chemist named Dan
Always followed his nose to the can.
    He judged people best
    By the urinal test,
As to race and to sex and to clan.

                                               1941*

691

There was a faith-healer of Deal
Who said, " Although pain isn't real,
    When, frightened by chance,
    I unload in my pants,
I dislike what I fancy I feel. "

                                               1941.

692

There was an old person of Delhi
Awoke with a pain in his belly,
    And to cure it, 'tis said,
    He shit in his bed,
And the sheets were uncommonly smelly.

                                               1870.

693

There was a young lady of Dexter
Whose husband exceedingly vexed her,
    For whenever they'd start
    He'd unfailingly fart
With a blast that damn nearly unsexed her.

                                               1941.

694

There was a young lady of Dorset
Who went to an Underground closet.
    She screwed up her ass
    But passed only some gas,
And *that* wasn't tuppence-worth, was it?

                                             1941.

EXCREMENT

695

There was a young woman named Dottie
Who said as she sat on her potty,
   "It isn't polite
    To do this in sight,
But then, who am I to be snotty?"

1946A.

696

My neighbors, the dirty Miss Drews,
Stand on their door-step and muse,
   And tie up their tresses
    While the dogs make their messes,
And I am wiping my shoes.

1936*

697

There was a young fellow of Ealing,
Devoid of all delicate feeling.
   When he read on the door:
    "Don't shit on the floor"
He jumped up and shat on the ceiling.

1941.

698

The Marquesa de Excusador
Used to pee on the drawing-room floor,
   For the can was so cold
    And when one grows old
To be much alone is a bore.

1942A.

699

While watching some tragical farces,
The audience had a catharsis.
   Instead of real tears
    They wept with their rears,
Which proves that catharsis my arse is.

1942-1951.

700

There was a young lady of Fismes
Who amazingly voided four streams.
    A friend poked around
    And a fly-button found
Wedged tightly in one of her seams.
                                1941.

701

There was a young lady from France
Supposed to play at a dance,
    She ate a banana
    And played the piano
And music came out of her pants.
                               1946A.

702

There was a young lady of Ghat
Who never could sit but she shat.
    Oh, the seat of her drawers
    Was a chamber of horrors,
And they felt even fouler than that!
                                1941.

703

There once was a fellow named Glantz
Who on entering a toilet in France,
    Was in such a heat
    To paper the seat,
He shit right into his pants.
                                1941*

704

Alas for a preacher named Hoke,
Whose shit was all stuck in his poke.
    He farted a blast
    That left hearers aghast,
But nothing emerged but some smoke.
                                1941.

705

A professor who taught at Holyoke
Had a bung like a red artichoke.
    She was greatly annoyed
    That each ripe haemorrhoid
Always quivered whenever she spoke.

1942A.

706

There once was a builder named Howell
Who had a remarkable bowel.
    He built him a building
    Of brickwork and gilding
Using—what do you think—on his trowel.

1947B.

707

That illustrious author, Dean Howells,
Had a terrible time with his bowels.
    His wife, so they say,
    Cleaned them out every day
With special elongated trowels.

1932.

708

Here's to the State of Iowa
Whose soil is soft and rich.
    We need no turd
    From your beautiful bird,*
You red headed son of a bitch.

1928A.

709

There was a young man from Kilbryde
Who fell in a shit house and died.
    His heart-broken brother
    Fell into another,
And now they're interred side by side.

1925*-1941.

710

There was a young girl of La Plata
Who was widely renowned as a farter.
    Her deafening reports
    At the Argentine sports
Made her much in demand as a starter.
                                  1941.

711

Q. Flaccus in his third *liber* :
" The Romans have no wood-pulp fiber.
    A crapulent quorum
    Will squat in the Forum
And heave dirty stones in the Tiber. "
                                  1942A.

712

There was a young man of Loch Leven
Who went for a walk about seven.
    He fell into a pit
    That was brimful of shit,
And now the poor bugger's in heaven.
                                  1928.

713

An old G.I. custom long-rooted
Is to entering fledglings well-suited.
    In every latrine
    A bright sign is seen :
" Stand close, the next guy may be barefooted. "
                                  1943.

714

There was a young Georgian named Lynd
Who'd never in all his life sinned,
    For whenever he'd start
    He'd be jarred by a fart,
And his semen was gone with the wind.
                                  1941.

715

There was a young man named McBride
Who could fart whenever he tried.
    In a contest he blew
    Two thousand and two,
And then shit and was disqualified.

                         1945C.

716

There was a young man named McFee
Who was stung in the balls by a bee.
    He made oodles of money
    By oozing pure honey
Every time he attempted to pee.

                         1943A.

717

There was a young girl of Machias
Whose bloomers were cut on the bias,
    With an opening behind
    To let out the wind,
And to let the boys in once or twias.

                         1938.

718

There was a young fellow named Malcolm
Who dusted his ass-hole with talcum.
    He'd always use it
    Every time that he shit,
And found the sensation right welcome.

                         1943.

719

There was an old man of Madrid
Who went to an auction to bid.
    In the first lot they sold
    Was an ancient commode—
And, my god, when they lifted the lid!

                         1941.

720

There was a young Royal Marine
Who tried to fart " God Save the Queen. "
    When he reached the soprano
    Out came the guano,
And his breeches weren't fit to be seen.

1879-1928.

721

There is a professor named Martin
From whom I'm about to be partin',
    And on my way out
    He may hear me shout,
" It's your face I'd sure like to fart in. "

1943.

722

A movement once rose 'mongst the masses
To travel about with bare asses.
    At true lovers' parting
    The best form was farting,
With buttocks immersed in molasses.

1941*

723

A gay young blade from Milano
Was Count Galeazzo Ciano.
    Safe from the wars,
    He found that his drawers
Contained rich deposits of guano.

1946B.

724

There once was a lady named Muir
Whose mind was so frightfully pure
    That she fainted away
    At a friend's house one day
When she saw some canary manure.

1939A.

725

There was a young lady of Newcastle
Who wrapped up a turd in a parcel,
   And sent it to a relation
   With this invitation—
" It has just come out hot from my arsehole."

1870.

726

There was an old scholar named Nick
Who wrote Latin and Greek with his prick.
   He peed a paean
   In the snow by a john
In script more than three inches thick.

1941.

727

An eminent preacher named Nixon
Used to fart as he said benediction.
   The shy flock would smile
   As they trooped down the aisle:
" The arse on our parson needs fixin'."

1942A.

728

There was a young girl in Ohio
Whose baptismal name was Maria.
   She would put on airs
   And pee on the stairs,
If she thought that no one was nigh 'er.

1927.

729

There was a young lady of Pinner,
Who dreamt that her lover was in her.
   This excited her heart,
   So she let a great fart,
And shit out her yesterday's dinner.

1870.

730

There was an old man who could piss
Through a ring—and, what's more, never miss.
    People came by the score,
    And bellowed, " Encore !
Won't you do it again, Sir ? Bis! Bis! "

                              1928.

731

There was a young lady of Purdbright
Who never could quite get her turd right.
    She'd go to the closet
    And leave a deposit
Like a mouse or a bat or a bird might.

                              1941.

732

There was an old fellow of Pittwood
Who never was able to shit good.
    He'd leave small deposits
    On shelves and in closets,
As a very small pup or a kit would.

                              1949.

733

There was a young man of Rangoon
Whose farts could be heard to the moon.
    When least you'd expect 'em,
    They'd burst from his rectum
With the force of a raging typhoon.

                              1941.

734

There was a young man of Rangoon
Who farted and filled a balloon.
    The balloon went so high
    That it stuck in the sky,
And stank out the Man in the Moon.

                              1879.

EXCREMENT

735
There was an old fellow from Roop
Who'd lost all control of his poop.
    One evening at supper
    His wife said, " Now, Tupper,
Stop making that noise with your soup! "
               1927-1941.

736
The intestines of Dante Rossetti
Were exceedingly fragile and petty.
    All he could eat
    Was finely chopped meat,
And all he could shit was spaghetti.
               1932.

737
There was a young man from St. Paul
Who had really no scruples at all—
    He would fart when he'd talk,
    And shit when he'd walk,
And at night throw it over the wall.
               1943-1952.

738
There was an old soldier named Schmitt
Took a trip to the can for to shit.
    To his epic despair
    No paper was there,
So he simply continued to sit.
                1943-1951.

739
Tom, Tom, the piper's son,
Let loose a fart, and away he run.
    But Tom fell in
    An old shit bin
And ever since then Tom stinks like sin!
                1941*

740. THE FARTER FROM SPARTA

There was a young fellow from Sparta,
A really magnificent farter,
    On the strength of one bean
    He'd fart God Save the Queen,
And Beethoven's Moonlight Sonata.

He could vary, with proper persuasion,
His fart to suit any occasion.
    He could fart like a flute,
    Like a lark, like a lute,
This highly fartistic Caucasian.

This sparkling young farter from Sparta,
His fart for no money would barter.
    He could roar from his rear
    Any scene from Shakespeare,
Or Gilbert and Sullivan's Mikado.

He'd fart a gavotte for a starter,
And fizzle a fine serenata.
    He could play on his anus
    The Coriolanus :
Oof, boom, er-tum, tootle, yum tah-dah!

He was great in the Christmas Cantata,
He could double-stop fart the Toccata,
    He'd boom from his ass
    Bach's B-Minor Mass,
And in counterpoint, La Traviata.

Spurred on by a very high wager
With an envious German named Bager,
    He'd proceeded to fart
    The complete oboe part
Of a Haydn Octet in B-major.

His repertoire ranged from classics to jazz,
He achieved new effects with bubbles of gas.
    With a good dose of salts
    He could whistle a waltz
Or swing it in razzamatazz.

His basso profundo with timbre so rare
He rendered quite often, with power to spare.
    But his great work of art,
    His fortissimo fart,
He saved for the Marche Militaire.

One day he was dared to perform
The William Tell Overture Storm,
    But naught could dishearten
    Our spirited Spartan,
For his fart was in wonderful form.

It went off in capital style,
And he farted it through with a smile,
    Then, feeling quite jolly,
    He tried the finale,
Blowing double-stopped farts all the while.

The selection was tough, I admit,
But it did not dismay him one bit,
    Then, with ass thrown aloft
    He suddenly coughed...
And collapsed in a shower of shit.

His bunghole was blown back to Sparta,
Where they buried the rest of our farter,
    With a gravestone of turds
    Inscribed with the words :
" To the Fine Art of Farting, A Martyr. "

1938-1948A.

752

The damned Jap sons-a-bitches,
We made them wet their britches.
    We grabbed our gun,
    And made 'em run,
The goddamned sons-a-bitches.

1943*

753

There was a young man from Split
Who was thrilled with the thought of a shit.
    He was simply elated,
    Till he grew constipated,
But that took all the pleasure from it.

1943.

754

A keen-scented dean of Tacoma
Was awarded a special diploma
    For his telling apart
    Of a masculine fart
From a similar female aroma.

1947.

755

I sat by the Duchess at tea,
And she asked, "Do you fart when you pee?"
    I said with some wit,
    "Do you belch when you shit?"
And felt it was one up for me.

                        1928-1941.

756

When asked by the Duchess at tea
If an eggplant I ever did see,
    I said "Yes," rather bored;
    She said, "Sir, you've explored
Up a hen's ass much further than me."

                        1946B.

757

There was a young man from Ti' Juana
Who declared as he wallowed in guano,
    "It may seem imbecilic
    To be *so* coprophilic—
I indulge in it just 'cause I wanna."

                        1948A.

758

There was a young fellow named Twyss
Whose orgasms forced him to piss,
    And most girls objected
    To having injected
A flood of his piss 'midst their bliss.

But one girl—a smart little floozie—
Saw reason for being less choosey.
    Said this sensible miss,
    "Well, anyway, Chris,
Your piss certn'y cleans out my coosie."

                        1941.

760

" It's true, " confessed Jane, Lady Torres,
" That often I beg lifts in lorries.
    When the men stop to piss
    I see things that I miss
When I travel alone in my Morris. "

1947A.

761

There once was a sailor from Wales,
An expert at pissing in gales.
    He could piss in a jar
    From the top-gallant spar
Without even wetting the sails.

1941.

762

There was an old lady from Wheeling
Who had a peculiar feeling,
    She laid on her back
    And opened her crack
And pissed all over the ceiling.

1870-1925*

763

There was an old lady of Ypres
Who got shot in the ass by some snipers,
    And when she blew air
    Through the holes that were there,
She astonished the Cameron Pipers.

1941.

IX

GOURMANDS

764

There was a young sapphic named Anna
Who stuffed her friend's cunt with banana,
    Which she sucked bit by bit
    From her partner's warm slit,
In the most approved lesbian manner.
1934-1941.

765

There was a young girl of Antietam
Who liked horse turds so well she could eat 'em.
    She'd lie on their rumps
    And swallow the lumps
As fast as the beasts could excrete 'em.
1947B.

766

There was a young man had the art
Of making a capital tart
    With a handful of shit,
    Some snot and a spit,
And he'd flavor the whole with a fart.
1879.

767

There was an old man of Balbriggan,
Who cunt juice was frequently swigging,
    But even to this
    He preferred tom-cat's piss,
Which he kept a pox'd nigger to frig in.
1879.

768

There once was a midget named Carr
Who couldn't reach up to the bar,
    So in every saloon
    He climbed a spittoon,
And guzzled his liquor from thar.

1939A.

769

There was a young man from the coast
Who ate melted shit on his toast.
    When the toast saw the shit
    It collapsed in a fit,
For the shit was its grandfather's ghost.

1934.

770

There was an old man of Corfu
Who fed upon cunt-juice and spew.
    When he couldn't get that,
    He ate what he shat—
And bloody good shit he shat, too.

On clinkers his choice often fell,
Or clabbered piss brought to a jell.
    When these palled to his taste
    He tried snot and turd-paste,
And found them delicious as well.

He ate them, and sighed, and said, " What
Uncommonly fine shit and snot!
    Now really, the two
    Are too good to be true—
I would rather have et them than not. "

1879-1941.

773

A Dutchman who dwelt in Dundee
Walked in to a grocer's named Lee.
    He said, " If you blease,
    Haff you any prick cheese ? "
Said the grocer, " I'll skin back and see. "
                          1941-1948.

774

A coprophagous fellow named Fleam
Loved to drink a strong urinal stream.
    He seduced little gonsils
    Into spraying his tonsils
With the stuff he liked best on earth : cream.
                          1942.

775

There was a young fellow named Fritz
Who planted an acre of tits.
    They came up in the fall,
    Pink nipples and all,
And he chewed them all up into bits.
                          1941.

776

There was a young man of Glengarridge,
The fruit of a scrofulous marriage.
    He sucked off his brother,
    And buggered his mother,
And ate up his sister's miscarriage.
                          1934-1941.

777

A daughter of fair Ioway,
While at sport in the toilet one day,
    Swallowed some of her pee,
    "And hereafter, " said she,
" I'll do it at lunch every day. "
                          1946A.

778

A young lady who once had a Jew beau
Found out soon that he'd got a bubo,
    So when it was ripe
    She put in a pipe,
And sucked up the juice through a tube oh!

1870.

779

There was a young fellow of Kent
Who had a peculiar bent.
    He collected the turds
    Of various birds,
And had them for lunch during Lent.

1947B.

780

There was a young man of King's Cross
Who amused himself frigging a horse,
    Then licking the spend
    Which still dripped from the end,
Said, " It tastes just like anchovy sauce. "

1879.

781

A hypocritical bastard named Legman
When drinking piss-highballs puts egg in 'em.
    If he tells you you're queer
    To enjoy pissless beer,
Just say to him, " Quit pulling my leg, man! "

1952.

782

There was a young fellow from Leith
Who used to skin cocks with his teeth.
    It wasn't for pleasure
    He adopted this measure,
But to get at the cheese underneath.

1934-1938.

783

Said a busy young whore known as Mable,
Who at fucking was willing and able,
   " It's a pity to waste
    All that juicy white paste, "
So she served it in bowls at the table.
                           1942.

784

There once was a U.S. marine
Whose manners were slightly obscene.
   He loved to eat jizz,
    Both others' and his,
When served in a hot soup-tureen.
                           1941*

785

There was a young man from Marseilles
Who lived on clap juice and snails.
   When tired of these
    He lived upon cheese
From his prick, which he picked with his nails.
                           1927.

786

There was an old maid from Shalot
Who lived upon frog shit and snot.
   When she tired of these
    She would eat the green cheese
That she scraped from the sides of her twat.
                         1927-1943C.

787

There was an old sailor named Jock
Who was wrecked on a desolate rock.
   He had nothing to eat
    But the punk of his feet,
And the cheese from the end of his cock.
                           1941.

788

There once was a baker of Nottingham
Who in making éclairs would put snot in 'em.
    When he ran out of snot,
    He would, like as not,
Take his pecker and jack off a shot in 'em.
                                            1941.

789

There was a young fellow of Perth,
The nastiest bastard on earth,
    When his wife was confined
    He pulled down the blind,
And ate up the whole afterbirth.
                                            1941.

790

A mannerly fellow named Phyfe
Was greatly distressed by his wife,
    For whene'er she was able
    She'd shit on the table,
And gobble the shit—with her knife!
                                          1944A.

791

There were two little mice in Rangoon
Who sought lunch in an old lady's womb.
    Cried one mouse, " By Jesus,
    I'll wager this cheese is
As old as the cheese in the moon! "
                                            1941.

792

Where was a young lady of Rheims
Who was terribly plagued with wet dreams.
    She saved up a dozen,
    And sent to her cousin,
Who ate them and thought they were creams.
                                            1879.

793

An elderly rabbi named Riskin
Dines daily on cunt-juice and foreskin.
    And to further his bliss,
    At dessert he'll drink piss,
For which he is always a'thirstin'.
                          1946A.

794

There was a young man known as Royce
Who took an emetic by choice.
    He was fed, quite by chance,
    Half the crotch of the pants
Of a girl who kept crab-lice as toys.
                          1942-1952.

795

There was a young man of St. Just
Who ate of new bread till he bust.
    It was not the crumb,
    For that passed through his bum,
But what buggered him up was the crust.
                          1870.

796

There was an old man of Seringapatam
Besmeared his wife's anus with raspberry jam,
    Then licked off the sweet,
    And pronounced it a treat,
And for public opinion he cared not a damn.
                          1870.

797

There was a young lady of Totten
Whose tastes grew perverted and rotten.
    She cared not for steaks,
    Or for pastry and cakes,
But lived upon penis *au gratin*.
                          1938.

798

There was a young man of the Tweed
Who sucked his wife's arse thro' a reed.
    When she had diarrhoea
    He'd let none come near,
For fear they should poach on his feed.

1879.

799

There was a young pair from Uganda
Who were having a fuck on a veranda.
    The drip from their fucks
    Fed forty-two ducks,
Three geese, and a fucking big gander.

1942.

800

A hungry old trollop from Yemen
Did a pretty good business with he-men.
    But she gave up all fucking
    In favor of sucking,
For the protein contained in the semen.

1947B.

X

VIRGINITY

801

Sass Mädelein unter den Aestchen
Und spielt' mit dem Knäbleinmästchen,
    Dem niedlichen Zweck—
    Bald ist der Kranz weg:
Blieb nichts davon nur das Kästchen.
                           1942A.

802

A maiden sat under a tree
And played with the lad's fiddle-dee,
    His little wood post—
    Soon her jewel is lost
From the casket where it used to be.
                           1942A.

803

"Competition is keen, you'll agree,"
Said an ancient old flapper from Dee,
    So she dyed her gray tresses,
    Chopped a foot from her dresses,
And her *reason* you plainly can see.
                           1927.

804

The bride went up the aisle
In traditional virginal style,
    But they say she was nary
    An innocent cherry,
But a whore from the banks of the Nile.
                           1948A.

805

There was a young virgin named Alice
Who thought of her cunt as a chalice.
    One night, sleeping nude,
    She awoke feeling lewd,
And found in her chalice a phallus.

                  1941.

806

There was a young lady of Andover,
And the boys used to ask her to hand over
    Her sexual favor,
    Which she did (may God save her!)
For her morals she had no command over.

                  1951.

807

There was a young girl named Anheuser
Who said that no man could surprise her.
    But Pabst took a chance,
    Found Schlitz in her pants,
And now she is sadder Budweiser.

                1927-1932.

808

To the shrine which was Pallas Athena's
Young Bito (who'd learned about penis)
    Brought her needles and thread
    And scissors and said,
"You can stick them — I'm changing to Venus!"

                1942A.

809

There's a tiresome young girl in Bay Shore,
When her fiancé cried, "I adore
    Your beautiful twat!"
    She replied, "Like as not—
It's pretty, but what is it *for*?"

                1952.

810

There once was a tart named Belinda
Whose cunt opened out like a window.
    But she'd slam the thing shut,
    The contemptible slut,
Whenever you tried to get inda.

                                1941.

811

A lisping young lady named Beth
Was saved from a fate worse than death
    Seven times in a row,
    Which unsettled her so
That she quit saying "No" and said "Yeth."

                                1943A.

812

There was a young lady of Bhore
Who was courted by gallants galore.
    Their ardent protestin'
    She found interestin',
And ended her life as a virgin.

                                1943A.

813

There was a young fellow named Biddle
Whose girl had to teach him to fiddle.
    She grabbed hold of his bow
    And said, "If you want to know,
You can try parting my hair in the middle."

                                1942.

814

In Stokes lived an ugly bluestocking
Who declared the men's manners were shocking.
    Why, she'd never been diddled,
    Even fingered or fiddled...
So she finally moved over to Focking.

                                1942A.

815

There was a young virgin of Bude
Whose tricks, though exciting, were viewed
    With distrust by the males
    For she'd fondle their rails,
But never would let them intrude.
1941.

816

There was an old spinster named Campbell
Got tangled one day in a bramble.
    She cried, " Ouch, how it sticks!
    But so many sharp pricks
Are not met every day on a ramble. "
1942.

817

There was a young girl from the Cape
Who filled her hole with bicycle tape
    To ease up the pangs
    Caused by the whangs
Of gentlemen bent upon rape.
1939A.

818

There was a young Miss from Cape Cod
Who at soldiers would not even nod.
    But she tripped in a ditch
    And some son-of-a-bitch
Of a corporal raped her, by God!
1928B-1943A.

819

There once was a passionate Celte
Who'd an urge to know how a cock felt.
    One went in, hard and straight,
    But her heat was so great
That she found she had caused it to melt.
1941.

820

A Salvation Lassie named Claire
Was having her first love affair.
    As she climbed into bed
    She reverently said,
"I wish to be opened with prayer."

                     1943A.

821

An innocent maiden of Clewer
Incited her boy-friend to screw her.
    She tried to say no,
    A half-second slow—
Now when she sits down she says, "Oo-er!"

                       1952.

822

There was a young lady of Corbie
Who said, "Oh, the men really bore me!
    But I reckon, without 'em,
    Though I hate 'em and scout 'em,
There just would be no one to scour me."

                       1952.

823

There was a young lady of Crewe
Whose cherry a chap had got through,
    Which she told to her mother
    Who fixed her another
Out of rubber and red ink and glue.

                       1941.

824

There was a young princess called Dagmar
Who said, "I should so like to shag, Ma,"
    And says she, "If you speaks
    To the King of the Greeks,
He will lend me his own tolliwag, Ma."

                       1870.

825

There was a young girl of Dalkeith
With a hymen in need of relief,
    So she went to the doctor
    Who prodded and shocked her,
And stretched it with fingers and teeth.

1952.

826

A girl named Alice, in Dallas,
Had never felt of a phallus.
    She remained virgo intacto,
    Because, ipso facto,
No phallus in Dallas fit Alice.

1946B.

827

An ignorant virgin of Dee
Entertained a man's cock just to see
    If the darn thing would fit—
    It went off in her pit,
And she cried, " Hey! that's no place to pee!"

1941.

828

A young lady who taught at Devizes
Was had up at the local assizes
    For teaching young boys
    Matrimonial joys,
And giving French letters as prizes.

1941.

829

A complacent old don of Divinity
Made boast of his daughter's virginity.
    They must have been dawdlin'
    Down at old Magdalen—
It couldn't have happened at Trinity.

1938.

830

There was a young virgin of Dover
Who was raped in the woods by a drover.
    When the going got hard
    He greased her with lard,
Which felt nice, so they started all over.
                            1941.

831

There was a young girl of East Lynne
Whose mother, to save her from sin,
    Had filled up her crack
    To the brim with shellac,
But the boys picked it out with a pin.
                        1927-1941.

832

The first love of a lady named Ederle
Found her hymen obstructed him steadily,
    But he merely rubbed lard on
    The end of his hard on,
And then found he entered quite readily.
                            1941.

833

There was a bluestocking in Florence
Wrote anti-sex pamphlets in torrents,
    Till a Spanish grandee
    Got her off with his knee,
And she burned all her works with abhorrence.
                            1942A.

834

A homely old spinster of France,
Who all the men looked at askance,
    Threw her skirt overhead
    And then jumped into bed,
Saying, " Now I've at least half a chance. "
                            1941.

835. THE MISFORTUNES OF FYFE

There was a young fellow named Fyfe
Who married the pride of his life,
   But imagine his pain
   When he struggled in vain,
And just couldn't get into his wife.

Now the trouble was not with our hero,
Who, though no match for Epstein or Nero,*
   Had a good little dong
   That was five inches long,
And as stiff as a parsnip at zero.

But his efforts to poke her, assiduous,
Met a dense growth of hair most prodiguous.
   Well, he thought he might dint her
   By waiting till winter,
But he found that she wasn't deciduous.

Now here was this fellow named Fyfe,
Unable to diddle his wife—
   Which fact, sad but true,
   Left him nothing to do
But bugger the girl all his life.

For diversion this might have been funny,
And of course it *did* save him some money,
   But it angered our Fyfey
   To think that his wifey
Was hoarding her deep nest of honey.

He went whoring to find satisfaction,
But with whores, though accomplished in action,
    He never could capture
    That fine fucking rapture,
For the thought of his wife was distraction.

So here was our fellow named Fyfe
With a truly impervious wife.
    She was not worth a damn,
    Being close as a clam—
Why, he couldn't get in with a knife!

The problem that harassed his soul
Was : what kept him out of her hole?
    Was her hymen too tough?
    Was she stuffed up with fluff?
Was her coosie the home of a mole?

This was just what poor Fyfe couldn't tell,
For her prow was as sound as a bell.
    He'd have needed a gimlet
    To get into her quimlet,
And it made the poor guy mad as hell.

He applied to that fellow from Strensall
For help from his long, pointed pencil,
    But Strensy's tool now
    Was as blunt as the prow
Of a tug—he'd have needed a stencil.

Fyfe searched for the chap from New York
Who had punctured the hymen like cork,
    But *he* was quite coy
    For he now loved a boy,
And refused to help Fyfe with the stork.

Fyfe asked Durand how much he'd charge
(The fellow whose cock could contract or enlarge)
    To drill his way in
    With his prick like a pin,
And there make it slowly enlarge.

But Durand—though he'd fuck with no urgin'—
Warned, "Apart from the risk that she'll burgeon,
    Your pride must be low
    If you'll meekly forego
A crack at a genuine virgin."

In the spring in the woods Fyfe did wander late,
And saw couples preparing to copulate,
    But he could not abide
    The gay sight, and he cried
At the thought that the pigfuckers penetrate!

One couple he foolishly leapt on,
To examine the wound and the weapon.
    One was rigid, one deep—
    The snug fit made him weep,
And in shame and contrition he crept on.

In the meantime, Fyfe's wife, who had wed
With *some* thought to the pleasures of bed,
    Was becoming depressed,
    In fact damn near obsessed
By her terribly tough maidenhead.

She remarked, " When all joking is done,
What I honestly want is a son.
    I would like impregnation
    If not copulation—
But to wed and have neither's no fun. "

She grew worried and nervous and thin,
Till Fyfe said, " You would jump at a pin! "
    And these words, though unkind,
    Put the thought in her mind
That a pin-point *perhaps* might get in.

Thus she thought of synthetic conception,
Which at first seemed like basest deception,
    But her cunt was so sore
    From Fyfe's trying to bore,
That she gave the thought better reception.

And indeed, though it's sad to relate it,
Her first fuck was so sadly belated,
    That a poke by a pin,
    Though ever so thin,
Was a prospect that made her elated.

To be brief, the great action was done:
There was artfully planted, a son,
    Through a bodkin that filled her,
    And wonderfully thrilled her—
More fun than a son of a gun!

This syringe, which was long but quite thin,
Left a hole that Fyfe couldn't get in,
    But he kept right on busting
    And jousting and thrusting,
On account of his excess of vim.

While she mused on this synthetic screw,
The sperm got well-planted, and grew,
    And the great day approached
    When her breech would be broached,
But Fyfe, the poor wretch, never knew.

One night, while in sheer desperation
He prodded and poked like tarnation,
    His wife groaned with pain—
    She gave way!! Would he gain
The goal of three years' contemplation?

The head of his dingus went in!
He felt sure he was going to win!
    He thrust like a demon,
    He spilt all his semen,
And scraped off a square inch of skin.

But despite all his trying, he found
He was losing, not gaining, his ground.
    Though he clung to her thighs
      While he tried for the prize,
Each push *in* caused a greater rebound.

The harder the poor fellow tried,
The more her hold filled, from inside,
    Till he fell back quite spent,
      His prick battered and bent,
And a few minutes later—he died.

As he passed, a new life was begun,
And his tomb tells how he was undone:
    " Shed a tear for poor Fyfe,
      His imperforate wife
Did him in with the aid of their son. "

                        1938-1941.

863

A neuropath-virgin named Flynn
Shouted before she gave in:
    " It isn't the deed,
      Or the fear of the seed,
But that big worm that's shedding its skin! "

                        1942A.

864

There was a young fellow named Gluck
Who found himself shit out of luck.
    Though he petted and wooed,
      When he tried to get screwed
He found virgins just don't give a fuck.

                        1941.

865

There was an old spinster named Gretel
Who wore underclothes made of metal.
    When they said, " Does it hurt ? "
    She said, " It keeps dirt
From stamen and pistil and petal. "

          1942.

866

There were three young ladies of Grimsby
Who said, "Of what use can our quims be ?
    The hole in the middle
    Is so we can piddle,
But for what can the hole in the rims be ? "

          1928-1938.

867

There was a young lady of Harwich
Who said on the morn of her marriage,
    " I shall sew my chemise
    Right down to my knees,
For I'm damned if I fuck in the carriage! "

          1880.

868

I don't mind if a girl rides a hel'copter,
I don't mind if a girl rides a car,
    But the girl who rides straddle
    An old fashioned saddle
Is stretching things a bit too far.

          1945C.

869

There was a young girl from Hoboken
Who claimed that her hymen was broken
    From riding a bike
    On a cobblestone pike,
But it really was broken from pokin'.

          1945.

870

There was a young brave who got hot
And chased an old squaw who was not.
    So she stuffed her canal
    With some dried chapparal,
And sprinkled some sand on her twat.

                      1942A.

871

A lady of virginal humours
Would only be screwed through her bloomers.
    But one fatal day
    The bloomers gave way,
Which fixed her for future consumers.

                      1941.

872

A girl who lived in Kentucky
Said, " Yes, I've been awfully lucky.
    No man ever yet
    On my back made me get,
But sometimes I feel awful fucky. "

                      1927.

873

Exclaimed a young girl in Kildare,
As her lover's jock towered in air,
    " If that goes in me I
    Shall certainly die—
As I shall if it does not go there. "

                      1942A.

874

There was an old lady of Leicester,
And no man had ever caressed her,
    And all day she'd wriggle
    And giggle and jiggle,
As though seven devils possessed her.

                      1941.

875

A coon who was out with his Liz
Said, " Baby, let's get down to biz. "
    Said she, " That cain't be,
    Less you'se stronger'n me,
But, honey, I reckon you is. "

                               1927.

876

There was a young girl named McKnight
Who got drunk with her boy-friend one night.
    She came to in bed
    With a split maidenhead—
That's the last time she ever was tight.

                               1941.

877

That Jew-girl, the famed Virgin Mary,
Said, " Oh God, my quim's got all hairy!
    To hell with virginity,
    I'll fuck the whole Trinity!
I'm tired of vice solitary. "

                          1943B-1944A.

878

No one can tell about Myrtle
Whether she's sterile or fertile.
    If anyone tries
    To tickle her thighs
She closes them tight like a turtle.

                               1943.

879

There was a young widow of Nain
Who the bedclothes did frequently stain,
    With such great inflammation
    Came such menstruation,
Her cunt so long idle had lain.

                               1870.

VIRGINITY

880

A certain young sheik I'm not namin'
Asked a flapper he thought he was tamin',
" Have you your maidenhead ? "
" Don't be foolish, " she said,
" But I still have the box that it came in. "

1948.

881

There is a young girl from New York
Who is cautious from fear of the stork.
    You will find she is taped
    To prevent being raped,
And her ass-hole is plugged with a cork.

1947-1951.

882

There was a young girl of Ostend
Who her maidenhead tried to defend,
    But a Chasseur d'Afrique
    Inserted his prick
And taught that ex-maid how to spend.

1879.

883

There was a young fellow from Oudh
Whose mind was excessively lewd.
    He asserted, " All women
    Seen dancin' or swimmin'
Would rather be home gettin' screwed. "

1949.

884

A girl at whom no one made passes
No longer resents wearing glasses,
    For two F.B.I. men
    Demolished her hymen
On failing to find her New Masses.

1949.

885

There was a young virgin in Perth
Swore she'd do it for no one on earth,
    Yet she fell without scandal
    To a red Christmas candle
And was always less choosey henceforth.

                      1942A.

886

There was an old maid in Peru
Who'd a dog and a cat and a gnu.
    From a sailor named Harrot
    She bought an old parrot,
And he threw in a young cockatoo.

                      1941.

887

There was a young lassie named Phyllis
Was deflowered one night in a Willys.
    Before they were through
    Her spine was askew,
And I very much fear that it still is.

                      1943A.

888

A Newfoundland lad from Placentia
Was in love to the point of dementia,
    But his love couldn't burgeon
    With his touch-me-not virgin
'Til he screwed her by hand in absentia.

                      1947B.

889

There was a young lady from 'Quoddie
Who had a magnificent body,
    And her face was not bad,
    Yet she'd never been had
For her odor was markèdly coddy.

                      1949.

890

A pathetic appellant at Reno
Was as chaste as the holy Bambino,
    For she'd married a slicker
    Who stuck to his liquor
And scorned her ripe maraschino.

                        1947B.

891

There was a young man of St. Kitt
Who was screwing a spinster, but quit.
    Said she, " Don't be scary,
    It's only my cherry,"
But he said, " It feels more like a pit."

                        1941.

892

There was a young girl of Samoa
Who determined that no man should know her.
    One young fellow tried
    But she wriggled aside,
And spilled all the spermatozoa.

                      1928-1932.

893

Maggie is such a sad sack of shit
That no one will tickle her tit.
    It would make her so glad
    To be had by a lad,
Her drawers cream at the mere thought of it.

                      1943.

894

There was a young fellow named Simon
Who tried to discover a hymen,
    But he found every girl
    Had relinquished her pearl
In exchange for a solitaire diamond.

                      1941.

895

There was a T/5, name of Snyder,
Who took out a girl just to ride her.
    She allowed him to feel
    From her neck to her heel,
But never would let him inside her.

1943.

896

There was a young girl from Sofia
Who succumbed to her lover's desire.
    She said, " It's a sin,
    But now that it's in,
Could you shove it a few inches higher? "

1945.

897

There was a young girl of Spitzbergen
Whose people all thought her a virgin,
    Till they found her in bed
    With her quim very red,
And the head of a kid just emergin'.

1928.

898

An innocent soldier named Stave
Was almost seduced by a Wave.
    But he's still a recluse
    With all of his juice,
For he didn't know how to behave.

1944.

899

There was a young fellow named Sweeney
Whose girl was a terrible meanie.
    The hatch of her snatch
    Had a catch that would latch—
She could only be screwed by Houdini.

1941.

VIRGINITY

900

A proper young lady of Taos
Had her panties trimmed neatly with lace.
   But a vulgar young man
   Raped her roughly, and ran,
And left them pure panties in chaos.
                               1941.

901

There was a young girl of Topeka
Who from diddling grew weaker and weaker,
   Till a guy, name of Dick,
   Went and offered his prick,
So she tried it and shouted, " Eureka! "
                               1951.

902

There was an old spinster of Tyre
Who bellowed, " My cunt is on fire! "
   So a fireman was found,
   Brought his engine around,
And extinguished her burning desire.
                               1941.

903

There was an old maid in Van Nuys
Who went crazy from making mud pies.
   She would fill them with farts
   And pickled beef-hearts,
And bake them between her fierce thighs.
                               1942A.

904

There was a young girl named Venus
Who had never encountered a penis.
   When Van Stone threw his in
   It went up to her chin,
But the bore, not the stroke, was the meanest.
                               1945C.

905

A skinny old maid from Verdun
Wed a short-peckered son-of-a-gun.
    She said, " I don't care
    If there isn't much there.
God knows it is better than none. "

1927-1932.

906

There was a young virgin named Violet
Whose hope was to remain inviolate.
    But she let a man neck her
    And soon his hard pecker
Had wedged itself firmly in Violet.

*1941**

907

There was a young lady named Wilma
Who said, " Oh now, please do not kilma.
    I love your advances
    And what's in your pantses,
Do you think it could possibly fill-ma ? "

1951.

908

There was a young lady of Worcester
Who dreamt that a rooster seduced her.
    She woke with a scream,
    But 'twas only a dream—
A bump in the mattress had goosed her.

1932-1941.

909

There was a young lady called Wylde,
Who kept herself quite undefiled
    By thinking of Jesus,
    Contagious diseases,
And the bother of having a child.

1927-1928.

XI

MOTHERHOOD

910

There once was a Vassar B.A.
Who pondered the problem all day
    Of what there would be
    If C-U-N-T
Were divided by C-O-C-K.

A young Ph.D. passing by,
She gave him the problem to try.
    He worked the division
    With perfect precision,
And the answer was B-A-B-Y.

                  1928A-1941.

912

To a widow-bereaved of Barrientos
Her marital divertimentos
    Are so sentimental—
    Even things contraceptal,
That old fishskins are dearest mementos.

                  1944A.

913

There was a young girl who begat
Three brats, by name Nat, Pat, and Tat.
    It was fun in the breeding
    But hell in the feeding,
When she found there was no tit for Tat.

                  1941.

914

There was a young girl of Bombay
Who was put in the family way
    By the mate of a lugger,
    An ignorant bugger
Who always spelled CUNT with a K.

                      1927-1941.

915

An indolent vicar of Bray
Kept his wife in the family way,
    Till she grew more alert,
    Bought a vaginal squirt,
And said to her spouse, " Let us spray! "

                      1941.

916

There was a young man of Cape Cod
Who once put my wife into pod.
    His name it was Tucker
    The dirty old fucker,
The bugger, the blighter, the sod!

                      1927.

917

There was a young man of Cape Horn
Who wished he had never been born.
    And he wouldn't have been
    If his father had seen
That the end of the rubber was torn.

                      1927-1928.

918

There was a young pessimist, Grotton,
Who wished he had ne'er been begotten,
    Nor would he have been
    But the rubber was thin,
And right at the tip it was rotten.

                      1941.

919

There once was a modern young chick
Who wished above all to be chic.
    She thought it much neater
    (Not to mention discreeter)
To do it with a sheik with a " Sheik. "
                                1942.

920

There was a young girl of Claridge's
Who said, " What a strange thing marriage is,
    When you stop to think
    That I've poured down the sink
Five abortions and fifty miscarriages! "
                                1943B.

921

There was an old lady, God damn her,
She fucked herself with a hammer.
    The hammer was blunt
    And so was her cunt,
And out came a kid with a hop, skip, and jump.
                                1928B.

922

There was a young lady of Delhi
Who had a bad pain in her belly.
    Her relations all smiled
    C'os they found her with child
By his honour the C—f B—n K—y.
                                1870.

923

There was a young girl whose divinity
Preserved her in perfect virginity,
    'Til a candle, her nemesis,
    Caused parthenogenesis—
Now she thinks herself one of the Trinity.
                                1943A.

924

A pious young lady named Finnegan
Would caution her beau, " Now you're in again,
    Please watch it just right
    So you'll last through the night,
For I certainly don't want to sin again. "

                                              1941.

925

There was a young girl from the five-and-ten
Who diddled herself with a fountain pen.
    The top came off,
    The ink went wild,
And now she's the mother of a colored child.

                                      1928A-1941.

926

There was a young lady named Flo
Whose lover had pulled out too slow.
    So they tried it all night
    Till he got it just right...
Well, practice makes pregnant, you know.

                                              1941.

927

There was a young lady of France
Who went to the Palace to dance.
    She danced with a Turk
    Till he got in his dirk,
And now she can't button her pants.

                                             1941.

928

There once was a midwife of Gaul
Who had hardly no business at all.
    She cried, " Hell and damnation!
    There's no procreation—
God made the French penis too small. "

                                             1941.

929

My wife Myrtle's womb has a habit
Of expanding whenever I stab it.
    What's more, my wife Myrtle
    Is so wondrously fertile,
That she's giving me kids like a rabbit.

1944.

930

There once was a handsome Haitian,
The luckiest dog in creation.
    He worked for the rubber trust
    Teaching the upper crust
The science of safe copulation.

1941.

931

There was a young lady named Hall
Who went to a birth-control ball.
    She was loaded with pessaries
    And other accessories,
But no one approached her at all.

1938.

932

A medical student named Hetrick
Is learnèd in matters obstetric.
    From a glance at the toes
    Of the mother, he knows
If the fetus's balls are symmetric.

1943.

933

Old King Cole was a bugger for the hole,
And a bugger for the hole was he.
    He called for his wife
    And stuck her with a knife,
And out jumped a K-I-D.

1925*

934

There was a young man of Jesus
Who performed cheap abortions with tweezers.
    One night in a hunt
    Up a mummified cunt
He found a F. L. of Caesar's.

1941-1947B.

935

There was a young lady of Louth
Who suddenly grew very stout.
    Her mother said, "Nelly,
    There's more in your belly
Than ever went in through your mouth."

1928-1941.

936

There was a young lady from Thrace
Whose corsets got too tight to lace.
    Her mother said, "Nelly,
    There's things in your belly
That never got in through your face."

1932-1950.

937

Frankie and Johnny were lovers
Especially under the covers.
    When she pulled out his trigger
    She said, "Mmm, what a figger!
But it makes so many girls mothers."

1942.

938

There was a young girl of Madrid
Who thought she'd be having a kid.
    So by holding her water
    Three months and a quarter
She drowned the poor bastard, she did.

1941.

939. REDWING

There once was an Indian Maid,
A whore she was by trade,
    For two-bits a whack
    She'd lay on her back,
And let the cowboys ram it up her crack.

One day to her surprise
Her belly began to rise,
    And out of her jigger
    Jumped a cast-iron nigger
With balls between his eyes.

Oh, the moon shines tonight on Mrs. Porter,
    She had a daughter
    Who was a slaughterer,
She washed her cunt with caustic soda
    To keep the odor
    From growing strong.

1935*

942

There was a young lady of Maine
Who declared she'd a man on the brain.
    But you knew from the view
    Of the way her waist grew,
It was not on her brain that he'd lain.

1941.

943

There was an old whore of Marseilles
Who tried the new rotary spray.
    Said she, " Ah, that's better...
    Why here's a French letter
That's been missing since Armistice Day! "

1941.

944

A lazy young lady named May
Was a torrid but troublesome lay.
    She was prone to conceive,
    So made haste to achieve
A bed with a built-in Bidet.

1943A.

945

Said a girl to her friend from Milpitas,
"There's a doctor in town who will treat us
    For feminine ills
    And hot and cold chills,
Or even abort a young fœtus."

1945.

946

There once was an innocent miss
Who feared she'd conceived from a kiss.
    So, as a precaution,
    She had an abortion,
But naught was forthcoming but piss.

1941.

947

There was a young girl from New York
Who expected a call from the stork.
    So with infinite caution
    She performed an abortion
With an icepick, a spoon, and a fork.

1941.

948

There was a young man, Mussolini,
Who found he had seven bambini.
    He said, "If I thought
    That the griddle was hot,
I'd never have put in the weenie!"

1946B.

949

There was a young lady named Myrtle
Whose womb was exceedingly fertile.
    Her pa got contortions
    At all her abortions,
And bought her a chastity girdle.

1944A.

950

Said a young man of Novorossisk,
"I use vulcanization by Fisk.
    Of course it comes higher,
    But when it's time to retire
You can frisk with a minimal risk."

1951.

951

There was a young fellow named Oram,
A model of tact and decorum.
    When about to fuck Grishkin
    He pulled out a fishskin
From the leaves of the Keats variorum.

1942.

952

There was a young man of Penzance
Who rogered his three maiden aunts.
    Though them he defiled,
    He ne'er got them with child,
Through using the letters of France.

1870.

953

There was a young girl from Penzance
Who decided to take just one chance.
    So she let herself go
    In the lap of her beau,
And now all her sisters are aunts.

1941.

954

In Spring Miss May marries Perce,
'Til then their pash' they disburse :
    With a thin piece of rubber
    There's no need to scrub 'er—
Of course, there's no harm to rehearse.

                                          1927.

955

There was a young fellow named Peter
Who was laying his gal with a cheater,
    When the rubber thing broke
    And started to smoke
From the friction with her piss-hole (ureter).

                                          1946A.

956. SOCIALLY CONSCIOUS PORNOGRAPHY

We've socially conscious biography,
Esthetics, and social geography.
    Today every field
    Boasts its Marxian yield,
So now there's class-conscious pornography.

Oh, the worker is nobody's fool,
For by rights he's the man with the tool.
    His ponderous prick'll
    Arise with the sickle,
And bugger the Fascists who rule.

Miss de Vaughan was a maker of panties
For all girls from subdebs to grand-aunties.
    Her very best ad
    Was herself, lightly clad
In her three-ninety-five silken scanties.

So this wench is a capitalist,
She's our villain and ought to be hissed.
    But she's lush and she's plump,
      And a glimpse of her rump
Would teach Marx that there's something he's missed.

Now de Vaughan had resolved on a lock-out
To give Communist Labor the knock-out.
    She said, " Fuck the foul fools. "
      (She'd attended good schools),
And took a fresh bottle of Hock out.

Joseph Smith was a sturdy longshoreman
(And an eminent amateur whoreman).
    Just to be sympathetic
      He grew peripatetic,
' Til his picketing irked de Vaughan's doorman.

For this lout was a scab born and bred,
Who fainted whene'er he saw red:
    In distress he reported,
      But she only retorted,
" Run home and hide under your bed. "

For her plans were peculiar and wicked,
As she thought, " He's a man, if a picket. "
    She lured him inside
      And insidiously plied
The prick of the picket to lick it.

Joe's rod was as stiff as a rail,
But he couldn't let principles fail.
  " You degenerate bitch,
    That's a trick of the rich;
But the People prefer honest tail.

" You may tickle the cocks and the vanities
  Of the rich men who purchase your scanities,
    But the proud People's Front
    Calls for sound hairy cunt.
So it's *down* with de Vaughan's panty-wanities. "

He picked a soft couch in her office,
And tore off her pants and ripped off his.
    Then he showed her the rod
    Marks the difference, by God,
Between what a man and a toff is.

Now our Joe was the first proletarian
Who had filled with his sperm the ovarian
    Recess of de Vaughan,
    Which had sheltered the spawn
Of unnumbered Fascists, all Aryan.

Next day his friends said, "You've been soaring,
You're dead on your feet. Were you whoring?"
    He replied, " Starving masses
    Mean more than plump asses.
Last night from within I was boring. "

And de Vaughan thought her troubles were over,
Her picket had left (to recover),
    But he'd furnished her womb
    With incipient bloom :
A fact she had yet to discover.

So after nine months, to the day,
The employer in labor pains lay.
    As the boy hove in sight
    He yelled, " WORKERS UNITE! "
And the doctors all fainted away.

The moral of this is, my child,
By rich promises don't be beguiled.
    Remember that workers
    Are eminent firkers,
And go left, if you must be defiled.

                              1943A.

972

A grey-headed tutor named Porson
From some strange amatory contortion
    Believed he'd conceived
    A book, but relieved
Himself by a pamphlet abortion.

                              1942A.

973

Young girls of seductive proportions
Should take contraceptive precautions :
    Silly young Ermintrude
    Let one small sperm intrude...
Who's the best man for abortions ?

                              1938.

974

A cautions young husband named Rafe
Used to diddle his wife with a safe.
    Thus he thwarted God's wishes
    And fed his pet fishes,
Which he kept in a bedside carafe.

1941.

975

There was a young man from Rangoon
Who was born at least three months too soon.
    He hadn't the luck
    To be born of a fuck,
But was shoveled in cold on a spoon.

1938-1947B.

976

Said a pregnant young lady named Sally,
" I've learned that it's consummate folly
    To walk home from a dance
    Without any pants
When the way home leads over the Pali. "

1946.

977

There was a young girl of Samoa
Who plugged up her cunt with a boa.
    This strange contraceptive
    Was very deceptive
To all but the spermatozoa.

1941.

978

There was a young lady named Sharkey
Who had an affair with a darkey.
    The result of her sins
    Was quadruplets, not twins,
One white, and one black, and two khaki.

1927*-1943C.

979
A certain young man of St. Paul
Consistently practiced withdrawal.
   This quaint predilection
   Creation such friction,
He soon had no foreskin at all.

Withdrawal, according to Freud,
Is a very good thing to avoid.
   If practiced each day,
   Your balls will decay
To the size of a small adenoid.

Freud's opinion, said old Dr. Stekel,
Isn't worth a Confederate shekel.
   Withdrawal is fun—
   But beware lest the sun
Should cause the withdrawn parts to freckle.

                         1948A.

982
There was a young lady named Sheba,
Fell in love with an eager amoeba.
   This queer bit of jelly
   Crept into her belly,
And ecstatically murmured, " *Ich liebe!* "

                         1941.

983
Pity the spermatozoa!
His life leads him lower and lower.
   With fear in his belly
   He swims through the jelly,
But seldom increases the scoah.

                         1941.

984

A fearless young spermatozoa
Remarked to an ovum, "Helloa!
   We'd make a cute fœtus,
    But I fear she'd mistreat us—
By the smell of this place, she's a whoah."

1941.

985

There once was a lady who'd sinned,
Who said as her abdomen thinned,
   "By my unsullied honor,
    I'm *not* a madonna!
My baby has gone with the wind."

1947B.

986

A husband who craved to be sterile
Because of the pregnancy peril
   Said, "I've thought of vasectomy,
    But my wife then might hector me,
And threaten divorce when we quarrel."

1941.

987

There was a young lady of Wantage
Of whom the Town Clerk took advantage.
   Said the County Surveyor,
    "Of course you must pay her;
You've altered the line of her frontage."

1932.

988

There was an old codger named Wright
Who did nasty things just for spite.
   He knocked up his daughter
    And then tried to abort her
By biting her tits in the night.

1941.

XII

PROSTITUTION

989

There once was a girl from Alaska
Who would fuck whenever you'd ask her.
    But soon she grew nice
    And went up in price,
And no one could touch her but Jesus H. Christ,
Or possibly John Jacob Astor.
                          1927-1932.

990

A vicious old whore of Albania
Hated men with a terrible mania.
    With a twitch and a squirm
    She would hold back your sperm,
And then roll on her face and disdain ya.
                          1941.

991

There was an old whore of Algiers
Who had bushels of dirt in her ears.
    The tip of her titty
    Was also quite shitty,
She never had washed it in years.
                          1938-1941.

992

A guy met a girl in Anacostia
And said, " Darling, dare I accost ya?
    I got only a buck,
    Is that good for a fuck? "
She replied, " Not a fart will it cost ya. "
                          1943.

993

There once was a floozie named Annie
Whose prices were cosy—but canny:
   A buck for a fuck,
    Fifty cents for a suck,
And a dime for a feel of her fanny.

1943B.

994

Said an elderly whore named Arlene,
" I prefer a young lad of eighteen.
    There's more cream in his larder,
    And his pecker gets harder,
And he fucks in a manner obscene. "

1942.

995

When the Duchess of Bagliofuente
Took her fourteenth *cavaliere servente,*
    The Duke said, " Old chappy,
    I'll keep that quim happy
If I have to hire nineteen or twenty. "

1942A.

996

There was a young man from Berlin,
A patron of sexual sin,
    He crammed the small crease
    'Twixt the legs of his niece
With a foot of his old rolling pin.

1945.

997

There was a young chip from Brazil
Who fucked like a veritable mill.
    There was never a whore,
    When she'd finished her chore,
More prompt to present you her bill.

1942.

998

There was a young trucker named Briard
Who had a young whore that he hired
    To fuck when not trucking,
    But trucking *plus* fucking
Got him so fucking tired he got fired.
                              1941.

999

There was a young fellow called Cary,
Who got fucking the Virgin Mary.
    And Christ was so bored
    At seeing Ma whored
That he set himself up as a fairy.
                              1928.

1000

There once was a girl from the chorus
Whose virtue was known to be porous.
    She started by candling,
    And ended by handling
The whole clientèle of a whorehouse.
                              1943B.

1001

A hard-working waitress named Cora
Discovered that drummers adore a
    Titty that's ripe
    And a cunt that is tripe—
Now she doesn't work hard any more-a!
                              1941.

1002

A lady named Belle da Cunt Corrigan
Was the mistress of J. Pierpont Morigan,
    Till she handed the banker
    A hell of a chancre,
And now she is just a plain whore again.
                              1941.

1003

There was a young harlot of Crete
Whose fucking was far, far too fleet.
    So they tied down her ass
    With a long ton of brass
To give them a much longer treat.

When the Nazis landed in Crete
This young harlot had to compete
    With the many Storm Troopers
    Who were using their poopers
For other things than to excrete.

Our subversive young harlot of Crete
Was led to fifth-column deceit.
    When the paratroops landed
    Her trade she expanded
By at once going down on their meat.

Then here was this harlot of Crete,
She decided to be very neat.
    She said, " I'm too high class
    To ream common ass,
And I'll wash every prick that I eat. "

And at last this fine harlot of Crete
Was hawking her meat in the street.
    Ambling out one fine day
    In a casual way,
She clapped up the whole British fleet.

                              1943-1951.

1008

There was a young lady from Cue
Who filled her vagina with glue.
    She said with a grin,
  " If they pay to get in,
They'll pay to get out of it too. "

1947B.

1009

There was a young girl named Dale
Who put up her ass for sale.
    For the sum of two bits
    You could tickle her tits,
But a buck would get you real tail.

1942.

1010

To succeed in the brothels at Derna
One always begins as a learner.
    Indentured at six
    As a greaser of pricks,
One may rise to be fitter and turner.

1946B.

1011

There was a young girl from Des Moines
Who had a large sack full of coins.
    The nickels and dimes
    She got from the times
That she cradled the boys in her loins.

1945.

1012

A passion-swept dame called Dolores
Is the hottest of history's whores.
    Though we fuck her with zest,
    When we crawl home to rest,
Guess who's there waiting for us—
    Dolores, of cour-es!

1941.

1013

A young man, quite free with his dong,
Said the thing could be had for a song.
 Such response did he get
 That he rented the Met,
And held auditions all the day long.
       1942.

1014

A sempstress at Epping-on-Tyne
Used to peddle her tail down the line.
 She first got a crown,
 But her prices went down—
Now she'll fit you for ten pence or nine.
       1942A.

1015

There was a young lady of Erskine,
And the chief of her charms was her fair skin,
 But the sable she wore
 (She had several more)
She had earned while wearing her bare skin.
       1941.

1016

Two young girls who lived in Ft. Tunney
Decided to shop their dofunny.
 " We had papa tutor us
 To cash in on our uterus;
We park transients now, in each cunny!"
       1943B.

1017

Said the whore whom they called Geraldine,
" When I think of the pricks that I've seen,
 And all of the nuts
 And the ass-holes and butts,
And the bastards like you in between..."
       1942-1952.

1018

A notorious whore named Miss Hearst
In the weakness of men is well versed.
    Reads a sign o'er the head
    Of her well-rumpled bed:
"The customer always comes first."

1945.

1019

Said a pretty young whore of Hong Kong
To a long-prongèd patron named Wong,
    "They say my vagina's
    The nicest in China—
Don't ruin it by donging it wrong."

1941.

1020

There was a young man of Jaipur
Whose cock was shot off in the War.
    So he painted the front
    To resemble a cunt,
And set himself up as a whore.

1938.

1021

Since donning a uniform, Joe
Quit the floozies that he used to know.
    Says he, "Joan Bennett'll
    Tickle my genital
Every night at the old U.S.O."

1944.

1022

A shiftless young fellow of Kent
Had his wife fuck the landlord for rent.
    But as she grew older
    The landlord grew colder,
And now they live out in a tent.

1941.

1023

There was an old girl of Kilkenny
Whose usual charge was a penny.
   For the half of that sum
    You could finger her bum—
A source of amusement to many.

                     1928-1947B.

1024

Said a madam named Mamie La Farge
To a sailor just off of a barge,
   " We have one girl that's dead,
    With a hole in her head—
Of course there's a slight extra charge. "

                     1944A.

1025

Have you heard about Dorothy Lamour,
Whose lovers got fewer and fewer?
   When asked why she lost 'em
    She said, " I defrost 'em—
I guess I'm not made for a whore. "

                     1942-1952.

1026

In the city of York there's a lass
Who will hitch up her dress when you pass.
   If you toss her two bits
    She will strip to the tits,
And let you explore her bare ass.

                     1945.

1027

A harlot of note named Le Dux
Would always charge seventy bucks.
   But for that she would suck you,
    And wink-off and fuck you—
The whole thing was simply de luxe!

                     1941.

1028

There was an old hag named Le Sueur
Who just was an out-and-out whore.
    Between her big teats
      You could come for two bits,
And she'd fuck in any old sewer.
                              1946A.

1029

Any whore whose door sports a red light
Knows a prick when she sees one, all right.
    She can tell by a glance
      At the drape of men's pants
If they're worth taking on for the night.
                              1943.

1030

There was a young lady named Mable
Who would fuck on a bed or a table.
    Though a two-dollar screw
      Was the best she could do,
Her ass bore a ten-dollar label.
                              1944-1952.

1031

There was a young whore from Madrid
Who anyone could fuck for a quid.
    But a bastard Italian
      With balls like a stallion
Said he'd do it for nothing—and did.
                              1938.

1032

Les cocottes de la ville de Marseille
Sont brunettes de l'ardent soleil.
    Elles pissent du vin blanc,
      Couchent pour dix francs —
Mais où sont les patentes de santé?
                              1942A.

1033

The tarts in the town of Marseilles
Are brunette from the sun every day.
    White wine is their piddle,
    For ten francs they'll diddle—
But their tickets of health, where are they?
                   1942A.

1034

Unique is a strumpet of Mazur
In the way that her clientèle pays her:
    A machine that she uses
    Clamps on to her whoosis,
And clocks everybody that lays her.
                   1941.

1035

There was an old whore named McGee
Who was just the right sort for a spree.
    She said, " For a fuck
    I charge half a buck,
And I throw in the ass-hole for free. "
                   1944A.

1036

Said a dainty young whore named Miss Meggs,
" The men like to spread my two legs,
    Then slip in between,
    If you know what I mean,
And leave me the white of their eggs. "
                   1943.

1037

Said a naked young soldier named Mickey
As his cunt eyed his stiff, throbbing dickey,
    " Kid, my leave's almost up,
    But I feel like a tup;
Bend down, and I'll slip you a quickie. "
                   1951.

1038

A school marm from old Mississippi
Had a quim that was simply zippy.
    The scholars all praised it
    Till finally she raised it
To prices befitting a chippy.

1952.

1039

There was a young thing from Missouri
Who fancied herself as a houri.
    Her friends thus forsook her,
    For a harlot they took her,
And she gave up the role in a fury.

1952.

1040

There was a young lady named Moore
Who, while not quite precisely a whore,
    Couldn't pass up a chance
    To take down her pants,
And compare some man's stroke with her bore.

1941.

1041

A tired young trollop of Nome
Was worn out from her toes to her dome.
    Eight miners came screwing,
    But she said, " Nothing doing;
One of you has to go home! "

1941.

1042

There was a young woman of Norway
Who drove a rare trade in the whore way,
    Till a sodomite Viscount
    Brought cunt to a discount,
And the bawdy house belles to a poor way.

1870*

1043

Said Clark Gable, picking his nose,
" I get more than the public suppose.
    Take the Hollywood way,
    It's the women who pay,
And the men simply take off their clothes."

1939A.

1044

A chippy whose name was O'Dare
Sailed on a ship to Kenmare,
    But this cute little honey
    Had left home her money
So she laid the whole crew for her fare.

1946A.

1045

A sailor ashore in Peru
Said, " Signora, quanto por la screw?"
    " For only one peso
    I will, if you say so,
Be buggered and nibble it too."

1942A.

1046

A sprightly young tart in Pompeii
Used to make fifty drachma per lay.
    But age dimmed her renown
    And now she lies down
Fifty times for the same pay.

1942A.

1047

A soi-disant Mynheer Professor
Met a beat-up old whore from Odessa.
    She applied all her arts
    To his genital parts,
But they only grew lesser and lesser.

1948A.

1048

Says a busy young whore named Miss Randalls,
As men by the dozens she handles,
   "When I get this busy
    My cunt gets all jizzy,
And it runs down my legs like wax candles."
                            1942.

1049

A whorehouse at 9 rue de Rennes
Had trouble in luring in men,
   Till they got some fairies
   With pretty dillberries,
And their clientèle came back again.
                           1942A.

1050

There was a young lady in Reno
Who lost all her dough playing keeno.
   But she lay on her back
   And opened her crack,
And now she owns the casino.
                           1942.

1051

A prosperous merchant of Rhône
Took orders for cunt on the phone,
   Or the same could be baled,
   Stamped, labeled, and mailed
To a limited parcel-post zone.

DuPont, I. G., Monsanto, and Shell
Built a world-circling pussy cartel,
   And by planned obsolescence
   So controlled detumescence
A poor man could not get a smell.
                           1948A.

1053

There was a rich old roué
Who felt himself slipping away.
 He endowed a large ward
 In a house where he'd whored.
Was there a crowd at his funeral? I'll say!
        1948.

1054

There was a hot girl from the Saar
Who fucked all, both from near and from far.
 When asked to explain,
 She replied with disdain,
" I'm trying to buy me a car. "
        1943.

1055

There was a young girl from St. Cyr
Whose reflex reactions were queer.
 Her escort said, " Mable,
 Get up off the table;
That money's to pay for the beer. "
        1949.

1056

A licentious old justice of Salem
Used to catch all the harlots and jail 'em.
 But instead of a fine
 He would stand them in line,
With his common-law tool to impale 'em.
        1941.

1057

There was an old girl of Silesia
Who said, " As my cunt doesn't please ya,
 You might as well come
 Up my slimy old bum,
But be careful my tapeworm don't seize ya. "
        1927-1941.

1058

Ethnologists up with the Sioux
Wired home for two punts, one canoe.
    The answer next day
    Said, " Girls on the way,
But what the hell's a 'panoe' ? "

                      1946A.

1059

There was a young lady from Slough
Who said that she didn't know how.
    Then a young fellow caught her
    And jolly well taught her;
She lodges in Pimlico now.

                      1928.

1060

Said a girl from Staraya Russa,
Whom the war had made looser and looser,
    " Yes, I'm wormin' a German,
    A vermin named Hermann,
But his dink is a lollapalooza! "

                      1942.

1061

There was an old Count of Swoboda
Who would not pay a whore what he owed her.
    So with great *savoir-faire*
    She stood on a chair,
And pissed in his whiskey-and-soda.

                      1938-1941.

1062

There was an old man of Tagore
Who tried out his cook as a whore
    He used Bridget's twidget
    To fidget his digit,
And now she won't cook any more.

                      1941.

1063

There was a young whore from Tashkent
Who managed an immoral tent.
    Day out and day in
    She lay writhing in sin,
Giving thanks it was ten months to Lent.

1946B.

1064

A young girl who was no good at tennis,
But at swimming was really a menace,
    Took pains to explain,
    " It depends how you train :
I was a street-walker in Venice. "

1946.

1065

There was a young man from the War Office
Who got into bed with a whore of his.
    She took off her drawers
    With many a pause,
But the chap from the War Office tore off his.

1938.

1066

There was an old whore of Warsaw
Who fucked all her customers raw.
    She would thump with her rump,
    And punt with her cunt,
And lick every prick that she saw.

1941.

1067

There once was a knowledgeful whore
Who knew all the coital lore.
    But she found there were many
    Who preferred her fat fanny,
And now she don't fuck any more.

1948A.

1068

There once was a versatile whore,
As expert behind as before.
    For a quid you could view her,
    And bugger and screw her,
As she stood on her head on the floor.
                          1941.

1069

There was an old harlot of Wick
Who was sucking a coal-heaver's prick.
    She said, " I don't mind
    The coal-dust and grime,
But the smell of your balls makes me sick."
                       1882-1941.

1070

There once was a harlot at Yale
With her price-list tattooed on her tail,
    And on her behind,
    For the sake of the blind,
She had it embroidered in Braille.
                          1941.

XIII

DISEASES

1071

Remember those two of Aberystwyth
Who connected the things that they pissed with?
   She sat on his lap
   But they both had the clap,
And they cursed with the things that they kissed
   with.   1928B-1944A.

1072

A sultan named Abou ben Adhem
Thus cautioned a travelling madam,
   " I suffer from crabs
   As do most us A-rabs, "
" It's alright, " said the madam, " I've had
   'em. "   1946A.

1073

There was an old whore of Azores
Whose cunt was all covered with sores.
   The dogs in the street
   Wouldn't eat the green meat
That hung in festoons from her drawers.
                                    1941.

1074

There was a young fellow—a banker,
Had bubo, itch, pox, and chancre.
   He got all the four
   From a dirty old whore,
So he wrote her a letter to thank her.
                                 1911-1927.

1075. LUETIC LAMENT

There was a young man of Back Bay
Who thought syphilis just went away,
    And felt that a chancre
    Was merely a canker
Acquired in lascivious play.

Now first he got acne vulgaris,
The kind that is rampant in Paris,
    It covered his skin,
    From forehead to shin,
And now people ask where his hair is.

With symptoms increasing in number,
His aorta's in need of a plumber,
    His heart is cavorting,
    His wife is aborting,
And now he's acquired a gumma.

Consider his terrible plight—
His eyes won't react to the light,
    His hands are apraxic,
    His gait is ataxic,
He's developing gun-barrel sight.

His passions are strong, as before,
But his penis is flaccid, and sore,
    His wife now has tabes
    And sabre-shinned babies—
She's really worse off than a whore.

There are pains in his belly and knees,
His sphincters have gone by degrees,
   Paroxysmal incontinence,
   With all its concomitants,
Brings on quite unpredictable pees.

Though treated in every known way,
His spirochetes grow day by day,
   He's developed paresis,
   Converses with Jesus,
And thinks he's the Queen of the May.

                              1938-1941.

1082

There was a young girl of Bavaria
Who thought her disease was malaria.
   But the family doc
   Remarked to her shock,
"It is in the mercurial area."

                              1941.

1083

A noble young lord named Bellasis
Was a sad case of satyriasis,
   Till help psychiatric
   Brought the fucking fanatic
To a state of sexual stasis.

                              1947B.

1084

There was a young man of Berlin
Whom disease had despoiled of his skin,
   But he said with much pride,
   "Though deprived of my hide,
I can still enjoy a put in."

                              1879.

1085

There was a young man of Cashmere
Who purchased a fine Bayadere.
    He fucked all her toes,
      Her mouth, eyes, and her nose,
And eventually poxed her left ear.
                                1879.

1086

There was a young woman of Cheadle
Who once gave the clap to a beadle.
    Said she, " Does it itch ? "
    " It does, you damned bitch,
And burns like hell-fire when I peedle. "
                                1879.

1087

There was a young woman of Chester
Who said to the man who undressed her,
    " I think you will find
      That it's better behind—
The front is beginning to fester.
                             1927-1941.

1088

There was an old sarge of Dorchester
Who invented a mechanical whore-tester.
    With an electrical eye,
      His tool, and a die,
He observed each sore pimple and fester.
                                1944.

1089

There's a man in the city of Dublin
Whose pego is always him troubling,
    And it's now come to this,
      That he can't go to piss,
But the spunk with the piddle comes bubbling.
                                1870.

1090

There was a young priest of Dundee
Who went back of the parish to pee.
    He said, " *Pax vobiscum,*
      Why doesn't the piss come?
I must have the c-l-a-p. "

1928*-1941.

1091

There was an old party of Fife
Who suspected a clap in his wife.
    So he bought an injection
      To cure the infection,
Which gave him a stricture for life.

1870.

1092

There was a young rounder named Fisk
Whose method of screwing was brisk.
    And his reason was : " If
      The damned bitch has the syph,
This way I'm reducing the risk. "

1941.

1093

A horny young soldier named Frank
Had only his girl-friend to thank
    That he didn't catch clap,
      Gonorrhea or pap,
And wind up in an oxygen tank.

1943.

1094

A president called Gambetta
Once used an imperfect French Letter.
    This was not the worst,
      With disease he got cursed,
And he took a long time to get better.

1879.

1095

There was a young lady of Gaza
Who shaved her cunt clean with a razor.
    The crabs in a lump
    Made tracks to her rump,
Which proceeding did greatly amaze her.
                               1879.

1096

There was an old man of Goditch,
Had the syph and the clap and the itch.
    His name was McNabs
    And he also had crabs,
The dirty old son of a bitch.
                           1927-1941.

1097

There was a young lady from Ipswich
Who had syphilis, pox, and the itch.
    In her box she put pepper
    And slept with a leper,
And ruined that son of a bitch.
                           1945C.

1098

A lecherous fellow named Gould
Soliloquized thus to his tool:
    " From Cape Cod to Salamanca,
    You've had pox, clap, and chancre—
Now ain't you a bloody great fool?"
                         1939A-1946B.

1099

There was a young lady of Grotton
Had to plug up her coosie with cotton,
    For it was no myth
    That the girl had the syph—
She stunk, and her titties were rotten.
                             1941.

1100

There was a young woman of Hadley
Who would with an omnibus cad lie.
    He gave her the crabs,
      And besides minor scabs
The pox too she got very badly.
                        1870.

1101

A strapping young fellow named Herman
Had a ring round his prick that was permanent.
    All the old docs
      Said the ring was the pox,
But he swore it was lipstick or vermin.
                        1941.

1102

There was a young lady named Hitchin
Who was scratching her crotch in the kitchen.
    Her mother said, " Rose,
      It's the crabs, I suppose."
She said, " Yes, and the buggers are itchin'. "
                        1879-1941.

1103

Young Tom Doane, a promising jockey,
Laid up his spurs, feeling rocky.
    " I have got saddle-galls
      On both of my balls."
But the doctor wrote down : Gonococci.
                        1942A.

1104

There was a young girl of Kilkenny
On whose genital parts there were many
    Venereal growths—
      The result of wild oats
Sown there by a fellow named Benny.
                        1946A.

1105

There was a young maid of Klepper
Went out one night with a stepper,
    And now in dismay
    She murmurs each day,
" His pee-pee was made of red-pepper! "
                                                1927.

1106

The physicians of Countess van Krapp
Found a terrible rash on her map—
    Sores that opened and closed
    Which they soon diagnosed
As a case of perennial clap.
                                                1941.

1107

There was a young lady named Lea
Whose favors were frequent and free,
    And pants-pigeons flew
    Where her goose-berries grew,
And some of them flew onto me.
                                                1944A.

1108

He'll be there to inspect me,
With a big syringe to inject me—
    Oh, I'll be humpbacked
    Before I get back
To Ten-Ten-Tennessee...
                                          1919-1939*

1109

There was a young lady of Michigan
Who said, " Damn it! I've got the itch again. "
    Said her mother, " That's strange,
    I'm surprised it ain't mange,
If you've slept with that son-of-a-bitch again. "
                                                1941.

1110

There was an old man of Molucca
Who wanted his daughter, to fuck her.
    But she got the best
    Of his little incest,
And poxed the old man of Molucca.
                          1870.

1111

There was a young lady named Nance
Who had ants in the seat of her pants.
    When they bit her on bottom
    She yelled, " Jesus God rot 'em!
I can't do the St. Vitus dance."
                     1942-1952.

1112

There once was a Spanish nobilio
Who lived in a Spanish castilio,
    His *cojones* grew hot
    Much more often than not,
At the thought of a Spanish jazzilio.
                        1941*

1113

The wife of a Viking in Norway
Was caught taking a nap in a doorway.
    " When you make the attack,
    Let it be from the back,
Because lately the front way's the sore way."
                       1942A.

1114

Alack, for the doughty O'Connor
Who fucked like a fiend for his honor,
    Till a flapper named Rhea
    Colluded to be a
Mother to Leuco and Gonor.
                     1942A.

1115

A charming young lady named Randall
Has a clap that the doctors can't handle.
   So this lovely, lorn floozie,
    With her poor, damaged coosie,
Must take her delight with a candle.

                               1941.

1116

A rank whore, there ne'er was a ranker,
Possessed an Hunterian chancre,
   But she made an elision
    By a transverse incision,
For which all her lovers may thank her.

                               1870.

1117

There was a young lady of Reading,
Who got poxed, and the virus kept spreading.
   Her nymphae each day
    Kept sloughing away,
Till at last you could shove your whole head in.

                               1882.

1118

A girl to the druggist did say,
" I am bothered with bugs in my hay."
   " I see what you mean,
    You need Paris green
To be rid of the things right away."

The results of this piece of mischance
Were disastrous, you'll see at a glance.
   First died bugs, then went trees,
    Then her pet Pekinese,
And two gentlemen just in from France.

                               1948A.

1120

There was a young lady at sea
Who said, " God, how it hurts me to pee. "
   " I see, " said the mate,
   " That accounts for the state
Of the captain, the purser, and me. "
1925*-1927.

1121

A virile young G.I. named Shorty
Was lively, and known to be " sporty. "
   But he once made a slip
   And showed up with a " drip, "
And was red-lined (35-1440).
1943.

1122

A boy whose skin long I suppose is,
Was dreadfully ill with phymosis.
   The doctor said, " Why,
   Circumcision we'll try,
A plan recommended by Moses. "
1870.

1123

There was an old man of Tantivy
Who followed his son to the privy.
   He lifted the lid
   To see what he did,
And found that it smelt of Capivi.
1879.

1124

There was an old man at the Terminus
Whose bush and whose bum were all verminous.
   They said, " You *sale Boche!*
   You really must wash
Before you start planting your sperm in us. "
1928.

1125

There was a young girl of Uttoxeter,
And all the young men shook their cocks at her.
    From one of these cocks
    She contracted the pox,
And she poxed all the cocks in Uttoxeter.
                       1870-1941.

1126

A fellow who slept with a whore
Used a safe, but his pecker got sore.
    Said he with chagrin,
   "Selling these is a sin."
Said the druggist, "*Caveat emptor.*"
                           1946.

1127

Full ninety years old was friend Wynn
When he went to a hookshop to sin.
    But try as he would
    It did him no good.
For all he had left was the skin.
                       1927-1948.

1128

There was a young lady of Yap
Who had pimples all over her map.
    But in her interstices
    There lurked a far worse disease,
Commonly known as the clap.
                           1947B.

XIV

LOSSES

NOTE

[*Losses through the agency of animals
will be found in Chapter VII, "Zoophily."*

*Losses in connection with masturbation
will be found in Chapter XV, "Sex Substitutes."*]

1129

There was a young lady of Alnwicke
Whom a stranger threw into a panic.
    For he frigged her and fucked her,
    And buggered and sucked her,
With a glee hardly short of satanic.

                  1941.

1130

I lost my arm in the army,
I lost my leg in the navy,
    I lost my balls
    Over Niagara Falls,
And I lost my cock in a lady.

                    1939*

1131

An explorer returned from Australia,
Reported lost paraphernalia:
    A Zeiss microscope
    And his personal hope,
Which had vanished with his genitalia.

                    1942A.

1132

There was a young sailor named Bates
Who did the fandango on skates.
    He fell on his cutlass
    Which rendered him nutless
And practically useless on dates.

1944-1952.

1133

There was an old maid from Bermuda
Who shot a marauding intruder.
    It was not her ire
    At his lack of attire,
But he reached for her jewels as he screwed her.

1950.

1134

There was a young fellow named Bill
Who took an atomic pill.
    His navel corroded,
    His asshole exploded,
And they found his nuts in Brazil.

1948.

1135

While pissing on deck, an old boatswain
Fell asleep, and his pisser got frozen.
    It snapped at the shank,
    And it fell off and sank
In the sea—'twas his own fault for dozin'.

1941.

1136

There was a young fellow named Bob
Who explained to his friends with a sob,
    " The size of my phallus
    Was just right for Alice
Till the night that she bit off the knob. "

1941.

1137

There was a young fellow from Boston
Who rode around in an Austin.
    There was room for his ass
    And a gallon of gas,
But his balls hung outside, and he lost 'em.
                             1938.

1138

A miner who bored in Brazil
Found some very strange rust on his drill.
    He thought it a joke
    Till the bloody thing broke—
Now his tailings are practically nil.
                             1942A.

1139

An eccentric young poet named Brown
Raised up his embroiderèd gown
    To look for his peter
    To beat it to metre,
But fainted when none could be found.
                             1941A.

1140

A Bavarian dame named Brunhilde
Went to bed with a jerry-built builder.
    The end of his john
    Was so badly put on
That it snapped in her bladder and killed her.
                             1941.

1141

There was a young man of Calcutta
Who tried to write " Cunt " on a shutter.
    He had got to " C-U- "
    When a pious Hindu
Knocked him arse over tip in the gutter.
                           1879-1928.

1142

There was a young man of Canute
Who was troubled by warts on his root.
    He put acid on these,
    And now, when he pees,
He can finger his root like a flute.

                                     1941.

1143

Another young man, from Beirut
Played a penis as one might a flute,
    Till he met a sad eunuch
    Who lifted his tunic
And said, " Sir, my instrument's mute."

                                     1947B.

1144

There was a young girl in a cast
Who had an unsavory past,
    For the neighborhood pastor
    Tried fucking through plaster,
And his very first fuck was his last.

                                     1948A.

1145

There were two young men of Cawnpore
Who buggered and fucked the same whore.
    But the partition split
    And the gism and shit
Rolled out in great lumps on the floor.

                               1928-1949.

1146

The wife of a red-headed Celt
Lost the key to her chastity-belt.
    She tried picking the lock
    With an Ulsterman's cock,
And the next thing he knew, he was gelt.

                                     1944.

1147

There was an old lady of Cheadle
Who sat down in church on a needle.
    The needle, though blunt,
    Penetrated her cunt,
But was promptly removed by the beadle.

                             1879-1941.

1148

The wife of an athlete named Chuck
Found her married life shit-out-of-luck.
    Her husband played hockey
    Without wearing a jockey—
Now he hasn't got what it takes for a fuck.

                             1941*-1952.

1149

There was a young lady of Clewer
Who was riding a bike, and it threw her.
    A man saw her there
    With her legs in the air,
And seized the occasion to screw her.

                             1941.

1150

There was a young man of Coblenz
The size of whose balls was immense.
    One day, playing soccer,
    He sprung his left knocker,
And kicked it right over the fence.

                             1941.

1151

An unfortunate bugger named Cowl
Took a shit while as drunk as an owl.
    He stumbled, alack!
    And fell flat on his back,
And his ballocks slipped into his bowel.

                             1941.

1152

There was a young girl from the Creek
Who had her periods twice every week.
    "How very provoking,"
      Said the Vicar from Woking,
"There's no time for poking, so to speak."

                      1927-1945C.

1153

The wife of a chronic crusader
Took on every man who waylaid her.
    Till the amorous itch
    Of this popular bitch
So annoyed the crusader he spayed her.

                      1942.

1154

There was a young lady of Dee
Who went down to the river to swim.
    A man in a punt
    Stuck an oar in her eye,
And now she wears glasses, you see.

                      1941A-1948A.

1155

There was a young fellow named Dick
Who was cursed with a spiralling prick,
    So he set out to hunt
    For a screw-twisted cunt
That would match with his corkscrewy dick.

He found one, and took it to bed,
And then in chagrin he dropped dead,
    For that spiralling snatch
    It never would match—
The damn thing had a left-handed thread!

                      1934*-1941.

1157

There was a young girl named Dinwiddie
With a brace of voluptuous titty.
    But the boys squeezed them so
    That they hung down below,
And one drooped behind and got shitty.

                                        1941.

1158

There was a young lady named Dowd
Whom a young fellow groped in the crowd.
    But the thing that most vexed her
    Was that when he stood next her
He said, " How's your cunt ? " right out loud.

                                        1941.

1159

There was a young lady named Duff
With a lovely, luxuriant muff.
    In his haste to get in her
    One eager beginner
Lost both of his balls in the rough.

                                        1941.

1160

There was a young lady named Eva
Who went to a ball as Godiva.
    But a change in the lights
    Showed a tear in her tights,
And a low fellow present yelled, " Beaver! "

                                  1927-1941.

1161

There was an old fellow of Ewing
Who said, " It's computing I'm doing.
    By leaving my drawers on
    While clambering whores, on
The whole I've lost ten miles of screwing. "

                                       1946A.

1162

There was a man from Far Rockaway
Who could skizzle a broad from a block away.
    Once while taking a fuck,
    Along came a truck
And knocked both his balls and his cock away.

1945C.

1163

There was a young fellow named Förster
Who fucked a young girl till he burst 'er.

[*The only two-line limerick.*]

1947B.

1164

And then there's a story that's fraught
With disaster—of balls that got caught,
    When a chap took a crap
    In the woods, and a trap
Underneath... Oh, I can't bear the thought!

1941.

1165

A careless old hooker in Frisco
Got turpentine mixed in her pisco,
    And scalded with steam
    A muff-diver's dream
Because he refused to let puss go.

1942A.

1166

There was a young man from Glenchasm
Who had a tremendous orgasm.
    In the midst of his thralls
    He burst both his balls
And covered an acre with plasm.

1943A.

1167

There was an old person of Gosham
Who took out his ballocks to wash 'em.
    His wife said, " Now, Jack,
    If you don't put them back,
I'll step on your scrotum and squash 'em."

1938-1941.

1168

A gallant young Frenchman named Grandhomme
Was attempting a girl on a tandem.
    At the height of the make
    She slammed on the brake,
And scattered his semen at random.

1938.

1169

There was a young lady named Hall,
Wore a newspaper dress to a ball.
    The dress caught on fire
    And burned her entire
Front page, sporting section, and all.

1941.

1170

There was an old sheik named Al Hassid
Whose tool had become very placid.
    Before each injection
    To get an erection
He had to immerse it in acid.

1949.

1171

There was a young man in Havana,
Fucked a girl on a player piano.
    At the height of their fever
    Her ass hit the lever—
Yes! He has no banana!

1941.

1172. ANNE COOPER HEWITT

I'm only a sterilized heiress,
A butt for the laughter of rubes.
    I'm comely and rich
      But a venomous bitch—
My mother—ran off with my tubes.

Oh, fie on you mother, you dastard!
Come back with my feminine toys.
    Restore my abdomen
      And make me a woman—
I want to go out with the boys!

Imagine my stark consternation
At feeling a surgeon's rude hands
    Exploring my person
      (Page Aimée McPherson)
And then rudely snatching my glands.

Oh, fie on you medical monsters!
How could you so handle my charms?
    My bosom is sinking,
      My clitoris shrinking—
I need a strong man in my arms!

The butler and second-man snub me,
No more will they use my door key.
    The cook from Samoa
      Has spermatozoa—
For others, but never for me.

Oh, fie on you fickle men-servants!
With your strong predilection to whore.
  Who cares for paternity?
  Forgive my infirmity—
Can't a girl just be fun any more?

What ruling in court can repay me
For losing my peas-in-the-pod?
  My joyous fecundity's
  Turned to morbundity—
Like Pickford, I'll have to try God.

Oh, fie on you, courthouse and rulings!
I want my twin bubbles of jest.
  Take away my hot flashes
  And menopause rashes,
And let me feel weight on my chest!

1938*-1946A.

1180

There was a young man with a hernia
Who said to his surgeon, "Gol-dernya,
  When carving my middle
  Be sure you don't fiddle
With matters that do not concernya."

1870-1939*

1181

A marine being sent to Hong Kong
Got his doctor to alter his dong.
  He sailed off with a tool
  Flat and thin as a rule—
When he got there he found he was wrong.

1942A.

1182

There was a young fellow named Hyde
Who took a girl out for a ride.
   He mucked up her fuck-hole
   And fucked up her muck-hole,
And charged her two dollars beside.

1941.

1183

Consider the case of Charles the Insane
Who had a large cock and a very small brain.
   While fucking his sister
   He raised a large blister
On the tip of his whip and her pubic terrain.

1945.

1184

There was a young Scotchman named Jock
Who had the most horrible shock:
   He once took a shit
   In a leaf-covered pit,
And the crap sprung a trap on his cock.

1941.

1185

The Conquering Lion of Judah
Made a prayer to the statue of Buddha.
   " Oh, Idol, " he prayed,
   " May Il Duce be spayed,
And all his descendants be neuter! "

1946B.

1186

There was a young couple named Kelly
Who had to live belly to belly,
   Because once, in their haste,
   They used library paste
Instead of petroleum jelly.

1938.

1187

There was a young man of Khartoum
Who lured a poor girl to her doom.
    He not only fucked her,
      But buggered and sucked her—
And left her to pay for the room.
                        1938.

1188

Said old Mr. Wellington Koo,
" Now what in the Hell shall I do ?
    My wife is too hot,
      I can't fill up her slot— "
So he screwed her to bits trying to.
                        1952.

1189

A crooner who lived in Lahore
Got his balls caught in a door.
    Now his mezzo soprano
    Is rather piano
Though he was a loud basso before.
                        1942A.

1190

There was a young Marquis of Landsdowne,
Who tried hard to keep his great stands down.
    Said he, " But that I thought
    I should break it off short,
My penis I'd hold with both hands down."
                        1870.

1191

Did you hear about young Henry Lockett?
He was blown down the street by a rocket.
    The force of the blast
    Blew his balls up his ass,
And his pecker was found in his pocket.
                        1946B.

1192

There was a young girl named Louise
With a marvelous vaginal squeeze.
    She inspired such pleasure
    In her lover's yard measure,
That she caused his untimely decease.

1941.

1193

There was a young man of Madras
Who was fucking a girl in the grass,
    But the tropical sun
    Spoiled half of his fun
By singeing the hair off his ass.

1928-1941.

1194

There was a young man of Malacca
Who always slept on his left knacker.
    One Saturday night
    He slept on his right,
And his knacker went off like a cracker.

1941.

1195

Growing tired of her husband's great mass,
A young bride inserted some glass.
    The prick of her hubby
    Is now short and stubby,
While the wife can now piss through her ass.

1941*

1196

A girl of as graceful a mien
As ever in London was seen,
    Stepped into a pub,
    Hit her man with a club,
And razored to shreds his machine.

1946A.

1197

There was a young man of Missouri
Who fucked with a terrible fury,
    Till hauled into court
    For his besti-al sport,
And condemned by a poorly-hung jury.

                              1951.

1198

All winter the eunuch from Munich
Went walking in naught but a tunic.
    Folks said, " You've a cough;
    You'll freeze your balls off! "
Said he, " That's why I'm a eunuch. "

                              1939A.

1199

There was a young lady named Nance
Whose lover had St. Vitus dance.
    When she dove for his prick,
    He wriggled so quick,
She bit a piece out of his pants.

                              1941.

1200

There was a young lady in Natchez
Who fell in some nettle-wood patches.
    She sits in her room
    With her bare little moon,
And scratches, and scratches, and scratches.

                              1927.

1201

There was an old man from New York
Whose tool was as dry as a cork.
    While attempting to screw
    He split it in two,
And now his tool is a fork.

                              1952.

1202

A bridegroom at Niagara Falls,
His fate was sad, and it appalls:
    His bride refused to fuck him,
    Or bugger, frig, or suck him;
So he went nuts—cut off his putz,
    And then bit off his balls.
                                1941.

1203

When Abelard near Notre Dame
Had taught his fair pupil the game,
    Her uncle—the wag—
    Cut off Peter's bag,
And his lectures were never the same.
                              1942A.

1204

A young man of Novorossisk
Had a mating procedure so brisk,
    With such super-speed action
    The Lorentz contraction
Foreshortened his prick to a disk.
                           1946-1951*

1205

There once was a Frenchman from Pau
Who went for a slide on the snow.
    He traveled so fast
    That he skinned off his ass,
And the cuticle now has to grow.
                          1940*-1946A.

1206

A nudist by name Roger Peet,
Loved to dance in the snow and the sleet,
    But one chilly December
    He froze every member,
And retired to a monkish retreat.
                              1939A.

1207

There was a young lady named Perkin
Who swallowed an extra-large gherkin.
    Now she doesn't spend much
    On kotex and such,
On account of her drain isn't workin'.

                  1941.

1208

There was a young man of Porcellian,
A rotter, a shit-heel, a hellion.
    But the X-ray revealed
    That his sperm was congealed,
And both of his balls in rebellion.

                  1941.

1209

A bibulous bishop would preach
After sunning his balls on the beach.
    But his love life was ended
    By a paunch so distended
It annulled, *ipso facto,* his reach.

                  1945.

1210

There was a young fellow named Puttenham
Whose tool caught in doors upon shuttin' 'em.
    He said, " Well, perchance
    It would help to wear pants,
If I just could remember to button 'em."

                  1949-1952.

1211

One evening a workman named Rawls
Fell asleep in his old overalls.
    And when he woke up he
    Discovered a puppy
Had bitten off both of his balls.

                  1941.

1212

A horny young fellow named Redge
Was jerking off under a hedge.
    The gardener drew near
    With a huge pruning shear,
And trimmed off the edge of his wedge.

                                  1941.

1213

There once was a girl at the Ritz
Who liked to have men bite her tits.
    One good Fletcherizer
    Made her sadder but wiser
By chewing them up into bits.

                              1932-1941.

1214

A geologist named Dr. Robb
Was perturbed by his thingamabob,
    So he took up his pick
    And whanged off his wick,
And calmly went on with his job.

                                  1942A.

1215

There was an old man from Robles
Who went out to dine with some nobles.
    He would risk his life,
    And fucked the host's wife,
And now, so 'tis said, he has no balls.

                                  1927.

1216

When the White Man attempted to rule
The Indians made him a fool.
    They cut off his nuts
    To hang in their huts,
And stuffed up his mouth with his tool.

                                  1943.

1217

There was a young singer named Springer,
Got his testicles caught in the wringer.
    He hollered with pain
    As they rolled down the drain,
(*falsetto*) : " There goes my career as a singer! "
                                    1943.

1218

There was an old man of Stamboul
With a varicose vein in his tool.
    In attempting to come
    Up a little boy's bum
I burst, and he *did* look a fool.
                                    1928.

1219

There was an old rake from Stamboul
Felt his ardor grow suddenly cool.
    No lack of affection
    Reduced his erection—
But his zipper got caught in his tool.
                                    1943B.

1220

There was a young girl of high station
Who ruined her fine reputation
    When she said she'd the pox
    From sucking on cocks—
She should really have called it " fellation. "
                                    1941.

1221

When the Bermondsey bricklayers struck,
Bill Bloggins was 'aving a fuck.
    By uni-on rules
    He 'ad to down tools—
Now wasn't that bloody 'ard luck!
                                    1947A.

1222

Said a doleful young man with a stutter,
" M-my wife don't allow me to butt her.
    It's-ts-ts-'tsall right,
    B-b-but, but some night
I'll t-tie down the bitch, and g-gut her! "

A less violent chap with a stammer
Said, " M-mine too—she won't let me ram her.
    What's s-soured me on life
    Is not f-fucking my wife,
D-d-d-d-d-d-d-dammer! "

1941.

1224

There was a young man from Tahiti
Who went for a swim with his sweetie,
    And as he pursued her
    A blind barracuda
Ran off with his masculinity.

1947.

1225

I'd rather have fingers than toes,
I'd rather have ears than a nose,
    And a happy erection
    Brought just to perfection
Makes me terribly sad when it goes.

1948A.

1226

There was a young fellow named Tom
Who ran screaming home to his mom.
    The fear of the Bomb
    Scared him back in the womb—
The bastard, he wasn't so dumb!

1950.

1227

There was a young lady of Tring
Who sat by the fire to sing.
   A piece of charcoal
    Flew up her arsehole
And burnt all the hair off her quim.

                      1870.

1228

There was a young man of Tyburnia
Who was fucking a girl with a hernia.
   When he shot in her twat
    Why, she also shot—
All over him! Wouldn't that burn ya?

                      1948A.

1229

An athletic young fellow in Venice
Got the stone from straining at tennis.
   When his jock wouldn't stand
    She who had it in hand
Said, " These out-door sports are a menace."

                      1942A.

1230

A lady was once heard to weep,
" My figure no more I can keep.
   It's my husband's demand
    For a tit in each hand,
But the bastard will walk in his sleep!"

                      1943A.

1231

There was a young lady of Wheeling
Who professed to lack sexual feeling.
   But a cynic named Boris
    Just touched her clitoris,
And she had to be scraped off the ceiling.

                      1941.

1232

There was a young lady named White
Found herself in a terrible plight:
   A mucker named Tucker
    Had struck her, the fucker—
The bugger, the bastard, the shite!

1927-1941.

XV

SEX SUBSTITUTES

1233

A man in the battle of Aix
Had one nut and his cock shot away,
    But found out in this pickle
    His nose could still tickle,
Though he might get the snuffles some day.
                      1942A.

1234

Nymphomaniacal Alice
Used a dynamite stick for a phallus.
    They found her vagina
    In North Carolina,
And her ass-hole in Buckingham Palace.
                    1942-1951.

1235

A lesbian lassie named Anny
Desired to appear much more manny.
    So she whittled a pud
    Of mahogany wood,
And let it protrude from her cranny.
                      1943A.

1236

There once was a young Aztec
Who was fond of reading Steinbeck.
    When asked where she read,
    She said, " Always in bed,
Especially when wearing Ko-tex. "
                      1942.

1237

There was a young man of Bagdad
Who was dreaming that he was a shad.
    He dreamt he was spawning,
    And then, the next morning,
He found that, by Jesus! he had.
1944A.

1238

There was a young man of Balbriggan
Who was fearfully given to frigging,
    Till these nocturnal frolics
    Played hell with his bollox,
And killed the young man of Balbriggan.
1870.

1239

An eunuch frequenting Bangkok
Used to borrow the deified jock
    From a local rain-god
    When he went for a prod—
You could hear the girl yell for a block.
1942A.

1240

When a girl, young Elizabeth Barrett
Was found by her ma in a garret.
    She had shoved up a diamond
    As far as her hymen,
And was ramming it home with a carrot.
1932.

1241

There was a young girl of Batonger,
Used to diddle herself with a conger.
    When asked how it feels
    To be pleasured by eels,
She said, " Just like a man, only longer."
1941.

1242

A nudist resort at Benares
Took a midget in all unawares.
   But he made members weep
   For he just couldn't keep
His nose out of private affairs.

1949.

1243

There was a young man from Bengal
Who got in a hole in the wall.
   " Oh, " he said, " It's a pity
   This hole is so glitty,
But it's better than nothing at all. "

1946A.

1244

There was an asexual bigot
Whose cock only served as a spigot,
   Till a jolly young whore
   Taught him tricks by the score;
Now his greatest delight is to frig it.

1944.

1245

There once was a horny old bitch
With a motorized self-fucker which
   She would use with delight
   All day long and all night—
Twenty bucks : Abercrombie & Fitch.

1941-1952.

1246

There was a young man of Bombay
Who fashioned a cunt out of clay,
   But the heat of his prick
   Turned it into a brick,
And chafed all his foreskin away.

1879.

1247
A squeamish young fellow named Brand
Thought caressing his penis was grand,
    But he viewed with distaste
    The gelatinous paste
That it left in the palm of his hand.
                            1942.

1248
There was a young fellow named Bream
Who never had dreamt a wet dream,
    For when lacking a whore
    He'd just bore out the core
Of an apple, and fuck it through cream.
                            1941.

1249
There was a young man from the Bronx
Who when offered a piece said, "No thonx."
    He said, "I declare,
    I prefer solitaire,
And all that I do is just yonx."
                            1939A.

1250
There was a young naval cadet
Whose dreams were unusually wet.
    When he dreamt of his wedding
    He soaked up the bedding,
And the wedding ain't taken place yet.
                          1942-1952.

1251
There was a young man of Calcutta
Who jerked himself off in the gutter.
    But the tropical sun
    Played hell with his gun
And turned all his cream into butter.
                          1941-1951.

1252

A young jacker-off of Cawnpore
Never felt a desire for more.
    In bold self-reliance
    He cried out his defiance
Of the joys of the fairy and whore.

                       1942.

1253

There was a young fellow named Chisholm
Afflicted with skin erotism.
    In bathing, he'd rub
    His prick in the tub
Till the water was soapy with jism.

                       1942.

1254

There were two young ladies from Claversham
Who allowed two buck niggers to ravish 'em.
    Said May to Elize,
    " If we just close our eyes,
We'll imagine they're Hackett and Faversham! "

                       1943B.

1255

There was a young girl of Cohoes
Who jerked herself off with her nose.
    She said, " Yes, I done it,
    But just for the fun it
Afforded the folk of Cohoes. "

                       1952.

1256

There once was a fabulous Creole
Whose prick had a wide-open pee-hole.
    This carrot so orange
    Got caught in the door-hinge
When he tried to bugger the key-hole.

                       1941*

1257

There was a young woman of Croft
Who played with herself in a loft,
    Having reasoned that candles
    Could never cause scandals,
Besides which they did not go soft.

                              1927-1949.

1258

Said another young woman of Croft,
Amusing herself in the loft,
    " A salami or wurst
    Is what I should choose first—
With bologna you know you've been boffed. "

                              1941-1952.

1259

There was a young lady of Dallas
Invented a singular phallus.
    It came and it went,
    And when it was spent
It proceeded to fill up the chalice.

                                    1943A.

1260

There was a young fellow from Dallas
Who enjoyed doing things with his phallus.
    So many tricks did he try
    It became, by and by,
Little more than a leather-tough callus.

                                    1943.

1261

There was a young man from Darjeeling
Whose dong reached up to the ceiling.
    In the electric light socket
    He'd put it and rock it—
Oh God! What a wonderful feeling!

                                    1946A.

1262

A geneticist living in Delft
Scientifically played with himself,
    And when he was done
    He labeled it : *Son,*
And filed him away on a shelf.

                  1942A.

1263

A certain young fellow named Dick
Liked to feel a girl's hand on his prick.
    He taught them to fool
    With his rigid old tool
Till the cream shot out, white and thick.

                  1942.

1264

An agreeable girl named Miss Doves
Likes to jack off the young men she loves.
    She will use her bare fist
    If the fellows insist
But she really prefers to wear gloves.

                  1942.

1265

A lecherous Northumbrian druid,
Whose mind was filthy and lewd,
    Awoke from a trance
    With his hand in his pants
On a lump of pre-seminal fluid.

                  1945.

1266

There was an old Chinaman drunk
Who went for a sail in his junk.
    He was dreaming of Venus
    And tickling his penis,
Till he floated away in the spunk.

                  1879.

1267

There was a young man from Oswego
Who fell in love with a Dago.
    He dreamt that his Venus
    Was jerking his penis,
And woke up all covered with sago.

1946A.

1268

There was a gay Countess of Dufferin,
One night while her husband was covering,
    Just to chaff him a bit
    She said, " You old shit,
I can buy a dildo for a sovereign."

1870.

1269

The modern cinematic emporium
Is by no means the merest sexorium,
    But a highly effectual
    Heterosexual
Mutual masturbatorium.

1943*

1270

As Apollo was chasing the fair
Daphne she vanished in air.
    He could find but a shrub
    With thick bark on the hub
And not even a knot-hole to spare.

1942A.

1271

There were three young ladies of Fetters,
Annoyed all their elders and betters
    By stuffing their cock-holders
    With proxies for stockholders,
Old bills, and anonymous letters.

1941.

1272

There was a young parson of Goring
Who made a small hole in the flooring.
    He lined it all round,
    Then laid on the ground,
And declared it was cheaper than whoring.

1879.

1273

A fair-haired young damsel named Grace
Thought it very, very foolish to place
    Her hand on your cock
    When it turned hard as rock,
For fear it would explode in her face.

1946A.

1274

There was a young lady of Harrow
Who complained that her cunt was too narrow,
    For times without number
    She would use a cucumber,
But could not accomplish a marrow.

1879.

1275

There was a young parson of Harwich,
Tried to grind his betrothed in a carriage.
    She said, " No, you young goose,
    Just try self-abuse.
And the other we'll try after marriage. "

1879.

1276

There was a young lady named Hatch
Who doted on music by Bach.
    She played with her pussy
    To " The Faun " by Debussy,
But to ragtime she just scratched her snatch.

1943-1952.

1277
There was a young man from Havana
Who continually played the " piana."
   ' Til one day his finger slipped,
    And his fly it ripped,
And out slipped a hairy banana.
                             1950.

1278
A water-pipe suited Miss Hunt,
Who used it for many a bunt,
   But the unlucky wench
    Got it caught in her trench—
It took twenty-two men and a big Stillson wrench
To get the thing out of her cunt.
                             1941.

1279
At Vassar sex isn't injurious,
Though of love we are never penurious.
   Thanks to vulcanized aids
    Though we may die old maids,
At least we shall never die curious.
                             1941.

1280
The swaggering hips of a jade
Raised the cock of a clerical blade.
   Hell-bent for his fun
    He went home on the run,
And diddled his grandmother's maid.
                             1941.

1281
A neurotic young man of Kildare
Drilled a hole in the seat of a chair.
   He fucked it all night,
    Then died of the fright
That maybe he wasn't " all there."
                             1946A.

1282

There was a young lady from Kincaid
Who covered it up with a band-aid.
    The boy-friend said, " Shit,
    I can't find the slit! "
And helped himself out with a hand-aid.

1948A.

1283

An amorous Jew, on Yom Kippur,
Saw a shiksel—decided to clip her.
    " I'll grip her, and strip her,
    And lip her, and whip her— "
Then his dingus shot off in his zipper!

1943B.

1284

There was a young fellow named Klotz
Who went looking for tail in New Lots.
    Of tail he found nary
    A piece, but a fairy
Suggested he try some ersatz.

1942-1947B.

1285

There was a young man of Kutki
Who could blink himself off with one eye.
    For a while though, he pined,
    When his organ declined
To function, because of a stye.

1947B.

1286

Since the girls found no joys in her lap,
Pete chopped off her big brother's tap.
    At his death she did not repent,
    But fixed it with cement
And wore it in place with a strap.

1942.

1287

An innocent boy in Lapland
Was told that frigging was grand.
    But at his first trial
    He said with a smile,
"I've had the same feeling by hand."

1927.

1288

She made a thing of soft leather,
And topped off the end with a feather.
    When she poked it inside her
    She took off like a glider,
And gave up her lover forever.

1948A.

1289

There is a young fellow from Leeds
Whose skin is so thin his cock bleeds
    Whenever erect,
    This dermal defect
Often scares him from sowing his seeds.

1947.

1290

There was a young fellow from Lees
Who handled his tool with great ease.
    This continual friction
    Made his sex a mere fiction,
But the callus hangs down to his knees.

1947.

1291

There was a young man from Liberia
Who was groping a wench from Nigeria.
    He said, "Say, my pet,
    Your panties are wet."
"Sorry, sir, that's my interior."

1947B.

1292

There was a pianist named Liszt
Who played with one hand while he pissed,
   But as he grew older
   His technique grew bolder,
And in concert jacked off with his fist.
                             1941A.

1293

There was an old parson of Lundy,
Fell asleep in his vestry on Sunday.
   He awoke with a scream:
   "What, another wet dream!
This comes of not frigging since Monday."
                             1879.

1294

A soldier named Dougall McDougall
Was caught jacking off in his bugle.
   Said they of the army,
   "We think that you're barmy,"
Said he, "It's the new way to frugle."
                             1939A.

1295

A thrifty old man named McEwen
Inquired, "Why be bothered with screwing?
   It's safer and cleaner
   To finger your wiener,
And besides you can see what you're doing."
                             1942A.

1296

There was a young man from McGill
Who was always seen walking uphill.
   When someone inquired,
   "My man, aren't you tired?"
He said, "No, it makes my balls thrill."
                             1939A.

1297

There was a young man named M'Gurk
Who dozed off one night after work,
    He had a wet dream
    But awoke with a scream
Just in time to give it a jerk.

1927-1941.

1298

Have you heard of Professor MacKay
Who lays all the girls in the hay?
    Though he thinks it's romantic
    He drives them all frantic
By *talking* a wonderful lay.

1942-1952.

1299

A horny young girl of Madras
Reclined with a monk in the grass.
    She tickled his cock
    With the end of a rock
Till it foamed like a bottle of Bass.

Another young lady named Hicks
Spent all her time thinking of pricks,
    And it was her odd whim
    To tickle her quim
Till it foamed like a bottle of Dicks.

1941-1951.

1301

A lusty young woodsman of Maine
For years with no woman had lain,
    But he found sublimation
    At a high elevation
In the crotch of a pine—God, the pain!

1941.

1302

There was a young lady named Mandel
Who caused quite a neighborhood scandal
   By coming out bare
   On the main village square
And frigging herself with a candle.
                                  1943B.

1303

There was a young girl named Maxine
Whose vagina was wondrously clean:
   With her uterus packed
   She kept safe from attack
With a dill pickle, papulous, green.
                                  1942A.

1304

There was a young lady named May
Who frigged herself in the hay.
   She bought a pickle—
   One for a nickel—
And wore all the warts away!
                                  1927.

1305

In all of the Grecian metropolis
There was only one virgin—Papapoulos;
   But her cunt was all callous
   From fucking the phallus
Of a god that adorned the Acropolis.
                                  1941.

1306

There were two Greek girls of Miletus
Who said, " We wear gadgets that treat us,
   When strapped on the thigh
   Up cozy and high,
To constant, convenient coitus. "
                                  1941.

1307

There was an aesthetic young Miss
Who thought it the apex of bliss
    To jazz herself silly
    With the bud of a lily,
Then go to the garden and piss.

                          1928.

1308

There was a young girl of Mobile
Whose hymen was made of chilled steel.
    To give her a thrill
    Took a rotary drill
Or a Number 9 emery wheel.

                      1938-1941.

1309

There was a young man from Montrose
Who could diddle himself with his toes.
    He did it so neat
    He fell in love with his feet,
And christened them Myrtle and Rose.

Oh, that supple young man of Montrose
Who tickled his tail with his toes!
    His landlady said,
    As she made up his bed,
"My God! How that man blows his nose!"

                      1927-1941.

1311

There was a young lady from Munich
Who was had in a park by a eunuch.
    In a moment of passion
    He shot her a ration
From a squirt-gun concealed 'neath his tunic.

                      1943A-1945.

1312

There was a young girl from New York
Who diddled herself with a cork.
    It stuck in her vagina—
    Can you imagina
Prying it out with a fork!

                                       1938.

1313

There was a young man in Norway,
Tried to jerk himself off in a sleigh,
    But the air was so frigid
    It froze his balls rigid,
And all he could come was frappé.

                                1938-1941.

1314

A bobby of Nottingham Junction
Whose organ had long ceased to function
    Deceived his good wife
    For the rest of her life
With the aid of his constable's truncheon.

                                       1941.

1315

A nymphomaniacal nurse
With a curse that was worse than perverse
    Stuck a rotary drill
    Up her twat, for a thrill—
And they carted her off in a hearse.

                                     1939*

1316

Peter, first Duke of Orange
Was limited to a miserable four-inch,
    But technique in a keyhole
    Developed his P-hole
'Til at last it got caught in the door-hinge.

                                     1946.

1317

The young things who frequent picture-palaces
Have no use for this psycho-analysis.
    And although Doctor Freud
    Is distinctly annoyed
They cling to their old-fashioned fallacies.
                                      1927*

1318

There was a young fellow named Perkin
Who always was jerkin' his gherkin.
    His wife said, " Now, Perkin,
    Stop jerkin' your gherkin;
You're shirkin' your ferkin'—you bastard! "
                            1938-1944A.

1319

There was a young girl from Peru
Who badly wanted a screw.
    She tried a broom-handle
    And the end of a candle,
But threw them away for a Jew.
                                    1946A.

1320

There was a young man named Pete
Who was a bit indiscreet.
    He pulled on his dong
    Till it grew very long
And actually dragged in the street.
                                    1939A.

1321

A eunuch who came from Port Said
Had a jolly good time in bed,
    Nor could any sultana
    Detect from his manner
That he used a banana instead.
                                    1947B.

1322

Quoth the coroner's jury in Preston,
"The verdict is rectal congestion."
    They found an eight-ball
    On a shoemaker's awl
Halfway up the major's intestine.

                    1942A.

1323

When Paul the Apostle lay prostrate,
And leisurely prodded his prostate,
    With pride parabolic
    His most apostolic
Appendage became an apostate.

                    1947.

1324

There was a young lady named Psyche
In bed with a fellow named Ike.
    Said he, "Now don't worry,
    Or hurry or flurry,
But that ain't my prick—it's a spike."

                    1941.

1325

There was a young man from Racine
Who invented a fucking machine.
    Concave or convex
    It would fit either sex,
With attachments for those in between.

                    1927-1938.

1325 A

And was perfectly simple to clean.
With a drip-pot to catch all the cream.
And jerked itself off in between.
The God-damndest thing ever seen.
And guaranteed used by the Queen.

                    1928-1950.

1326

There was a young man from Aberdeen
Who invented a jerking machine.
    On the twenty-fifth stroke
    The God damn thing broke
And beat his balls to a cream.
                                1950.

1327

There was a young lady named Rackstraw,
Titillated herself with a hack-saw.
    As a result of this action
    She no longer has traction,
And a penis feels just like a jackstraw.
                             1945-1952.

1328

There was a young girl named Miss Randall
Who thought it beneath her to handle
    A young fellow's pole,
    So instead, her hot hole
She contented by means of a candle.
                                 1947.

1329

There was an Archbishop of Rheims
Who played with himself in his dreams.
    On his night-shirt in front
    He painted a cunt,
Which made his spend gush forth in streams.
                                 1879.

1330

A cardinal living in Rome
Had a Renaissance bath in his home.
    He could gaze at the nudes
    As he worked up his moods
In emulsions of semen and foam.
                                 1942A.

1331. HYDRAULIC INTERLUDE

There was a young lady named Rose
Who'd occasionally straddle a hose,
   And parade about, squirting
   And spouting and spurting,
Pretending she pissed like her beaux.

She was seen by her cousin named Anne,
Who improved the original plan.
   Said she, " My dear Rose,
   In this lowly old hose
Are all the best parts of a man. "

So, avoiding the crude and sadistic,
She frigged in a manner artistic:
   At the height of her pleasure
   She turned up the pressure,
And cried, " Ain't it grand and realistic! "

They soon told the Duchess of Fyfe,
And her crony, the alderman's wife;
   And they found it so pleasing,
   And tickling and teasing
That they washed men right out of their life.

It was tried by the great Mrs. Biddle,
And she said to her husband, " Go fiddle!
   Here's double the fun,
   And you get three in one—
A ducking, a douche, and a diddle. "

It was tried by the dancer, Di Basle,
Whose cunt was just made for a nozzle.
    She said, " I admit
    It's an elegant fit,
But of course it won't do for the arse 'ole. "

It was tried by the Duchess of Porter,
And passed on by her to her daughter,
    Who said, " With a leman
    You're fearful of semen,
But a fuck's as effective with water. "

Thus writes Lady Vanderbilt-Horsett,
Who invented the Lonely-Maid Corset :
    " I thought all vicarious
    Fucking precarious.
I was wrong. It's a whiz. I endorse it. "

Soon in Paris, on the Boulevard Salique,
You could purchase *(complet avec talic,*
    Pour soixante francs cinq)
    A short hose and a tank,
And they called it *Le Fuckeur Hydraulique.*

                      1938-1941.

      1340
There was a young lady named Rose,
With erogenous zones in her toes.
    She remained onanistic
    Till a foot-fetichistic
Young man became one of her beaux.
                     1941*-1946B.

1341

There once was a eunuch of Roylem,
Took two eggs to the cook and said, "Boil 'em.
    I'll sling 'em beneath
    My inadequate sheath,
And slip into the harem and foil 'em."
1947B.

1342

There was a young fellow named Rule
Who went to a library school.
    As he fingered the index
    His thoughts ran to sex,
And his blood all ran to his tool.
1942.

1343

There was a young fellow named Rummy
Who delighted in whipping his dummy.
    He played pocket pool
    With his happy old tool
Till his shorts and his pants were all comey.
1942.

1344

There was a young man of St. Paul's
Possessed the most useless of balls.
    Till at last, at the Strand,
    He managed a stand,
And tossed himself off in the stalls.
1879.

1345

There's a pretty young lady named Sark,
Afraid to get laid in the dark,
    But she's often manhandled
    By the light of a candle
In the bushes of Gramercy Park.
1946A.

1346

There was a young man of Savannah,
Met his end in a curious manner.
    He diddled a hole
    In a telegraph pole
And electrified his banana.

                                1941.

1347

Cried her partner, " My dear Lady Schmoosing,
While I'll own that stinkfinger's amusing,
    Still, this constant delay
    Tends to hold up the play,
And this goom on the deck's most confusing. "

                                1945.

1348

Girls give Jim's stiff penis a spasm
Whenever he sees 'em or has 'em.
    He likes them so well
    He needs only to smell
Them, to have a spontaneous orgasm.

                                1942.

1349

There was a young man of high station
Attached to the Chinese Legation.
    He liked to be fucked,
    And adored being sucked,
But he revelled in pure masturbation.

                            1879-1947B.

1350

A milkmaid there was, with a stutter,
Who was lonely and wanted a futter.
    She had nowhere to turn,
    So she diddled a churn,
And managed to come with the butter.

                                1941.

1351

A girl by the green Susquehanna
Said she would do it mañana,
    But her lover got sore
    And sailed off to Ladore...
And now she must use a banana.

1942A.

1352

There was a young genius in Texas
Who could flex his own solar plexus.
    It made his ding bounce,
    And he caught every ounce
Of his magical spraying of sexus.

1952.

1353

A decayed, witty old frump of Thrace
Substituted rubber in her personal place.
    She developed the trick,
    When you pulled out your prick,
Of snapping the guck in your face.

1943.

1354

There was a young lady of Thyme
Who swore she'd hold out for all time.
    So she stifled the crave
    For a cock in her nave,
And insisted a candle was fine.

1946A.

1355

A virgin felt urged in Toulouse
Till she thought she would try self-abuse.
    In search of a hard on
    She ran out in the garden,
And was had by a statue of Zeus.

1942A.

1356

Under the spreading chestnut tree
The village smith he sat,
    Amusing himself
    By abusing himself
And catching the load in his hat.

                      1941.

1357

There was a young man from Vancouver
Whose existence had lost its prime mover.
    But its loss he supplied
    With a piece of bull's hide,
Two pears, and the bag from the Hoover.

                      1941.

1358

There was a young fellow named Veach
Who fell fast asleep on the beach.
    His dreams of nude women
    Had his proud organ brimming
And squirting on all within reach.

                      1947B.

1359

A widow whose singular vice
Was to keep her late husband on ice
    Said, " It's been hard since I lost him—
    I'll *never* defrost him!
Cold comfort, but cheap at the price. "

                    1947B.

1360

Don't dip your wick in a Wac,
Don't ride the breast of a Wave,
    Just sit in the sand
    And do it by hand,
And buy bonds with the money you save.

                    1948.

1361

There was a young man named Walljasper
Who invented a furlined ballclasper.
    A half turn to the right
    Would bring squeals of delight
To the most sterile, im*p*otent whoremaster.

1947B.

1362

There was a young man from Winsocket
Who put a girl's hand in his pocket.
    Her delicate touch
    Thrilled his pecker so much,
It shot off in the air like a rocket.

1942-1952.

1363

There was a young fellow from Yale
Whose face was exceedingly pale.
    He spent his vacation
    In self-masturbation
Because of the high price of tail.

1927-1941.

XVI

ASSORTED ECCENTRICITIES

1364

Floating idly one day through the air
A circus performer named Blair
   Tied a sizeable rock
   To the end of his cock
And shattered a balcony chair.
                       1941.

1365

There was a young fellow of Alltree
Whose parts were but puny and paltry,
   But he knew how to do
   A neat gobbledegoo
[. . . . . *cetera desunt*]
                       1946A.

1366

There was a young lady of Asia
Who had an odd kind of aphasia.
   She'd forget that her cunt
   Was located in front,
Which deprived her of most of the pleasure.
                       1949.

1367

There was a young girl of Asturias
With a penchant for practices curious.
   She loved to bat rocks
   With her gentlemen's cocks—
A practice both rude and injurious.
                       1941.

1368

There was a young man of Australia
Who painted his ass like a dahlia.
    The drawing was fine,
    The color divine,
The scent—ah, that was a failure.

                            1928-1932.

1369

A lecherous fellow named Babbitt
Asked a girl if she'd fuck or would nab it.
    Said she, " From long habit
    I fuck like a rabbit,
So I'd rather cohabit than grab it."

                            1941.

1370

A reformer who went out to Bali
To change the sartorial folly
    Of the girls now admits,
    " A pair of good tits
In season can seem rather jolly."

                            1942A.

1371

There was a young Queen of Baroda
Who built a new kind of pagoda.
    The walls of its halls
    Were festooned with the balls
And the tools of the fools that bestrode her.

                          1938-1941.

1372

There was a young fellow of Barrow
Whose whang-bone was lacking in marrow.
    To accomplish a rape
    He wound it in tape,
And feathered the shaft like an arrow.

                            1941.

1373
The Reverend Henry Ward Beecher
Called a girl a most elegant creature.
    So she laid on her back
    And, exposing her crack,
Said, "Fuck *that*, you old Sunday School Teacher!"
                              1948.

1374
There was a young man of Belgravia
Who cared neither for God nor his Saviour.
    He walked down the Strand
    With his prick in his hand
And was jailed for indecent behavior.
                              1870–1932.

1375
A vigorous fellow named Bert
Was attracted by every new skirt.
    Oh, it wasn't their minds
    But their rounded behinds
That excited this loveable flirt.
                              1948A.

1376
A lazy, fat fellow named Betts
Upon his fat ass mostly sets.
    Along comes a gal
    And says, "*I*'ll fuck you, pal."
Says he, "If you'll do the work, let's."
                              1941.

1377
There was a young fellow named Bliss
Whose sex life was strangely amiss,
    For even with Venus
    His recalcitrant penis
Would never do better than t
                             h
                             i
                             s
                             .

1378

There once was an actress of Bonely,
And the men never let her be lonely.
   So she hung out in front
   Of her popular cunt
A sign reading: " Standing Room Only. "

1941.

1379

There was a gay Countess of Bray,
And you may think it odd when I say,
   That in spite of high station,
   Rank and education,
She always spelt Cunt with a K.

1879.

1380

There was a young lady in Brent,
When her old man's pecker it bent,
   She said with a sigh,
   " Oh, why must it die?
Let's fill it with Portland Cement. "

1927.

1381

There was a young lady named Bruce
Who captured her man by a ruse:
   She filled up her fuselage
   With a good grade of mucilage,
And he never could pry himself loose.

1941.

1382

There was an old man from Bubungi
Whose balls were all covered with fungi.
   With his friends, out at lunch,
   He tore off a bunch
And said, " Now divide this among ye. "

1941A.

1383

On a bridge sat the Bishop of Buckingham
Thinking of twats and of sucking 'em,
   And watching the stunts
   Of the cunts in the punts,
And the tricks of the pricks that were fucking 'em.
                      1941-1950.

1384

There was a young maid of Cardiff,
Whose father one day asked if
   To church she would walk
   To hear some good talk,
When the young maid replied, " Ax my spiff."
                      1870.

1385

On guard by the bridge of Carquinez
With his eyes on the evening star, Venus,
   With the sky full of blimps,
   And the town full of pimps,
And an incredible length in his penis

Stood a soldier of just 22
Thinking of his leave-night screw. . .
. . . .
. . . . *[cetera desunt]*
                      1942.

1387

There was a young fellow named Chick
Who fancied himself rather slick.
   He went to a ball
   Dressed in nothing at all
But a big velvet bow round his prick.
                      1944A.

1388

There was a young lady from China
Who mistook for her mouth her vagina.
    Her clitoris huge
    She covered with rouge
And lipsticked her labia minor.

                          1948.

1389

The ancient orthographer, Chisholm,
Caused a lexicographical schism
    When he asked to know whether
    'Twere known which was better
To use—g or j—to spell "jism."

                          1941.

1390

There was a young man from the Coast
Who received a parcel by post.
    It contained, so I heard,
    A triangular turd
And the balls of his grandfather's ghost.

                      1946B-1950.

1391

There was a young girl of Connecticut
Who didn't care much about etiquette.
    Whenever she was able
    She'd piss on the table,
And mop off her cunt with her petticoat.

                          1952.

1392

An ignorant maiden named Crewe-Pitt
Did something amazingly stupid:
    When her lover had spent
    She douched with cement,
And gave birth to a statue of Cupid.

                          1941.

1393

The Duchess of Drood's lewd and crude,
And the men think her terribly rude.
    When they swim by the docks
    She tickles their cocks
And laughs when the red tips protrude.
                                 1941.

1394

A certain young lady named Daisy
Who is really infernally lazy
    Said, " I haven't the time
    To wipe my behine,
But the way I can hump drives 'em crazy."
                                 1941.

1395

There was a shy boy named Dan
Who tickled his girl with a fan.
    She started to flirt
    So he lifted her skirt
And gave her a fuck like a man.
                                 1950.

1396

There was a young man of Datchet
Who cut off his prick with a hatchet.
    Then very politely
    He sent it to Whitely,
And ordered a cunt that would match it.

THE REPLY

" There is a young girl here at Vassar
    And none, for your needs, could surpass her.
        But she cannot detach it
        And much less dispatch it.
You'll still have to bach it.   Alas, sir!"
                                1927-1949.

1398. SOCIAL POISE — SIC TRANSIT

There was a young fellow named Dick
Who perfected a wonderful trick:
   With a safe for protection
   He'd get an erection,
And then balance himself on his prick.

'Twas a fearful and wonderful sight,
And the ladies all shrieked with delight,
   But the men were less zealous
   For it made them all jealous,
And they said that it wasn't polite.

But that night each one tried it and failed,
While their wives looked on helpless and wailed,
   For either they'd teeter
   And fall on their peter,
Or they'd find themselves getting derailed.

So Dick was the toast of the town,
There was nothing too good for the clown,
   And the wives all came flocking
   To sample his cocking,
While the husbands deplored his renown.

Then along came a fellow from France
Whose success you'd foretell at a glance,
   For his cock didn't dangle
   But stayed at right angle,
Which gave him an excellent stance.

With a flourish he took off his clothes,
And assumed Dick's remarkable pose,
   But the chief of his talents
   Was keeping his balance
While he juggled his balls with his toes.

Then came the best part of all,
That always would bring down the hall,
   For his finishing trick
   Was to straddle his prick,
And wheel out of sight on one ball.

The ladies all ran and told Dick
That the Frenchman had bettered his trick,
   So he straddled and struggled
   And finally juggled,
But he knocked out his prop with a kick.

And the tragedy didn't end there,
For as he whirled down through the air
   His prick became tied
   In a knot that defied
All attempts to untangle its snare.

Most men would have died of remorse,
But Dick found another resource:
   For pretzels he'd pose
   With his twisted up hose,
And he made a nice income, of course.

1938-1941.

1408

Meat-rationing did not terrify Miss Davey,
She got married to a sailor in the Navy,
    For she knew between his legs
    He had ham and he had eggs,
A big wienie, and oodles of white gravy.

                                  1942.

1409

There was a young priest named Delaney
Who said to the girls, " *Nota bene,*
    I've seen how you swish up
    Your skirts at the bishop
Whenever the weather is rainy. "

                                  1937*

1410

A surly and pessimist Druid,
A defeatist, if only he knew it,
    Said, " The world's on the skids,
    And I think having kids
Is a waste of good seminal fluid. "

                                 1943A.

1411

The grand-niece of Madame DuBarry
Suspected her son was a fairy.
    " It's peculiar, " said she,
    " But he sits down to pee,
And stands when I bathe the canary. "

                                 1944A.

1412

In his garden remarked Lord Dunedin,
" A fig for your diggin' and weedin'.
    I like watching birds
    While they're dropping their turds,
And spyin' on guineapigs breedin'. "

                                 1947A.

1413

I dined with the Duchess of Dyches,
Who said, " God! how my bottom-hole itches! "
   So she passed around switches
   And took down her britches,
And soon her dinner-guests had her in stitches.

                                    1944A.

1414

There was a young girl of East Anglia
Whose loins were a tangle of ganglia.
   Her mind was a webbing
   Of Freud and Krafft-Ebing
And all sorts of other new-fanglia.

                              1942-1948A.

1415

Said Einstein, " I have an equation
Which science might call Rabelaisian.
   Let P be virginity
   Approaching infinity,
And U be a constant, persuasion.

" Now if P over U be inverted
  And the square root of U be inserted
   X times over P,
   The result, Q.E.D.
Is a relative, " Einstein asserted.

                                      1947B.

1417

A pretty young girl Eskimo
Thought it very patriotic to sew
   Ballock-warmers for those
   Who were fighting the foes,
And on whom the North wind would blow.

                                    1946A.

1418

There was a young man from Eurasia
Who toasted his balls in a brazier
    Till they grew quite as hot
    As the glamorous twat
Of Miss Brenda Diana Duff Frazier.

1939*

1419

A psychoneurotic fanatic
Said, " I take little girls to the attic,
    Then whistle a tune
    'Bout the cow and the moon—
When the cow jumps, I come. It's dramatic.'

1946.

1420

There was an old fellow named Fletcher,
A lewd and perverted old lecher.
    In a spirit of meanness
    He cut off his penis,
And now he regrets it, I betcha.

1941.

1421

A mystical painter named Foxx
Once picked up a girl on the docks.
    He made an elliptic
    Mysterious triptych,
And painted it right on her box.

1941.

1422

There was a young cowboy named Gary
Who was morbidly anxious to marry,
    But he found the defection
    Of any erection
A difficult factor to parry.

1941.

1423

A proper young person named Gissing
Announced he had given up kissing.
   " I strike out at once
     For something that counts,
And besides my girl's front teeth are missing."
1942A.

1424

A young baseball-fan named Miss Glend
Was the home-team's best rooter and friend,
   But for her the big league
     Never held the intrigue
Of a bat with two balls at the end.
1943.

1425

I love her in her evening gown,
I love her in her nightie,
   But when moonlight flits
     Between her tits,
Jesus Christ, almighty!
1927.

1426

The favorite pastime of grandfather
Was tickling his balls with a feather.
   But the thing he liked best
     Of all the rest
Was knocking them gently together.
1939A.

1427

A company of Grenadier Guards
While traversing the park, formed in squads,
   Saw two naked statues
     At three-quarter pratt views,
Which perceptibly stiffened their rods.
1941.

1428

There was a young athlete named Grimmon
Who developed a new way of swimmin':
    By a marvellous trick
    He would scull with his prick,
Which attracted loud cheers from the women.

                      1941.

1429

An old Jap samurai named Haki
Once pickled his penis in saki.
    When the thing was quite dead
    He cried with bowed head,
"Banzai! *Requiescat in pace.*"

                      1948A.

1430

A Biblical party called Ham
Cried, "Cuss it, I don't give a damn!
    My father's yard measure
    I view with great pleasure,
Such a bloody great battering ram!"

                      1870.

1431

There once was a lady hand-letterer
Who thought of a program to better her.
    She hand-lettered each
    Of the parts she could reach,
The bosoms, the navel, et cetera.

                      1947B.

1432

There was a young girlie named Hannah
Who loved madly her lover's banana.
    She loved pubic hair
    And balls that were bare,
And she jacked him off in her bandanna.

                      1942.

1433

A sensitive fellow named Harry
Thought sex too revolting to marry.
    So he went out in curls
    And frowned on the girls,
And he got to be known as a fairy.

1941A.

1434

A fine Southern lady named Hentz
Preferred colored boys when she'd yentz.
    She explained, " When they're black
    They've a spring in their back,
And their tools are most always immense. "

1941.

1435

An ingenious young fellow named Herman
Tied a bow on the end of his worm, and
    His wife said, " How festive! "
    But he said, " Don't be restive—
You'll wriggle it off with your squirmin'. "

1941.

1436

There was an announcer named Herschel
Whose habits became controversial,
    Because when out wooing
    Whatever he was doing
At ten he'd insert his commercial.

1949.

1437

There was a young lady named Hicks
Who delighted to play with men's pricks,
    Which she would embellish
    With evident relish,
And make them stand up and do tricks.

1941.

1438

There was a young girl from Hong Kong
Whose cervical cap was a gong.
    She said with a yell,
    As a shot rang the bell,
" I'll give you a ding for a dong. "

                                      1945.

1439

There was a young man in Hong Kong
Who grew seven fathoms of prong.
    It looked, when erect,
    About as you'd expect—
When coiled it did not seem so long.

                                     1948A.

1440

There was a young man named Ignatius
Who lived in a garret quite spacious.
    When he went to his auntie's
    He always wore panties,
But alone in his garret—good gracious!

                                     1939A.

1441

There was a sad prude out in Iowa
Who would say, " Please say it my way :
    Do not say fuck,
    It don't rime with duck.
Say untcay and itshay and uckfay. "

                                     1952.

1442

A sweet young strip dancer named Jane
Wore five inches of thin cellophane.
    When asked why she wore it
    She said, " I abhor it,
But my cunt juice would spatter like rain. "

                                     1934.

1443. BACK FROM BOHEMIA

Said a slant-eyed young jade of Japan,
"I must study under Gauguin!"
    Though he taught her at first,
    Soon their places reversed,
And *she* became Yin, and he Yan.

That horny old rascal, Manet,
While buggering a boy on the Quay,
    Was attacked by a crick
    In the tip of his prick—
"*Merde!*" he cried, "Quick! Baume Bengué!"

A ten-sous *grisette* named Cécile
Thus cautioned another *jeune fille*:
    "Now Dali is jolly,
    But watch him, by golly!
Or he'll stuff up your ass with an eel."

Regardez-vous Toulouse-Lautrec,
Though at first glance an ambulant wreck,
    He could fuck once a week
    A la manière antique,
And once in a while *à la Grecque.*

A lively young thing from Bryn Mawr
Was raped by an ape in the Bois.
    Picasso appeared...
    He coughed lightly and leered,
"*Carajo! C'est Matisse, par ma foi!*"

Van Gogh found a whore who would lay,
And accept a small painting as pay.
    " *Vive l' Art!* " cried Van Gogh,
    " But it's too fucking slow—
I wish I could paint ten a day! "
                                  1941.

1449

For sculpture that's really first class
You need form, composition, and mass.
    To do a good Venus
    Just leave off the penis,
And concentrate all on the ass.
                                 1947B.

1450

There is a young nurse in Japan
Who lifts men by their pricks to the pan,
    A trick of jujitsu,
    And either it shits you
Or makes you feel more like a man.
                                 1942A.

1451

There was a young lady whose joys
Were achieved with incomparable poise.
    She could have an orgasm
    With never a spasm—
She could fart without making a noise.
                                  1941.

1452

Der alt' Philosoph genannt Kant
Hat die reine Vernunft als Trabant.
    Zeit war seine Buhle,
    In seinem Nachtstuhle
Ward die Zukunft des Weltraums gekannt.
                                  1942A.

1453

" Remind me, dear, " said Sir John Keith,
" As soon as I've finished my teeth,
    To take down this glass
    And examine my ass
From behind—and of course from beneath. "

                              1947A.

1454

There was a young lady named Kerr
Whose step-ins were made out of fur.
    When they asked, " Is it fun ? "
    She replied, " It's a son-
of-a-gun to make pussy purr! "

                              1946A.

1455

The prick of a young man of Kew
Showed veins that were azure of hue.
    Its head was quite red
    So he waved it and said,
" Three cheers for the red, white, and blue. "

                            1941*-1951.

1456

A young man who lived in Khartoum
Was exceedingly fond of the womb.
    He thought nothing finer
    Than the human vagina,
So he kept three or four in his room.

                             1943C.

1457

The last time I dined with the King
He did quite a curious thing :
    He sat on a stool
    And took out his tool,
And said, " If I play, will you sing ? "

                                1941.

1458

There was a young lady named Knox
Who kept a pet snake in her box.
    It was trained not to hiss
    When she sat down to piss,
But would nibble the noggins off cocks.

                        1941.

1459

A clever inventor named Krupp
Wore a belt when he wanted to tup.
    His mighty dry cells
    Made her tits buzz like bells,
And lighted the hall-entrance up.

                        1942A.

1460

A whore grown too old to get laid
Turned *parfumeuse,* finding it paid
    To concoct *Fleur de Floozie*
    From the juice of her coosie
(Substantial discount to the trade).

                        1941.

1461

There was a young laundress of Lamas
Who invented high amorous dramas
    For the spots she espied
    Dried and hardened inside
The pants of the parson's pajamas.

                        1941.

1462

There once was a spinsterish lass
Who constructed her panties of brass.
    When asked, " Do they chafe ? "
    She said, " Yes, but I'm safe
Against pinches, and pins in the ass."

                        1951.

1463

A patrician young fellow named Lear
Used to wash off his bollox with beer.
    Said he, " By the gods,
    This is good for the cods—
It will lengthen my fucking career. "

          1941.

1464

A big woolly dog named Lee
Had a host of friends to see.
    So he paced the street
    On all four feet
But visited mostly on three.

          1946A.

1465

A once-famous gatherer of leeches
Has taken to combing the beaches,
    Where he helps all the aunties
    On and off with their panties,
And they help him off with his breeches.

          1942.

1466

There once was a peon named Leon
Who had such a face you could pee on.
    When he said, " Sí, sí, "
    We all made pee-pee
On the face of that peon named Leon.

          1944*

1467

A sadist who lived in Limoges
Used to beat up his wife with his hose.
    He declared, " It is fun
    Before I've begun
To warm her from scalp-lock to toes. "

          1942A.

1468

There once was a girl named Louise
Whose cunt-hair hung down to her knees.
    The crabs in her twat
    Tied the hair in a knot,
And constructed a flying trapeze.

                                         1944.

1469

The team of Tom and Louise
Do an act in the nude on their knees.
    They crawl down the aisle
    While fucking dog-style,
And the orchestra plays Kilmer's " Trees. "

                                         1945.

1470

A cheerful old party of Lucknow
Remarked, " I should just like a fuck now! "
    So he had one and spent
    And said, " I'm content.
By no means am I so cunt-struck now. "

                                         1879.

1471

Have you heard about Magda Lupescu,
Who came to Rumania's rescue?
    It's a wonderful thing
    To be under a king—
Is democracy better, I esk you?

                                         1941.

1472

A golfer named Sandy MacFarr
Went to bed with a Hollywood star
    When he first saw her gash he
    Cried, " Quick, goot muh mashie!
Uh thunk uh c'n muk it in par. "

                                         1946A.

1473

While Titian was mixing rose-madder,
His model posed nude on a ladder.
    Her position, to Titian,
    Suggested coition,
So he climbed up the ladder and had 'er.

          1941.

1474

When Angelico worked in cerise,
For the angel he painted his niece.
    In a heavenly trance
    He pulled off her pants,
And erected a fine altar-piece.

          1942A.

1475

There was a young lady of Maience
Who bade Adolf Hitler defiance.
    She'd lurk in dark halls
    And nip at his balls
With a patent-applied-for appliance.

          1943.

1476

A mason, one of the Malones
Put a coat of cement on his stones.
    " They keep warmer at night,
    And are bound to hang tight,
And not bruise themselves on my knee-bones. "

          1942A.

1477

There was a young girl named Maxine
Who found a new use for the bean.
    As a vaginal bearing
    She found it long-wearing,
And it varied her fucking routine.

          1941.

1478

Beneath a tree one rainy day in May,
A lover and his swooning lady lay.
   He was in her to the hilt,
   And though she was nearly kilt,
She loved it, and kept hollering, " Hooray! "

                                    1941.

1479

A bus-man named Abner McFuss
Liked to suck off small boys on his bus,
   Then go out and sniff turds
   And the assholes of birds—
He sure was a funny old cuss.

                                    1941.

1480

There was an eccentric from Mecca
Who discovered a record from Decca,
   Which he twirled on his thumb
   (These eccentrics are dumb)
While he needled the disc with his pecca.

                                    1951.

1481

There once was a young English miner
Who prospected a bit in North China.
   He described a crevasse in an igneous mass,
   That ran horizontal and sparkled like glass,
As a petrified Chinese vagina.

                                    1945.

1482

There once was a pretty young miss
Who enjoyed watching her lover piss.
   She made him drink water
   Much more than he oughter,
While Pilsner assured her of bliss.

                              1941*-1952.

1483

There was a young man from Mobile
Who wondered just how it would feel
    To carry a gong
      Hanging down from his dong,
And occasionally let the thing peal.

So he rigged up a clever device,
And tried the thing out once or twice,
    But it wasn't the gong
    But rather his prong
That peeled, and it didn't feel nice!

                      1941.

1485

Había una joven modesta
Qui antes se protegia con protesta.
    Pero ahora confiesa
    Que la picha tiesa
Es la cosa lo menos molesta.

                      1944A.

1486

There died an old man of Moldavia,
Well known for his bawdy behaviour.
    When the priest thought him shriven,
    And fitted for heaven,
He cried, " Go and bugger the Saviour! "

                      1870*

1487

There was a young girl of Moline
Whose fucking was sweet and obscene.
    She would work on a prick
    With every known trick,
And finish by winking it clean.

                      1941.

1488

A young Nordic lass in Mombassa
Demanded a piece of hot ass-a,
    But she flew in a rage
    And locked her cunt in a cage
When they brought her King Haile Selassie.

1945.

1489

A musicienne in gay Montebello
Amused herself playing the cello,
    But not a solo,
    For she used as a bow
The dong of a sturdy young fellow.

1942A.

1490

There was a young man named Morel
Who played with his prick till he fell.
    When to get up he started
    He suddenly farted,
And fell down again from the smell.

1943-1951.

1491

There was a young man named Moritz
Who was subject to passionate fits,
    But his pleasure in life
    Was to suck off his wife
As he swung by his knees from her tits.

1941.

1492

There was a young man named Murray
Who made love to his girl in a surrey.
    She started to sigh
    But someone walked by,
So he buttoned his pants in a hurry.

1950.

1493

A young man whose sight was myopic
Thought sex an incredible topic.
    So poor were his eyes,
    That despite its great size,
His penis appeared microscopic.
                                   1941*

1494

A cartographer, Harrison by name,
By projection of balls gained his fame.
    The walls of *his* halls
    Were hung not with balls,
But peculiar distortions of same.
                              1947B-1951.

1495

There was a young farmer of Nant
Whose conduct was gay and gallant,
    For he fucked all his dozens
    Of nieces and cousins,
In addition, of course, to his aunt.
                                     1879.

1496

There was an old girl of Nantucket
Who went down to hell in a bucket,
    And the last words she spoke
    Before the rope broke,
Were: " Ass-hole, you buggers, and suck it! "
                                  1879-1941.

1497

There was a young man from Naragansett
Who colored his prick to enhance it.
    But the girls were afraid
    That ere they got laid
'Twould lose all its color in transit.
                                     1943C.

1498

There was a young lady named Nelly
Whose tits could be joggled like jelly
    They could tickle her twat,
    Or be tied in a knot,
And could even swat flies on her belly.

                    1941.

1499

An Esquimau living near Nome
Erected a sign by his home:
    He hung on his totem
    A jock and a scrotum,
And the hair wore a walrus-tusk comb.

                    1942A.

1500

A hermit who had an oasis
Thought it the best of all places:
    He could pray and be calm
    ' Neath a pleasant date-palm,
While the lice on his ballocks ran races.

                    1942A.

1501

On his honeymoon sailing the ocean
A tightwad displayed much emotion
    When he learned, one fine day,
    He'd been fucking away
What could have been bottled as lotion.

                    1948A.

1502

Have you heard about Molly O'Day
Who always had the time (so they say):
    She opened her crotch
    And pulled out a watch,
Which usually made the boys gay.

                    1942.

1503

There was in Connecticut once
A chap who went strongly for runts.
    Midget parts he collected
    Were all hand-selected
And framed, within miniature cunts.

                    1952.

1504

There was a young man named O'Neill,
Used to play on the old Campanile.
    He made the gong bong
    With the end of his dong—
Now he's trying to get it to heal.

                    1942-1952.

1505

Have you heard of the Widow O'Reilly
Who esteemed her late husband so highly
    That in spite of the scandal,
    Her umbrella handle
Was made of his *membrum virile*.

                    1941.

1506

There was a young student of Oriel
Who flouted the ruling proctorial.
    He ran down the Corn
    With a hell of a horn,
And buggered the Martyrs' Memorial.

                    1941.

1507

There once was a gay young Parisian
Who came to an awful decision:
    For his sexual joys
    He'd have women and boys,
And snakes too—and no supervision!

                    1941.

1508

A young man from Peloponnesus
Seduced all his nephews and nieces.
    At the point of a sword
    He married his ward,
And was the father of triplets, by Jesus.

1941-1947B.

1509

There was an old priest of Penrang,
Wound a spiked ampallang round his whang.
    When they asked, " Why'd you do it ? "
    The priest said, " Oh, screw it!
It's just for the young girls I bang. "

1941.

1510

On May Day the girls of Penzance,
Being bored by a lack of romance,
    Joined the workers' parade
    With this banner displayed:
" What The Pants of Penzance Need Is Ants. "

1941.

1511

There was a young girl of Peru
Who had nothing whatever to do,
    So she sat on the stairs
    And counted cunt hairs—
Four thousand, three hundred, and two.

1941.

1512

As His Holiness signed my petition
He said, " I take this position :
    Here shines a clean mind,
    For nowhere can I find
A single lubricious omission! "

1942A.

1513

For the prick-naming prize of Pinole
This year's winner was Daniel O'Dole.
    He will tell you with bonhommie,
    "I call mine 'Metonymy,'
Because it's the part for the whole."

        1943.

1514

There was a young man of Pitlochry
Whose morals were simply a mockery,
    For under the bed
    He'd a woman, instead
Of the usual item of crockery.

        1941.

1515

There was a young girl with a pretty-ass,
And her habits were neat but invidious.
    She would wipe with a taper
    Of scented blue paper,
Since she was so very fastidious.

Then when she had wiped off her bung
Of the clinkers that thereunto clung,
    She would singe off the hair
    That had sprouted down there,
And would lick her twat clean with her tongue.

        1941.

1517

There was a young fellow named Price
Who dabbled in all sorts of vice.
    He had virgins and boys
    And mechanical toys,
And on Mondays... he meddled with mice!

        1941.

1518

A detective named Ellery Queen
Has olfactory powers so keen,
    He can tell in a flash
    By the scent of a gash
Who its previous tenant has been.

          1945.

1519

There once were a couple of queers
Who loved going on basketeers.
    One preferred, you may guess,
    The right, to left-dress,
But for hangs-in-the-middle—just jeers!

          1942-1952.

1520

There was a young man from Racine
Who was weaned at the age of sixteen.
    He said, " I'll admit
    There's no milk in the tit,
But think of the fun it has been. "

          1947B.

1521

The cock of a fellow named Randall
Shot sparks like a big Roman candle.
    He was much in demand,
    For the colors were grand,
But the girls found him too hot to handle.

          1946A.

1522

A widow who lived in Rangoon
Hung a black-ribboned wreath on her womb,
    " To remind me, " she said,
    " Of my husband who's dead,
And of what put him into his tomb. "

          1941.

1523

There was a young angel named Rayloe
Who hard by his arse wore his halo.
    When asked its intent
    He replied, as he bent,
" It sanctifies those who would play low. "
                  1944A.

1524

There was a young girl named Regina
Who called in a water-diviner,
    To play a slick trick
    With his prick as a stick,
To help her locate her vagina.
                  1941*

1525

There once was a boring young Reverend
Who preached till it seemed he would never end.
    His hearers, en masse,
    Got a pain in the ass,
And prayed—for relief of their nether end.
                  1942*

1526

There was a queer fellow named Rice
Whose sex life was colder than ice,
    But a kindly relation
    Restored his sensation
By covering his penis with lice.
                  1941A.

1527

A prudish young damsel named Rose
Is particular how men propose.
    To " Let's have intercourse, "
    She says gaily, " Of course, "
But to " Let's fuck, " she turns up her nose.
                  1942.

1528

A perverted old barber once said,
" I never can trim a man's head,
   ' Cause I wish that his jowls
    Were nearer his bowels,
And his nose were a pecker instead. "

                                  1941.

1529

There was a young man of St. James
Who indulged in the jolliest games :
   He lighted the rim
    Of his grandmother's quim,
And laughed as she pissed through the flames.

                                  1938.

1530

Said the venerable Dean of St. Paul's
" Concerning them cracks in the walls—
   Do you think it would do
    If we filled them with glue ? "
The Bishop of Lincoln said : " Balls! "

                                  1928.

1531

There was a young man from St. Paul's
Who read *Harper's Bazaar* and *McCall's*
   Till he grew such a passion
    For feminine fashion
That he knitted a snood for his balls.

                                  1944A.

1532

There were three young girls in St. Thomas,
Arrived at a dance in pajamas.
   They got screwed by the drummer,
    And this went on all summer—
I'm surprised that by now they ain't mamas.

                                  1941.

1533

There was a young fellow named Scott
Who took a girl out on his yacht,
    But too lazy to rape her
    He made darts of brown paper,
Which he languidly tossed at her twat.
                      1941.

1534

Said the gay Chatelaine of Shalott,
" I wish I had teeth in my twat.
    For just think, " said she,
    " How nice it would be
To keep all the pricks that I got. "
                      1941.

1535

There was an old man of Shamokin,
Fucked his wife with his wooden leg oaken.
    So quick did he stick her,
    Pretending to prick her,
That he soon had her cunt all a-smokin'.
                      1952.

1536

Said a certain sweet red-headed siren,
" Young sailors are cute—I must try one! "
    She came home in the nude,
    Stewed, screwed, and tattooed
With lewd pictures and verses from Byron.
                      1944A.

1537

A fantastic young Prince of Sirocco
Had erotical penchants roccoco :
    The prick of this Prince
    Was flavored with quince,
And he seasoned his semen with cocoa.
                      1941-1952.

1538

There was a young lady named Smith
Whose virtue was largely a myth.
    She said, " Try as I can
    I can't find a man
Who it's fun to be virtuous with."

                               1945C.

1539

There was once a young man from Snodgrass
Who had dingleberries hanging from his ass.
    He threw them at people
    And shouted from the steeple,
" I fuck you all up the ass! "

                               1950.

1540

There once was a Monarch of Spain
Who was terribly haughty and vain.
    When women were nigh
    He'd unbutton his fly,
And screw them with signs of disdain.

                             1949-1952.

1541

A swami once took Spanish fly
And ran clean amok to Delhi,
    Where he jumped in the Ganges
    And used his phalanges
To comfort the cunts swimming by.

                               1942A.

1542

When the judge, with his wife having sport,
Proved suddenly two inches short,
    The good woman declined,
    And the judge had her fined
By proving contempt of the court.

                               1942A.

1543

"I'll admit," said a lady named Starr,
"That a phallus is like a cigar;
    But to most common people
    A phallic church-steeple
Is stretching the matter too far."

1946.

1544

There was a composer so swell
Who thought screwing to music was hell.
    Everything went fine
    Till he got out of time—
"Say, this isn't Bach, it's Ravel!"

1942.

1545

An erotic neurotic named Syd
Got his Ego confused with his Id.
    His errant libido
    Was like a torpedo,
And that's why he done what he did.

1949-1951.

1546

There was a young fellow named Thrale
Who was hardly what you could call male.
    His libido wasn't channelized
    So he got psychoanalyzed,
And now he can't get enough tail.

1952.

1547

There was a young man named Treet
Who minced as he walked down the street.
    He wore shoes of bright red,
    And playfully said,
"I may not be strong, but I'm sweet."

1944.

1548

There was a young fellow named Tucker
Who rushed at his mother to fuck her.
    His mother said, " Damn!
    Don't you know who I am?
You act like a regular mucker! "

          1952.

1549

A neurotic young man from Tulane
Caused his mother considerable pain.
    He poured nitroglycerin
    Where his dad put his pisser in,
And then threw her under a train.

          1945.

1550

The Vizier of Stamboul, a Turk,
Had an emerald hilt on his dirk.
    But his dong set with rubies
    Drove crazy the pubes
Of ladies who lightened his work.

          1942A.

1551

There was a young tinker of Turkey
Whose rhythm at diddling was jerky.
    At six-eight and four-four
    He was good, and no more,
But he really was great at mazurky.

          1941.

1552

To an ancient divine of Tyrone
Was the art of rebushing cunts known.
    In each cunt he would ram
    A fine, prime raw ham,
And then deftly extracted the bone.

          1941.

1553

There was a young man up in Utah
Who constructed a cundum of pewter.
   He said, " I confess
   You feel nothing or less,
But it makes you as safe as a neuter."

                                1942.

1554

There was a young man from Venice
Who played a good game of lawn tennis.
   But the game he liked best,
   Far more than the rest,
Was played with two balls and a pennis.

                               1945C.

1555

The mathematician Von Blecks
Devised an equation for sex,
   Having proved a good fuck
   Isn't patience or luck,
But a function of y over x.

                                1949.

1556

There was a young female named Ware
Who cut off her pubical hair.
   Then to save the men trouble
   She razored the stubble,
But none of them really did care.

                                1942.

1557

A finicky young whippersnapper
Had ways so revoltingly dapper
   That a young lady's quim
   Didn't interest him
If it hadn't a cellophane wrapper.

                                1941.

1558

Antoinette was a beautiful whore
Who wore fifty-six beads—nothing more.
    They sneered, "Unrefined!"
    When she wore them behind,
So she tactfully wore them before.

1942.

1559

There was a young man who said, "Why
Can't I bugger myself, if I'm spry?
    If I put my mind to it
    I'm sure I can do it—
You never can tell till you try."

1941.

1560

Hickory is the best of wood,
Fucking does a woman good,
    It spreads her thighs,
    Opens her eyes,
And gives her ass good exercise.

1928A-1939*

1561

It's a hell of a situation up at Yale,
It's a hell of a situation up at Yale,
    It's a hell of a situation,
    They are sunk in masturbation,
For there ain't no fornication up at Yale.

Oh, the freshmen get no tail, up at Yale,
Oh, the freshmen get no tail, up at Yale,
    Oh, the freshmen get no tail,
    So they bang it on the rail,
It's the asshole of creation up at Yale.

1928C-1952.

1563. OVER THERE

Oh, the peters they grow small, over there,
Oh, the peters they grow small, over there,
   Oh, the peters they grow small,
   Because they work 'em for a fall,
And then eats 'em, tops and all, over there.

Oh, the pussies they are small, over there,
Oh, the pussies they are small, over there,
   Oh, the pussies they are small,
   But they take 'em short and tall,
And then burns their pricks and all, over there.

Oh, I wish I was a pimp, over there,
Oh, I wish I was a pimp, over there,
   Oh, I wish I was a pimp,
   For I'd give the boys a crimp,
With all my whorey blimps, over there.

Oh, they had a squirt for clap, over there,
Oh, they had a squirt for clap, over there,
   Oh, they had a squirt for clap,
   It was a potent clap trap,
And it burnt our pecker's cap, over there.

1927.

1567. IN MOBILE

Oh, the men they wash the dishes, in Mobile,
Oh, the men they wash the dishes, in Mobile,
   Oh, the men they wash the dishes,
   And they dry them on their britches,
Oh, the dirty sons-of-bitches, in Mobile!

Oh, the cows they all are dead, in Mobile,
Oh, the cows they all are dead, in Mobile,
   Oh, the cows they all are dead,
   So they milk the bulls instead,
Because babies must be fed, in Mobile!

Oh, they teach the babies tricks, in Mobile,
Oh, they teach the babies tricks, in Mobile,
   Oh, they teach the babies tricks,
   And by the time that they are six,
They suck their fathers' pricks in Mobile!

Oh, the eagles they fly high, in Mobile,
Oh, the eagles they fly high, in Mobile,
   Oh, the eagles they fly high
   And from way up in the sky,
They shit squarely in your eye, in Mobile!

1927.

XVII

WEAK SISTERS

1571

There was a young woman from Aenos
Who came to our party as Venus.
   We told her how rude
   'Twas to come there quite nude,
And we brought her a leaf from the green-h'us.
                                            1907*

1572

There was an old man of Boolong
Who frightened the birds with his song.
   It wasn't the words
   That frightened the birds
But the horrible *dooble ong-tong*.
                                            1924*

1573

A girl attending Bryn Mawr
Committed a dreadful faux pas.
   She loosened a stay
   In her decolleté,
Exposing her je-ne-sais-quoi.
                                            1942*

1574

A fanatic gun-lover named Crust
Was perverse to the point of disgust.
   His idea of a peach
   Had a sixteen-inch breech,
And a pearl-handled 44 bust.
                                            1944*

1575

A daring young maid from Dubuque
Risked a rather decided rebuke
    By receiving a prude
    In the absolute nude,
But he gasped, " IF you only could cook! "
                                     1948A.

1576

A wonderful fish is the flea,
He bores and he bites on me.
    I would love, indeed,
    To watch him feed,
But he bites me where I cannot see.
                                     1927.

1577

A lady athletic and handsome
Got wedged in her sleeping room transom.
    When she offered much gold
    For release, she was told
That the view was worth more than the ransom.
                                     1944.

1578

There was a young lady of Joppa
Who came a society cropper.
    She went to Ostend
    With a gentleman friend
—The rest of the story's improper.
                                  1928A-1951*

1579

There was a young girl of Oak Knoll
Who thought it exceedingly droll,
    At a masquerade ball
    Dressed in nothing at all
To back in as a Parker House roll.
                                  1940*-1949.

1580

The cross-eyed old painter McNeff
Was color-blind, palsied, and deaf.
   When he asked to be touted
   The critics all shouted:
" This is art, with a capital F! "

                              1942*

1581

There was a young maid from Madras
Who had a magnificent ass;
   Not rounded and pink,
   As you probably think—
It was grey, had long ears, and ate grass.

                              1940*

1582

In La France once a clevair young man
Met a girl on the beach down at Cannes.
   Said the mademoiselle,
   " Eh, m'sieu, vot ze 'ell?
Stay away where eet ees not son-tan! "

                              1943A.

1583

There was a young maid of Boston, Mass.
Who stood in the water up to her knees.
   (If it doesn't rhyme now,
   It will when the tide comes in.)

                              1941A.

1584

There was an old sculptor named Phidias
Whose knowledge of Art was invidious.
   He carved Aphrodite
   Without any nightie—
Which startled the purely fastidious.

                              1903*

1585

There's a man in the Bible portrayed
As one deeply engrossed in his trade.
    He became quite elated
    Over things he created,
Especially the women he made.

1945.

1586

A king sadly said to his queen,
" In parts you have grown far from lean."
    " I don't give a damn,
    You've always liked ham,"
She replied, and he gasped, " How obscene!"

1943A.

1587

A bather whose clothing was strewed
By winds that left her quite nude,
    Saw a man come along,
    And unless we are wrong
You expected this line to be lewd.

1944*

1588

I sat next to the Duchess at tea.
It was just as I feared it would be:
    Her rumblings abdominal
    Were simply phenomenal,
And everyone thought it was me!

1924*

1589

There's a sensitive man in Tom's River
Whom Minsky's causes to quiver.
    The aesthetic vibration
    Brings soulful elation,
And also is good for the liver.

1946A.

1590

There was a young person of Tottenham
Whose manners, Good Lord! she'd forgotten 'em.
    When she went to the vicar's,
     She took off her knickers,
Because she said she was hot in 'em.
                                  1903*

1591

There was a young lady of Trent
Who said that she knew what it meant
    When he asked her to dine,
     Private room, lots of wine,
She knew, oh she knew!—but she went!
                             1940*-1950.

1592

There once was a fellow named Trete
Who from birth was inclined to be neat.
    He became extra fussy
     When he thought his pants mussy,
And would throw them away in the street.
                                   1939A.

1593

A handsome young widow named Vi
Seduced all the wardens nearby.
    When the siren said: " Woo! "
     What else could they do
To extinguish the gleam in her eye?
                                     1942.

1594

There was a young lady from Waste
Who fled from a man in some haste.
    She tripped as she ran,
     And fell flat on her pan—
She sometimes still dreams that she's chaste.
                                      1942*

1595

There was a young lady from Wheeling
Who was out in the garden a-kneeling,
    When by some strange chance
    She got ants in her pants,
And invented Virginia reeling.

                              1944A.

1596

There was a young woman from Wilts
Who went up to Scotland on stilts.
    When they said, " Oh, how shocking
    To show so much stocking! "
She answered, " Well, how about kilts? "

                            1903-1908*

1597

Said a printer pretending to wit:
" There are certain bad words we omit.
    It would sully our art
    To print the word f—,
And we never, oh never, say sh—! "

                                1940*

XVIII

CHAMBER OF HORRORS

1598
A plump English prof. from Atlanta
Was bloated with bawdy, bold banter.
    He'd sit on his ass
    And let fly his gas
Whenever he sniffed a decanter.
                              1938.

1599
There once was a gangster named Brown,
The wiliest bastard in town.
    He was caught by the G-men
    Shooting his semen
Where the cops would all slip and fall down.
                              1938.

1600
There was a cute quirp from Calcutta
Who was fond of churning love-butta,
    One night she was heard mutta
    That her quim was a-flutta
For the thing she called " Utterly-Utta! "
                              1943.

1601
An unfortunate fellow named Chase
Had an ass that was not quite in place,
    And he showed indignation
    When an investigation
Showed that some people shit through their face.
                              1941.

1602

A young man from famed Chittagong
Worked hard at the stool and worked long.
    He felt a hard mass
    Obstructing his ass,
Then shit and cried, " I shit a gong! "
                              1942.

1603

There was a stout lady of Cuttack
Posteriorly pecked by a wild duck
    Who pursued her for miles
    And continued his wiles
Till he completely demolished her buttock.
                              1943*

1604

It was on the 7th of December
That Franklin D. took out his member.
    He said, like the bard,
    " It will be long and very hard,
Pearl Harbor has given me something to remember. "
                              1942.

1605

There was a young fellow from Eno
Who said to his girl, " Now, old Beano,
    Lift your skirt up in front,
    And enlarge your old cunt,
For the size of this organ is keen-o. "
                              1927.

1606

A maiden who dwells in Galena
Has bubbies of graceful demeanor,
    And whenever she preens
    These astounding poitrines,
She insists upon Simoniz Kleener.
                              1938.

1607

It's a helluva fix that we're in
When the geographical spread of the urge to sin
    Causes juvenile delinquency
    With increasing frequency
By the Army, the Navy, and Errol Flynn.
                            1947B.

1608

To Italy went Sinclair Lewis
Documenting the life led by loose
    American drunks,
    But he unpacked his trunks
' Cause Florence slipped him a goose.
                            1948A.

1609

There was a young fellow named Louvies
Who tickled his girl in the boovies,
    And as she contorted,
    He looked down and snorted,
" My prick wants to get in your movies! "
                            1927.

1610

A person of most any nation
If afflicted with bad constipation,
    Can shove a cuirass
    Up the crack of his ass,
But it isn't a pleasing sensation.
                            1941.

1611

I got this from the fellow what own it :
He declared that he boasted one mo' nut
    Than most people sport,
    But was terribly short
In the part you might stick through a doughnut.
                            1948A.

1612

Said my wife as she stood on a rostrum,
"I don't mind if I don't have colostrum,
    But I'll take an option
    If your child's for adoption—
Though I cannot bear kids, I can foster 'em."
                                 1951.

1613

There was a young man in Schenectady,
And he found it quite hard to erect, said he,
    Till he took an injection
    For deficient erection,
Which in just the desired way effected he!
                               1942-1952.

1614

There was a young student of Skat, ah me!
Who said, "What have these wenches got o' me?
    I have lost father's knees,
    Likewise my pancreas,
And I fear I shall die of phlebotomy."
                                   1938.

1615

An untutored Southwestern solon
Couldn't tell his behind from a hole in
    That good Texas ground
    Till the day that he found
That oil wouldn't come out of his colon.
                                 1948A.

1616

A hopeful young lady of Sukker Barrage
Possessed a big swelling she hoped would assuage.
    On her way to the train,
    She was caught in the rain—
Oh, what a sad tale of hopeless Miss Carriage!
                                   1943*

1617

A horrid old lady of Summit,
Every time she got laid had to vomit,
    And although she would groan
    When her man got a bone,
" Give it here, " she would say, " and I'll gum it. "
                                           1952.

1618

There was a young girl from Vistula
To whom a friend said, " Jeff has kissed you, la! "
    Said she, " Yes, by God!
    But my arse he can't sod,
Because I am troubled with fistula. "
                                           1879.

1619

There was a young man from Wanamee
Well schooled in the technique of sodomy.
    He buggered with glee
    An old man in a tree,
And remarked with a shrug, "Won't you pardon me?"
                                          1946B.

1620

Said a platinum blonde from Warsaw,
As she looked at herself in the raw,
    " 'Neath my umbilicus
    (And as like Mike as Ike is)
There's a picture of George Bernard Shaw. "
                                          1941.

XIX

ADDENDA

1621. LITTLE ROMANCES

The limerick form is complex
Its contents run chiefly to sex.
    It burgeons with virgeons
    And masculine urgeons,
And swarms with erotic effex.
                           1944.

1622

There was a young girl whose frigidity
Approached cataleptic rigidity
    Till you gave her a drink,
    When she quickly would sink
In a state of complaisant liquidity.
                           1945.

1623

There was a young fellow named Lancelot
Whom his neighbors all looked on askance a lot.
    Whenever he'd pass
    A presentable lass,
The front of his pants would advance a lot.
                           1944.

1624

A self-centered young fellow named Newcombe
Who seduced many girls but made few come
    Said, " The pleasures of tail
    Were ordained for the male.
I've had mine. Do I care whether you come ? "
                           1944.

1625

She egged him on with her charms,
And wriggled right into his arms.
    She promised him bliss
    With her first little kiss,
And they soon found themselves in a barn.

She slid under his much-muscled torso
And guided his shaft to her morceau.
    He drilled till she ran
    And dripped into a pan—
She was filled like she'd wished, only more so.

                  1946A.

1627

There was a young lady of Paris
Whom nothing could ever embarrass
    Until one fine day
    In a sidewalk café
She abruptly ran into Frank Harris.

                  1945.

1628. ORGANS

There was a young lady named Alice
Whose ass was as big as a palace.
    Her dresses were tight
    And she made quite a sight
To quicken the pulse of the callous.

                  1944.

1629

In the speech of his time, did the Bard
Refer to his prick as his " yard ,"
    But sigh no more, madams :
    ' Twas no longer than Adam's
Or mine, and not one half so hard.

                  1944-1952.

1630

There was a young fellow named Chubb
Who joined a smart buggery club,
    But his parts were so small
    He was no good at all,
And they promptly refunded his stub.

                      1951.

1631

There was a young girl named Dalrymple
Whose sexual equipment was so simple
    That on examination they found
    Little more than a mound
In the center of which was a dimple.

                      1944.

1632

There was a young lady named Grace
Who had eyes in a very odd place.
    She could sit on the hole
    Of a mouse or a mole
And stare the beast square in the face.

                      1944.

1633

There was a young fellow, McBride,
Who preferred his trade long, thick, and wide.
    But he never rejected
    Anything that erected,
For " Peter is peter, " he sighed.

                      1952.

1634

There once was a writer named Mark
Who encountered a cunt in the dark.
    He said, " Now, by thunder,
    It's a Natural Wonder—
I declare this a National Park! "

                      1944-1952.

1635

Il y avait un jeune homme de Provence
Dont les couilles étaient vraiment immenses.
   " C'est un grand avantage, "
     Disait-il, " quand je nage,
Mais ça gêne quand je baise ou je danse. "
1952.

1636

There was a young man of Provence
Whose bollocks were simply immense.
   " They're an excellent float
     In a bathtub or boat,
But, " said he, " what a bore when I yentz. "
1952.

1637

The nipples of Sarah Sarong,
When excited, are twelve inches long.
   This embarrassed her lover
     Who was pained to discover
She expected no less of his dong.
1944.

1638

A damsel who lives at The Springs
Had her maidenhead ripped into strings
   By a hideous Kurd,
     And now, she averred,
" When the wind blows through it, it sings. "
1944.

1639

A guy with a build that was stallionate
Found it harder than Hades to copulate.
   When sexually charged,
     His appendage enlarged
To the girth of the girl he took out to date.
1952.

1640

A gun-shy recruit from Visalia
Was an absolute infantry failure.
    But he wasn't so dumb
    When it came to a come,
And he knew how to use genitalia.

1942.

1641

A Chinaman hailing from Wusih
Once laid an American floozie.
    " How different, " he cried,
    As he slid it inside,
" To diddle a vertical coozie! "

1944.

1642. STRANGE INTERCOURSE

An opera singer named Black
Would fuck anything with a crack:
    Sidewalks and board fences,
    Young goats and cheese blintzes,
And the cheekiest man in his claque.

1945.

1643

There was a young fellow named Bouch
Who inveigled a girl to a couch.
    He said, " Pretty young miss,
    I will take you, I wiss,
Horizontally, vertically, crouch. "

1945.

1644

The dong of a fellow named Grable
Was as pliant and long as a cable.
    Each night while he ate,
    This confirmed reprobate
Would screw his wife under the table.

1945.

1645

Down in Berne, Minister Grew,
There's nothing that fellow won't screw—
    From queens down to cooks
    They're all on his books,
And he dabbles in sodomy too.

                                     1923*

1646

There was a young person of Kent
Who was famous wherever he went.
    All the way through a fuck
    He would quack like a duck,
And he crowed like a cock when he spent.

                                     1951.

1647

An ardent young man from Naragansett
Was accustomed to fucking in transit.
    He'd catch something neat
    In a Pullman retreat,
Say " How do you do ? " and then pants it.

                                     1945.

1648

There once were two Siamese twins
Who, though plural, had singular sins.
    One preferred buggery,
    The other skullduggery,
Which involved fucking both " widdershins! "

                                  1943-1952.

1649. ORAL, AND BUGGERY

Tiberius sat in his patio
And said, " I don't care for fellatio,
    Nor yet cunnilingus
    Or whatever the thing is—
This headwork is mighty damn rash o' you! "

                                  1943-1952.

1650

A prim young fellatrix named Prue
Said, " There's one thing a nice girl won't do.
    You may *not* touch my rear end,
    But if my up-here end
Appeals, there's a hole in that too. "

                                     1945.

1651

There once was a writer named Twain
Who had a peculiar stain
    Surrounding the head
    Of his prick: it was red,
And was said to wash off in the rain.

                                     1944.

1652

There once was a writer named Clemens
Whose balls were a pair of large lemons.
    To flavor his tea,
    He would jack off with glee,
And drink it down, *tremens et gemens*.

                                     1944.

1653

In the soap-operas heard in Gomorrah,
The heroine wakes up in horror
    To find that a prick
    Nearly three inches thick
Is halfway up her tune-in-tomorrow.

                                     1944.

1654

There was a young man from Peru
Who attempted to bugger a gnu.
    Said the gnu, " Pederasty
    Is decidedly nasty,
But you may slip up my slew for a sou. "

                                     1944.

1655

There was a young lady who said,
As her bridegroom got into the bed,
   "I'm tired of this stunt
    That they do with one's cunt,
You can get up my bottom instead."

                      1951.

1656. ABUSES OF THE CLERGY

A priest from the Isle of Choiseul
Was inordinately proud of his tool,
   So this clerical stallion
    Bred a labor battalion
To build him a chapel and schule.

                      1944.

1657

When the Bishop of Solomons diocese
Was stricken with elephantiasis,
   The public beheld
    His balls as they swelled
By paying exorbitant priocese.

                      1944.

1658

A synod of Anglican friars
Were discussing their carnal desires.
   Said the priest from Tulagi,
    "The Marys are baggy,
But a coconut truly inspires."

                      1944.

1659

A Mexican nun named Sor Juana
Was hot as a wop primadonna,
   But when the old bishop
    Could not get his fish up,
She said, "Anyhow, I don' wanna."

                      1952.

1660

Astute Melanesians on Munda
Heard a Padre discussing the wunda
   Of Virginal Birth;
   They debated its worth,
Then tore the poor Padre asunda.

                                 1944.

1661

The Bishop of Ibu Plantation
Wrote a thesis on Transfiguration
   For the Christian Review
   (As good Bishops do)
Whilst practicing miscegenation.

                                 1944.

1662

The Bishop of Tassafaronga
Could stand his seclusion no longa.
   His habits monastic
   Were very elastic—
But, unhappily, so was his donga.

                                 1944.

1663. ZOOPHILY

There once was a Bactrian camel
Who was bound by no fetter or trammel.
   When he tried to make hay
   In his Bactrian way,
His wife said, "Make me; I'm a mammal."

                                 1943.

1664

There was a young girl from Decatur
Who was fucked by an old alligator.
   No one ever knew
   How she relished that screw,
For after he fucked her, he ate her.

                                 1944.

1665

A zoologist's daughter in Ewing
Gave birth to a bottle of bluing.
    Her father said, "Flo,
    What I want to know
Isn't *whether,* but *what* you've been screwing."

When the girl replied, quick as a wink,
"My child isn't bluing, it's ink,"
    The professor said, "Ah!
    Then, no doubt, its papa
Is the squid that I keep in the sink."

                  1944.

1667

There was a young person of Jaipur
Who fell madly in love with a viper.
    With screams of delight
    He'd retire each night
With the viper concealed in his diaper.

                  1944.

1668

A disgusting young man named McGill
Made his neighbors exceedingly ill
    When they learned of his habits
    Involving white rabbits
And a bird with a flexible bill.

                  1944.

1669

There was an old maid in Nantucket,
Had an asshole as big as a bucket.
    While bent over the oven,
    A-dreamin' of lovin',
Her goat seized the moment to fuck it.

                  1952.

1670

There was a young man who preferred
Having sex with some kind of a bird.
    The rarer the species,
    And the fuller of feces,
The better—that guy really loved turd.
                      1951-1952.

1671

There once was a fellow named Siegel
Who attempted to bugger a beagle,
    But the mettlesome bitch
    Turned and said with a twitch,
" It's fun, but you know it's illegal. "
                            1943.

1672

There was a young fellow named Spratt
Who was terribly sassy and fat.
    He sat amusing himself
    By abusing himself,
While his trained leopard licked at his pratt.
                            1944.

1673

On the plains of north-central Tibet
They've thought of the strangest thing yet:
    On the ass of a camel
    They pour blue enamel,
And bugger the beast while it's wet.
                            1944.

1674

A milkmaid of Warnesby Fair
Was an expert at riding bulls bare.
    Oh how the bulls gallop
    To give that dear trollop
A bounce on the sweet derry-air.
                            1945.

1675

In the quaint English village of Worcester
Lived a little red hen and a rooster.
    A coquettish glance
    She acquired in France
Gave him ants in his pants, and he goosed her.
1944.

1676. EXCREMENT

There's always some one around
Who'd object if I rifted with sound.
    But out in the park,
    At least after dark,
I can make the welkin resound.
1951.

1677

There was a young student of art
Who made a strange anatomical chart:
    In place of the chest
    A grease spot on the vest,
And in place of the asshole a fart.
1944.

1678

There was an old maid from Bruton
Who had the bad habit of pootin'.
    Her sphincter was weak,
    Her wind she couldn't keep—
This tootin' old spinster from Bruton.
1951.

1679

Said a snuff-taking Turk, "Why, with ease
I can stifle the noisiest sneeze."
    But at prayers one day
    His ass-hole gave way,
And the shit filled his drawers to the knees.
1952.

1680

A flatulent nun of Hawaii
One Easter eve supped on papaya,
    Then honored the Passover
    By turning her ass over
And obliging with Handel's Messiah.

1944.

1681

There was a young man from Montmartre
Who was famed far and wide for his fart.
    When they said, " What a noise! "
    He replied with great poise,
" When I fart, sir, I fart from the heart. "

1945.

1682

There was a young man named O'Malley
Who was fucking his gal in the alley,
    When right at the start
    She let a small fart,
Said O'Malley to Sally, " Now r'ally! "

1951.

1683

A stingy old man of St. Giles
Saved his shillings with miserly wiles.
    Just to save a few bob
    He would wipe with a cob,
And that way he got piles and piles!

1941.

1684

Lord Randall, on top of his tart,
Let a horrible, fizzling fart.
    Said the tart, " Now, m'lord,
    I'm taking your word
You did not follow through on the spot. "

1952.

ADDENDA

1685. VIRGINITY, MOTHERHOOD

Down in Rome, Washburn Child,
A lecherous fellow and wild—
   Like his buddy, King Vic,
   He likes thrusting his prick
Into twats hitherto undefiled.

          1923*

1686

There was a marine on Palau
Who looked for a girl to deflower.
   But to his surprise
   The Jap girls run sidewise—
To deflower on Palau takes know-how.

          1944.

1687

The life of a clerk of the session
Was strangled in psychic repression,
   But his maladies ceased
   When his penis uncreased
In straight geometric progression.

          1943-1952.

1688

There was a young lady named Sue
Who preferred a stiff drink to a screw.
   But one leads to the other,
   And now she's a mother—
Let this be a lesson to *you*.

          1945.

1689

The chief charm of a whore in Shalott
Was the absence of hair on her twat.
   She kept it smooth-looking
   Not by shaving or plucking,
But by all of the fucking she got.

          1951.

1690. DISEASES & LOSSES

The rosy-cheeked lass from Dunellen
Whom the Hoboken sailors call Helen,
    In her efforts to please
    Spread social disease
From New York to the Straits of Magellan.
                              1944.

1691

There was a young girl of Mauritius
Who declared, "That last screw was delicious.
    But the next time you come,
    Won't you come up the bum?—
That wart on your cock looks suspicious."
                              1952.

1692

There was a young lady named Bigger
Who said as she squeezed on the trigger,
    "You son of a bitch
    My cunt has the itch,
And *in morte* you may attain *rigor*."
                              1945.

1693

There was a young man of Calcutta
Whose balls were turning to butter.
    In a day of great heat
    The folks had a treat
As his testicles flowed down the gutter.
                              1952.

1694

There was a young woman named Jones
Who midst her screams, her howls and her groans,
    Was raped by a nigger
    Whose tool was no bigger
Than yours or mine—hence the groans!
                              1952.

1695

There was a young man from Kilgore
Who wasted his life on a whore.
    To get an erection
    He took an injection
And shot out his wad on the floor.

                     1942.

1696

There was a young fellow of Rhodes
Whose testicles turned into toads.
    He, horrified, wept,
    As they struggled and leapt:
"Give me back my quiescent old nodes!"

                     1945.

1697

There was a young fellow named Runyan
Whose pecker came down with a bunion.
    When he had an erection
    This painful infection
Gave off a faint odor of onion.

                     1952.

1698

A lady on climbing Mount Shasta
Complained as the mountain grew vaster,
    That it wasn't the climb
    Nor the dirt and the grime,
But the ice on her ass that harassed her.

                     1944.

1699

Œdipus Œdipus Œdipus Smith
Could copulate only with kin and/or kith,
    Till they cut off his penis
    And thereafter Venus
To him was a beautiful, innocent myth.

                     1948A.

1700

There was an old goddess named Venus
Who loved young Adonis' penis.
    When Jupiter, the fool,
      Cut off the boy's tool,
She remarked, " Please don't come between us."
                                      1952.

1701. SEX SUBSTITUTES

There was a young lady named Alice
Who purchased a hard-rubber phallus.
    Since she learned its perfections
      She shuns doctors' inspections—
It is *such* an odd place for a callus.
                                      1944.

1702

There was a young girl named Dalrymple
Whose sexual needs were so simple
    She enjoyed the full spasm
      Of a perfect orgasm
By frigging herself on a pimple.
                                      1944.

1703

To the mountains went sweet Dolly Dare
Intent upon having an affair,
    But her plans they miscarried—
      The guys were all married,
But you can bet she played no solitaire.
                                      1951.

1704

There was a young woman of Geneva
Whose life was all joie de vivre.
    When she grew too old to joie
      She employed a young boy
To restore the joie to her vivre.
                                      1952.

1705

There was a young fellow named Goff
Whose amusement was jacking it off.
    He pulled it so hard
    It stretched out a yard,
And turned to bright blue and fell off.
                                1944.

1706

A morbid young lady named Jean
Was known as the Masochist Queen.
    She used thistles and cacti
    In pursuit of her practi,
In a manner both odd and obscene.
                             1943-1944.

1707

There was a young fellow at Jesus
Who developed a phallic prosthesis.
    He made use of this tool
    To thoroughly fool
All girls who were known as P.T.'s's.
                                1944.

1708

There was a young caveman named Ug
Who stuck his plug in a jug.
    Said Ug with a shrug
    As he gave it a tug,
"Now ain't this a hell of a fug!"
                                1944.

1709. ASSORTED ECCENTRICITIES

There is an old fellow named Brougham
Who reminds me of someone—but whom?
    If only I knew
    I'd get both the two
Together some night, and I'd screw'm.
                                1952.

1710

There was a young fellow named Edward
Who preferred a live trope to a dead word.
    He never would speak
    Of taking a leak,
But instead said his urge was to headward.

                              1950.

1711

Er was eens een juffrouw in Groningen
Die had gruwelijk het land aan verschoningen.
    Zij waste haar fluit
    Maar eens per jaar uit,
En dat was met Driekoningen.

                              1944.

1712

A tea-swilling bookman, Magee,
When he has distant clients to see,
    Always travels by plane
    And if pressed to explain
Says, "I dote on T W A tea."

                              1945.

1713

There was a young man of Manhasset
Whose life seemed excessively placid.
    One day, just for fun,
    He raped an old nun,
And filled up her crevice with acid.

                              1952.

1714

Said a prominent lecherous Nazi,
"Our program may sound hotsy-totsy,
    But a girl, when you diddle her,
    Spreads her thighs with *Heil Hitler!*
And it all seems a little ersatzy."

                              1943.

1715

There was a young lady named Peaches
Who frequented the very best beaches.
    She refused the life-guard,
      Though he breast-stroked her hard—
She preferred to be sucked off by leeches.
                            1952.

1716

A nudist girl wearing three raisins,
A masquerade prize was her goal.
    The judges said, " Lookie,
      From the front she's a cookie,
From the back she's a Parker House roll. "
                            1944*

1717

There was an old fellow named Rapp
Who had a job all considered a snap.
    In the insane asylum
      He'd grade cunts and file 'em,
And bi-weekly he'd rub up their nap.
                            1944.

1718. ADDENDA

Said an old-fashioned god named Anubis,
" I know about pubes and boobies,
    But I've no impression
      About the Eustachian,
Or where the Fallopian tube is. "
                            1952.

1719

There once was a sensitive bride
Who ran when the groom she espied.
    When she looked at his swiver
      They had to revive her,
But when he got it well in, she just sighed.
                            1952.

1720

Ein lustiger Geck namens Franz,
Er zerrte einmal seinen Schwanz.
    Um sein männliches Glied
    Verband er ein Ried,
Nun also ficken er kanns.

                           1952.

1721

Said the horrible whore of Lahore
While ape-fucking against a door,
    " This orang-utang
      Is better than bhang—
The penis of man is quite a bore. "

                    1918*-1952.

1722

There once was a young man named Lanny
The size of whose prick was uncanny.
    His wife, the poor dear,
    Took it into her ear,
And it came out the hole in her fanny.

                           1952.

1723

Two pretty young twins named Mahony
Once tickled a horse's baloney.
    With a spurt and a splash
    They fell with a crash,
And no one knew which had the Toni.

                           1952.

1724

There was a young lady of Norway
Who hung by her heels in a doorway.
    She said to her beau,
  " Look at me, Joe,
I think I've discovered one more way. "

                           1952.

1725

There was a young girl from Odessa,
A rather unblushing transgressor.
    When sent to the priest
    The lewd little beast
Began to undress her confessor.

                  1952.

1726

A scandal involving an oyster
Sent the Countess of Clewes to a cloister.
    She preferred it in bed
    To the count, so she said,
Being longer, and stronger, and moister.

                  1952.

1727

There was a young man from Peru
Whose lineage was noble all through.
    Now this isn't crud
    For not only his blood
But even his semen was blue.

                  1952.

1728

A lecherous priest from Peru
Fucked the deacon's wife in a pew.
    " I'll admit I'm not pious, "
    He said, " I've a bias—
I think it diviner to screw. "

                  1952.

1729

Cleopatra, while helping to pump,
Ground out such a furious bump
    That Antony's dick
    Snapped off like a stick,
And left him to pump with the stump.

                  1952.

1730

A certain young lady named Rowell
Had a musical vent to her bowel.
    With a good plate of beans
    Tucked under her jeans
She could play To a Wild Rose by MacDowell.

              1947B.

1731

The parish commission at Roylette
Bought their vicar a pristine new toilet.
    But he still voids his bowels
    On a heap of old towels,
He's so very reluctant to soil it.

              1949.

1732

There was a young man named Royal
Whose ambition was to be a *moyhel*.
    He worked and he toiled
    But was finally foiled
When he tried it out on a goil.

              1943*

1733

There was a young lady named Shriver
Who was screwed in the ass by the driver,
    And when she complained
    He said, " Sorry you were pained, "
And gave her a fiver to bribe her.

              1952.

1734

A muscular Turk of Stamboul
Tried to screw a recalcitrant mule.
    He climbed on a haystack
    Overlooking a racetrack,
And dived in all covered with drool.

              1952.

1735

There once was an artist named Thayer
Who was really a cubist for fair.
    He looked all his life
    To find him a wife
Possessed of a cunt that was square.
                              1952.

1736

A frugal young fellow named Wise
Gets the most from the dead whores he buys.
    After sporting a while
    As a gay necrophile,
For dessert he has maggot surprise.
                              1952.

1737

A certain professor named Yarrow
Had trouble seducing a sparrow.
    When he'd given up hopin'
    He pried her jaws open,
And filled up her bill with his marrow.
                              1952.

1738. CHAMBER OF HORRORS

A bishop there was of Pyongyang
Who offered an actress his dong.
    She cried, " 'Pon my Seoul
    I have a huge hole,
But your thing's just comme-ci Kumsong."
                              1952.

1739

There was a young man from Saskatchewan
Whose pecker was truly gargantuan.
    It was good for large whores
    And small dinosaurs,
And sufficiently rough to scratch a match upon.
                              1952.

NOTE

The following 16 limerick-sequences, and ballads more or less in the limerick form, are included:

	NUMBER
Alice Blue Gown	43, 45
I Wonder What My Wife Will Want	106
In the Shade of the Old Apple Tree	111
They A' Do't	369
Royal Spasm in Five Fits	510
The Good Ship Venus	523
The Farter from Sparta	740
The Misfortunes of Fyfe	835
Redwing	939
Socially Conscious Pornography	956
Luetic Lament (Venereal Ode)	1075
Anne Cooper Hewitt	1172
Hydraulic Interlude	1331
Social Poise — Sic Transit	1398
Back from Bohemia	1443
Up at Yale, Over There, In Mobile	1561

BIBLIOGRAPHY

Anecdota Americana. Being, explicitly, an anthology of tales in the vernacular. Elucidatory Preface by J. Mortimer Hall [*pseud.*] Anecdotes collected and taken down by Mr. William Passemon [*pseud.*] Pen and ink drawings by Anton Erdman. Woodblocks drawn & cut by Bruce MacAile. Printed and published by Humphrey Adams for The Association for the Asphyxiation of Hypocrites, solely on subscription of its members. 'Boston' [New York: Printed by Guy d'Isère for David Moss, 1927]. (2), xxv, 202 p. 8vo.

Limericks at numbers 200, 206, 211, 428, 436, 479, 481. Reprinted [New York, 1928?] with an extra poem, p. 202, beginning " When I was young, " and the large phallophoric initial A of the original edition (p. 1) omitted. (Note : The pen and ink drawings attributed here to 'Anton Erdman' are reproduced from a French [1920's] edition of Verlaine's *Œuvres libres*.) Expurgated edition (New York, 1933); reprinted, omitting the Preface (1934); revised as *The New Anecdota Americana* (New York, 1944). The first of these contains nineteen limericks expurgated from 'Falmouth'; the revision contains nine.

Anecdota Americana. An Anthology of tales in the vernacular. Edited without expurgation by J. Mortimer Hall [*pseud.*] Second Series. 500 more. With 37 illustrations. 'Boston: Humphrey Adams' [New York] 1934. 224 p. 8vo.

Limericks at numbers 33, 438, 440-446, 503. Not compiled by the editor of the original series.

Anthropophyteia. See SUSRUTA.

A Book of Anglo-Saxon Verse. See DRAKE.

Cleopatra's Scrapbook. 51 B.C. 'Blue Grass, Kentucky' [Wheeling, W.Va.?] 1928 Edition. (4), xxxii, 119 p. 16mo.
    Includes pages 45A-H, and two inserts: a " P Ticket " and a foldover transparency showing a daisy-chain. See note on Limerick 1090.

The Cremorne. A Magazine of wit, facetiae, parody, graphic tales of love, etc. London: Privately Printed [Cameron] '1851' [1882]. 8vo.
    A sequel to *The Pearl* (1879-80). First issue, August 1882, dated 'January 1851.' Issue no. 3 ('March 1851') contains five limericks, p. 87. No later issues have been examined.

Cythera's Hymnal, or Flakes from the Foreskin. A collection of songs, poems, nursery rhymes, quiddities, etc. etc. Never before published. 'Oxford: Printed at the University Press, for the Society for Promoting Useful Knowledge' [London] 1870. (Cum Privilegio.) 85 p. 8vo.
    Contains fifty-one erotic limericks (titled " Nursery Rhymes ") p. 70-82. See 'Pisanus Fraxi' [H. Spencer Ashbee], *Index Librorum Prohibitorum* (London, 1877) p. 185.

[DAVIS]. *The International Set: A Gallery of limerick portraits,* based on a research study by Eric E. St. Aye Scott [pseud.] Boston, 1946. (3), iv, 52 p. 16mo.
    115 limericks, arranged partly by subject, partly by frequency and form, with expurgation of erotic terms (restored here) or substitution of the verb " scrog."

DOUGLAS, Norman (1868-1952). *Some Limericks.* Collected for the use of Students, & esplendour'd with Introduction, Geographical Index, and with Notes explanatory and critical, by Norman Douglas.

[Florence : G. Orioli] Privately Printed, 1928. 97 p. lg.8vo.

Limitation, p. 2 : " This Edition is issued to Subscribers only. It consists of one hundred and ten copies, numbered and signed by the Author, numbers 1-10 being on special paper priced at ten guineas each, and numbers 11-110 at five guineas each. The price of both sets will be doubled after January 31, 1929. The type has been distributed. This copy is No. [*numbered and signed in ink*]. " Bound in gold rough linen.

—*same*. [New York : Printed by Guy d'Isère for David Moss, 1928.] 97 p. lg.8vo.

Limitation, p. 2 : " This book is issued to *Subscribers only*. It is not for sale. The Edition consists of seven hundred and fifty numbered copies, of which three hundred and fifty are for English and four hundred for American collectors. The type has been distributed. This copy is Number —. " Printed on cream-colored heavy wove paper; bound in brown rough linen in imitation of the Florence edition.

There are two further issues of this edition : one [Chicago, c. 1929] on cream laid paper, bound in dark brown buckram; the other [New York, 1940] on white wove paper, bound in gray rough linen.

—*same*. [Philadelphia, 1931] 96 p. 8vo.

Printed on india-colored laid paper; bound in orange cloth, top stained green, cover-title in Black Letter. Point in limitation notice, p. 2 : " Edittion. "

—*same*. [Paris ?] 1929. 97 p. lg.8vo.

Limitation, p. 2 : " This edition is limited to one thousand copies. The type has been distributed. This is number [*machine-numbered*]. Printed in Germany ." (Title-page lacking in copy collated.)

—*same*. [Paris : Obelisk Press] Privately Printed, 1939. 118 p. sm.8vo.

Limitation, p. 6 : " This integral edition, printed for and with the licence of the author, is complete and unexpurgated, and limited to one thousand copies. This is number [*machine-numbered*]. Printed in France." Colophon, p. 118 : Georges Frère, Tourcoing. In copy no. 713, sent by Douglas to a friend in America in 1950, the words in the limitation, "*printed for and with the licence of the author,*" are underlined, with a marginal asterisk and the note, "What next!" In the same copy, p. 84 (in the original edition, p. 67; Limerick 489* here), the misprint of " to the pure all things are puer " (with two "pures") is marked.

—*same.* 'Boston : Nicholson and Whitney, 1942' [Paris : Obelisk Press ? c. 1950]. 118 p. sm.8vo.

Copyright [!] p. 8 : " Copyright, 1928, By Hutchinson & Poole. Printed in the U.S.A." Limitation, p. 118 : " One thousand copies of this edition were printed by The Brownbent Press, Boston, Mass. Copy No. [*machine-numbered*]."

Note : A mimeographed edition, stitched, made in San Francisco, c. 1947, has been reported but not seen. See also *From Bed to Verse* (1945). All editions of Douglas contain 68 limericks.

[DRAKE]. *A Book of Anglo-Saxon Verse.* Newly arranged and edited. With notes by various hands. 'Nantucket' [Oakland, Cal.] 1949. (66), 32 p. 8vo.

Unbound sheets. 161 limericks, with an Index of Rimes. " Printed on the Concavo-Convex Press in Racine."

'FALMOUTH, John.' *Ninety-five Limericks.* A Contribution to the folk lore of our time. Collected and edited by John Falmouth [*pseud.*] Suffern, N.Y. : Limerick Press, 1932. (10), xcv p. 16mo.

Publicly published. Erotic terms letter expurgated with xxxx's (restored here). All but fifteen of the limericks are from Douglas and *Immortalia.*

Farmer Gray. [Overseas? U.S. Marine Aircraft Group 94, c. 1945.] 9 p. mimeographed.
   Seventy limericks, numbers 9, 42, and 54 missing in transcript used. See Note 496.

From Bed to Verse. An unabashed anthology. Being a collection af [*sic*] the world's best-loved feelthy limericks, collected with diligence and industry by divers idle hands for the amusement and delectation of some members of the Army of Occupation in Germany, and their friends. [Wiesbaden,] Germany: Very privately printed, 1945. 20 p. sm.8vo.
   Douglas' limericks, without his notes, followed by fourteen others.

'HALL, J. Mortimer.' See *Anecdota Americana*.

'HARDER, Richard Offenbach.' See WOOD.

[HARRISON]. MS., New York, 1947.
   A general collection, including fifty limericks, probably original, not found elsewhere.

Heated Limericks. 'Paris' [Havana]: Privately printed for Erotica Biblion Society, 1933. 12 p.
   Not seen. Possibly a reprint of 'Falmouth' or Douglas.

Immortalia. An Anthology of American ballads, sailors' songs, cowboy songs, college songs, parodies, limericks, and other humorous verses and doggerel now for the first time brought together in book form. By A Gentleman About Town. [Philadelphia:] One thousand copies ... privately printed for subscribers. None is for general sale. 1927. (1), iii, 184 p. lg.4to.
   103 limericks, p. 156-176, in a separate roman-numeralled series, much poorer in quality than the rest of the collection. Offset reprint [New York, c. 1932] 8vo.

Index Limericus. MS., Berkeley, Cal., 1941-47.
  Card index, including all the limericks in *Immortalia*, Douglas, 'Falmouth,' *Pornographia Literaria, That Immoral Garland, Unexpurgated*, and *Farmer Gray*, with 330 new examples from the transactions of the American Limerick Society, in Berkeley, 1942-47.

An Investigation into the epistemology and classification of limericks. [Rochester, N.Y. : U.S. Army Medical Corps, 1943.] Mimeographed.
  A small but spirited collection.

'JONES, Dave E.' *A Collection of sea songs and ditties* from the stores of Dave E. Jones [pseud.; U.S., c. 1928]. (2), 48 p. sq.16mo.
  Mostly ballads, including eleven limericks. Hole for padlock through outer edges of pages and canvas wrapper.

LA BARRE, Weston. "The Psychopathology of drinking songs," in *Psychiatry* (Washington, May 1939) v. 2 : p. 203-212.
  No examples. Quoted in the present text from MS. (104 limericks, mostly from *Immortalia*) with additions to 1946.

Lapses in Limerick. MS., Ann Arbor, Michigan, 1935-38.
  Includes all the limericks in *The Pearl, Immortalia*, Douglas, 'Falmouth,' and *Anecdota Americana* II, with 350 new examples orally collected—" all metrically perfect " [*n.b.*] Quoted here from the partial revision, N.Y., 1941.

[MORSE]. *The Limerick : A Facet of Our Culture.* A study of the history and development of the limerick, ensplendor'd with over two hundred examples of the immortal verse form, commentaries, and index. Annotated and unexpurgated. Privately printed. For private circulation to subscribers only. No copies for general sale. 'Mexico City : Cruciform Press, 1944' [U.S., 1948]. (6), vii, 157 p. 8vo.

Errata-slip tipped to p. *149a.* Date 1948, p. 11; and other dates after 1944, *passim.* 276 limericks, mostly from *Immortalia,* Douglas, and *The Pearl.* There is a companion volume, *Folk Poems And Ballads: An Anthology* ('Mexico City: Cruciform Press, 1945') published simultaneously.

N.Y., 1941 (MS.)

A partial revision of *Lapses in Limerick,* enlarged (to 658 examples) with about 100 new examples orally collected, 1938-41. An additional group, collected N.Y., 1944-52, is included here.

The Pearl. A monthly journal of facetiae and voluptuous reading. 'Oxford: Printed at the University Press' [London: Cameron] 1879-80. 3 v. 8vo.

Edited and partly written by the publisher, Cameron. Eighteen monthly issues, from July 1879 through December 1880, the first six containing 61 (of 65) limericks, titled "Nursery Rhymes." All issues are erroneously dated 1880 in the American reprint, c. 1932 ('London: Printed for the Society of Vice, 1880'). See also *The Cremorne.*

Poems, Ballads, and Parodies. A volume of collected verse hitherto unpublished. 'Benares—Paris: Published for distribution among members only, and not for sale, by Benardin Society, 1923' [Detroit: McClurg? c. 1928]. 60 p. 12mo.

Includes ten limericks. Union label, p. 3: "Allied Printing Trades Council. Union Label. Detroit, Mich."

Pornographia Literaria. [U.S., c. 1941] Mimeographed.

In spite of the similar number of limericks (68), an entirely different collection from Douglas'.

'SCHWEINICKLE, O. U.' *The Book of a Thousand Laughs.* By O. U. Schweinickle [pseud.] "Oh, die Gedanken, wie die stanken, Aus des Arschlock eines Kranken." [Wheeling, W.Va.? 1928.] cover-title, 96 p. 12mo.

Begins with seventeen limericks, p. 1-6, and Skinner (Limerick 97*), p. 41; followed by jokes, reprinted from *Anecdota Americana,* and ending with twelve " Frau Wirtin " verses (see WELLS) and " Baron Mikosch " anecdotes in Pennsylvania Dutch.

' SCOTT, Eric E. St. Aye. ' See DAVIS.

Songs My Mother Never Taught Me. [New York: Pershing Rifles, City College, 1944.] Mimeographed.
With a short section of limericks, titled " Shitty Ditties. "

SUSRUTA II, Dr. in S. " Englische Volklieder aus Indien, " in *Anthropophyteia* (Leipzig, 1910) v. 7: p. 375. — " Englische Soldatenlieder aus Zentralindien, " *same* (1911) v. 8 : p. 374.
Six limericks collected in India.

That Immoral Garland. Being a collection of previously unpublished limericks from the literary remains of my uncle, who gave me permission to offer them ten years after his death. From the Sign of the Lampadophore, 1941. [MS., Berkeley, Cal., 1942.]
Introduction signed, ' Norman Douglas, Amalfi, 1917 '. " Apology of the Executor " dated 1942. 106 original limericks, only three beginning with the inactive " There was. " With excursi to the first sixty, Index, and Bibliography in the manner of Douglas. See also Limericks 229, 1659, 1718.

Unexpurgated. Bidet Press [Los Angeles, 1943]. (8), 65 p. 8vo.
169 limericks, followed by " Socially Conscious Pornography, " a limerick-sequence in fifteen stanzas and chorus (Limericks 956-971). Reprinted without title: " Edited by R. Schloch, Ph.D. [*pseud.*] " The Open Box Press [California, *ante* 1951]. (5), 64 p. 8vo.

WELLS, F. L. "Frau Wirtin and associates: A note on alien corn," in *American Imago* (South Dennis, Mass., March 1951) v. 8 : p. 93-97.

No examples. Parallels the German "Frau Wirtin" verses (see SCHWEINICKLE) with rhyme-words and themes of 57 English-language limericks. See Note 1730.

[WOOD, Clement, 1888-1950]. *The Facts of Life — In Limericks.* Erotologically classified. With a Preface by Richard Offenbach Harder, Ph.D. [*pseud.*; Delanson, N.Y., 1943]. 26 p. (including cover-title) 8vo.

92 limericks, arranged by subjects.

Yale Tales. [Pittsfield, Mass., 1952.] 4 f., f°.

Mimeographed. 80 limericks (about 15 new), followed by "The Good Ship Venus." No title. See Limericks 1722-1739.

NOTES & VARIANTS

NOT-QUITE LIMERICKS: Here's To It, 367; It's Only Human Nature, 368; Berries, 452; Calcutta Curio, 459; Who'll Bugger the Turk? 521; The Dean Undressed, 572; The Book of God, 573; Gracie Allen, 648; Iowa, 708; Tom, Tom, the Piper's Son, 739; Sons-a-Bitches, 752; Helicopter, 868; God Damn Her, 921; Five-and-Ten, 925; Old King Cole, 933; Ten-Ten-Tennessee, 1108; The Spanish Nobilio, 1112; I Lost My Arm, 1130; Screwy Dick, 1155; The Village Smith, 1356; Don't Dip Your Wick, 1360; The Girl I Left Behind Me, 1425; Grandfather's Balls, 1426; Hickory Wood, 1560; Boston, Mass. 1583; Parker House, 1716.

LITTLE ROMANCES

1. ABERYSTWYTH (Abersquith, Allawisquith, Aquistwith, Drisquith, Ipswich, Ipswith, Twistwith). Attributed to Swinburne by Norman Douglas (1928) giving lines 1-2 only, and to George Bernard Shaw by 1943. Variants: a " young man "—

   He found there a lass
   Whom he laid on her ass   [1946A.

A " young couple "—

   They fell on the track
   And she lay on her back,
And they connected the things that they pissed with.
                                        [1928B.

(This version is followed by the gonorrheal sequel, Limerick 1071.)

There was a young pair of Aberystwyth
Who united the organs they kissed with.
  But as they grew older
  They also grew bolder,
And united the organs they pissed with.   [1938.

Who had some friends they played whist with.
  They were accustomed, when able,
  To reach under the table
And tickle the things that they pissed with. [1941A.

  One day they were found
  Lying flat on the ground
Playing games with the things that they pissed with.
           [1943C.

2. Who said, " Do you call that a hard-on ? "
           [1952.

4.   But I find when I fuck her,
   Her cunt's lost its pucker   [1941.

5. BERLIN (Flynn, Lynn, Wynn).

  But try as he might
  To do the job right   [1949*

6. She was shrewd, but I proved myself shrewder.
           [1943C.

  The girl was a virgin
  And needed no urgin'—   [1941.

  One night on the Lido
  She aroused my libido—   [1943B.

10. Who thought he'd at last found a tight 'un.
  He said, " Oh my love,
  It fits like a glove "—   [1927.

There was a young lady of Brighton
Whose C.U.N.T. was a tight 'un.
   If you give a good shove
   It will fit like a glove,
But excuse me, you're not in the right 'un.   [1882.

13. Lines 1-4 in Aldous Huxley's *Eyeless in Gaza* (1936).

16. Double pun on kiddie-car and " par " (father, also the proper number of strokes — in golf).

17. The place where my pisser and farter is.   [1927.

18. CHESTER (Leicester, Lester). Compare Limerick 7. A clean version is used as a sample in the New York Sunday *News* $1,000 limerick contest, June 10, 1951, suburban ed., p. 3, with illustration showing the bride in bed looking daggers at her mother, who is saying :

  " This man that you've won
    Should be just loads of fun.
  Since tea he's kissed me and your sister. "

19. The favorite limerick of the compiler's wife.

20. *The Country Plumber's Catalog* (Minneapolis, c. 1935) gives last line as : " Who played all her soft little ditties. "

21. A sexagenarian colonel
Considered himself ever-vernal.
   It was thought, though, his prick
   Was as soft as a wick,
And lifeless, except in a urinal.   [1944.

23. There was a young lady of Diss
Who went to the river to piss.
   The men in the punt
   Shoved the pole up her cunt,
And gave her most exquisite bliss.   [1870.

25. Amorous Bachelor: "Let's go out in the gloaming."— Practical Widow: "It'll be more comfortable on the sofa."

28. DUMFRIES (Breeze, Louise, St. Bees, Tees). Ambisextrous: "There was a young *girl*..."

> He said to her, "Miss,
> Take a firm hold of this,
> But be devilish careful of these." [1945.

> It would double my bliss
> If while pulling on this
> You would rub round and round upon these. [1952.

30. "To teach thee, I am naked first; why then, What needst thou have more covering than a man." —John Donne, *Elegies* (MS. c. 1595; ed. 1669) XIX. "To his Mistris Going to Bed."

31. And one went so far
    As to wave from his car [1943B.

> There was one so depraved
> That he actually waved [1946B.

First publicly printed in *The World's Best Limericks* [ed. Peter Beilenson] (Mount Vernon, 1951).

32. "Here's one thing that Roosevelt can't ration!" [1943.

34. FLYNN (Lynn, Min). *Immortalia* (1927): "Who thought that to love was a sin." Falmouth (1932), expurgating this, gives: "Who thought that to XXXX was a sin." On the expurgation that creates sexual terms where none existed, see Kendall Banning's Censored *Mother Goose Rhymes* (N.Y., 1926) and *Purified Proverbs* (N.Y., 1930); and Robert Carlton ("Bob") Brown's *Gems : A Censored Anthology* (Cagnes-sur-Mer, 1931).

41. There was a young girl from Granada
    Who swore no man ever had made her.
        But they found on the grass
        The marks of her ass,
    And the knees of the last one who'd laid her.
    [1943B.

44. (2nd verse):
    Then he turned her around to the front
    And he took a good look at her cunt   [1950.

45. Version B of "Alice Blue Gown," from *North Atlantic Squadron* (caption-title, mimeo, Gander Bay, Newfoundland, 1944).

47. It's winter outside, the winds roar,
    While inside you sneeze and you snore.
        You can't go canoein'
        To get in your screwin'
    But a lot can be done on the floor.   [1941.

48. And a voice from the thicket said, "Thanks!"
                                                 [1944.

51. HUGHES (Clewes, Toulouse).

56. KHARTOUM (Bloom, Broom, Brougham, Groom, Muldoon, Rangoon). Limerick version of the Oscar Wilde joke: "H'all right, guv'nor, but 'oo does wot to 'oo, an' 'oo pyes?"

    There was a hot twot from Khartoum
    Took a cocksucker up to her room.
        She said, "Now we're here
        Let's get this all clear—   [1943B.

        And they argued a lot
        About who would do what
    And how and with which and to whom.   [1941.

        "Why you son of a bitch,
        You don't know which is which,
    Who does what, why, and to whom!"   [1939A.

[373]

57. With her petticoats up, in the hay. [1952.

" Maidenheads are for ploughboys."— Dr. Johnson.

60. LEIGH (Dee, Dundee, Lea, Lee). One of the most famous limericks, noted as his favorite by Arnold Bennett, in Langford Reed's *The Complete Limerick Book* (1924; ed. 1926) p. 116. The plumber's response varies greatly in the texts : " Don't worry —Don't be silly—If anyone's coming—Hurray—Never mind (*or* fear)—Keep on fucking—Aha—*and* O.K. " Also told, mid-1930's, as a joke, of Marlene Dietrich accepting flowers in the nude in her dressing-room from a messenger boy : " Run along now, I hear somebody coming. "—" You have wonderful hearing, Miss Dietrich—it's me! " Compare John Wilmot, Earl of Rochester, *Sodom* (MS. 1668? ed. Paris, 1904) p. 28-9, Princess Swivia, wishing to excite her brother, Prince Pricket, to a second try, suggests :

Stroke cunt and Thigh... Now kiss my Dear Feel on my breasts... Oh never fear, Thrust out your spirits with all might and main. I hear one coming, put it in again.
(*Enter* CUNTICULA, *drunkish*.)

61. FRANÇOIS (Blois, Dubois). Often given in English, as the preceding limerick, with the rhymes " François, " " in the Bois, " and " C'est moi. "

62. There was a young plumber named Grinnig
Who was plumbing his girl *recht wahnsinnig*.
    When the girl said, " Stop plumbing,
    I hear someone coming! "
Said the plumber named Grinnig, " *Das bin ich!* "
[1945.

64. MCGUZZUM (Van Guzen).

65. With tag-ends for lines 1, 2, 5 : " Ph.D., " " N.B.C. " (National Baking Company), and " P.D.Q. " (pretty damn quick).

[374]

66. A bitch and a fake and a fraud.
        At a dance, I am told,
        She'd wear pants, and act cold,
    But on the veranda—my God!   [1948A.

71. Noblesse oblige.

72. NAHANT (Grant, the Levant).

73.   She said, " You're lazy! "
        He said, " You're crazy—"   [1952.

74.   He went out one day,
        For a damned long way—
    Right up the Suez Canal.   [1928.

77.   Said he, " Yes, it's a fuck,
        And you're shit out of luck—"   [1941.

78.   Said the girl, very rude,
    " I enjoy being screwed—"   [1941.

80. PITLOCHRY (Dockery, Pittochery). " U.S.A. version : "
      She said, " Oh, you've shot
        All over my twat—"   [1948A.

82. Obviously a reaction to the more exotic types. Compare Limerick 52.

86. Unorthodox rhyme. Compare Limerick 55, and the group listed before Note 1. " Stewed, screwed, and tattooed : a sailor's good time. " (Compare Limerick 1536.) Also : " A shower, a shave, and a shit. "

87. " Frigging " here seems to mean fucking.

91. Thomas Hamilton, Earl of Haddington, *Select Poems on Several Occasions* (c. 1730) Tale 37, " The Rebuke, " (ed. 1824) p. 198, ends :

"Thy p—k," she cry'd, in great surprise,
"A p—k, and of so small a size!
It either is your little finger,
Or you're a vile Italian singer."

95. Man on top of woman
Hasn't long to stay,
His head is full of nonsense
His ass is full of play.
He goes in like a lion,
He comes out like a lamb,
And when he buttons up his pants
He isn't worth a damn.   [New Jersey, 1942.

97. As first recorded, in *Anthropophyteia* (1911), the extra line, "The dinner, not Skinner!" is already present. The explanatory seventh line first in *Pornographia* (c. 1941); the Tupper-topper—Skinner as repeated by an Englishman—first in *Unexpurgated* (1943).

99. Written by the compiler, 1939. First printed by Davis (1946) with first line: "My dear Mrs. Ormesby-Gore." Variant from England, 1947:

"It's no good," said Lady Maud Hoare,
"I can't concentrate any more.
   You're all in a sweat
   And the sheets are quite wet,
And just look at the time—half past four."

101. Many texts give "*no* education." Variant:

Making love to a bitch
In—I won't say a ditch—
But terrain having *no* elevation.   [1941.

102. STONE (Bayonne, Joan, Scone, Sloan).

106. Slightly expurgated version, "I wonder what my wife will want to eat [!] tonight," in *The Country*

[376]

Plumber's Catalog (Minneapolis, c. 1935), an illustrated toilet-paper packet.

116. Two little girls from Twickenham,
Two little boys with their prick in 'em,
    They lay on the sward
    And prayed to the Lord
To lengthen and strengthen and thicken 'em.
[1941.

117. In a hammock a fellow named Bliss
Was screwing a cautious young miss.
    She wriggled and squirmed
    So as not to get spermed,
And they ended up something like this. [1941.

120. "Little Brown Jug," a popular American jig song in praise of a jug of whiskey. Compare Alexander Pope, *The Rape of the Lock* (ed. 1714) IV. 54: "And maids turned bottles, call aloud for corks." See also the girl's invitation, (ed. 1712) II. 19, to "seize Hairs less in sight, or any hairs but these!" (ed. 1714, end of Canto IV.)

ORGANS

126. Adam's activity varies: "Disporting himself with his madam—Stroking the thighs—Caressing the rump—And played with the butt—Caressing the tits—Fondling the breasts of his madam."

    No one else in creation
    Could enjoy such sensation. [1942.

Morse (1948) notes the relation to the "Ode on the Antiquity of Fleas" (Adam had 'em).

127. Said she, "I am not!
I've a sweet little twat,
And a *very* nice, neat little figua!" [1941.

[377]

Re-parodied (from a clean original):

There was a young man from Antigua
Who said to his girl, " What a prig you are!
    Whenever we lay
    You refuse to display
The nethermost parts of your figuah! "   [1948A.

128. Compare Limericks 144, 160.

130. BENGAL (Nepal, St. Paul). Morse (1948) notes the reminiscence of the ballad " No Balls At All, " a bawdy parody (of unknown age) of William Allen Butler's " Nothing to Wear, " in *Harper's Weekly* (1857), with which compare:

    But some meddlesome bitches
    Once pulled down his breeches,
When lo! He'd no bollocks at all.   [1870.

    His wife grew suspicious
    And pulled down his britches

    Some women took pity
    And formed a committee

    Till frenched in the shade
    By a sharp-toothed maid   [1942-44.

A graduate student named Sol
Was accused of having one ball.
    He shrieked, " It is true,
    But what can one do,
When to Pater one has given one's all? "   [1944.

131. *That Immoral Garland* (1942) giving variants:

She could oil it in case it got rough.
And could slide up and down like a cuff.
And was caked like an old powder-puff.
—but she couldn't contract it enough.

134. On the acoustical aspect, compare Dr. Zuck, Limerick 365. On size, compare the following variant with Limerick 246:

>   It was so deep and so wide
>   You could go camping inside,
> Provided you brought your own tent. [1948.

136. I've a question to ask you, Miss Russell,
   Is all that development muscle?
     Or can that enormity
     Be a deformity—
   For instance an out-of-place bustle? [1944A.

On the much-publicized bosom of the movie actress, Jane Russell, but compare the equally busty and far more famous Lillian Russell, Note 1645.

138. BULGARIA (Bavaria). Variants in the couplet: Peru (Baloo, Corfu).

141. CHINA (South Carolina).

145. See Note 1637.

152. DETECTIVE (Bective). Often "lynx-eyed detective." A version beginning "Said the duke to the duchess, elective," is publicly printed in Francis Leo Golden's *For Doctors Only* (N.Y., 1948) chap. V, "Calling Doctor Kinsey."

   Said the Duke to the Duchess of Bective,
  "Though foreshortened, of course, in perspective,
     Ain't your easterly tit
     Just the teentsiest bit
   To the west—or's my eyesight defective?" [1941.

153. An obvious clean-up is printed in Clement Wood's *A Book of Humorous Limericks* (Girard, Kansas, 1926; Little Blue Book 1018), calling the original "entirely unprintable" (p. 8):

[379]

>   Her lips she'd compress
>   To a pin-point, or less,
> Or roll them out round, like a quoit.

155. DEVIZES (Assizes, Charizes, Das Vizes, Vinsizes).
Variant line 4:

>   It went twice round his knees   [1947B.

156. Translating the variant of Limerick 155:

>   One was so small
>   It was nothing at all,
> The other took numerous prizes.   [1928.

160. FLORIDA (Ecuador).

There once was a gay young toreador
Who married a lousy old whoreador.   [1939A.

Got stuck on a nasty old, horrid whore.   [1927A.

>   When she opened her thighs
>   He exclaimed in surprise: [1932-1941.

>   He got up in the dark
>   And was heard to remark: [1927.

>   But exclaimed with disgust
>   At the very first thrust: [1949.

>   He probed her vagina
>   And fell clear through to China
> Shouting, " This ain't a cunt, it's a corridor! "
>   [1948A.

166. GLENGOZZLE (Dolmossal, Jossyl, Mosul, Schnossel, Throstle, Wrossil).

167.   And preserved every stool,
           Which he wound on a spool   [1949.

[380]

And his wife was quite pleased
For it tousled and teased
And tickled her twat in the scrimmage.   [1941.

169. HALL (Gaul, Paul, St. Gall, St. Paul, Trinity Hall). The texts show great variation in both the form of the ball (hexagonal, elliptical, rectangular, triangular, and simply, " mathematical ") and the exact fraction of fuck-all: one third (also two thirds) of three fourths, four fifths of five fourths, three eighths of five twelfths, nine tenths of two thirds, and eight times the sine. Compare the masturbation (" five against one ") numbering poem:

Six times six are thirty-six
And one are thirty-seven—
I don't care if I go crazy,
As long as I get to heaven.   [Pa., c. 1934.

170. There was a young fellow of Harrow
Who feathered his cock like an arrow.
" And there's room for improvement, "
Said his girl, " in the movement—
Make it flutter about like a sparrow. "   [1941.

172. With this Venus' fly-trap compare Limericks 228, 301, and 1498.

174. Which allowed him to fuck
While enjoying a suck,
With reserves in case aught should go wrong. [1949.

The author writes, in Drake's notes (1949), concerning the erroneous version above: " Since this is not only my own composition, but my favorite of all my works in this form, I am hardly capable of an unprejudiced judgment; but I must protest this rewrite... what I seriously object to is the change in the young man's character. Here he becomes shrewdly calculating; in the original he represented a fine acme of carefree abandon. Here he resembles a miser; in the original he was like the man who, having money over and above the needs of his existence, delightfully squanders it on the absurdities of pleasure."

178. KANSAS (Costanza, Fort Franza). General Carranza: a well-bewhiskered luminary of the 1911 revolution in Mexico.

183. LAHORE (Bangore, Belgore, Bryn Mawr, Samoa, Tagore). Compare Limerick 1020.

> Who got his prick caught in the door.
>   The stump fitted key-holes
>   And debutante pee-holes [1941.

185. Clement Wood, whose Little Blue Book collection (1926) gives a clean-up, ending "And he couldn't sit down for the weeds," gives, in his privately printed collection (1943B), a version with a young lady:

> She'd a fine growth of grass
> On her tits and her ass,
> But her cunt was all covered with weeds.

187. One of the few Learic last lines—adjective and all—in this collection, and *it* is wrong! (The young lady of the first line becomes old in the last.)

191. There was a princess of Bengal
Whose cunt was excessively small.
>   She said, " It would be
>   Much simpler for me
> To do without fucking at all." [1941.

195. MADRAS (Alsace, Belfast, Cass, Glass).

> Whose bollox were made of cut-glass. [1941.
>
>   They would tinkle and swing
>   And play " God Save the King " [1952.

And his wife was quite pleased
For it tousled and teased
And tickled her twat in the scrimmage. [1941.

169. HALL (Gaul, Paul, St. Gall, St. Paul, Trinity Hall). The texts show great variation in both the form of the ball (hexagonal, elliptical, rectangular, triangular, and simply, " mathematical ") and the exact fraction of fuck-all: one third (also two thirds) of three fourths, four fifths of five fourths, three eighths of five twelfths, nine tenths of two thirds, and eight times the sine. Compare the masturbation (" five against one ") numbering poem:

Six times six are thirty-six
And one are thirty-seven—
I don't care if I go crazy,
As long as I get to heaven. [Pa., c. 1934.

170. There was a young fellow of Harrow
Who feathered his cock like an arrow.
 " And there's room for improvement, "
 Said his girl, " in the movement—
Make it flutter about like a sparrow. " [1941.

172. With this Venus' fly-trap compare Limericks 228, 301, and 1498.

174. Which allowed him to fuck
 While enjoying a suck,
With reserves in case aught should go wrong. [1949.

The author writes, in Drake's notes (1949), concerning the erroneous version above: " Since this is not only my own composition, but my favorite of all my works in this form, I am hardly capable of an unprejudiced judgment; but I must protest this rewrite... what I seriously object to is the change in the young man's character. Here he becomes shrewdly calculating; in the original he represented a fine acme of carefree abandon. Here

New York State Medical Society (1866) p. 256-61, and figs. 39-43; stated to be, p. 258: "a Gipsey, about 22 years of age, and with extraordinary animal passions; the sight of a female is sufficient to excite his amorous propensities. He functionates with both the penes, finishing with one, and then continues with the other..." The record of the same case in *The Lancet* (London, 1865) v. 2: p. 124, takes a more moderate view: "It is true that the right penis is somewhat smaller in circumference than the left, but he [Dos Santos] states that they were originally of the same size. He habitually uses the left in sexual intercourse."

204. A young lady of immoral proclivity
Had an odd perineal sensitivity. [1943C.

205. There was a young fellow named Thwart
Whose prick, although thick, was quite short.
   But to make up this loss
   He had balls like a horse,
And he never spent less than a quart. [1941.

213. "Good healthy example."—Prof. LaBarre (1946). But compare Note 1637.

216. Amenities of the honeymoon.

222. "A young man whom we'll designate X" (1946A). Morse (1948) gives the variant "Who was constantly troubled with sex," noting the origin of the limerick in the judge's obiter dictum (legal maxim: The law does not concern itself with trifles) on the United Mine Workers' suit for portal-to-portal pay in the 1940's.

224.   For when it was hard
   He would grease it with lard
And deflower the Straits of Carquinez. [1944.

229. By the author of *That Immoral Garland* (1942A), as also Limerick 1659. Miss Scott is an ice-skating

champion. The pose complained, of is the arabesque usually photographed for the magazines from three-quarters behind on the leg-up side, to show the most possible thigh, pantie-crotch, scalloped breasts, and fixed grin.

232. Fiddle-fucking: sub-axillary (New Jersey, 1939).

233. When firmly implanted within her. [1941.

242. 'Twas the shock of his life
When it went through his wife [1941.

It went through an actress,
Three sheets, and the mattress,
And wound up in the bedroom utensil. [1941.

244. So long are their things
They can tie them with strings
And dispose of the surplus for weenies. [1944.

There was a cock-teaser named Jeanie
Whose boy-friends all called her a meany.
When out necking at night
She would close her legs tight
And do nothing but play with your weenie.
[1943-1952.

249. There was a young lady named Hooton
Whose cunt you could put a top-boot in.
So her husband divorced her
And married a worster,
With a cunt that an oak-tree could root in.
[1941.

256. Compare Limerick 164.

258. WARWICK (Yorick). "He had a selection..."

261. Compare the much older catch-phrase: "Ain't heard swearin' like that (*or* Ain't seen so much commotion) since Maw caught her tit in the wringer." Faked photographic novelty card (N.Y. 1952)

[385]

of a fat woman with one breast going through a washing-machine wringer, with caption (borrowed from novelty card of cow stepping on teat, 1951): "So you think YOU got troubles!" Ambivalent anti-breast sadism (homosexual slapping of women in movies, originally with rejected food) to be compared with the growing American breast-fetichism and masochistic oral dependence.

263   His wife was the same,
        For attached to her frame
Were one rubber bub, and one rubbable.   [1951.

STRANGE INTERCOURSE

265. Il y avait un jeune homme de Dijon,
    Qui n'avait que peu de religion.
        Il dit, " Quant à moi,
            Je m'encule tous les trois—
Le Père, et le Fils, et le Pigeon. "   [1928-1939A.

266. Spanish-speaking peoples have a fine sacrilegious style of oath and invective, swearing, for instance, " By the twenty-four testicles of the twelve Apostles of Christ! "   " By the ass-hole of God! " or " By the blessed cunt of the Virgin Mary, which I would have fucked if I had had the time! " For another Spanish limerick, see 1485.

268. On the movie-actress Mary Astor, whose sex-diary ("Twenty minutes—I don't know how he does it! ") was published in the New York tabloids during her divorce in the 1930's.

269. On Auden and Isherwood, minor British poets of the period.

271. Parodied in Limerick 1643

273.   His twenty inch peter
       (A triple repeater)
    Would come like the Biblical Flood!   [1948.

274. Note the obscene public interest in the sex life of famous cripples: the man in the iron lung, President Franklin D. Roosevelt (Note 32) etc.

276.   Said the king, as he came,
       To this cow-cunted dame: [1941.

In his *Quaderni d'anatomia,* folio 7 recto, note 5, Leonardo da Vinci gives a burlesque demonstration that the cunt of a woman is proportionately three times as large as that of a cow. Compare the burlesque discussions of the "Intronati" in Antonio Vignale's *La Cazzaria* (1530), MS. translation by Samuel Putnam, who discusses the work in *Encyclopaedia Sexualis* (N.Y. 1936) p. 491-2.

278.   But 'tweren't the Almighty
       That lifted her nightie   [1941.

       Though she had been worked over
       'Twas not by Jehovah,
    But a man with a fifteen-inch rod.   [1949.

282. COAST (Boast). Variant: "Said the wan ectoplasm," heightening the note of wistful sadness. Compare Limerick 691, and Philippe Quinault's *The Amourous Fantasme* (English translation, 1661).

       A terrible spasm
       Passed over her chasm
    While the fellow was browning his toast.   [1948.

285.   Not a murmur was heard,
       Not a sound, not a word   [1943A.

287. Limerick version of an incest theme well-known in folk tales, often with the revenge element of

transmitting venereal disease to a male enemy by these (repressed homosexual) means.

290. Nil desperandum. Compare Limerick 1020.

291. This is of course the opening of Sterne's *Tristram Shandy* (1760). Much material exists on the clock as Conscience (Freud, *Collected Papers*, 2 : 158-9; and A. M. Meerloo, in *Psychiatric Quarterly*, 1948-50) and on Father Time as Kronos the castrator. Improved :

> He buggered the clock
> With the end of his cock,
> And wound up his wife with the key. [1946A.

> He cut off his cock
> In winding the clock,
> So he fucked his wife with the key. [1939A.

292. Apocryphal whore's boast (Pa. 1940): "I can suck you off, jerk you off, or take out my glass eye and wink you off." Hirschfeld (1914) quotes from Rohleder, "coitus in cavitatem oculi extracti."

293. Three ingenious young siblings called Biddle
Indulged in a three-cornered diddle.
> Though those on each side
> Were well satisfied,
All fought for dual joys in the middle. [1942.

Punch-line of a well-known joke, becoming a catch-phrase: "Lucky Julius (*or* Pierre), always in the middle!" The name has been used alone, as a recondite bawdry, in *Time* and in Al Capp's "Li'l Abner."

301. Robert Ripley, *Believe It Or Not* (1929) p. 169 : "The Empress Marie Louise [Napoleon's second wife] could fold her ears at will — and also turn them inside out!" The under side of the upper crust. Compare Limericks 172, 228, and 1498.

302. Who lost it one night in Peoria.
          Then she lost some more cherries
          At Pierre's and at Sherry's,
But most at the Waldorf-Astoria.   [1943B.

Song: " She Had To Go and Lose It At the Astor " (music by " John Doe & Joe Doaques, " 1939).

306. A reporter named Archibald Symes
      Lured girls on to infamous crimes.
          " I give them, " he'd boast,
          " Two Globes and a Post,
      And God knows how many Times. "   [1942.

This joke, on how many newspapers of these names a newsgirl can hold between her legs, illustrated in *Broadway Brevities* (Oct. 10, 1932).

308. HILDA (Brunnhilde, Ilder). See Limerick 1140.

310. Parodying a famous original by Cosmo Monkhouse.

311.   To Betty-Jane Kuntz
          Who took three men at once—   [1941.

This heroine appears under the name Lyde (as noted in *Index Limericus*) in an epigram in the Greek Anthology, V. 49, translated into Latin thus:

Lyde, quae tribus viris eadem celeritate inservit, Huic supra ventrem, illi subter, alii a postico. Admitto, inquit, paediconem, mulierosum, irrumatorem. Si festinas, etiam si cum duobus ingressus sis, ne te cohibeas.

Compare Martial IX. 32, also Limerick 1145, and the recent Purim poem (1947) beginning:

    Oh, Esther was a three-way queen,
    She wasn't very moral.
    She took the king in every way—
    Vaginal, anal, oral.

313. One of the most famous limericks, with gag variant: "And instead of coming he sneezed, or shit, or jacked off" (1938*).

314. KILDARE (Astaire, BelAir, Bulgair, Carstair, Clair, Eau Claire, Klare, MacNair, Montclair, nowhere). Compare the geographical variants of Limerick 202, and, with the version below, the mathematical variants of Limerick 169. The number of the crucial stroke varies from the twenty-first in *Immortalia* (1927) to the sixty-third in Douglas (1928) as below:

>Who was having a girl in a chair.
>   At the sixty-third stroke
>   The furniture broke,
>And his rifle went off in the air.   [1928.

315. As every schoolboy knows, this is an abbreviation of the Welsh name Llanfairpwllgwyngyllgogerychwyrndrobwylltysiliogogogoch, on which Langford Reed, *The Complete Limerick Book* (2 ed., 1926) p. 189*, asks for a "hero to venture an example."

316. Stacked-chairs position. Compare Variant 311.

319. Compare: "Wife: an attachment you screw on the bed to get the housework done."

328. Actually Young had only 21 wives. His reputation as a man of parts may not, however, have been entirely without foundation. At his birthplace in Whitingham, Vermont, a simple marker records: "Brigham Young, born on this spot 1801, a man of much courage and superb equipment."

330.   And, being quite lewd
>   She asked to be screwed
>In the ass by her friend John O'Rourke.   [1946A.

333.   And he hadn't much patience
>   With the girl's objurgations.   [1941.

335. PENZANCE (France). The original of both theme and rhyme is Limerick 90, sixty years before. The texts vary greatly, one version making it a train, not a bus, and ending : " The engineer shit (*not* shot) in his pants. "

336. " Perhaps the colloquial comparative, ' hotter than a Persian fuck, ' should be changed to ' longer. . . ' "
—*Lapses in Limerick* (1938).

338. Possibly the lunar climate. See Limerick 323.

339. Generally said to refer to Mrs. Wallis Warfield Simpson, " who fucked the King of England out of the throne " (1936).

  When she said to her swain,
 " Let's do it again! "   [1941.

  Said the driver, " Encore! "
  But the man just got sore   [1949.

There was a young lady named Ransom
Who was ravished three times in a cab.
  When she cried out for more,
  Came a voice from beneath :
" Lady, my name is Sanders, not Sandow. " [1944.

344. On newspaper correspondent Walter Duranty's *I Write As I Please* (1935).

346. This ugly autobiographical fantasy appears only in Clement Wood's *The Facts of Life in Limericks* (1943). The theme is repeated, in a slightly glozed form, in a new story added to the reprint of his collection of short stories, *Flesh,* before his death.

348. SPAIN (Lorraine, Steubén). Variants : " Who was raped by an ape on a train " (1944), " Who delighted to pee in the rain " (1952); but the text form has the real Gothic flavor.

[391]

350. "The last line should be read with leering envy."
—*Index Limericus* (1943). Variant:

There was a young fellow of Sydney
Who with women and wine ruined his kidney.
   He screwed and he boozed,
   And his innards all oozed,
But he had a good time of it, didn' he?   [1941.

351. TIBET (Turkish cadet). Wells, 1951, notes a "religious motif" in this, suggesting a variant on a Tibetan *priest*.

    With the greatest of ease
    He could rape six Chinese   [1948A.

353. There was a young man from Toledo
Who traveled about incognito.
   The reason he did
   Was to bolster his id
While appeasing his savage libido   [1949.

355. With a cockswain or two, for good measure. [1941.

357.   Till one day with a cousin
    He ripped off a dozen   [1948A.

359. Omitting the Man in the Moon limericks (323 and 338) from the consideration, this and the preceding are the first science-fiction limericks.

361. Compare "fish, fuck, faint, and fall over," *fish* referring to oragenitalism, *fall over* to passive pedication (N.Y. 1939), and the song "Mary Lou" (in *North Atlantic Squadron,* Gander Bay, Newfoundland, 1944, mimeographed), ending: "She can ride, fart, fight, fuck, shoot the shit and drive a truck, That's the kind of a sonovabitch that's gonna marry me."

363. Y.T.: Young Thing. Variant. "There was a young twirp of Ave. B." (1943B).

367. Toast (by a Lady): "In with it, and out with it, and God work his will with it."—*The Pearl*, no. 16 (Oct. 1880).

> Here's to it and from it
> And to it again.
> May the man who got to it
> And then didn't do it,
> May he never get to it
> To do it again. [N.Y. 1939.

368. To line a pretty girl against the wall,
> To stick your continuation
> In her communication—
> It's human nature, that's all. [1943.

369. "They A' Do't." From *The Pearl*, no. 8 (Feb. 1880), intruded in Part IV of "Lady Pokingham, or They All Do It," with note: "to the tune of ' A man's a man for a' that'." The origin of this Scottish song is a mystery. It does not appear in the first edition of Robert Burns' *Merry Muses of Caledonia* (Dumfries, c. 1800), but is included by Duncan M'Naught (*Merry Muses,* ed. 1911, Introduction) in a list of additions first published in the edition "Dublin: Printed for the Booksellers, 1832," which has not been available for collation. The asterisked line in the second verse is a forgery by the present editor to fill an apparent lacuna in the text.

ORAL IRREGULARITY

379. ARDEN (Barden, Bellardon, East Arden, Hardon, Varden). Clean original—with the "I beg pardon" conclusion—in Carolyn Wells' *Folly for the Wise* (1904) p. 167.

> Said the man, somewhat gruff,
> "Do you swallow that stuff?" [1941.

        And when she was through
        He said, " Let's see the goo "   [1948A.

        When he asked with a squirm,
     " What's become of the sperm ? "   [1948.

        The sailor asked, " Punk,
        Do you swallow that junk ? "   [1949.

        When asked what she did
        With that thumping big quid,
   She replied, " (Er-ug-gulp) I beg pardon ? "   [1941.

386. He said, " This is fun,
      But let's try a new one—
  As the snobs like to call it : Fellatio. "   [1948A.

387. And spit all the shit on her chest.   [1941.

388. Wrote a treatise on cunts and on fucking 'em.
      A learned Parsee
      Taught him Gamahuchee,
  So he added a chapter on sucking 'em.   [1879.

Gamahuchee : a French word, *gamahucher,* of unknown derivation (possibly from the Japanese *gamaguchi,* purse), referrring to oragenitalism. The first half of a monograph on the subject has been published : *Oragenitalism :* An Encyclopaedic outline of oral technique in genital excitation, Part I : Cunnilinctus, by ' Roger-Maxe de La Glannège ' [pseud.; New York] 1940. 63 p. 8vo. The announced Part II : Fellation & the Sixty-Nine, was never written, the author not having the courage to do the research.

      But a lady from Wales
      Took the wind from his sails   [1947B.

      But an unknown French jerk
      Eclipsed this great work
With a pamphlet on peckers and sucking 'em.
                                       [1949.

391. Morse (1948) p. 76, objects to Douglas' erudite pun on *Ecce homo!* — Behold the homo. (*John*, 19:5.)

393.   He said, "Now, you scum,
           Gobble some of my come!"
       "When you've buggered my bum, sir," said Mary.
                                                    [1944A.

396. Has almost as many historical errors as the Old Lady of Wheeling (Limerick 762) has physiological. Variant: "Used to blow the Imperial tars, Till the sailors revolted . . ." (1952).

401. Who would not take a prick in her "place."
         But though she'd not fuck it,
         She'd kiss and she'd suck it,
     And let it go off in her face.   [1948.

404. Famous American murder trial of the 1920's. Theora Hix bit Dr. Snook's penis during fellation in an automobile, and he killed her with a hammer, his testimony to this effect being hawked semi-publicly at the time in a 32do pamphlet.

405. Cf. variant mispronunciation of "fellatio" in 386.

413. 'George Archibald Bishop' [Aleister Crowley], "Sleeping in Carthage," in his *White Stains* [London] 1898, p. 106:

   The month of thirst is ended.   From the lips
       That hide their blushes in the golden wood
   A fervent fountain amorously slips,
       The dainty rivers of thy luscious blood...
   Divinest token of sterility,
       Strange barren fountain blushing from the womb.

417. See Note 459.   Variant:

       He said with a grunt,
     "If my ear was a cunt
       I'd sit right down here and I'd fuck it."   [1928B.

[395]

426. Though present here only for the rhyme, the castratory-homosexual barber (Mad Barber of Fleet Street) is not an uncommon theme, handled by—among others—George Meredith, Lafcadio Hearn, and Jack Woodford.

428. Compare Limerick 415. Cunnilinctus joke in *Broadway Brevities* (Oct. 1932) : Chorus girl : "Oh, Mr. Zilch, please remove your glasses!" Gag photograph, reported from Florida, 1952, of a girl's crotch with a pair of horn-rimmed spectacles caught between her thighs.

431. He rushed to the doc,
Who looked at his cock [1945*

432. But never would screw
On account of the view
That her method was neater and sweeter. [1949.

433. There once was a King, Hal the Bluff. [1944.

438. Franchot Tone, stage and motion-picture actor, début (?) in *Pagan Lady*, 1930. Widely disliked. Involved in a triangle fracas, 1951, explained by a photograph presumably of his wife, Barbara Payton, circulated in 1952, showing her wildly laughing while a man engages in cunnilinctus on her. Called "the famous 'joy in cunnilingus' photograph," in *Exposé* (N.Y., Oct. 1952) p. 6/4.

BUGGERY

451. Nautical advice : "No frigging in the rigging!" Compare Limerick 500.

456. Clean original in *Peter Pauper's Limerick Book* (ed. 1942) p. 25, with a drawing, by Herb Roth, of the lady being pinched in the rear by a two-tailed triton with magnificent pubic hair, but no penis.

458.   You must be in a rut,
            Unfastidious, but—   [1948A.

There was a young man from Le Havre
Who cornered a lovely cadaver.
    And though our young Stanley
    Realized it unmanly,
He knew when he wished he could have her.   [1940*

459. The fantasy of auto-sodomy is of great psychological interest, as both an acceptance of passive homosexuality and a simultaneous defiance of it. See Limericks 1559, 448, 461, 494 (and the more famous but basically identical 417). The conclusion here—one of the commonest of folk-taunts, but considered less insulting than the similar advice to fuck one's mother—is also used in Don Marquis' privately printed *Ode to Hollywood* (1929), ending: " Go fuck thy suffering self! "

463. DAVE (Belgrave, Mohave). One of the most frequently heard limericks. The *ne plus ultra* of the extenuating circumstance (itself formerly a disgrace)—" I only do it for the money. " Compare the same theme in Limerick 537, and a variant in 493. Clean original of the couplet in a limerick on the unpronounceability of Russian names, in Ethel Watts Mumford's *Smiles in Rime* (1904) p. 97: " . . . My name, I admit, Is a sneeze and a spit, But thank God it's not &c. "

            When asked if ashamed,
            He said, " I can't be blamed "   [1927.

            He said, " I confess
            It's a bit of a mess "   [1943A.

            He said, " It's the shits,
            The worms eat her tits "   [1942.

    " It isn't so nice
        With the vermin and lice,
But think of the money I save! "   [1944.

464. DELRAY (Bombay, L.A., Torbay, Torquay). There is some error here. Delray is in Michigan, while "nothing to pay" is a traditional Welsh phrase. Falmouth (1932) changes the "young Jew" to a "young man."

465. Davis (1946) for some reason gives "Estrekko." For a similar musical dénouement, see Limerick 92.

468. Drake (1949) drops "futter" for "Sutter." Compare Limerick 1315 for disposal of the victim.

471. The terrible cymbal-clash in the "Dance of the Furies" from Gluck's *Orpheus* is probably meant.

473. Apparently to be pronounced *Dy*-grace. Should be in the "Chamber of Horrors."

476. A variant of Limerick 1218, and compare 241.

479. Yiddish: *reb*, rabbi; *toches*, buttocks; *kosher*, ritually permissible; *broches*, benedictions. *Kadoches* is not a place, but means a fit or seizure (used as a curse).

481. This variant of Limerick 1186 was the subject of a forty-page presidential address, by the compiler of *Index Limericus,* written for the third meeting of the American Limerick Society, Berkeley, Cal., October 30, 1942—the all-time record for limerick annotation.

482. British approximation of the Kentucky dialect.

483. Although Prof. Alfred C. Kinsey, whose famous defense of homosexuality and premature ejaculation, *Sexual Behavior in the Human Male* (in collaboration with two boy-associates, Philadelphia, 1947) omits all reference to the 3500 penis measurements taken in connection with it—no vaginas have been depth-gauged for his more recent volume on the "Human Female"—these will be found charted in

[398]

Robert L. Dickinson, *Human Sex Anatomy* (2 ed., 1949) p. vi-a and Fig. 112 : " Human Penis, Forms, Dimensions and Angles : Data from G series by Dickinson & Legman. "

485. The late General George S. Patton reported as saying to his medical officers (c. 1945) : " Open the whore-houses. A man that won't fuck won't fight. "

489. Douglas (1928) gives the variant, which he calls " a little gross " : " And he out with his cock, and he did. " Most reprints erroneously give two " pures " in the polluted proverb in Douglas' note here (p. 67) : " To the pure all things are puer. "

496. MAG 94 : U.S. *Marine Aircraft Group*. This is the last limerick in *Farmer Gray* (mimeographed, c. 1945). The sudden change of tense from past to present in the last line, indicating MAG 94 as the probable source of the collection, is the same error—also made in almost the last line (" return of the repressed ")—as that upon which the higher critical destruction of the Bible's authority was originally begun by Thomas Hobbes : " . . . but no man knoweth of his [Moses'] sepulchre unto *this* day. "—*Deuteronomy*, 34 : 6.

498. For it seems that meanwhile,
Though a wart cramped his style   [1941.

502. PERU (Purdue, Kalamazoo, Kew). Often " by a gnu, " with which compare Limerick 1654. Purifying Douglas, 'Falmouth' leaves the Jew (compare Note 464), but makes his consort a girl. The real question, how a person could know, during the moment of buggery, the religion of the bugger (there are some moments when even the longest of foreskins retract), remains unanswered.

503. A nigger, a bugger, a Jew.   [1946A.

505. Clean original (Weston) in *Unexpurgated,* from Morris R. Bishop ['W. Bolingbroke Johnson']'s limerick murder-mystery, *The Widening Stain* (1942) p. 159.

509. (line 2 :) The same shape in back as in front. [1952.

510. The King of Siam (verse 1) and the Bey of Algiers—reversing couplets—were first printed in *Anthropophyteia* (1910-11), the King of Spain first in Douglas (1928). With the " odd-o'-me sodomy " rhyme compare Limericks 443 and 569. Many variants of the " fat-bottomed boy " couplet : " The height of my joys Is bungholing boys " (1939A), " For whole-hearted joy I'll take a round-bottomed boy " (1941A), " I get all my joy From the ass of a boy " (1942), " I have for my toys Little round-bottomed boys " (1942), and a complete variant (1939A-1944) :

I'm the King of Siam, I am, I am,
For women I don't give a damn.
   The ass-holes of boys
   Is what I enjoys—
I am the King of Siam, God Damn!

Note that all these reverse the sentiment of the original :

512. " There may be some joy
   In the arse of a boy,
But I prefer women. "—*Loud cheers.*   [1911.

" I am old and well stricken in years,
   And my language is blunt,
   But a cunt *is* a cunt,
And fucking *is* fucking "—(*loud cheers*).   [1928.

" I've given up sodomy,
   Boys no longer bodder me.
From now on we fuck. "—*Loud cheers.*   [1943C.

Who said to his harem, " My dears,
    I know what you're expecting
    With your clitori erecting,
But this morning 'twill be up your rears. "   [1947B.

" Outside there are urchins
    Who are waiting for virgins.
This is your day off. "—*Loud sneers!*   [1952.

514. Who said, " You boys and girls fuck about,
    But I get my spunk
    From an elephant's trunk— "
(*Cries of* " Fraud!   Lousy cheat!   Throw him out!)
    [1947B.

516. Continuing the theme of Limerick 1057.

517. Sadistic concept of coitus, the woman being killed simply by anal coitus. Compare Limerick 1713, and the punitive pedication of the Bishop of Buckingham in Limerick 535.

519. Pidgin-English limerick presented at the American Limerick Society, Jan. 26, 1946.

521. *The Pearl*, no. 13 (July 1880), captioned : " A Propos of the Naval Demonstration. "

522. Senator Walsh was caught frequenting male prostitutes in a Brooklyn peg-house staffed by German spies. Compare the pronunciation of the *u*'s in Limerick 1689.

528. " The Cabin-Boy " (Little Roy, Tommy Tripper, from Sochipper). Although the two-couplet verse form is probably the original of the limerick as we know it—and explains the non-rhyme or mere geographical rhyme in the first line—the attempt is generally made to compress two-couplet forms into pure limerick shape. (See the list of Not-Quite Limericks preceding Note 1.) G. Legman, " Rationale of the Dirty Joke, " in *Neurotica* (N.Y.,

1951) no. 9: p. 56-7, notes: "A single stanza expressing the Ganymede revenge theme [" of the dangerous anus that hurts the penis of the dominating (pedicating) male"] is all that is popularly remembered of a modern ballad... "'The good ship's name was Venus'," quoting the "*He* filled his ass" line common to all the limerick versions but not to the ballad, and dating the verse U.S. 1928. Judge Learned Hand, famous for his liberal decisions in sex-literature cases in the 1930's, is described by Philip Hamburger, "The Great Judge," in *Life* (Nov. 4, 1946), reprinted in his *The Oblong Blur* (1949) p. 25, as being "prevailed upon to sing a ribald song of the sea, entitled *The Cabin Boy*. When they left Holmes [Oliver Wendell Holmes, who "relished his repertoire"], Hand turned to [Felix] Frankfurter and said, 'I fear the old man thinks I am a mere vaudevillian'."

A la santé de Jacques, le garçon de cabine,
Le petit éventreur impur.
    Son can il remplit
    De la verre rompie,
Et il a circoncisé le patron.   [1947B.

ABUSES OF THE CLERGY

530.   She committed this deed
        From a natural need   [1943A.

        But it is the belief
        That she peed for relief.

        But I hasten to mention
        From vesicular tension   [1947B.

534.   As they knelt in their stalls
        They tickled the balls   [1941A.

There was a young Bishop of Birmingham
Who deflowered young girls while confirming 'em.
  ' Mid liturgical chants
  He would take down their pants
And release his episcopal sperm in 'em.   [1941.

  There were roars of applause
As he yanked off their drawers   [1943B.

  He'd lift up his cassock
And kneel on a hassock   [1942.

With their backs to the altar
  They sullied the psalter,
As he eased the episcopal worm in 'em.   [1942.

535. The British public (*i.e.* private) school being unfamiliar to American reciters, it is commonly varied to: "a swank Eastern school" (1941A), "parochial school" (1943A), "a large public school" (1943C), etc. Wood (1943B) gives the Bishop "*yards* of episcopal tool," with which compare Limerick 548. The theme of buggery as punishment is very notable here, and see Note 517.

536. This limerick was not originally a part of the Buckingham sequence preceding, but is generally added as the perfect conclusion. Variant last lines: "And much more amusing than you" (1943), "And two inches (four inches, six inches, nine inches, ten inches) longer than you!" Compare Thomas Hamilton, Earl of Haddington, *Select Poems on Several Occasions* (c. 1730) Tale 40, "The Dying Toast [i.e. Beauty]", where the "dying toast" rouses herself from her death-bed on hearing "two virtuous virgins, fair and young" arguing, the eldest that:

" Our parson's is by far the best,
  'Tis full ten inches long,
It upwards to his belly press'd,
  'Tis stiff, 'tis hard, 'tis strong. "

[403]

To which the younger replies:

> "Your long and thin are but a joke,
>   Such baubles I have try'd.
> Our curate's is by far more strong,
>   'Tis his alone can charm,
> For, though it is not quite so long,
>   'Tis twice as thick's my arm."

(The erotic riddles and contests in sexual brag at death-beds, wakes, and weddings, are an interesting *rite de passage,* common in the Hispanic countries and elsewhere.)

538. When reproached by the nuns for not fucking 'em,
    Replied, "Though my dick
    Is sufficiently thick,
Your slits are poor fits. Put a tuck in 'em." [1949.

540. Her protruding breast
    And the way that she dressed [1948.

543. Episcopal preachers,
    The lecherous creatures— [1941.

Itinerant monks,
The libidinous skunks— [1941.

545. This was the first limerick in the present collection, and is given in the form transcribed at Ann Arbor, Michigan, 1935. Compare Limerick 421.

546. A jack in the box. "Big Catholic Layman" (B.C.L.), one making heavy contributions to the church. Monsignor Fulton J. Sheen, a fashionable proselytizing priest.

549. Compare Limericks 299 and 573, and Note 534.

Used a Chinaman's ass for an altar.
    He said, "Nostradamus!
    My god, what an anus!"
As he wiped off his cock on the psalter. [1951.

551. —A faith surpassing belief! [1928.

560. See the *Dissertatio theologica de sanctificatione seminis Mariae Virginis in actu conceptionis Christi*, by Samuel Schrœer (Leipzig, 1709), compared with which the famous confessorial manual, *De Matrimonio*, by Thomas Sanchez, is said to be " un modèle de discrétion pudibonde. "

561. A better-known variant (compare Limerick 532):

From a niche in the crypt at St. Giles
Issued screams that re-echoed for miles.
    Said the vicar, " Good gracious!
    It's Brother Ignatius;
He forgets that the bishop has piles."
[1940-1945.

563.   So one night after prayers
    He bolted upstairs,
And buggered the Lady Superior. [1879.

Cleaned up versions are commonly printed, as in Max Miller's *Fog and Men on Bering Sea* (1936), *Peter Pauper's Limerick Book* (ed. 1942), and, most absurdly, in *Six Limericks for Mezzo Soprano or Baritone*, with pianoforte accompaniment by Edward B. Manning (N.Y.: Boosey & Co., 1911), with title-page caution: " The public performance of any parodied version of these songs is strictly prohibited. "

565. Compare the rhymes in Limericks 1657 and 1128.

572. On the two-couplet limerick form see Note 528. American reciters generally miss the pun on " old school tie " as not merely the physical necktie (with its usual symbolic phallicism, as in fly- and tie-ripping—" displacement of lower to upper "), but as " A phrase applied to Public School associations, influences, importance, memories. "—Eric Partridge, *A Dictionary of Clichés* (1940).

573. Schweinickle (1928) p. 80, gives as a joke, with prologue: " A girl was going to be baptised. The preacher pulled down the blinds, stuffed the keyholes, then told her to strip to her naked skin, which, to comply with the parson's request, she did. He opened up the Bible and told her to lay on it. Then he mounted her and said: 'The Holy Book [etc., ending:] Now wwiggle yyour ass to ssave your ssoul'." Compare *Bishop Percy's Folio Manuscript* (c. 1620, ed. F. J. Furnivall, 1867) Loose and Humorous Songs, p. 35, " Off a Puritaine ":

> It was a puritanicall ladd
>   that was called Mathyas,
> & he wold goe to Amsterdam
>   to speake with Ananyas.
> he had not gone past halfe a mile,
>   but he mett his holy sister;
> hee layd his bible under her breeche,
>   and merylye hee kist her.
>
> " Alas! what wold they wicked say? "
>   quoth shee, " if they had seene itt!
> my Buttocckes thé lye to lowe : I wisht
>   appocrypha were in itt! "

A longer version appears in Thomas Hamilton, Earl of Haddington, *Select Poems* (c. 1730) Tale 17.

ZOOPHILY

577. 'George Archibald Bishop' [Aleister Crowley], *White Stains* [London] 1898, p. 109, " With Dog and Dame ":

> I yield him place : his ravening teeth
>   Cling hard to her—he buries him
> Insane and furious in the sheath
>   She opens for him—wide and dim
> My mouth is amorous beneath...

[406]

579.   Just for a whim
       He dressed up as a quim   [1928.

       He made up as a tree
       Having failed to foresee
       Being pissed on by dogs, cats, and all.   [1949.

580. Christina Stead, *Letty Fox: Her Luck* (N.Y., 1946) p. 293-4, describing a party at which dirty jokes etc. are being told by both women and men: "The Washington miss... said, with timid eagerness, 'That's very good. Do you like limericks? We go in more for limericks in Washington'." With a variant of the present example, ending "And leaves them alone with Mamma," and the implication that mild types like these are not "really good." A similar scene on the telling of dirty jokes appears in Viña Delmar's *Bad Girl* (1928) p. 37-8; and compare Richard Waterman, "The Role of obscenity in the folk tales of the 'intellectual' stratum of our society," in *Journal of American Folklore* (April 1949) v. 62: p. 162-5.

582. BRUNO (Buno, Guantanamo, San Bruno, Yuno). All members of the American camel family appear in variants of the last line: alpaca, guanaco, &c.

584. Douglas very correctly notes, from the *Sketches of Moral Philosophy* by Sydney Smith (d. 1845), "We shall generally find that the triangular person has got into the square hole... and a square person has squeezed himself into the round hole." Compare also the Biblical injunction (*Matthew*, 5: 22) that "whosoever shall say, Thou fool, shall be in danger of hell fire."

       Said she, "You damned shit,
       You can't fuck a bit"   [1879.

       Said the ape, "Something's wrong
       With the shape of your prong"   [1941.

[407]

> Said the ape, " Sir, your prick
> Is too long and too thick,
> And something is wrong with the shape." [1928.

589 The fice or feist-hound (lap dog), so called from its farting habits (feist: a wet fart).

594. Collected as verse 1 only of a " Ballad of Artificial Insemination " (N.Y., 1945A), the remainder being lost.

595. DUNDEE (Capri, McGee, Paree, Pooree). An extremely popular limerick with many variants as to " the result, " all apparently intended to explain the rainbow-assed monkey.

> There once was a heathen Chinee
> Who briggled an ape in a tree. [1948A.

>   The result of the fuck
>   Was a bald-headed duck, [1946A.

> Blue ass and a purple J.T. (*John Thomas*) [1943B.

> There was a young man from Bombay
> Who raped a baboon in the hay.
>   The results were most horrid—
>   All ass and no forehead,
> Three balls and a purple toupée. [1942.

> There was a young girl of the Cape
> Who had an affair with an ape.
>   The result was quite 'orrid,
>   All ass, and no forrid,
> And one of its balls was a grape! [1951.

599. EAU CLAIRE (Kildare, Knair, McNair, St. Clair).

> Made friends with a cinnamon bear,
>   But the treacherous brute
>   Made a pass at his fruit,
> And left only buttons and hair. [1945.

601. Non-zoophilous couplet and conclusion:

>   But really she burned for it,
>   Squirmed for it, yearned for it,
> Cried for it nightly in torrents. [1941.

602. Compare Limericks 586 and 1238.

603. Variant, apparently on Miss Madeleine Slade, recipient of Gandhi's *Bapu's Letters to Mira,* with a fine colloquial rhyme in the couplet:

> Woke up one morning quite randy.
>   He called for Miss Slade,
>   Or a goat instead [1942.

> Whose clothes were exceedingly scanty.
>   To scratch his left ball
>   Was no trouble at all—
> In fact, 'twas convenient and handy. [1951.

604. Compare Limerick 1069, and, with Note 595:

> There once was a maid from Geneva
> Who kept a giraffe to relieve her.
>   The result of this fuck
>   Was a four-legged duck,
> Three eggs, and a spotted retriever. [1932*-1950.

605. Something of an inevitable rhyme; compare in Henry Miller's *The Booster* (later *Delta,* November 1937), back cover:

>   Out of the gorse
>   Came a homosexual horse.

Other name variants: Dorse, Morse. Two variant conclusions referring to Robinson Jeffers' *Roan Stallion* (1925), both with female protagonists:

>   A roan stallion charged her
>   And so much enlarged her
> That her husband applied for divorce. [1941.

>   "I used to love heifers
>   Until I read Jeffers,
> But now I could go for this horse!"   [1938*

619 "I've found in the course of philanderin'"   [1942*

620. Burlesque book-title: *The Wildcat's Revenge*, by Claude Balls. (List of 185 such titles, Utah 1952.)

621. She did so becuz
         She imagined the buzz   [1943.

622. Next morning at dawn
         She started to spawn   [1945C.

>   When nine months had passed
>   She had crabs up her ass   [1943B.

>   What she conceived was a sin,
>   All beard and no chin   [1952.

>   With motions phenomenal
>   And contortions abdominal,
>   The turtle made Myrtle fertile.   [1948.

623. Said the pig with a grunt,
       "Get away from my cunt—"   [1944.

630. So he sat on a mat
         And fucked the cat   [1939A.

>   So he whipped out his carrot
>   And diddled a parrot
>   —The offspring reminds me of you!   [1944A.

631. Consciously borrowing the couplet of Limerick 658. Variant: "An heir to the Portuguese crown" [1943A.

638. Compare with Limerick 503:

>   He tripped on a rug
>   And buggered a bug,
>   But the bug hardly minded at all.   [1944A.

[410]

640. Douglas (1928) p. 73, giving lines 1-4 only, a number of Learic last lines have been cobbled together by various hands, on the style of: "And fooled (foiled?) that old man of Santander." Limerick 641 (Toulouse) first in *Anecdota Americana* II (1934) with the Santander couplet.

642. Boulton and Park, two homosexuals of the period, put on trial in April 1870. A contemporary cut showing them in women's clothes and men's, is reproduced in Michael Sadleir's *Forlorn Sunset* (N.Y., 1946) chap. 26, pt. 2, p. 305. On talking pigs and pig-fuckers, see Limericks 623 and 626.

652. One of ten similar "Limericks About Children, For Children, by One who doesn't like 'em," this being the only one at all approaching the erotic element. A sample of the others, with the castratory fear—quite clear in the last line—displaced on the mother-image, as in *Hänsel and Gretel* (the witch who bites the child's finger to see if he's plump enough to eat):

An old Irish witch named Maloney
Cackled, "Chicken is terribly bony.
    But a son or a daughter
    Will make your mouth water,
And is boneless as fresh-cut baloney."   [1948A.

Compare a bus-advertisement for Hebrew National Kosher delicatessen, in the Jewish sections of New York, 1952, showing an enormous knife cutting into a large bologna (flanked by olives), with the caption: "For the SLICE of Your Life!" See also Isaac Rosenfeld, "Adam and Eve on Delancey Street," in *Commentary* (Oct. 1949) v. 8: p. 385-7.

654. See Note 622.

658. "Mayor of Southampton" (also of Southbridge), "Bishop of Oxford" (Avery, Bavory, Chats-

worth, or Worcester), Earl Lavery, of Waverly. In *Life in a Putty-knife Factory* (1943) p. 144, H. Allen Smith notes a fondness for the couplet here (obviously from Limerick 387) in " John Steinbeck [who] had two thirds of the bottle of brandy inside of him by that time... and every few minutes he'd take another sip and cry out:

> *With lecherous howls,*
> *I deflower young owls!* "

EXCREMENT

668. Castoria: a patent laxative for babies.

675. There's an end to his wit
'Twas a handful of shit   [1948A.

676. Cleaned up couplet in *Peter Pauper's Limerick Book* (ed. 1942) p. 24: " She didn't dare bend, For fear she'd offend." LaBarre (1939) p. 209 erroneously notes: " A fat lady of Bryde was afraid to re-tie her shoe-laces for fear of incontinence of feces [!] "

677. Variant conclusion: " It's longer than marster's —and hairier! " (1945), with which compare a similar dénouement to a game of " Bride's Buff " in the kitchen, in *The Last of the Bleshughs* ' by the Marquis de Fartanoys ' [Roy McCardell; New York, c. 1928], reprinted, with erotic illustrations added, from *Secret Memoirs* (1928) v. 2: p. 481-499. McCardell's erotic work includes " The Quimbo Lexicon, " in *Observations of An Old Man in Love* ('Philadelphia,' 1929), pretendedly an interlude from Frank Harris' *Life and Loves* (see Limerick 1627).

679. Compare " Calcutta Curio, " Limerick 459.

680. Punning on the World War II phrase, "shit for the birds," meaning lies, buncombe.

683. On the need to "learn, read, or accomplish other tasks during defaecation," see Karl Abraham, *Selected Papers* (1927), International Psycho-Analytical Library, v. 13: p. 385, "Contributions to the Theory of the Anal Character."

686. CHISELHURST (Hazelhurst, Thistlehurst). Better-rhyming, more castratory, and probably the original conclusion:

And before he remembered, his pizzle burst. [1947.

The effect of whistling on the genitals in easing urination, is noted at least as far back as the original *Mother Goose's Melody* (intra 1768-80) ed. 1791, p. 48, the editor—apparently Oliver Goldsmith, a physician as well as a writer—noting, concerning the famous non-sequitur song, "Three children sliding on the ice": "There is something so melancholy in this song, that it has occasioned many people to make water. It is almost as diuretic as the tune which John the coachman whistles to his horses.—Trumpington's *Travels*." Compare Shakespeare's *Henry IV*, Part II, Act III. ii. 346.

694   But having got there
      (S)he let out only air   [1949.

696   By George Moore, as cited by Padraic Colum, in *Esquire* (March 1936) p. 62.

697. The Old Lady, alias of Ealing, will be found under Wheeling, Limerick 762.

698 "Excusado," Spanish for toilet, and not for "excuse me" or similar; therefore the occasion of many traveler's tales of embarrassing confusion.

699.   From pity and terror
       They committed the error
   Of weeping—alas!—from their arses.   [1942.

700 A similar odyssey of a fly-button is used with telling effect in Norman Douglas' *South Wind* (1917). Variant: " With the aid of a sound... "

701. Compare the music-hall song, " I 'ad a banana with Lydy Diana. "

702. *Lapses in Limerick* notes, in " And they felt even fouler than that, " an admirable avidity for empiric research.   Compare Limerick 438.

706. In other words : a shit brickhouse.

707. Compare Limerick 474.

708. Schweinickle (1928) p. 61, as a reply by the Congressman from Iowa to the following toast by the Congressman from Maine :

  " Here's to the American Eagle,
   That beautiful bird of prey :
   He flies from Maine to Mexico,
   And he shits on Iowa. "

An encounter almost as desperate is recorded in " The Rival Toasts, " in *The Pearl* no. 1 (July, 1879)—just preceding the first batch of limericks—in which " Captain Balls... of the Yankee frigate " offers as a toast, on an English man o' war : " Here's to the glorious American flag : Stars to enlighten all nations, and Stripes to flog them. " To which Jack, " the old ship's steward " on the Englishman, egged on by his captain, offers the reply : " Then here's to the ramping, roaring, British Lion, who shits on the stars, and wipes his arse on the stripes. "

[414]

709. Langford Reed, *The Complete Limerick Book* (1925) p. 210, the only off-color specimen Reed allows himself — possibly out of sheer misunderstanding.

712. Douglas notes briefly, "As to the victim being now in Heaven—we must take our poet's word for that. I think, unless they have fished him out, he will be found where he was."

714. On *Gone With the Wind*—from Dowson's *Cynara* —popularized by the novel (1936) by the Georgian writer, Margaret Mitchell.

715. The plot essentials of a party-record called "The Farting Contest" (Canada, c. 1940) with superlative sound effects and the same last line.

717. MACHIAS (Matthias, Mount Tamalpais, Tobias).

> They were fixed with a loop
> Through which she could poop   [1946A.
>
> With a slit in the middle
> Through which she could piddle   [1940*

719. Compare Limerick 685.

720 Douglas notes that the soprano is the part beginning, "Send her victorious..." Compare, in "The Star-Spangled Banner," the equally impossible passage for soprano beginning "Whose broad stripes and bright stars..." On musical farting generally, see Limerick 740.

723. Ciano: a minor Fascist functionary, married to Mussolini's daughter, Edda, and executed by his father-in-law in 1944.

725.   And sent it to Spain
       With a note to explain
   That it came from his grandmother's arsell.   [1928.

>   Received a remarkable parcel:
>   In a box with three locks
>   Were two cocks with the pox,
>   And a quim, and the brim of an arsehole.   [1941.
>
>   In it, I've heard,
>   Was a transparent turd   [1952.

Compare: *a blivet*: two pounds of shit in a one-pound bag (thrown out an upper-story window to splatter on the pave when one has no toilet—also called "sending the air-mail"), *a trivet*: a pound of shit stuffed in the toe of an old sock, and used as a blackjack; and *a rivet*: a mashed-potato turd stuffed down a sink. (1952).

729.   She woke with a start
        And let a loud fart,
    Which was followed by luncheon and dinner.
                                                    [1928.

Douglas notes the strict logic of the excretion (p. 71), with which compare " To the Critics and Poets," in *The New Boghouse Miscellany, or A Companion for the Close-stool* (1761) p. 207-15:

>   There was a jovial butcher,
>   He liv'd at Northern-fall-gate,
>   He kept a stall
>   At Leadenhall,
>   And got drunk at the boy at Aldgate.
>
>   He ran down Hounsditch reeling,
>   At Bedlam he was frighted,
>   He in Moorfields
>   Besh-t his heels
>   And at Hoxton he was wiped.

The anonymous critic noting (p. 214) how in the second verse "The geography of the places where the action happened, is strictly observed..." Although the limerick form can be traced to "Tom o' Bedlam's Song" (c. 1610) and "Sumer is icumen in" (c. 1300); this example, "To the Critics" (which may be reprinted from Newbery's magazine *The Midwife*, c. 1750), is the earliest "geographical" limerick as yet discovered, and has certainly enough place-names, false rhymes, and even a "There was..." to satisfy any historian.

731-32. First Egyptologist (on finding a pile of fresh shit in the unopened tomb): "Dr. Carter, do you think possibly a cat crept into the crypt and crapped and crept out again?" Second Egyptologist: "No, I think it was the pup popped into the pit and pooped and then popped out."

733. Variant: "With a roar like a double bassoon" (1941). The bassoon is the typical farting instrument of the orchestra, consciously so used in Richard Strauss' "Tyl Eulenspiegel" to show Tyl's fright at the scaffold. Lady: "Does the bassoonist really make that noise with his mouth?" Conductor: "I hope so." (Dr. Paul Englisch, *Das skatologische Element in Literatur*, 1928, p. 57.)

737. And at night piss all over the hall. [1943.

739 Quoted by Morse (1948) p. 9, from *The Eternal Eve* [Cleveland?] 1941, p. 166.

740. He could fart anything
      From God Save the King   [1938.
      (From Stravinsky to swing)   [1952.

As observed by *Index Limericus*, "St. Augustine, in his *De Civitate Dei* (d. 430), refers to an individual possessed of this talent." The themes of music and farting (Notes 715, 733) are perhaps inseparable. Sándor Ferenczi, "On Obscene Words," in his *Contributions to Psycho-analysis* (Boston, 1916) p. 143, notes, concerning a homosexual flatophile: "The infantile interest for the sounds accompanying the emission of intestinal gas was not without influence on his choice of profession. He became a musician." See Limericks 139 (variant: "... an accordion-pleated vagina; With the aid of a fart, She could render in part"), 667, 686, 701, 710 (on the present rhymes), 763, and Douglas' note, p. 40, on 720, the *vox humana* and "pétophone." See also 1730.

752. Quoted by William Martin Camp, *Retreat, Hell!* (1943) p. 52, with note: "It was a little ditty we made up in Shanghai," apparently on the pattern of the non-limerick song, "The Pioneers," (also varied as "The Engineers"):

The pioneers have hairy ears
    They piss through leather britches;
They wipe their ass on broken glass,
    Those hardy sons-of-bitches!...   [1927.

753. A masochistic young man of Split
Ate his peaches complete with the pit.
    'Twas not for the stone,
    He claimed, but alone
For the smart that remained when he shit.

[1944-1952.

755. Douglas, p. 71, notes the almost complete lack of polysyllables. Variant: "Which, I think, left the honors with me" (1943A).

762. There was a young lady of Ealing,
    Who had such a curious feeling,
        She'd lie on her back
        And tickle her crack,
And spend right bang up to the ceiling.   [1870.

The original of the first limerick I ever heard (c. 1925). Drake calls it "the schoolboy limerick par excellence, crammed with droll errors of psychology, physiology, and anatomy." (1949). Variants: Darjeeling, free wheeling.

Remember that old lady from Wheeling?
Well she STILL has that pecu-li-ar feeling,
   And she STILL lays on her back
   And opens her crack,
And you ought to see the god-damn ceiling!
                                                                 [1952.

763. Ypres: " Wipers, " of course.

GOURMANDS

764. In a list of fruits inserted into and eaten out of the vagina during cunnilinctus: " strawberries or cherries (sweet, pitted cherries), or sections of an orange (a seedless orange), or slices of apple deliciously dipped in honey," in *Oragenitalism : Pt. I. Cunnilinctus,* by 'Roger-Maxe de La Glannège,' [New York] 1940, p. 38, the banana is omitted!

769. Compare Limericks 725 and 1390.

770. And a bloody good substitute, too.   [1928.

775. FRITZ (Biarritz, Cadiz, Fitts, Hitz, McFitz, Moritz, Ritz, St. Kitts). With this standard oral-incorporative fantasy of the nursing period, compare Limerick 1213. Davis (1946) p. 41, notes the interesting repressed variant: " Last line sometimes massacred to: ('No last line: what would you do with an acre of tits?') ". *Lapses* (1941): " But the real thrill in titiculture is running around barefoot over the budding bubbies. " Intended as a joke, this has been translated into merely gruesome quasi-fact in the " Falsie-Mat, " sold in New York bar-appliance shops, 1950, and composed of unseparated false breasts of foam rubber, to be used as a bath mat. See the advertisement in *Billboard* (N.Y., Jan. 7, 1950), quoted by Albert Ellis, *The Folklore of Sex* (1951) p. 113, beginning: " ACRES AND ACRES OF 'EM! " in clear reminiscence of this limerick.

776. The last item in *Anecdota Americana II* (1934) with the note, concerning the author: "What a mind!" Compare Limerick 789. Variants: "A son of a bitch by marriage" (1950), "Whose actions, no doubt, you'll disparage" (1946b).

781. Query: "hypercritical"? Written by a committee, and presented with apologies for the poor rhyme.

782. LEITH (Dalkeith, Galbreathe, Keith, Leaf). Compare Limerick 384, a much earlier version.

785. *Index Limericus* (1946) comments: "Couldn't he get any government relief, or OPA, or something?"

786. When these grew humdrum
 She would suck up the scum [1941.

788. From the bellies of birds
 (S)he squeezed little turds,
 And tickled dogs' cocks till they shot in 'em. [1943b.

790. At formal affairs
 She'd shit on the stairs [1952.

793. From the whole tone, impossible rhyme, etc. of this apotheosis of the theme of the Jew-as-castrator, one would really expect "blood" not "piss" in the couplet.

796. Compare the added-foot form of Limericks 437 and 394.

798. "The poor fellow was living in typographical error. He had evidently mistaken colitis for coitus."—*Lapses in Limerick* (1938).

800. Compare Limerick 392. Depression joke (c. 1932): "Are times tough? Listen, in Philadelphia they're sucking cocks for food."

VIRGINITY

807. But a fellow named Gibbons
      Untied her Blue Ribbons   [1948A.

Based on popular brand-names (here of beers)—a macaronic form common in erotic "novelties." Beilenson (*World's Best Limericks,* 1951) gives a clean-up erroneously mixing in a whiskey:

But Old Overholt
Gave her virtue a jolt—

812. A catch, the rhyme requiring "whore." Variant:
"Whom a bevy of blades did adore"   [1930-1944.

815. With distrust by the men
      For she'd frig them, and then
When they wanted to fuck her—she sued!   [1941.

816. "Don't kick against the pricks."—*Acts,* 9 : 5 and 26 : 14, after Æschylus' *Agamemnon.*

818. Compare Limericks 101 and 606.

820. In the throes of her first love affair,
      Said, " Let's join in a hymn
      As you enter my quim— "   [1944.

825. Freud, in one of his great speculative papers, "The Taboo of Virginity" (1918), *Collected Papers,* v. 4: p. 217-235, discusses the peculiar psychological depths of ritual defloration, which still survives in the "marriage counsellor's" pre-marital stretching, burlesqued in the present limerick. Vaginismus as an expression of the bride's hostility against her husband is discussed by Karl Abraham, "The Female Castration Complex," in his *Selected Papers* (1927) p. 355.

[421]

826. Had a cunt as big as a palace.
　　　Though they searched far and wide,
　　　And many were tried　　　　　　　[1952.

833. Compare Limerick (and Note) 601.

835. By the compiler of *Lapses in Limerick* (1938), on a two-line beginning set by Douglas (1928) p. 17. Compare Limericks 37-39, a tryout of the rhymes. Limerick 298 also appears to be by the same hand. The allusion to the sculptor Epstein in the second stanza is to his wiggly-dick statue of Adam, displayed in America, about 1940, as a peep-show. On Strensall see Limerick 242; the "chap from New York," 331; Durand, 154.

864. Limerick version of the novelty "definition" (c. 1940): "*virgin* : a girl that don't give a fuck." In the same form: "*pimp* : nookie-bookie, a crack salesman"; "*necking* : uptown shopping for a downtown bargain."

866. Douglas (1928) p. 20, lines 1-2 only. To be recited with extravagantly rolled r's. Compare Limerick 809.

867. Was preparing her trousseau for marriage.
　　　Said she, "If you please,
　　　Make it tight in the knees"　　　　[1947B.

872. Compare Limerick 482, on the same rhyme.

875. A willing young lady of Siam
　　　Remarked to her lover, to try him:
　　　"To screw me, of course,
　　　You would have to use force,
　　But God knows you're stronger than I am!"　[1941.

　　With variants in line 2: Young Priam, Omar Khayyam.

884. On the famous lines by Dorothy Parker: "Men seldom make passes, At girls who wear glasses." F.B.I.: Federal Bureau of Investigation, the U.S. secret police. *New Masses*: a Communist magazine.

885. And did it for all she was worth. [1942A.

886. Suitable for recitation in mixed company. Compare Philip Heseltine's "fallacies" limerick 1317.

887. Willys: an American automobile.

890. Maraschino: i.e. "cherry," virginity.

892. Who vowed she'd not fuck any more,
    Till a man at a dance
    Pulled down her pants,
And filled her with spermatozoa. [1939A.

895. T/5: technical sergeant, U.S. Army.

896. Children's riddle (Pa., c. 1925): "What's the difference between a sin and a shame?—It's a sin to put it in, but it's a shame to take it out."

897. Troubled by the forthright lack of rhyme, *Unexpurgated*, Morse, and Drake give the variants Spurgeon and Sturgeon. Spitzbergen is correct.

901.   Till a fellow named Dick
    Inserted his prick,
And she wept, screamed, and shouted "Eureka!"
[1951.

903. Schweinickle (1928) p. 40: "A man goes into a butcher shop and grocery store and asks for some beef hearts. 'I haven't any,' answered the proprietor, 'but I got some beans. Take those; they'll be farts in the morning'." The author notes the *Nonnenfürzchen* and *pets des nonnes* pastries. Compare the English love-charm (surviving as a children's game) of *cockelty-bread*, described in John

[423]

Aubrey's *Remaines* (1687) as "A wanton sport, which they call moulding of cockle-bread; they gett upon a table-board, and then gather-up their knees and their [petti-]coats with their hands as high as they can, and then they wabble to and fro with their buttocks as if they were kneading of dough... The maids when they have put themselves into the fit posture say thus—'My granny is sick and now is dead, We'll go mould some cockle-bread'." See G. L. Gomme, *Games* (1894) p. 74, and the material collected in Joseph Wright's *English Dialect Dictionary* (1898) s.v.

905. God bless her.—Drake.

906. Single-rhyme limerick, on the song "In Violet Time" by William Soskin, in *The Bedroom Companion* (N.Y., 1935) p. 209-11, beginning: "Oh, violate me in violet time, In the violest way you know..."

908. WORCESTER (Brewster, Felusta, Wooster). Very commonly heard, with variant couplets: "She awoke with a cry, But found with a sigh" (1932); "But awakened to find, 'Twas all in her mind" (1940*); "She woke with a scare, To find no one there" (1941A); "She woke up in bed, To find out instead" (1941*); "In spite of all urgin' She stayed grimly virgin, And fainted when anyone goosed her" (1943A); "She awoke with a glow, But alas! 'twas not so!" (1945C); "But when she awoke, She found it a joke" (1946A); "She awoke with a smile, And enjoyed it a while" (1949); "She found out instead That a spring in the bed Had poked through the mattress and goosed her" (1946B).

There was a young virgin of Worcester
Who said, when her boyfriend seduced her,
  "With his cock and his eggs
    In between my spread legs,
I felt like a hen with a rooster."   [1942.

909.   By ice-cold ablutions
       And nightly pollutions
    Which she'd had since a very small child.   [1952.

MOTHERHOOD

914. BOMBAY (Back Bay, Bray, Calais, Cape May, Le Hay, Malay). Swift's *Tale of a Tub* (1704, MS. 1697) Sect. II, begins with three sons who, attempting to find the letters of the word "shoulder-knot" in their father's will, cannot find a K anywhere in it, and finally satisfy themselves that "it was a gross mistake in our language to spell 'knot' with a K; but that from henceforward... it should be writ with a C."—which leaves it perilously close (*totidem literis,* as Swift puts it) to "cunt."

917. CAPE HORN (Vaughan). Variants: "But the rubber was thin" (1927A); "That the bloody French letter was torn" (*From Bed to Verse,* 1945, p. 68). Compare: *Allerlei saftige und seltene Mikosch-Anekdoten* (3 Auflage, Pressburg, 1892) no. 85, in a group of "heights" and other burlesque queries: "Was ist Zufall?—Wenn man sein Leben einem geplatzten Condon verdankt." (What is luck? — When a man owes his life to a busted condom.)

919. "Sheik": a brand of condom; now no longer the slang term for an attractive young man, as temp. H. M. Hull's novel of the same name (1921).

922. "Chief Batsman Kelly"?

923. The Virgin Mary is not one of the Christian Trinity, though she obviously belongs there, but was removed at the Council of Ephesus in 431. If the woman vote gets important enough, She will very likely be restored, the preliminary

step of raising Her to heaven having been made in 1950.

924. *The Week-End Book* (London: Nonesuch Press, ed. 1928) p. 316, notes, on a mild song "Michael Finnigin," "Other verses, with lines ending sin-igin and in-igin, are believed to exist."

925. Variant (beginning " St. Louis woman, she had a yen for men ") : " And now she's nursing a boggy-woggy child " (1950).

    A German girl on the river Rhine
    Went out with a Yank for a hell of a time.
        The stripper broke,
        The juice flew out,
    And now he's the father of a square-head kraut.
                                      [1952.

927.   His manner was Gallic,
       His purposes phallic   [1941.

931.   She bought all the devices
       At *fabulous* prices   [1942*

933. Old King Cole was a bugger for the hole,
With a buckskin belly and a rubber ass-hole.
    When his wife had a kid
    He stuck her in the shit
And said, " That's enough—*fa'n'gul!* "   [1952.

The first two lines (independently) recorded, Pa., 1925. " *Fa'n'gul!* " an Italian oath or threat of pedication—here as birth control.

934. F.L.: French Letter (punning on those beginning " All Gaul... ") Compare Limerick 943.

939. Short version. A longer, very castratory version of this popular parody exists. On the refrain here, compare the milder form in T. S. Eliot's *The Waste Land* (1922) III—" The Fire Sermon, " *Collected Poems* (N.Y., 1936) p. 79 :

[426]

O the moon shone bright on Mrs. Porter
And on her daughter
They wash their feet in soda water.

944. *Unexpurgated,* Bidet Press [Los Angeles, 1943] Dedication, p. iii. Compare: Mark Antony—"Madam, I am not inclined to talk." Cleopatra—"Sir, I am not prone to argue."

949. If she went with a gent
Who on screwing was bent,
It meant a new girdle for Myrtle. [1947B.

951. On an anti-Semitic passage by T. S. Eliot, "Whispers of Immortality," *Collected Poems* (N.Y., 1936) p. 62: "Grishkin is nice... Uncorseted, her friendly bust Gives promise of pneumatic bliss... The sleek Brazilian jaguar Does not in its arboreal gloom Distil so rank a feline smell As Grishkin in a drawing room."

954. There was a young lady of Hub,
Went with her beau to a pub.
But her mamma spied her,
To the bathroom hied her,
And Oh, how she made that girl scrub. [1927.

972. On the male-motherhood of authorship, see (in excelsis!) the Introduction to Kurt M. Stein's *Gemixte Pickles* (Chicago, 1927): "Bei den Quantitäts von neuen Books zu judgeh wo daily geadvertised werden, sollt man denken es iss a dernsight easier a Brainchild zu haben denn a neun pount Baby. In a way iss dass so, aber net entirely. Der main Reason dafür iss becahs in dieser Line haben die Ladies plenty competition. Das andere Bissness haben sie pretty solid bei'm tail und aufgesewed, but an Gehirnkindern haben sie noch kei exclusive Patent..."

975. RANGOON (Dragoon, June, McGoon, Moon). Variants: "But a wet dream (*or*, But jacked off and)

[427]

poured in with a spoon " (1941), " But was scraped off the sheet with a spoon " (1946B).

978. *The Week-End Book* (London: Nonesuch Press, ed. 1927) p. 157, entitled " The Mendelian Theory. "

982. SHEBA (Bathsheba, Beersheba, Rheba). Clean-up couplet, " The affectionate creature Had little to teach her, " in Christina Stead, *Letty Fox: Her Luck* (N.Y., 1946) p. 293.

983. ' Mid the drumming of bums
      To the scrimmage he comes   [1941.

984. We're here on a rape,
      And all pushed out of shape,
      And still she keeps begging for moah!   [1941.

PROSTITUTION

989. ALASKA (Doncaster, Lancaster, Master). Added line limerick. Compare Limericks 188, 1278. Variant: " But when she got spliced " (1927).

990. *Coitus Saxonius,* a contraceptive measure described in Magnus Hirschfeld's *Sexualkunde,* effected by clamping a thumb and forefinger over the base of the man's penis just as he begins to ejaculate, forcing the semen into the bladder. The hateful elements are of course obvious.

991. The tail of her shirty
      Was also quite dirty   [1927.

1002. On Miss Belle da Costa Greene, the elder Morgan's librarian.

1010. Polluted proverb: " If at first you don't succeed—keep sucking! " (1940).

[428]

1012. On a popular song of the 1920's; ultimately from Swinburne's masochist ballad, "Dolores."

1014. A reply to the rising prices of Limerick 989, and 1023.

1017. Typical catch: two outer persons, of three walking abreast, ask each other: "Do you feel like a ball?" (Both answer yes.) "Then there must be a prick between us." "No, a prick is a part of a man!"

1020. JAIPUR (Cawnpore, Debwar, Jodhpur, Lahore, Tanjore). Compare Limericks 175, 183, 509.

1021. Joan Bennett: a movie-star of the period, apparently kinder than most. U.S.O. (United Service Organization): "A civilian movement for giving cookies to soldiers in need of a screw."

1025.   She took her sarong
      And wrapped up each dong,
And sent it on an explorative tour.   [1942.

1032. The last line a parody of Villon's "Mais où sont les neiges d'antan" (But where are the snows of yore?)

1035. Chinatown price-list from Herbert Asbury's *The Barbary Coast* (1933) p. 177: "Two bittee lookee, flo bittee feelee, six bittee dooe!" (a bit being an imaginary coin worth 12 ½ cents), preceded by "China girl nice! You come inside, please?" to which is "invariably added... this extraordinary information, seldom, if ever, correct: 'Your father, he just go out!'" to which Asbury adds the pre-analytic note: "Some of the Chinese considered it an honor to possess a woman whom their fathers had also possessed." (Apocryphal Shanghai brothel-sign: "Sholt-time piecee—1 buck Mex. Long-time piecee—1 buck 'Melican. Ass-hole flee if stay all night.")

[429]

1037.   Said a naked young sailor, named Chuck,
To his cunt, "Kid, I'm shit out of luck.
I'm due back at the dock,
But I've got a stiff cock;
Spread your legs, and I'll throw you a fuck."

[1951.

1040.   Compare Limerick 904.

1042.   This is the first recorded erotic limerick, printed in *Cythera's Hymnal, or Flakes from the Foreskin* ('Oxford,' 1870) p. 70, headed "Nursery Rhymes," and followed by fifty others, to p. 82. *Poor,* in the last line, is to be pronounced dialectally, *pore.*

1046.   *That Immoral Garland* (1942) noting, "This is from Ovid," which, though unlikely, points up the direct line of descent of the limerick from the obscene verse epigrams of the Greek Anthology, Martial, and other satirists of the Graeco-Roman period, through Antonio Beccadelli of Palermo (d. 1471, to whose *Hermaphroditus,* or collection of erotic epigrams, the more famous *Manual of Classical Erotology* of Forberg—Latin original, 1824—is merely a commentary), to the *Sinngedichte* of Lessing (d. 1781) Bk. II: "The unjust mob falsely imputed love of boys to the righteous Turan. To chastise the lies what else could he do but—sleep with his sister."

1054.   During World War II in the United States, new automobiles were purportedly difficult to buy.

1057.   Compare Limerick 516.   Variant:

And if you don't mind
You may try my behind—   [1927.

1058.   A well-known joke (spoonerism) in limerick form. Note telegraphic answer: ten words.

1059.—She's a Salvation Army lass now.   [1949.

1061. SWOBODA (Baroda, Bogota, Dakota, Pajoder, Minnesota, Rhoda). With variants : " So she jumped from the couch In a helluva grouch, " " She grew very sore, Rose up from the floor " (1948A); " So she wiggled her ass To the edge of his glass, And crapped in his whiskey and soda " (1942).

1063. Variant : " With her kith and her kin, She lay writhing in sin. " Compare Limerick 1699.

1065.   As if in a trance
    She pulled off her pants   [1950.

    In the manner of whores
    She never wore drawers
And he sucked all his spunk from her orifice.
                                                             [1943B.

1067. On the legend of the " knowledgeful whore, " see the lost love-books of the Greek and Roman matriarch-prostitutes (hetaira) listed in Iwan Bloch's *Die Prostitution*. One magnificent " restoration " of a " lost " love-book of this sort is *Die Weisheiten der Aspasia* by ' Fritz Thurn ' [Fritz Foregger] privately printed in Vienna, 1923, probably the finest erotic work since Chorier's *Luisa Sigea* (c. 1659).

1068. Joke, of the impotent old man who married an acrobat: she'd stand on her head and he'd drop it in.

1069. Compare Limerick 384. Variant:

While sucking her grandfather's prick,
    Exclaimed, " I don't funk
    The taste of your spunk
It's the smell of your arse makes me sick. "   [1882.

1070. YALE (Gale, Grail, Hale, MacPhail, Marseille, St. Gail, Thrale). One of the most popular limericks in America over the last decade. Publicly published in *Peter Pauper's Limerick Book* (ed. 1942), and in William DuBois' *The Island in the Square* (1947) p. 186, with the remark: " Let's swap limericks, and enjoy ourselves for a change. " Variant: " On the tits of a hooker named Gale, Was tattooed the price of her tail " (1946A). Homosexual variant: " On the chest of a gob from Marseille " (1951).

DISEASES

1071. A sequel to Limerick 1.

1073. The slimy green cheese
Hung down to her knees
And congealed at the end of her drawers.   [1941A.

1074. BANKER (Bangkor, Casablanca, Salamanca). Compare Limericks 1098 and 1116.

1075. A variant published, as " Venereal Ode, " in the " Tonics and Sedatives " department of the *Journal of the American Medical Association* (Jan. 31, 1942) v. 118: no. 5: p. 24, with Jesus expurgated to Croesus (!) in the last stanza; lacking the fifth stanza here, and with the sixth thus :

He aches from his head to his toes,
His sphincters have gone where who knows,
    Paradoxal incontinence
    With all its concomitance
Brings forth unpredictable flows.

1087. CHESTER (DePeyster, Esther, Hester, Leicester, Nor'wester, Port Chester, Winchester). See 1691*.

1090. Variant conclusions : " I must have a D-O-S-E " (1934), " As he banged his jappap on his knee "

(1946A). Drake (1949) finds in the couplet an "elaborately disguised pun on the English meaning of the word 'pax'." (Street preacher: "Peace on you, brother." Italian peddler: "Pees on you too, you sonamabitch!") *Cleopatra's Scrapbook* (1928) p. iii, varies the following version:

"I have'e God Dam'ee hard'ee."

There was once a heathen Chinee
Who went out in the Backyard to Pee.
    Said he, "What is thisee?
    My cockee no pissee,
Hellee, God Damee, chordee."   [1928A.

There was a young man from St. Trap
Who contracted a dose of the clap.
    He said, "*Pax vobiscum,*
    Why don't my piss come?
These nuns are too much for a chap!"   [1952.

1094. The earliest politico-erotic limerick. Compare Limericks 521, 581, 603, 922. A bitter anti-Semitic caricature and editorial (ending with the accusation of dirtiness—compare Note 951) appears in *Vanity Fair* (London, Oct. 19, 1872) "Statesmen, No. 127."

1095. Crabless in Gaza.

1098. "You've stolen my wealth,
    You've ruined my health"   [1943.

    "You cost all I had
    And it wasn't half bad,
But now you've quit fucking, you fool!"   [1939A.

1108. Parodying the song "My Home in Tennessee." In *Preface to an Unprintable Opus* ["Christopher Columbo"] by 'Pedro Pococampo' (Walter Klinefelter; Portland, Maine, 1942) p. 4, an even shorter fragment is given, Mr. Klinefelter recollecting privately (1944) a section of the stanzaic portion—

not in the limerick metre — from hearing it sung
"about 25 years ago":

>   The doctors round the door
>   They to each other swore
>   They never saw before
>   Such a tool as I wore.

1112.   His *cojones* were furious
        For pleasures injurious   [1941.

Cojones furiosos: "hot nuts". A limerick version of the opening stanza of a well-known ballad, "The Spanish Nobilio," of which the tune is similar to that to which limericks are sung.

1114. Joke, of the Negro mother who names her children SyPHILis and GoNORRhea, explaining that she found these pretty names on their birth certificates.

1117. Unpleasant schoolboy versions, such as this, of the standard womb-return fantasy are common. Joke (Pa., c. 1925), on two big Irish icemen who cannot make the widow come, but the little wizened Jew can, explaining: "I just stuck my head in and puked."

1120. Frank Harris, *My Life* (Nice, 1925) v.2: p. 362.

1121. "Red-lined" and "35-1440" refer to the withholding of U.S. Army ("G.I.") pay because of venereal disease.

1123. Capivi *(copaiba)*: a remedy for gonorrhea.

1124.   Said the girls, "Oh my gosh,
        You really must wash"   [1952.

        They said, "You old dub,
        You really must scrub"   [1949.

1125. Variants: "And she valued so highly, Each *membrum virile*" (1939A; compare Limerick 1505), "She should have known better Than to refuse a French letter" (1946B).

> Their pricks she oft sucked,
> Was oft buggered and fucked,
> And at last came to grief—for the pox ate her. [1870.

1126. Safe: a condom, called "French safes" in *Jim Jam Jems* (N. Dakota, Sept. 1916) p. 23. Joke: "These condoms are guaranteed.—What happens if they break?—The guarantee runs out."

LOSSES

1132. BATES (Gates, States, Yates). Variants: "A Russian sword-dancer" (1951), "A young pirate named Bates, Was fencing one day with his mates" (1950). Joke, on a gentleman named Bates introducing his family to Abraham Lincoln: "My wife, Mrs. Bates; my daughter, Miss Bates; and my son, Master Bates." Lincoln: "Why brag about it?"

1137. Austin: a diminutive automobile of the 1930's.

> His balls hung so low
> That they swung to and fro,
> And got caught on a rock and he lost 'em. [1950.

1139. Compare the lines by Francis Jeffrey, editor of the *Edinburgh Review* (1803-29) and author of the devastating criticism of Wordsworth's *The Excursion* (1814) beginning "This will never do": "On Peter Robinson—Here lies the preacher, judge and poet, Peter, Who broke the laws of God, and man, and metre."

1141. " I don't like to see—it's a fact that I utter
That nasty word [CUNT] written up on a shutter;
And I don't like to see a man, drunk as an Earl,
Getting into a lamp-post thinking it's a girl. "—

The Pearl, no. 17 (Nov. 1880), the 13th of 15 verses titled " Things I don't like to see." (The present limerick had appeared in number 1 of *The Pearl.*) Compare the exactly similar quatrains of Pierre Louÿs' posthumous *Pybrac* (1928), each of the 256 examples beginning, " Je n'aime pas à voir... "

There was a young man from Wamsutter
Who attempted to shit on a shutter.
    There were roars of dismay
      When the shutter gave way,
And he finished his shit in the gutter.   [1952.

1142. Joke, involving " holes in the penis of a war veteran, who is recommended to see a piccolo teacher, who will teach him to ' finger that stump' so he won't urinate on strangers. Under the pretence of mere callousness, a second castration (' veteran's re-education' by the piccolo teacher) is clearly contemplated. "—G. Legman, " Rationale of the Dirty Joke, " *Neurotica,* no. 9 (1951) p. 59.

A Wagnerian tenor named Knut
Sailed a brig from Bayreuth to Beirut.
    [*Couplet from Limerick* 1132]
Now he sings in duets with a flute.   [1944.

1146. The fantasy of the chastity-belt (infibulation: female castration) here combined with castration of the male. That the chastity-belt is a fantasy, and has no historical existence, will not be argued here.

1147. [Aleister Crowley], *White Stains : The Literary Remains of George Archibald Bishop, a Neuropath of the Second Empire* (1898) p. 10 : " One flash alone illumines the darkness of his boyhood; in 1853, after being prepared for confirmation, he cried out in full assembly, instead of kneeling to receive the blessing of the officiating bishop, 'I renounce for ever this idolatrous church'; and was quietly removed."

1152. CREEK (Barking Creek, East Creek, Peek, West Creek, Wokingham Creek). Variant in the couplet: WOKING (Hoboken).

1155. Limerick version of the poem "Screwy Dick with the Spiral Prick." *Index Limericus* notes: "The boar pig takes his time very leisurely, his penis being of a corkscrew shape."—William Acton, *The Functions and Disorders of the Reproductive Organs* (1858) p. 30.

1160. "Beaver!" (also "Zitz!"): a street cry when a beard is seen. Variant:

Filled up the bath tub to receive her;
   She took off her clothes
   From her head to her toes,
And a voice at the keyhole yelled, "Beaver!" [1927.

1161. Parodying the limerick-metre poem "The Time I've Lost in Wooing" by Thomas Moore (c. 1810), with an obvious pun in "on the whole." Variant: "By wearing my drawers While climbing on whores."

1162. Compare the long-penis castration story of the man who takes too strong an aphrodisiac, whereupon his penis grows so long that it follows a girl across the street and up the stairs "—and here comes the STREETCAR!" Variant:

Who claimed he could smell cunt a block away.
   He picked up a quiff
   Who gave him the syph,
And it rotted the tip of his cock away.   [1945A.

1163. Other two-line attempts: 1357*, 1583.

1164. A joke, "The Patience of Job," in *The Pearl*, no. 5 (Nov. 1879), about a farmer reprimanded for swearing by his wife, with a reminder of the patience of Job. "Blast that damned Job... he never had his balls caught in a rabbit trap!" A. Irving Hallowell, "Aggression in Saulteaux Society," in *Psychiatry* (1940) v. 3: p. 395-407: "Some years ago... several Berens River Indians who were out hunting came upon the traps of an Indian of the Sandy Lake Band... One of the hunters, egged on by his companions, defecated on one of the traps. Then he sprung the trap so that a piece of feces was left sticking out. Such an act was an insult to the owner of the trap and a deterrent to any animal that might approach it." Compare Limerick 1184.

There was a young fellow named Bell
Whose tale is heart-breaking to tell.
    He once took a crap
    In the woods, and a trap
Underneath—oh, it's tragic as hell!   [1941.

1169. Printed on a U.S. comic post card (Boston, Mass.: Tichnor Bros., no. 651, *ante* 1948).

1171. "YES! We Have No Bananas" (1923), a phenomenally successful castratory "nonsense" song. Compare Limericks 1277, 1346.

1172. Attributed to the Hollywood biographer, Gene Fowler (a version without the second and third choruses), as is a remarkable castration novelette, *The Demi-Wang* by 'Peter Long' (New York: Privately Printed, 1931). This work is casually discussed in Herbert Kerkow's *The Fateful Star Murder* (1931) p. 197-8. It contains probably the largest number of nonce-synonyms for the penis and sexual intercourse to be found in any fictional piece in English. (Compare the strikingly similar erotic verbalization in the castration poem, *The Loves of Hero and Leander,* 1651, by J[ames] S[mith].) Both "Anne Cooper Hewitt"—first published as "The Sterilized Heiress" in *Unexpurgated* (1943) p. 45, and based on a newspaper sensation of the 1930's—and *The Demi-Wang* contain satirical references to the actress Mary Pickford, whose book *The Demi-Widow* is parodied in the title.

1180. Who suffered from inguinal hernia.
  When offered a truss
  He said with a cuss,
"Just you mind the things that concern you."
              [1870.
The text-form printed in Samuel Hopkins Adams' *A. Woollcott: his life and his world* (1945) p. 122, as Heywood Broun's "unprinted surgical limerick" (d. 1939).

1181. *That Immoral Garland* (1942), noting it as "another instance of the enduring quality of that silly legend" as to the obliquity of the Oriental vagina. Compare Limericks 198, 1481, 1641, 1686.

1183. King Jonathan Edward the third
  Was caught pederasting a bird.
    He'd rammed the thing through
    With his long, slender screw,
And had pushed out a seven-inch turd. [1952.

1185. Emperor Haile Selassie of Ethiopia, called "The Lion of Judah," driven from his throne by Mussolini in 1936.

1186. Noted in *Neurotica,* no. 9 (1951) p. 53, as a minced version of the vagina-dentata threat.

  Who was stuck for a week by the belly
    To a Jew who used glue,
    When he wanted to screw   [1944A.

1193. Compare Limerick 488. The psychoanalytic literature is rich in references to the sun as father-figure. See, in particular, "The Blazing Sun: A Psychoanalytic Approach to Van Gogh" by Jacques Schnier, in *American Imago* (July 1950), reprinted in *Neurotica,* no. 8 (1951).

1195. See Note 528.

1200. She took down her britches,
Said, " Ouch, but it itches. " [1948.

1202. Of the iambic-idiotic school. Note the suicidal-sadistic self-directed violence obviously intended for the bride.

1204. Compare Limerick 1092.

1206. A version printed in an Army joke-book, *Keep 'Em Laughing* (N.Y., 1942) by William Allan Brooks, captioned, " Sic Transit Gloria Mundi. "

1212. On the gardener, see *Genesis* 3 : 8.

1213. The original, and less sadistic version of Limerick 775. Horace Fletcher: an American businessman and nutrition crank who taught the thorough mastication — " fletcherizing " — of every mouthful of food.

1217. Compare Limerick 1189. Variant: " My God! " he exclaimed, " I perceive I am maimed. " [1943A.

1218. In attempting to bugger
A boy on a lugger [1932.

1220. Compare Limerick 439, and Notes 386, 405.

1225. Castration fantasy, parodying Gelett Burgess' famous " On Digital Extremities " (1901), itself a symbolization of the same fears.

[440]

1226. Rhymeless (anti-authoritarian: compare Whitman). On the fear of the Atom Bomb, the castratory nature of which is popularly perceived only as fear of "sterilization" after-effects. Compare the classic womb-return fantasy, with the incestuous element boldly prominent, in "The Wish" by the Earl of Rochester (d. 1680):

Oh, that I now cou'd by some Chymick Art
To Sperm convert my Vitals and my Heart,
That in one thrust I might my Soul translate,
And in the Womb my self regenerate:
There steep'd in Lust, nine Months I wou'd remain,
Then boldly fuck my Passage out again.

1230. Joke, about married men on a hunting trip, none of whom could get to sleep until the guide gave each of them a hairbrush to hold.

SEX SUBSTITUTES

1234. Variant: "And part of a tit out in Dallas" (1946B). Protracted ballad of the dynamiting of a pregnant woman's vagina by two obstetricians, "The Ballad of Chambers Street," by Dr. Fritz Irving, with the climactic stanza: "Proud Aetna in her salad days, on that Sicilian shore, Did not erupt much more abrupt than did that Hebrew whore. With mangled child she much defiled the waters of the bay; His balls fell short of Cambridge port; his cod struck there to stay."

1238. Compare Limericks 586, 602.

1246. The first limerick printed in *The Pearl,* no. 1 (July 1879), captioned "Nursery Rhymes." Often printed and collected since.

1251. See Note 1193.

1258. She said, "A bologna
 Is the real corona,
Because it never gets soft." [1927.

1266. There once was a dissolute monk
 Who fell asleep on a trunk.
  He dreamt that Venus
  Was pulling his penis,
 And woke up all covered with gunk. [1941.

1269. Is not just a super-sensorium. [1952.

1272. He lined it with hair
 And fucked it with care [1941.

 Into which he would stick
 His episcopal prick [1945.

1274. Query: "encompass"?

1276. To jizz-jazzm-spasm
 She had her orgasm
At least twice as quickly—but natch! [1952.

There was a young woman named Margo
Who came when they played Handel's Largo.
 But when they played Liszt
 She farted and pissed
Just to show what she thought of such cargo.
  [1952.
There is a young lady named Hatch
Who constantly scratches her snatch.
 'Tis not for sensation
 Of sweet masturbation,
But because of some crabs she can't catch. [1943A.

1280. His fly-buttons busted
 And he ran home disgusted [1952.

1281. "All there": the threatened insanity of masturbation, plus the equally traditional threat of castration.

[442]

1284. Limerick version (made abysmally worse in *Unexpurgated*, 1943A) of a joke far more succinct: Homosexual *(to whore)*: " Prostitute! " Whore *(to homosexual)*: " Substitute! "

A fancy young pansy, Paul Potts,
Met a whore in a store down in Watts.
 Sneered the queer, " Shoo, you floosie! "
 Roared the whore, " Don't be choosy!
After all, my dear Paul, you're ersatz! " [1943A.

1287. Compare Limerick 1247.

1288. She neighed like a filly
  ' Cause it tickled her silly,
And kept her ass warm in cold weather. [1951.

1292. Compare Note 1276.

1297. Morse (1948) p. 138, notes: " There is a case recorded of a man who masturbated in his sleep. He had a wire cage made in which he locked himself at night by strapping it around his middle, and throwing the key onto the floor. (Max Hühner, *Sexual Debility in Man*, p. 103-4.) This prevented him from giving it that last lick. "

1298. When he pulls out his needle
  They yell, " Hi, diddle deedle,
This is no fag, but a fay. " [1942.

1304. She used a dill pickle,
  Explaining, " The tickle
Is swell till the warts wear away. " [1941.

1307. To fuck herself silly
  With the stem of a lily,
And sit on a sunflower to piss. [1928A.

1311. He did it by hand
  With a synthetic gland
Which he hid in the folds of his tunic. [1943A.

1313. NORWAY (Bombay, Calais, Cambrai, Cape May, Great Bay, Hudson's Bay).

> As his penis arose
> The temperature froze
> And he shot a vanilla frappé. [1952.

1315. Compare Limericks 468, 1234, and 1308.

1316. From the Dawn Club, San Francisco, 1946. Compare Limerick 1256.

1317. By P[hilip] H[eseltine], in *The Week-End Book* (London: Nonesuch Press, ed. 1927) p. 157, captioned "The Jung Idea." In the 1928 edition "old-fashioned" becomes "long-standing." Douglas (1928) p. 80, spells out the pun on "phalluses," with a delicious burlesque Freudian letter. *Index Limericus* notes the source of the rhymes here in Gilbert & Sullivan's *Gondoliers* (1889):

> I'm aware you object
>   To pavilions and palaces,
> But you'll find I respect
>   Your Republican fallacies. (Act I, *ad fin.*)

1318. One of the most popular limericks. Compare the surprise ending of Limerick 98. Usually ends, "Your gherkin's for ferkin', not jerkin'." Also: "You're shirking your furking — get working, John Perkins!" (1939A). The rhymes are perhaps inevitable ("Of course, five cents in those days... bought a firkin of gherkins or a ramekin of fescue or a pipkin of halvah"—S. J. Perelman, "So little time marches on," in his *Keep It Crisp,* 1946, p. 49), but the ultimate source may well be the limerick-metre "Song to Ceres" by Leigh Hunt (d. 1859), published in Emerson's *Parnassus* (1875):

> Laugh out in the loose green jerkin
> That's fit for a goddess to work in,
>   With shoulders brown
>   And the wheaten crown
> About thy temples perking...

[444]

Index Limericus marvellously notes Dexter Perkins' history of the Monroe Doctrine, called *Hands Off* (Boston, 1941).

1325. RACINE (McLean). This is the limerick most frequently encountered in this research. The principal variant endings are given in the text as 1325A. First publicly printed in "The Human Machine" by John Del Torto, in *Neurotica* no. 8 (1951) p. 23, delicately modified to a "screwing machine," and with the clank-mechanical ending: "And could wank itself off in between." Del Torto also gives, as analogue, a passage from Thomas Nash, his *Dildo* (MS. 1601), first printed in John S. Farmer's *Merry, Facetious, and Witty Songs and Ballads* (1895) [v. 1:] p. 22:

"He bendeth not, nor fouldeth any deale, but standes as stiffe as he were made of steele; (And playes at peacock twixt my leggs right blithe And doeth my tickling swage with manie a sighe;) And when I will, he doth refresh me well, and never makes my tender belly swell." Poore Priapus, thy kingdom needes must fall...

The theme of the sex machine has a long history and a complex psychological background which cannot be handled here. But see Victor Tausk's "On the Origin of the 'Influencing Machine' in Schizophrenia" (1919) translated in *Psychoanalytic Quarterly* (1933) and abridged in *Neurotica* no. 8 (1951) with additional notes of relevance to science fiction. Examples of the sex machine fantasy will be found in De Nerciat's *Les Aphrodites* (1793), in "The New Patent Fucking Machine," a ballad at the end of v. 2 of *The Pearl*, no. 12 (June 1880), in Eddy Smith's *Zehn Radierungen* (Berlin, 1921)—drawings of forms for both male and female, reprinted in the "Ergänzender Bilderteil" to Hirschfeld and Linsert's *Liebesmittel* (Berlin, 1930)—in *Memoirs of a Russian Princess* 'by Katoumbah Pasha' (London-Paris, 1890) Pt. 6, the machine being named

Belphegor [!]; in two pictorial "novelties" circulated in the U.S. about 1930 and 1940: "The Delighter" (on a Ford chassis), and the "Rape-all" (with cunt-lapper and titsucker "Attachments" on the style of the present limerick); in a modern ballad, "The Great Wheel" (to the hymn-tune: "Oh Master, Let Me Walk With Thee"), beginning: "A sailor told me ere he died, I don't know whether the bastard lied, His wife had had a cunt so wide, She never could ever be satisfied" (Yale, 1939); and in Limericks 365, 1459, 1326, and limerick-sequence 1331 here. Among the endless other curiosa of the subject may be mentioned the novel *The Magnificent MacInnes* (1949) by Shepherd Mead, pocket reprinted (c. 1951) as *The Sex Machine*. (And see Drake's colophon in the bibliography here.)

Il y avait un jeune homme de Boyer
Qui fabrique une machine à futoyer.
    Concave ou convexe,
    Pour plaire aux deux sexes,
Et extrêmement simple à nettoyer.   [1941.

Homo ingenius Racina
Coitus invenit machina.
    Adapta convexus
    Utrosque pro sexus
Dispendit cum omne vagina.   [1941.

1328. "her hot hole": compare the opening line of John Marston's *The Insatiate Countesse* (1613): "What should we doe in this Countesses darke hole?"

1342.   It arose to a stand
        And insisted his hand
    Should caress it and play pocket-pool.   [1942.

1349.   When asked if he screwed
        He replied that he would,
    But he greatly preferred masturbation.   [1943.

1350. Oliver St. John Gogarty, *As I Was Going Down Sackville Street* (N.Y., 1937) chap. vi, p. 113: "I am deep in the folk-lore of the churn... the awful tragedy of it is that no one realizes what is being lost. The sea chanties were nearly all gone until a few late-comers collected half-a-dozen Bowdlerised stanzas or so. But the churn! Only one song of butter-making remains... Father Claude overheard it in Tipperary, when a buxom maid was churning, as she thought, all alone. She had buttocks like a pair of beautiful melons. Her sleeves were rolled up. She had churned from early morning. Her neck was pink with exercise. Her bosom laboured, but she could not desist, for the milk was at the turn. Up and down, desperately she drove the long handle: up and down, up and down and up and up for a greater drive. The resistance grew against the plunger. Her hips and bosom seemed to increase in size while her waist grew thin. In front of her ears the sweat broke into drops of dew. She prayed in the crisis to the old forgotten gods of the homestead! Twenty strokes for ten! Gasping, she sang:

'Come, butter!
Come, butter!
Come, butter,
Come!
Every lump
As big as
My bum!'"

1354. And fixed her thoughts on the sublime. [1952.

1356. Variants: La Platte, Spratt, Tatt; "the village idiot sat." Compare Limerick 1672.

There was a young fellow named Pratt
Who was terribly sassy and fat   [1944A.

There once was a priest, Father Pat,
Who would roar out the *Magnificat*   [1943B.

[447]

1357. Unfinishable variant (or two-line limerick, compare 1163) proposed at the American Limerick Society, c. 1944 :

> There was a young girl from Vancouver
> Who was raped by President Hoover.

1358. He woke screaming defiance
      Of religion and science   [1952.

1360. Morse (1948) p. 140, noting this as a short-lived patriotic number of World War II on the various U.S. Women's Auxiliary Corps, adds " the story about the men who were comparing notes. One asked, ' Which would you rather have : A Wac in a shack, A Spar in a car, or a Wave in a cave ? ' The other replied, ' A sheep in a jeep '. " Add (c. 1944) the soldier who was busted out of the service for putting Wacs on the floor, and the sailor who was sucked under the boardwalk by a big Wave.

1362. As she felt his cock swell
      She exclaimed, " What the hell! "
So he went to the doctor's to dock it.   [1942.

ECCENTRICITIES

1368. The color was there,
      The likeness quite fair,
But the odor—my god, what a failure.   [1928c.

> It was rounded and rosy
> And *looked* like a posy,
> But the scent, on the whole, was a failure.   [1941.

1369. Single-rhyme limerick. Compare 1226, 1318, and 1413.

1371. BARODA (Bogota, Fashoda, Rhoda, Yahoda). Professor LaBarre is particularly disturbed—as who would not be—by this limerick, mentioning it in his 1939 article three times (the maximum for any other limerick is twice), and coming back to it in "The Apperception of Attitudes," in *American Imago* (1949) v. 6: p. 35, in reference to a resentful Gypsy woman pictured with sewing hoop and needles in William Steig's *The Lonely Ones* (1942) p. 84-5. (See the reply in Limerick 1494.)

> She covered the walls
> With millions of balls,
> And papered the ceiling with scrota.   [1952.

1372. Compare Note 170.

1377. California, 1948.

1379 The original of Limerick 914.

1382. This catch-phrase, usually rallying one's own fart (delivered on leaving a group) survives from at least Chaucer's time ("Somnour's Tale," 1400, l. 440) and the similar bequest in *Gyl of Braintfords Testament,* printed by Robert Copland about 1560 from a much older manuscript, and reprinted for private circulation by F. J. Furnivall (1871; Ballad Society, 7-a).

1384. I.e. "ask my arse," a type of wit called "selling bargains," and dating from at least the time of Queen Anne. Pope notes, in his *Bathos, or The Art of Sinking in Poetry* (1727) Swift-Pope Miscellanies, "last" vol., p. 111: "The principal branch of the *alamode* is the Prurient... It consists... of selling of bargains, and *double entendre.*" According to Francis Grose, *A Classical Dictionary of the Vulgar Tongue* (1788) *s.v.* bargain: it is "frequently alluded to by Dean Swift, who says the maids of honour often amused themselves with it. It consisted in the seller naming his or her hinder parts, in answer to the question, What? which the buyer was artfully led to ask. As a specimen, take the following instance: A lady would come into a room full of company, apparently in a fright, crying out, It is white, and follows me! On any of the company asking, What? she sold him the bargain, by saying, Mine a—e."

1389. The etymology is an even more vexed problem, than the question of whether to spell "jism"— as meaning semen (also courage: compare "spunk")—with a *g* or a *j*. It appears to be the final syllable of the word "orgasm." There is also some (later?) connection with the word "jazz" (meaning both a type of music and sexual intercourse), which is believed to be of African Negro origin. The phrase "jizz-jazzm-spasm," combining both (see Note 1276 here) has been reported, perhaps apocryphally, as a placard on a New Orleans carnival street band, about 1915.

1390. A variant of Limerick 769, with further variants in Note 725.

1398. Stanza 7 often occurs separately (variants: Halls, Niagara Falls, St. Paul's, Sioux Falls), and ending: "His favorite trick Was to skin back his prick, And slide off the stage (rollerskate off) on his balls" (1939A), followed by:

And this WAS a wonderful sight
And the ladies just swooned with delight.
    The men felt so blue
    At the things he could do
That they jacked themselves off, out of sight.
[1947B.

1409. Oliver St. John Gogarty, *As I Was Going Down Sackville Street* (N.Y., 1937) chap. XX, p. 295: lines 1-2 only, attributing the limerick to James

[450]

Joyce, but adding "I have heard that 'not once or twice in our rough island's story'." (Compare Note 1350, and the couplet of Limerick 1659.) The text version is corrupt. Original:

> 'Twould tempt the archbishop
> The way that you swish up
> Your skirts when the weather is rainy.

1410. Compare Limerick 1265.

1414. Lines 1-2 in Aldous Huxley's *Eyeless in Gaza* (1936), with reference, p. 98, to " a whole dictionary of national biography " of limericks.

1415. Compare Limerick 1555. Blue-print obscoenum (Brooklyn, 1951): [*Under a four-line formula* :] " The angle of the dangle decreases with the sag of the bag and increases with the heat of the meat in proportion to the mass of the ass and the beauty of the cutie. "

1418. And he prayed to his Maker
      For Gloria Baker, Or...   [1941.

    And he thought in his lust
      Of the beautiful bust   [1939A.

    And then, quite undaunted
      Declared that he wanted   [1941.

    He said, " Nothing will do
      But a screw or else two, From...   [1941.

Another variant involves the penis instead :

Who notched his cock with a razor.
    He made it so rough
    He scuffed the tough muff   [1948.

In the following variants, the first involves two young men; the second a shepherd :

> The size of whose dinks would amaze ya.
>> They plugged with their cocks
>> The glamorous box [1941.

> "I'd much rather sleep
>> With one of my sheep
> Than bed down with Diana Duff Frazier." [1948A.

As can be seen, many industrious minds have toyed with this epic. Miss Frazier was the first of the glamour débutantes, at whose début in 1938 some thirty thousand dollars were spent in a single night.

1425. A variant of one of the verses of "The Girl I Left Behind Me," a parody of a Civil War song, beginning: "Oh she jumped in bed And covered up her head, And said I couldn't find her, But she knew damn well She was lying like hell, 'Cause I jumped right in behind her" (Mich., 1935).

1430. "...the Talmudic version of the sin of... Ham is not that he *saw* or even laughed at his father's drunken nakedness (*Genesis*, 9: 22, and compare Lot's, *Genesis*, 19: 31 ff.), but that he castrated his father *(Sanhedrin, 70a)* in order that there be no further heirs to share the earth."—G. Legman, in *Neurotica*, no. 9 (1951) p. 62.

1431. Compare Shakespeare's similar euphemism in *Romeo and Juliet* (1597) II. i. 38:

Ah *Romeo* that she were, ah that she were
An open *Et caetera,* thou a poprin Peare.

The word expurgated is "arse," *open-arse* being, in the slang of the time, "that kinde of fruite As maides call Medlers when they laugh alone," since medlars split open when ripe and are then thought to look and smell like the vulva.

1436. Drake (1949) notes this as "An example of the curious phenomenon that any word whatever may be used to denote certain organs or acts, without the faintest danger of ambiguity." On the other hand, the verb "insert" in the present limerick rather points the way.

1441. Pig-Latin.

1443. This sequence is by R. S., author of probably the best American erotic novel, *The Devil's Advocate* 'by Wood C. Lamont' ('Chicago' [New York], 1942), 200 p., mimeographed. The pseudonym used was intended to suggest authorship by Clement Wood. Revised mimeo reprint, 1951.

1452. *That Immoral Garland* (1942) with the literal translation: "The old philosopher named Kant had pure reason for his playmate, time was his paramour, and in his night-stool the future of cosmic space could be read."

1457. Compare Limerick 1227, of which the last word should probably be "thing."

1465. See, in the New York tabloids, Summer 1950-51, the high farce of the anti-homosexual police at Jones Beach and Fire Island in bathing suits, with their badges pinned to the backs of their ukeleles. Since when: Orgy (for Orchard) Beach.

1466. "Shitty Ditties," in *Songs My Mother Never Taught Me* (N.Y., 1944). Political variant:

A little French poodle named Leon
Was looking for something to pee on.
    With human acumen
    He picked Harry Truman,
Upon which we all can agree on.   [1952.

1468. Joke, on girl who pays a thousand dollars to a doctor so she'll scream and carry on like a virgin on her wedding night. Later asks the doctor how he did it. "Simple. Knots in the hair."

1471. On Mme. Lupescu, mistress of King Carol of Roumania, see *Life,* Feb. 19, 1940, and the *Times Literary Supplement,* Aug. 8, 1942, p. 386. *Index Limericus* notes Mary Mills Patrick's *Under Five Sultans* (N.Y., 1929).

1473. An extremely popular limerick, and the only non-original example given in *That Immoral Garland* (1942) which continues the theme with Limerick 1474. On the dream and other symbolic equivalence of ladders or stairs and forbidden coitus, compare *Genesis,* 28 : 10-12, and 32 : 24-32. (On the thoughtless "unto this day" in the last cited passage—which, unto *this* day, forbids sirloin, T-bone, and porterhouse steaks to all Jews except the temple priests—compare Note 496.)

1478. Compare Limerick 901.

1480. Girl (*to music-store clerk*) : " Have you got Hot Lips on a 10-inch Decca ? " Clerk : " No, but I've got hot nuts on a 9-inch pecker. " Girl : " Is that a record ? " Clerk : " Well, it's better than average. "

1483. Compare Limerick 1504.

1485 Transmitted with this brutal translation into false rhymes :

There once was a girl sweet and modest,
Who protected her jewel with much protest.
    But now she admits
    That a prick that just fits
Is the thing that her least does molest.   [1952.

1486. The last limerick in *Cythera's Hymnal* (1870).

1487. On ocular intercourse compare Limericks 292 and 1285.

1495. Parodying Gilbert and Sullivan's *Pinafore* (1878).

[454]

1496. When asked to come out
       She replied, with a shout   [1928.

       When she got there
       And they asked for her fare   [1941.

       The neighbors came round
       And they thought he was drowned
Till he stuck up his cock and said, " Suck it. "
                                                   [1928B.
1502. Joke : Lady (*to milkman*) : " Have you the time ? "
      Milkman : " Yes, but who'll hold the horse ? "
      (Variant, with the suggestion of impotence, as in
      Note 944 : " Yes, but not the inclination. ")

1505. The widow of old Philip Wylie   [1948A.

1509. Speared an ampallang spang through his whang.
         Oh the piercing sensation,
         The wild titillation
      Of this fierce sort of Balinese bang!   [1941.

1510. With this earliest recorded socially conscious limerick, compare limerick-sequence 956 and 1221. An amazing ballad collection, combining even more clearly than *Unexpurgated* (Los Angeles, 1943) sex and socialism, is Hamish Henderson's *Ballads of World War II* (Glasgow : Caledonian Press, 1945), which includes, without any expurgation, the great " Ballad of King Faruk and Queen Farida " which was sung by English troops in Egyptian movie-theatres to the tune of *Salaam el Malik,* the national anthem, with the chorus : " O you can't fuck Farida if you don't pay Faruk. "

1512. The last limerick in *That Immoral Garland.* Three additions, ten years later, are Limericks 229, 1659, 1718.

1513. The same pun on " the part for the whole " is present, though perhaps too well hidden, in : " Tear-

[455]

fully weak, most women find it easier to effect the necessary castration symbolically, unconsciously; running off, not with the envied penis, but—by a foolish metonymy—with the pants."— G. Legman, *Love and Death : A Study in Censorship* (N.Y., 1949) p. 76.

1518. The erotic murder-mystery, *The Crimson Hairs* 'by Whidden Graham' (New York, 1934), 160 p., one of the most peculiar products of the erotica-publishing period of the 1930's depression in New York, has just some such plot.

1520. Parodying Limerick 463.

1525. There once was a preacher named Blind
Who preached out of all time and mind.
    His poor congregation
    To prevent constipation
Put fire-crackers up his behind. [1952.

1527. Limerick version of the most popular erotic ballad of the 1940's in America, " Ode to the Four-Letter Words," ending : "For the girl isn't born yet who'll stand for ' Let's fuck '. "

1528. To add to Note 426 (which rightly belongs here), a story by Russell Wilsey, on a castratory-homosexual barber, almost specifically so described, appears in *Which Grain Will Grow* (edited by Don M. Wolfe, N.Y., 1950) p. 169-76.

1529.   He set fire to the hair
    On his sweetie's affair [1939A.

    He lit a match
    To his grandmother's snatch [1950.

    He lit up the front
    Of his grandmother's cunt [1952.

1530. BALLS, *and Another Book for Suppression,* by Richard Aldington (London: E. Lahr, 1931).

1531. Polish and other first-generation immigrant people in America give Christmas candy in a "prick-sweater," sometimes with a red tip, a knitted bag for the testicles, drawstring and all, as though to wear. They hit each other with it, pose phallically as in Callot's *Balli di Sfessania* (c. 1623), etc. An Americanized red-flannel version of this is currently sold as a novelty "Tool-Warmer."

1533. Not mentioned in G. Legman's *Bibliography of Paper-Folding* (Malvern, 1952).

1537. Compare Limerick 1550, with this variant:
    He painted his tool
    To resemble a jewel   [1941.

1540. Duke *(to whore who is kissing him)*: "Now, I say! If you're going to get familiar, I jolly well shan't fuck you."

1542.   It completely unnerved her
    And his honour served her
With papers for contempt of the court.   [1942A.

1544.   He hoped to ring the gong
    But out slipped his dong,
And he went off in the air, pell mell.   [1942.

1549. Although a large number of limericks do end disastrously (see Chapter XIV here), the anti-sexual sadism of this example, as also of Limericks 1529 and 1713, is more typical of the perfectly pure "Little Willie" quatrains.

1553.   He said, "Their employment
    Cuts down [!] my enjoyment"   [1949.

1554. In Ruth Herschberger's *Adam's Rib* (1948), an attack on men, the position is seriously taken that the clitoris is superior to the penis even etymologically: that "clitoris" should really be pronounced with a long vowel, *clite-oris,* and "penis" with a short one: *pennis.*

1556. On the quasi-castration of pubic shaving, see the story "Hair" (originally titled "Midsummer Sorcery") in *Neurotica,* no. 5 (1949) p. 17.

1561. Also: "Oh they don't know navigation on the Teal" (1928C). "Over There" and "In Mobile" (also "In Cheyenne," 1947A) are parodies of the clean but castratory Spanish-American War song "The Monkeys Have No Tails in Zamboanga" (also parodied as "The Ladies Wear No Pants in San Fernando" by Robert J. Casey, as illustrated in Sterling North & Carl Kroch's *So Red the Nose* N.Y., 1935).

WEAK SISTERS

1571. Thomas Bailey Aldrich (d. 1907) in a MS. on sale at *Goodspeed's,* Boston. See *The Month at Goodspeed's Book Shop* (Jan. 1945) v. 16: p. 102.

1572. There was a bright fellow of Vendre
Whose transgressions the whole world did ponder.
    To gossips and press
    He'd tell all, but confess
The whole story in double entendres.   [1943A.

1573. In *Journal of the American Medical Association* (Jan. 17, 1942) v. 118: no. 3: p. 26, "Tonics and Sedatives." Compare Note 1075.

1579. Compare Limerick 1716.

1580. *Peter Pauper's Limerick Book* (ed. 1942).

1581. *Peter Pauper's Limerick Book* (ed. 1942) p. 93, the last limerick in the book, with tail-piece by Herb Roth showing a naked young woman with enormous buttocks riding on a donkey.

1584. In Ethel Watts Mumford's *The Limerick Up to Date Book* (San Francisco, 1903) "March 15th." Parodied in *The Pelican* (Oct. 23, 1903) with variant line 2: "Whose statues were perfectly hideous," and ending: "And we had to take something to stiddy us."

1587. Printed in various services magazines in 1944, e.g. Fort MacArthur *Alert* (June 23, 1944), and "Blitz-bits" in BMA *Blitz* (Ontario, Oct. 1944).

1588. Usually attributed to Woodrow Wilson. Compare Limericks 755-6.

1590. In Ethel Watts Mumford's *The Limerick Up to Date Book* (San Francisco, 1903) "Feb. 22nd," a Washington's Birthday special. Langford Reed, in his *Complete Limerick Book* (ed. 1926) p. 60, expurgates the "knickers" (British for panties) in the couplet to "mittens"— to rhyme with "Vicar's"!

1596. In Mumford, as above (1903) "July 1st," with illustration showing a red-bearded Highlander looking amazedly up the lady's dress. Compare, in Fred E. Woodward's *Line Lost Limericks* (1915):

There was a young woman named King
Who'd sit in a rocker and sing.
    She showed so much stocking
    They told her 'twas shocking,
But she said, "Come 'round when I swing."

1597. Printed as dedication to *Peter Pauper's Limerick Book* (Mount Vernon, 1940), with the double expur-

[459]

gation "*t—*" and "*sp—!*" but even so omitted from later editions, which are dedicated instead " To the memory of those we did not dare to print " by the editor-publisher, Peter Beilenson. The weakest sister of them all.

CHAMBER OF HORRORS

1600. " From an English Colonel who promises more. " —*Index Limericus*.

1603. H. A. Kharas, *Limericks of India* (Bombay).

1604. " Why is a prisoner about to be sentenced like a bride on her wedding night?—They both know it's going to be hard, but they don't know how long. "

1607. Errol Flynn, movie actor, involved in a sensational rape case believed to have been cooked up to restore fading public belief in his maleness. Since when, his name a synonym for ravishment. Parody, " Errol Flynn's Hymn " (on the war song " Praise the Lord and Pass the Ammunition ") with lines: " Praise the Lord, she gave me her permission, I'm too old to wait around a-swishin' " (Denver, 1943).

1609. LaBarre, p. 208, and Morse, p. 108, agree that " boovies " is " a corruption of... boobies or bubbies... a woman's breasts. " Compare Hamlet's jest to Ophelia, " I could interpret the love you beare, if I sawe the poopies dallying " (First Quarto, 1603, III. ii. 258).

1613. Ted had a prick that, erected, he
Could reach from New York to Schenectady.
    This tube in the air
    Made everyone stare,
And the women all wished they could neck Teddy.
[1942.

1616. H. A. Kharas, *Limericks of India* (Bombay).

1618. Another attempt on the same rhymes (with variant couplet: " Since a badly-aimed lay, She pissed shit every day ") :

There was a young girl from the Vistula
Who developed a bad fecal fistula.
    A lad from Alsace
    Rammed his rod up her ass—
He aimed at her cunt but he missed—Ooh la la!
[1943-1952.
Francis Grose, *A Classical Dictionary of the Vulgar Tongue* (1785) *s.v.* Pit: " To lay pit and boxes into one; an operation in midwifery or copulation, whereby the division between the anus and vagina is cut through and demolished; a simile borrowed from the playhouse ." Also, *s.v.* Eye-sore : " A disagreeable object. It will be an eye-sore as long as she lives; said by a man whose wife was cut for a fistula in ano. " A list of similar Wellerisms or " Proverbial Witticisms " (" as the man said when... ") will be found in Vincent Lean's *Collectanea* (1903) v. 2 : pt. 2 : p. 741-752.

1620. A joke version, with the White Russian general complaining that the whore has pulled up her skirt and shown him only Karl Marx' whiskers, is given in E. E. Cummings' *Eimi*, p. 309-310.

ADDENDA

1621. By a woman reader after looking through the *Unexpurgated* collection (1943A). That women are generally the villains in limericks (e.g. 1371 and 1475) has also been complained of. And compare the anti-woman sadism in folklore discussed in Notes 261, 1234, and 1549.

1624. A Boston sub-deb named Brooks
Whose hobby was reading sex books,
   She married a Cabot
   Who looked like a rabbit
And deftly lived up to his looks.   [1952.

Jack-rabbits are famous for their quick orgasm, à la Kinsey. Compare Limerick 483.

1625. From an epic, the rest fortunately lost, ending:

   And her dream made come true
   By feeding the dript goo
To her pussy: mousse de la Big Prick, now dead.

1627. Frank Harris, a literary character of the turn of the century, who made himself ridiculous in his last years with an erotic autobiography, *My Life and Loves* (1922-27), largely untrue.

1630. Compare the club in Limerick 264.

1632. Proctoscope joke ("Proctology is not a specialty; it is a perversion"): Doctor, *to a man who has swallowed his glass eye:* "I've been looking up these things for forty years, and this is the first one that ever looked back!" Also: What's the matter, Smith, don't you trust me?

1637. La Barre (1939) p. 208, on Limerick 145: "The female breasts, curiously, are spoken of only... in contexts [equating them] with the penis [in erectibility etc.].. there is no mention whatever of the physiological function of the breasts." (Exception: Limerick 1520.)

1645. From "Hawley's Diplomatic Series," an unpublished group of limericks on American diplomats in Europe, c. 1923. Here on Joseph Grew, minister to Switzerland. Compare Limerick 1685, on Richard Washburn Child, U.S. ambassador to

[462]

Italy. These are the only examples of the Diplomatic Series recovered, with a recollection (1952) of another beginning, "In Madrid..." on Alexander Pollock Moore, ambassador to Spain and husband of Lillian Russell, who figures in the limerick. (Compare Note 136.)

1650. Little Girl: "My mother says I must never let a boy put his hand up my dress. But you can put your hand *down* my dress, in back—it's the second hole you come to."

1652. Of Mark Twain's erotic and facetious pieces, "1601" is well known, and "I Thank Thee for the Bull, O God" was privately published in the 1930's by Merle Johnson, Twain's bibliographer (the verses only, but with no more than a fragment of the covering letters, which have since been discovered). The principal piece as yet unpublished is Twain's "Address to the Stomach Club of Paris, 1879: Some Remarks on the Science of Onanism," ending with a reference to the Paris Commune of 1871: "... in concluding, I say, 'If you *must* gamble away your lives sexually, don't play a Lone Hand too much.' When you feel a revolutionary uprising in your system, get your Vendôme Column down some other way—don't jerk it down."

1656. "Schule": Yiddish for synagogue.

1658. "Mary": a native woman.

1673. Vying with Limerick 351.

1674. "derrière": advertising cant for arse.

1675. The Little Red Hen and rooster are protagonists of various non-limerick folk verses.

1676. My occupation after dark
Is goosing statues in the park.
If Sherman's horse can take it
Why can't you?
("Humoresque," 1944A.)

1679. Clean original illustrated in A. B. Frost's *Stuff and Nonsense* (1888) p. 89. Compare Burton's note on the man-cannon or *Adami-top,* his rectum loaded with peppercorns and fired by a pinch of snuff applied to the nose, in the *Arabian Nights,* v. 10 : p. 235-6. (Burton Club ed., v. 10 : p. 203-4.)

1682. 1930's wit in this contretemps : " Pardon my Southern accent. " (From a Gracie Allen erotic cartoon booklet.)

1683. The identity of money and feces par excellence.

1685. See Note to Limerick 1645.

1688. " What do they call a girl who doesn't believe in contraception ? " " Mother ."

1689. " Plooking, " of course. Compare the rhymes on Brooklyn in Limerick 522, and Note 1556.

1691. On the folk notion that venereal disease cannot be transmitted via the mouth or rectum, compare Limericks 419, 1087.

1692. Slightly glozed version of the female dream of castrating men, by a lady professor :

There was a young lass hight Camilla
Who had a magical pillow.
    She'd lure men to her bed
    And when it touched their head,
Their wands would droop like a willow.   [1950.

1703. But you can bet she gave six brides a scare. [1951.

1706. She used thistles and cactuses
    In pursuit of her practices   [1943.

1707. " P.T. " : Prick-Teaser. Also C.T., cock-teaser.

1708. Joke (1951) on Tallulah Bankhead being introduced to Norman Mailer, in whose war novel, *The Naked and the Dead,* "fug" is the euphemism-of-choice: "Mailer? Mailer? Oh *yes,* dahling — you're the boy that can't spell fuck!"

1710. "Head": the privy on a ship.

1711. "Not a good limerick, belonging entirely to the genre of the obscene word introduced... at any rate the reputation of Groningen, a rural district of Holland, for general dirtiness gives the verse a point to Dutchmen."—*Index Limericus.* (However, the implication that the limerick form is used by other than English-speaking peoples is open to doubt. The examples in the present collection are certainly inauthentic.)

1712. Limerick version of a joke, itself a recent variant of the "See you when tea is ready" telegram, of which the point seems to have escaped the editor of *Anecdota Americana* [1927] p. 151*.

1714. A bit far-fetched, yet under the Nazi régime all even semi-official letters (as from business firms) closed with "Heil Hitler!" where we might say "Yours truly."

1716. Attributed to Ken Krueger by Walt Liebscher, in VoM (Dec. 1944) no. 37: p. 4. Compare 1579.

1721. "This big chimpanzee
    Is a comfort to me—"   [1952.

  "This ape has a lingam
    That's something to swing on—   [1952.

1722. Reversing the direction of entry in the usual long-penis and bride jokes: "Be careful dear; you know my weak heart.—I'll go easy passing the heart." Also: "Deep enough?—No, deeper.

—Deep enough now?—No, deeper!—*Now* is it deep enough?—Ugg ugg." With this "sadistic concept of coitus" compare Limerick 351 (*en brochette* in Tibet).

1723. On the series of advertisements showing two women posed with, and handling each other, captioned "Which twin has the Toni?" (a brand of hair-wave), which gave the go-ahead to open Lesbianism in American advertising since World War II. A novelty card, so captioned, shows twin girls in a bathtub with an Italian plumber.

1730. F. L. Wells, in *American Imago* (March 1951) v. 8 : p. 93, quotes a similar "Frau Wirtin" verse (the German counterpart of the English-language limerick — see Hayn-Gotendorf-Englisch, *Bibliotheca Germanorum Erotica et Curiosa,* 1929, v. 9 : p. 632-3, "Das Wirtshaus an der Lahn"):

> Frau Wirtin hatte 'nen Student
> Der war in furzen ein Talent.
> Er furzt' "Die letzte Rose,"
> Doch als der Sang an Aegir kam
> Da schiss er in die Hose.

1731. Many examples of "The Anal Character" hardly less absurd are cited by Karl Abraham, *Selected Papers* (1927) p. 383-6. And compare Note 683.

1732. "Folklore aside... rabbis do not customarily perform circumcisions, this being done by a minor functionary called a *mohel,* self-appointed to the work."— G. Legman, in *Neurotica* (1951) no. 9 : p. 59.

1735. Screwy Dick (Limerick 1155) revised.

1736. The Hermit of the Mohave (Limerick 463) revised for an oral-neurotic generation. See Note 261.

1738. The first literary product of the Korean War.

INDEX OF RHYMES

Limerick numbers for the names given here will be found in the main Index, following. Asterisks indicate non-rhyming first lines in the text.

A

A : *see* AY.
ABIT : Babbitt, habit.
ABLE : Grable, Mable.
ACE : Chase, Grace, Thrace.
ACES : oasis.
ACID : Manhasset.
ACIOUS : Ignatius.
ACK : Black, Brac, Karnak, Mac, Mack.
ACKER : Malacca.
ACKSTRAW : Rackstraw.
AD : Bagdad, sad.
ADAM : Adam.
ADDER : rose-madder.
ADDLE : Seattle.
ADE : jade, laid, maid, portrayed.
ADEN : Aden.
ADER : crusader.
ADLY : Hadley.
AFE : Rafe.
AGMAR : Dagmar
AGO : Oswego.
AH : bizarre.
AID : Kincaid.
AIL · Dale, Thrale, Yale.
AILYER . Australia.
AIM : Dame, name.
AIN : again, Blaine, insane, Jane, Maine, Nain, Spain, Touraine, Tulane, Twain.
AINS : Rains.
AINY : Delaney.
AIR : Adair, air, Bergère, Claire, Dare, Fair, Isère, Kildare, Lehr, O'Clare, O'Dare, Thayer, there, Ware.
AIRIER : Bavaria, Bulgaria.
AIRS : Benares.
AIRSKIN : Erskine.
AIRY : Cary, Du Barry, Harry, Mary, *see also* ARY.
AKE : Lake.
AKER : Baker.
AL : Cal., Natal.
ALCUM : Malcolm.
ALE : Braille, Dale, Thrale, Yale.
ALEM : Salem.
ALER : Taylor.
ALES : Marseilles, Wales.
ALIA : Australia, Visalia.
ALIS : Alice, Dallas.
ALISES : palaces.

[467]

ALL : all, Bengal, Gaul, Hall, McCall, Paul, Saul, Transvaal.
ALLS : Falls, Rawls, Paul's.
ALLY : O'Malley.
ALSH : Walsh.
ALTER : Gibraltar.
AM : am, Ham, Seringapatam, Siam.
AMAS : Lamas, Thomas.
AMBLE : Campbell.
AME : Dame, name.
AMES : Ames, James.
AMIN : namin'.
AMITER : McNamiter.
AMMEL : camel.
AMMER : God damn her, stammer.
AN : Afghanistan, Dan, Japan, man, Spokane.
ANA : Anna, Hannah, Havana, Louisiana, Savannah, Susquehanna.
ANCE : France, Nance, Penzance, see also ANTS.
ANCELOT : Lancelot.
AND : Brand, Durand, Lapland.
ANDA : Uganda.
ANDER : Santander.
ANDERIN : mandarin.
ANDING : Landing.
ANDLE : Mandel, Randall.
ANDLES : Randalls.
ANDOM : Grandhomme, Zaandam.
ANDOVER : Andover.
ANDY : Andy, Gandhi.
ANE : see AIN.

ANEY : Delaney.
ANG : Penrang.
ANGER : whanger.
ANGLE : Wrangle.
ANGLIA : Anglia.
ANIA : Albania.
ANIC : Alnwicke.
ANK : Frank.
ANKER : banker, ranker.
ANKS : Hanks.
ANNY : Annie, Lanny.
ANO : Milano.
ANSIT : Naragansett.
ANSOM : handsome, Ransom.
ANT : Kant, Nahant, Nant.
ANTA : Atlanta.
ANTAGE : Wantage.
ANTS : Franz, Glantz, see also ANCE.
ANTY : Ashanti, shanty.
ANUS : veteramus*.
ANZAS : Kansas.
AOS : Taos.
AP : Krapp, lap, Rapp, Yap.
APE : Cape.
APLESS : Minneapolis.
APPER : whippersnapper.
AR : Carr, helicopter, MacFarr, Saar, Starr.
ARBER : Harbor.
ARD : Bard.
ARDEN : Arden.
ARE : see AIR.
ARGE : LaFarge.
ARGLE : McFargle.
ARIA : Bavaria, Bulgaria.
ARIO : Ontario.
ARIS : Paris.

ARK : Mark, Sark, Wark.
ARKY : Sharkey.
ARL : Arles.
ARMER : Parma.
ARMS : charms.
ARRET : Barrett.
ARRIDGE : Barrage, Glengarridge, Harwich.
ARRIDGES : Claridges.
ARROW : Barrow, Harrow, Yarrow.
ARS : czars.
ARSEL : Newcastle.
ARSIS : farces.
ART : art, Bart, Montmartre, tart.
ARTA : see ARTER.
ARTED : Charted.
ARTER : Carter, La Plata, Sparta.
ARTERIS : Charteris.
ARTIN : Martin.
ARUM : geminarum.
ARY : Gary, Harry, see also AIRY.
ASHIO : Boccaccio, Horatio, patio.
ASHION : fashion, see also ATION.
ASIA : Asia, Eurasia.
ASIAN : Rabelaisian.
ASKER : Alaska.
ASKET : Nantasket, Trasket.
ASM : enthusiasm, Glenchasm, protoplasm, spasm.
ASPER : Walljasper.
ASS . Alsace, Arras, class, lass, Madras, Mass, Rheims*, Snodgrass.
ASSA : Mombassa.
ASSES : Masses, passes.
ASSER : Vassar.
ASSIS : Bellasis.
AST : Belfast, cast, vast.
ASTE : Waste.
ASTED : Gasted.
ASTER : Astor, pastor, Shasta.
ASTY : Grasty.
AT : ambulabat, begat, Bhogat, chestnut tree*, Ghat, Mount Himavat, Spratt.
ATCH : Hatch.
ATCHES : Natchez.
ATCHET : Datchet.
ATCHEWAN : Saskatchewan.
ATER : see ATOR.
ATES : Bates.
ATIC : fanatic.
ATIO : see ASHIO.
ATION : Haitian, nation, Plantation, station, see also ASHION.
ATIOUS : Ignatius.
ATOR : Decatur, tubulator.
ATS : Flats.
ATTLE : Seattle.
AUD : Maud.
AVE : Cave, Dave, Stave, Wac*.
AVEN : New Haven.
AVER : cadaver.
AVERSHAM : Claversham.

AVEY : Davey.
AVIOR : Belgravia, Moldavia.
AVISH : McTavish.
AVORY : unsavory.
AW : Bryn Mawr, DeFauw, Shaw, Warsaw.
AWL : *see* ALL.
AWN : swan.
AY : Aix, Bay, Bombay, Bray, Delray, Iowa, Kay, lay, MacKay, Manet, Marseilles, May, Norway, O'Day, Pompeii, roué, say, Shea, Vassar B.A.
AYLO : Rayloe.
AZER : Gaza, Mazur.
AZY : Daisy.

E

EBAT : ridebat.
ECCA : Mecca.
ECK : Aztec, Lautrec.
ECKS : *see* EX.
ECKTADY : Schenectady.
ECTIVE : detective.
ED : Fred, Said.
EDDING : Reading.
EDGE : Redge.
EDILY : Ederle.
EDWARD : Edward.
EE : agree, Altree, army, Capri, Dee, Dundee, flea, Lee, Leigh, McFee, McGee, Magee, me, quay, sea, tea, tree, Y.T.
EEBA : Sheba.
EECE : cerise, Greece, Nice.
EECH : preach, Veach.
EECHER : Beecher.
EECHES : leeches, Peaches.
EECONSFIELD : Beaconsfield.
EED : Tweed.
EEDIN : Dunedin.
EEDLE : Cheadle.
EEDO : Toledo.
EEDS : Leeds.
EEF : Khief.
EEGION : Norwegian.
EEGLE : Siegel, Spiegle.
EEK : Creek, Meek, Tweak.
EEKA : Topeka.
EEL : Campanile, Cécile, Deal, Mobile, Teal.
EELING : Darjeeling, Ealing, Wheeling.
EELS : Peels.
EEM : Bream, Fleam.
EEMEN : seamen, Yemen.
EEMS : Fismes, Rheims.
EEN : Aberdeen, Arlene, Cheyne, clean, Dean, Gene, Geraldine, Jean, marine, Maxine, mien, Moline, queen, Racine, Sheen.
EENIES : Sweenies.
EENIS : Aenos, Athena's, Carquinez, McMeanus, penis, Salinas, Venus.
EENO : Eno, Reno.
EENY : Mussolini, Sweeney.
EEO : Rio.
EEOLE : Creole.

EEON : Leon.
EEP : Neep, weep.
EER : Cashmere, here, Lear, queer, St. Cyr.
EERS : Algiers, queers.
EESE : Dumfries, ease, Lees, Louise, Maltese, South Greece.
EESIA : Silesia.
EESUS : Croesus, Jesus, Peloponnesus.
EET : Crete, Peet, Pete, suite, sweet, Treet, Trete.
EETEM : Antietam.
EETER : Peter, Streator.
EETH : Blackheath, Dalkeith, Keith, Leith.
EETON : Eton.
EETUS : coitus, Miletus, Milpitas.
EETY : Tahiti.
EEVER : Eva, Geneva.
EEZERS : Jesus.
EF : McNeff.
EGGS : Meggs.
EGMAN : Legman.
EGO : Oswego.
ELL : Cattell, Cornell, hotel, Morel, Pell, swell.
ELLEN . Dunellen, Llewellyn.
ELLF : Delft.
ELLION : Porcellian.
ELLO : Montebello.
ELLY : Delhi, Kelly, Nelly.
ELT : Celt, Celte.
ELTEM : Eltham.
ELTINEM : Cheltenham.

EMBER . December.
EMENS : Clemens.
EN : Ben, five-and-ten, Rennes.
ENCE : Brienz, Coblenz, Hentz, Provence.
ENCH : Bench, wench.
END : Glend, Ostend, Bend.
ENDER : vendor.
ENNIS : tennis, Venice.
ENNY : Kilkenny.
ENS : pens.
ENSIL : Strensall.
ENT : bent, Brent, Ghent, Kent, Tashkent, Trent.
ENTED : presented.
ENTIA : Placentia.
ENTIS : Prentice.
ENTOS : Barrientos.
ENTY : Bagliofuente.
EPPER : Klepper.
ER : *see* UR.
ERIL : sterile.
ERK : *see* URK.
ERIOR : Liberia, Siberia.
ERRIER : *see* ARIA.
ERRIES : Berries.
ESHION : session.
ESKU : Lupescu.
ESS : Jess.
ESSARY : Jessary.
ESSER : Odessa, Professor.
EST : Brest, undressed.
ESTER : Chester, Dorchester, Leicester, Nestor.
ESTION : Hestion.
ESTON : Preston.
ET : cadet, met, Tibet.
ETAL : Gretel.

ETCHER : Fletcher.
ETH : Beth.
ETHER : grandfather*, Heather, leather.
ETICUT : Connecticut.
ETRICK : Hetrick.
ETS : Betts.
ETTER : Gambetta.
ETTERER : letterer.
ETTERS : Fetters.
ETTO : Estretto.
EVEREND : Reverend.
EVON : Devon, Loch Leven.
EW : Corfu, Kew, you, *see also* OO.
EWBIC : cherubic.
EWCUM : Newcombe.
EWD : Bude.
EWK : Dubuque.
EWNICK : Munich.
EWR : Muir.
EWRIN : Van Buren.
EWRY : Kewry, Missouri.
EWTER : Utah.
EWZING : Schmoosing.
EX : complex, Rex, sex, Von Blecks.
EXED : oversexed.
EXETER : Exeter.
EXTER : Dexter.
EXUS : Texas.
EZURE : treasure.

I

I : fly, Kutki, Vi, Why.
IA : Hawaii, Ohio.
IANCE : Maience.
IAR : choir.
IARSE : Havre de Grace.
IAS : Machias.
IBS : Cribbs.
ICE : Price, Rice, vice.
ICES : Isis.
ICH : *see* ITCH.
ICK : Chick, Dick, Nick, prick, Wick.
ICKINEM : Twickenham.
ICKS : Hicks.
ICKY : Mickey.
ICTOR : Victor.
ID : Hassid, kid, Madrid, Syd.
IDDLE : Biddle, fiddle, Riddle.
IDE : bride, Bryde, Hyde, Kilbryde, McBride, outside, pride, Shrovetide.
IDER : Schneider, Snyder.
IDIOUS : Phidias, pretty-ass.
IDITY : frigidity.
IDNY : Sydney.
IEF : Khief.
IF : Cardiff, If.
IFE : Fife.
IFFEN : Tiffan.
IG : Drumrig.
IGGER : Bigger, trigger.
IGGIN : Balbriggan.
IGGIT : bigot.
IGGLE : O'Figgle.
IGUA : Antigua.
IHIL : Byhill.
IKE : Psyche.
IKEY : Psyche.
IKING : Viking.

ILDER : Hilda, Brunhilde.
ILE : aisle, Rhode Isle.
ILED : Child, Wylde.
ILES : St. Giles.
ILEY : O'Reilly.
ILIO : nobilio.
ILL : Bill, Brazil, McGill, Rhyll.
ILLA : Priscilla.
ILLIS : Phyllis.
ILLY : Lily, Willie.
ILMA : Wilma.
ILTS : Wilts.
IM : Djim, Jim.
IMBLE : Kimble.
IMBY : Grimby.
IME : Thyme.
IMES : Grimes.
IMON : Simon.
IMMIN : Grimmon.
IMPLE : Dalrymple.
IMRICK : Limerick.
IMS : Simms.
IMSBY : Grimsby.
IN : Berlin, East Lynne, Flynn, in, Lynn, Prynne, Wynn.
INA : Carolina, China, Medina, miner, Regina.
INAGIN : Finnegan.
INCE : Prince.
INCH : Lynch.
INCHES : Lynches.
IND : Lynd, sinned.
INED : Blind, mind.
INDA : Belinda.
INDOO : Hindu.
INE : Tyne.

ING : Byng, Chungking, King, thing, Tring.
INGE : Inge.
INGER : Ringer, Springer.
INGLE : Llanfairpwllgwyngyll.
INGO : St. Domingo.
INGS : Kings, Springs.
INICH : Greenwich.
INISTER : Axminster.
INITY : Divinity.
INJERY : gingery.
INK : Brink, Link, think.
INKUN : Lincoln.
INNER : Pinner, Skinner.
INNIN : McLennin.
INNY : Virginny.
INS : twins.
INSEY : Kinsey.
INZ : Tinz.
IOCESE : diocese.
IOLET : Violet.
IPER : Chypre, Jaipur.
IPERS : Ypres.
IPPER : Yom Kippur.
IPPY : Mississippi.
IR : *see* UR.
IRE : attire, Kilkyre, Sofia, Tyre.
IRED : Briard, desired.
IRES : friars.
IRIL : Cyril.
IRMINGEM : Birmingham.
IRON : siren.
ISCO : Frisco.
ISE : *see* IZE.
ISH : pish.
ISION : Parisian.

ISK : Fisk, Novorossisk.
ISKIN : Riskin.
ISM : Chisholm.
ISS : Bliss, miss, piss, Twyss.
ISSING : Gissing.
ISSION : *see* ITION.
ISSLEHURST : Chiselhurst.
IST : cyst, Liszt.
ISTER : Bicester, sister.
ISTULA : Vistula.
ISTWITH : Aberystwyth.
IT : Kitt, Schmitt, split, wit.
ITCH : bitch, Goditch, Iowa*, Ipswich, itch, son-of-a-bitch.
ITCHES : Dyches, sons-a-bitches.
ITCHESTER : Chichester.
ITCHIGEN : Michigan.
ITCHIN : Hitchin.
ITE : light, McKnight, night, Purdbright, tonight, white, Wight, Wright.
ITERMAN : lighterman.
ITH : Smith.
ITIE : gown*.
ITION : condition, petition.
ITIONS : Sissions.
ITIUS : Mauritius, Titius.
ITON : Brighton.
ITS : Biarritz, Fritz, Kitts, Moritz, Pitts, Ritz.
ITTLECOCK : Shittlecock.
ITTIES : cities.
ITTY : Dinwiddie.
ITUS : write us.
IVER : Shriver.
IVIT : inevit*.
IVITY : nativity.
IVVER : Tom's River.
IVVY : chivy, Tantivy.
IX : fellatrix, Hix.
IXON : Nixon.
IZ : Liz.
IZE : thighs, Van Nuys, Wise.
IZER : Anheuser.
IZES : Devizes.

O

O : Doe, Eskimo, Flo, Glasgow, Joe, Pau, Po, Soho.
OA : Samoa, spermatozoa.
OAN : *see* ONE.
OAST : Coast, Post.
OAT : throat.
OB : Bob, Robb.
OBBY : Hobby.
OBLES : Robles.
OCHES : Kadoches.
OCK : Bach, Bangkok, flock, Jock, Locke.
OCKAWAY : Rockaway.
OCKED : shocked.
OCKERY : Pitlochry.
OCKET : Lockett, Winsocket.
OCKING : bluestocking.
OCKS : Cox, Fox, Knox.
OCKSETER : Uttoxeter.
OCKY : Haki, jockey.

OD : Cape Cod, Nod.
ODA : Baroda, Swoboda.
ODDEM : Wadham.
ODDY : 'Quoddie.
ODES : Rhodes.
ODOMY : Wadham, Wanamee.
ODS : Guards.
OFF : Goff.
OFFIN : McGoffin.
OFFIS : Office.
OFT : Croft.
OGG : Fogg.
OGRAFY : biography.
OI : soy, Troy.
OICE : Royce.
OID : Freud.
OIL : Royal.
OILEM : Roylem.
OILET : Roylette.
OINS : Des Moines.
OIS : joys.
OISTER : oyster.
OIT : Detroit.
OKE : bloke, Hoke, Roque.
OKEN : Hoboken, Shamokin.
OKINGEM : Wokingham.
OKO : Sirocco.
OKUM : Oakum.
OLE : hole, Knoll, Pinole, raisins*, soul, Woods Hole.
OLES : Dutch Bols.
OLESILL : Wohl's Hill.
OLLY : Bali, Molly, Sally*.
OLON : solon.
OM : Tom.
OMA : Oklahoma, Tacoma.

OME : Nome, Rome.
OMO : Como.
ONE (long) : Cajon, Rhône, stone, Tone, Tyrone.
ONELY : Bonely.
ONES : Jones, Malones.
ONG : Boolong, Chittagong, dong, Hong Kong, King Kong, Pyongyang, Sarong.
ONGA : Tassafaronga.
ONGER : Batonger.
ONINGEN : Groningen.
ONIX : Bronix.
ONNA : Juana.
ONOR : O'Connor.
ONS : St. Johns.
ONT : Vermont.
ONTO : Toronto.
ONX : Bronx.
ONY : Mahony, Tony.
OO : Crewe, Cue, De Vue, Grew, Jew, Kalamazoo, Kew, Koo, Lou, McPugh, Peru, Prue, Purdue, screw, Sioux, Sue, you, zoo, *see also* EW.
OOBIES : Anubis.
OOBO : Jew beau.
OOBS : heiress*.
OOD : Pittwood, wood.
OOD (long) : Bude, crude, Oudh, prude, strewed.
OODA : Judah.
OODED : deluded.
OODER : Bermuda.
OODY (short) : Goody.
OOER : Clewer.
OOGAL : McDougall.

OOGE : Bruges.
OOID : Druid.
OOIE : St. Louis.
OOIN : Bruin.
OOING : Ewing, Fitz-Bluing, McEwen.
OOIS : Louis.
OOK (*short*) : Tobruk.
OOL : Choiseul, Gould, Istamboul, O'Doole, Poole, rule, Stamboul.
OOLY : Beaulieu.
OOM : Brougham, Frome, Khartoum, Rangoon*.
OOMA : Montezuma.
OOMERS : humours.
OON : baboon, moon, Rangoon.
OONO : Bruno.
OOPID : Crewe-Pitt.
OOR : Jaipur, Jodhpur, Lamour, Le Sueur, Moore, Tours.
OORIUS : Asturias, injurious.
OORY : Missouri, *see also* EWRY.
OOSA : Russa.
OOSE : Bruce, Lewis, Spruce, Toulouse.
OOSTER : Brewster, Worcester.
OOT : Beirut, Canute, Chubut, do't, foot.
OOTED : long-rooted.
OOTER : neuter.
OOTH : Duluth, Ruth.
OOTIN : Bruton.
OOTING : Tooting.
OOVER : Vancouver.

OOVIES : Louvies.
OOZE : Drews, Hughes.
OOZY : floozie, Wusih.
OPE : Good Hope.
OPIC : myopic.
OPPER : Joppa.
OPPOLIS : metropolis.
ORA : Cora.
ORAL : immoral.
ORANGE : Orange.
ORE : Bangore, Bhore, Cawnpore, Excusador, Johore, Kilgore, Lahore, ninety-four, shore, sore, Tagore, war, whore.
ORES : Azores, Dolores.
ORGAN : Morgan.
ORIA : Astoria, Gloria, Peoria.
ORIC : Warwick.
ORIEL : Oriel.
ORIGAN : Corrigan.
ORING : Goring.
ORIUM : emporium.
ORK : New York, O'Rourke, York.
ORMEE : Corbie*.
ORN : Cremorne, Horn.
ORPS : Thorpes.
ORRA : Gomorrah.
ORRENCE : Florence.
ORRIDER : Florida.
ORRIS : Torres.
ORSE : Gorse.
ORT : Connaught, Court, sport.
ORTION : Porson*.
ORTIONS : proportions.
ORTON : Norton.

ORTS : Schwartz.
ORTY : Del Norte, Shorty.
ORUM : Oram.
ORUS : chorus.
ORWAY : Norway.
OSE : clothes, Cohoes, Limoges, Montrose, Mose, nose, Rose, toes.
OSHAM : Gosham.
OSIS : suppose is.
OSS : Cross.
OSSET : Dorset, Osset.
OSSIL : Glengozzle.
OST : Frost, *see also* OAST.
OSTATE : prostrate, 1323.
OSTEN : Boston.
OSTER : Gloucester.
OSTIA : Anacostia.
OSTRUM : rostrum.
OT : hot, Mott, Scott, Shalott.
OTA : Dakota, Minnesota.
OTH : cloth.
OTHERS : Carruthers.
OTINEM : Nottingham, Tottenham.
OTION : Goshen, ocean.
OTOMY : Skat*.
OTS : Klotz.
OTSY : Nazi.
OTTEN : Grotton, Totten.
OTTY : Dottie.
OU : *see also* OW.
OU : Slough.
OUA : Palau.
OUCH : Bouch, grouch.
OUD : Dowd.
OUDA : Browder.
OUGHT (AWT) : fraught.
OUGHTER : daughter.
OUL : Cowl.
OUN : Brown, gown, Landsdowne, Piltdown.
OUND : around.
OUNTIN : Mountain.
OUS : Strauss.
OUT : mahout.
OUTH : Louth.
OVER : Dover.
OW : *see also* OU.
OWEL : Howell, Rowell.
OWELS : Howells.
OWIN : Bowen.
OWIT : poet.
OWY : Chloe.
OX : *see* OCKS.
OY : *see* OI.
OZIN : boatswain.

U

U (EW) : *see* EW.
U (OO) : *see* OO.
UB : Chubb.
UBBABLE : Zerubbabel.
UBBABUB : Zerubbabub.
UBLIN : Dublin.
UBLY : East Wubley.
UCH : much.
UCK : Canuck, Chuck, Gluck, Kentuck, Luck, struck, Zuck.
UCKER : Molucca, Tucker.
UCKET : Nantucket, Pawtucket.

UCKINGHEM : Buckingham.
UCKNOW : Lucknow.
UCKS : Le Dux.
UCKSEM : Huxham.
UCKY : Kentucky.
UD : Blood.
UFF : Bluff, Duff, stuff, Tough.
UG : Ug.
UGGER : lugger, Ramnugger.
UM : Clombe.
UMMIT : Summit.
UMMY : Rummy.
UMP : pump.
UMQUE : verumque.
UMSK : Umsk.
UN : sun, Verdun.
UNCTION : Junction.
UNDA : Munda.
UNDY : Lundy.
UNG : Jung.
UNGI : Bubungi.
UNK : drunk, monk.
UNNY : Tunney.
UNT : Blount, blunt, cunt, Hunt, runt, Wohunt.
UNTS : cunts, Luntz, once.
UNYAN : Runyan.
UP : Krupp.
UPPER : Tupper.
UPS : Tupps.
UR : Kerr.
URCH : Birch.
URD : averred, preferred, third.
URDS : Cape Verdes.
URGIN : Spitzbergen.
URK : M'Gurk, Turk.

URKIN : Perkin.
URKLY : Berkeley.
URKY : Turkey.
URL : Burrell, girl.
URM : tapeworm.
URMER : Burma.
URMIN : Herman, vermin.
URMINUS : Terminus.
URNAL : colonel.
URNER : Derna.
URNYA : hernia, Tyburnia.
URRY : Murray.
URSE : nurse, Perce.
URSHEL : Herschel.
URSIA : Persia.
URSIANS : Persians.
URSON : McPherson.
URST : Hearst.
URSTER : Foerster.
URT : Bert.
URTH : Perth.
URTLE : Myrtle.
US : McFuss.
USH : tush.
USSELS : Brussels.
UST : Crust, St. Just.
USTARD : mustard.
USTIN : Augustin.
UTH : *see* OOTH.
UTTACK : Cuttack.
UTTER : Calcutta, futter, stutter, Wamsutter.
UTTINEM : Puttenham.
UTTON : Sutton.
UVRIN : Dufferin.
UVS : Doves.
UVVERS : lovers.
UX : *see* UCKS.
UZZIN : McGuzzum*.

INDEX OF NAMES

If the name wanted cannot be found here, consult the Index of Rhymes, preceding, for other possibilities. Asterisks refer to variants in the Notes. A table of Subjects, by their inclusive numbers, faces this page.

ABELARD, 1203.
Abercrombie & Fitch, 1245.
Aberdeen, 720, 1326.
Aberystwyth, 1, 1071.
Abou ben Adhem, 1072.
Absalom, 96.
Acropolis, 1305.
Adair, 574.
Adam, 126, 1629.
Aden, 74, 446.
Adhem, Abou ben, 1072.
Adolf Hitler, 1475, 1714.
Adonis, 1700.
Aenos, 1571.
Aestchen, 801.
Afghanistan, 666.
Afrique, 882.
after all, 368.
again, 367.
agree, 803.
ah me, 1614.
Aileen, 994.
air, 1364.
aisle, 804.
Aix, 1233.
Alaska, 989.
Albania, 990.

Algiers, 512, 991.
Alice, 284, 530, 805, 826, 1136, 1234, 1628, 1701.
Alice Blue Gown, 43, 45.
all, 368.
Allawisquith, 1.
Allen, Gracie, 648, 1682*.
Alltree, 1365.
Alnwicke, 1129.
Alsace, 195, 531, 1618*.
Am, I, 265, 511.
ambulabat, 309.
Amelia, 973.
American Eagle, 708*.
Ames, 667, 1529.
amoeba, 982.
Anacostia, 992.
anchor, 1074.
Andover, 806.
Andy, 524.
Angelico, 1474.
Anglia, East, 1414.
Anheuser, 807.
Anna, 764.
Anne, 1332.
Annheuser, 807.
Annie, 148, 993, 1235.

[479]

Antietam, 765.
Antigua, 127.
Antoinette, 1558.
Antony, 1729.
Anubis, 1718.
Aphrodite, 1584.
Apocrypha, 573*.
Apollo, 1270.
Apostle, Paul the, 166.
apple tree, 111.
Aquistwith, 1.
Arden, 2, 379.
Arlene, 994.
Arles, 447.
Armistice Day, 943.
army, 1130.
around, 1676.
Arras, 448.
art, 766, 1677.
Arthur, 709.
Ashanti, 380.
Ashton-on-Lynches, 267.
Asia, 1366, 1418.
Assizes, 155, 828.
Astaire, 314.
Asti, 472.
Astor, 268, 302, 303.
Astor, John Jacob, 989.
Astor, Mary, 268.
Astoria, 668.
Astoria, Waldorf-, 302.
Asturias, 1367.
Athena, Pallas, 808.
Athol, 1513, 1579.
Atlanta, 1598.
attire, 669.
Auden, 269.
Augustin, 532.
Austin, 1137.

Australia, 449, 575, 1131, 1368.
Avenue B., 363*.
averred, 269.
Avery, 658.
Axminster, 450.
Ayre, 59.
Azerbaijan, 666.
Azores, 1073.
Aztec, 1236.

B., AVENUE, 363*.
B. A., 910.
Babbitt, 270, 929, 1369.
baboon, 576.
Bach, 202, 744, 1276, 1544.
Back Bay, 914, 1075.
Bactrian camel, 1663.
bade her, 1473.
Bagdad, 1237.
Bager, 745.
Bagliofuente, 995.
Bagoda, 1061, 1371.
Baker, 128.
Balbriggan, 451, 767, 1238.
Baldwin, 303.
Bali, 1370.
balls, grandfather's, 1426.
Baloo, Duke of, 138.
Bambino, 890.
Banark, 1345.
Bancock, 202.
Bangkok, 202, 1239.
Bangkor, 1074.
Bangore, 183, 577.
banker, 1074.
Barbara Ann Scott, 229.
Barbary ape, 584.

Bard, 1629.
Barden, 379.
Barking Creek, 1152.
Baroda, 1061, 1371.
Barrage, 776.
Barrage, Sukker, 1616.
Barrett, Elizabeth, 1240.
Barrientos, 912.
Barrier, 677.
Barrington, 670.
Barrow, 1372.
Bart, 670, 671.
Bartok, 202.
Basle, Di, 1336.
Bass, 1299.
Bates, 381, 1132.
Bathsheba, 982.
Batonger, 1241.
Baume Bengué, 1444.
Bavaria, 138, 1082.
Bay, Back, 914, 1075.
Bay, Great, 1313.
Bay, Hudson's, 1313.
Bayadere, 1085.
Bayonne, 102.
Bayreuth, 1142*.
Bay Shore, 809.
Beaconsfield, 3.
beau, Jew, 778.
Beaulieu, 4.
Bective, 152*.
Bee, 23, 1154.
Beecher, Henry Ward, 1373.
Beese, St., 28.
Beethoven, 92, 740.
begat, 913.
Beirut, 1142*, 1143.
BelAir, 314.

Belfast, 195, 578.
Belgian, 658.
Belgore, 183.
Belgrave, 463.
Belgravia, 1374.
Belinda, 810.
Bell, 1164*.
Bellaire, 314.
Bellardon, 379.
Bellasis, 1083.
Beloit, 153.
Ben, 227.
Benares, 1242.
Bench, 129.
Bend, South, 234.
Bengal, 130, 191*, 579, 638, 1243.
Bengué, Baume, 1444.
Bennett, Joan, 1021.
Benny, 1104.
Bergère, Folies, 161.
Berkeley, 271.
Berlin, 5, 190, 382, 996, 1084, 1127.
Bermondsey 1221.
Bermuda, 6, 1133.
Berne, 1645.
berries, 452.
Bert, 1375.
best, 149.
Beth, 811.
Betts, 1376.
Bevin, 543.
Bewly, 4.
Bhogat, 383, 672.
Bhore, 812.
Biarritz, 673, 775.
Bicester, 7, 453.
Biddle, 226, 293*, 813.

Biddle, Mrs., 1335.
Bigger, 1692.
bigot, 1244.
Bill, 1134.
Bings, 553.
biography, 956.
Birch, 533.
Birmingham, 534, 666.
Bistre, 7, 453.
bitch, 1245.
bitch, son-of-a, 8.
bitches, sons of, 752.
Bito, 808.
bizarre, 580.
Black, 1642.
Black Bluff, 131.
Blackheath, 384.
blacksmith, village, 1356.
Blaine, 9.
Blair, 1364.
Blecks, Von, 1555.
Blind, 1525*.
Bliss, 117*, 1377.
Bloch, 202*.
Bloggins, Bill, 1221.
Blois, 61.
bloke, 272.
Blood, 273.
Bloom, 56.
Blount, 132.
blue, nightgown of, 45.
Blue Book Tragedy, 1172.
bluestocking, 814.
Bluff, Black, 131.
Bluff, Hal the, 433*.
Bluff, Tomahawk, 131.
blunt, 385.
Blyzes, 828.
Boast, 282.

boatswain, 1135.
Bob, 1136.
Boccaccio, 386.
Boche, 1124.
Bogota, 1061, 1371.
Bois, 61, 1447.
Bols, Dutch, 454.
Bomb, the, 1226.
Bombay, 455, 464, 595*, 914, 1075, 1246, 1313.
Bonanza, 178.
Bonely, 1378.
Boolong, 1572.
Boradda, 1473.
Boris, 1231.
Boston, 1137, 1583.
Bouch, 1643.
Boulogne, 1572.
Boulton, 642.
Bowen, 133.
boy, cabin-, 528.
Boyer, 1325*.
Brac, 274.
Braille, 1070.
Brand, 1247.
Brasty, 472.
Bray, 915, 1379.
Brazil, 997, 1134, 1138.
Bream, 774, 1248.
breast, 572.
Breeze, 28.
Brenda Frazier, 1418.
Brent, 134, 1380.
Brest, 387, 537.
Brewster, 674, 908.
Briard, 998.
bride, 1719.
Bridget, 1062.
Brienz, 275.

Brigham Young, 328.
Brighton, 10, 456.
Brink, Ten, 104.
British Lion, 708*.
Bronix, 135.
Bronx, 1249.
Brooklyn, 522.
Brooks, 1624*.
Broom, 11, 56, 1187.
Brother John, 645.
Brougham, 11, 56, 1709.
Browder, Earl, 581.
Brown, 1139, 1599.
Bruce, 675, 1381.
Bruges, 276.
Bruin, 12.
Brume, 1187.
Brunhilde, 308, 1140.
Bruno, 582.
Brussels, 136.
Bruton, 1678.
Bryce, 1517.
Bryde, 676, 709.
Bryn Mawr, 183, 1447, 1573.
Bubungi, 1382.
Buckingham, 388, 538, 1383.
Buckingham Palace, 1234.
Buddha, 666, 1185.
Bude, 137, 815.
Budweiser, 807.
Bulgair, 314.
Bulgaria, 138, 677.
Buno, 582.
Buntz, 311*.
Buren, Van, 659.
Burma, 13.
Burns, Robert, 369*.

Burrell, 583.
Busch, 807.
butcher, 729*.
Butte, 1142.
Byhill, 678.
Byng, 457.
Byron, 1536.

CABIN-BOY, 528.
Cabot, 1624*.
cadaver, 458.
cadet, 351, 1250.
Cadiz, 775.
Caesar's, 934.
Cah'lina, 139.
Cajon, 277.
Cal., 14.
Calais, 914, 1304, 1313.
Calcutta, 15, 459, 679, 1141, 1251, 1600, 1693.
California, 452.
Cambrai, 1313.
camel, 1663.
Cameron Pipers, 763.
Camilla, 1692*.
Campanile, 1504.
Campbell, 816.
Canal, Suez, 74.
Cannaught, 144.
Cannes, 1582.
Canuck, 389.
Canute, 1142.
Cape, 584, 595*, 817.
Cape Cod, 278, 585, 818, 916, 1098.
Cape Corn, 917.
Cape of Good Hope, 188, 304, 561.

Cape Horn, 188, 917.
Cape May, 914, 1313.
Cape Nod, 586.
Cape Verdes, 680.
Capri, 595, 681.
Cardiff, 1384.
Carlotta, 740.
Carolina, 139.
Carolina, North, 1234.
Carolina, South, 139, 141, 235.
Carquinez, 224*, 1385.
Carr, 16, 768, 1472.
Carranza, 178.
Carruthers, 460.
Carstair, 314.
Carter, 279, 740.
Cary, 999.
Casablanca, 1074.
Cashmere, 1085.
Cass, 195.
cast, 1144.
Castoria, 668.
Catherine, Dame, 267.
Cattell, 682.
Cave, 683.
Cawnpore, 1020, 1145, 1252.
Cécile, 1445.
Celesia, 1057.
Celt, 1146.
Celte, 819.
cerise, 1474.
Cetus, 588.
Chalot, 786, 1534, 1689.
Charizes, 155.
Charlotte, 786.
charms, 1625.
Charted, 684.

Charteris, 17.
Chase, 1601.
Château d'If, 475.
Chatsworth, 658.
Cheadle, 1086, 1147.
Cheddar, 362.
Cheever, 1160.
Cheltenham, 685.
Cheltingham-Pitts, 217.
Chelton, 545.
cherubic, 140.
chest, 572.
Chester, 18, 1087.
Chester, Port, 1087.
Chester assizes, 828.
Cheyne, 539.
Chichester, 540.
chick, 919.
Chick, 1155, 1387.
Child, Washburn, 1685.
China, 49, 139, 141, 198, 235, 1019, 1388, 1481.
Chinee, 595*, 1090*.
Chiselhurst, 686.
Chisholm, 280, 1253, 1389.
Chislehurst, 686.
Chittagong, 1602.
Chivy, 687.
Chizzlehurst, 686.
Chloe, 19.
choir, 281.
Choiseul, 1656.
chorus, 1000.
Chowder, 581.
Chris, 758.
Christ, 989, 999.
Chubb, 1630.
Chubut, 461.
Chuck, 1037*, 1148.

Chungking, 142.
Chypre, 688.
Ciano, 723.
Cilesia, 1057.
Circassian, 508.
cities, 20.
Claire, 314, 598, 599, 820.
Claire, Eau, 598.
Claire, St., 599.
C-L-A-P, 1090.
Claridge, 776, 867.
Claridge's, 920.
Clark Gable, 908*, 1043.
class, 390, 1449.
Claversham, 1254.
Cleator, 432.
Clee, 1090.
Clemens, 1652.
Cleo, 92.
Cleopatra, 1729.
Clewer, 821, 1149.
Clewes, 51, 1726.
Clombe, 122.
cloth, 541.
clothes, 587.
cluck, 864.
Clyde, 335*, 676, 709.
coast, 282, 769, 1390.
Coblenz, 143, 275, 1150.
coconut tree, 519.
Cod, Cape, 278, 585, 818, 916, 1098.
Cohoes, 1255, 1309.
coitus, 588.
Cole, Old King, 933.
colonel, 21.
Como, 391.
complex, 1621.
condition, 392.

Connaught, 144.
Connecticut, 1391, 1503, 1613*.
Contrary, Mary, 393.
Cooper, Gladys, 457.
Cooter, Lake, 1553.
Cora, 1001.
Corbie, 822.
Corfu, 138, 770.
Corinthian, 258.
Coriolanus, 743.
Cornell, 145.
Corrigan, 1002.
Corvallis, 1234.
Costanza, 178.
Court, Newminster, 626.
Cowl, 1151.
Cox, 283.
Cox, Isaac, 394.
Crap, 1106.
Crawford, Joan, 1028*.
Creek, Barking (East, West, Wokingham), 1152.
Cremorne, 462.
Creole, 1256.
Crete, 146, 567, 1003.
Crewe, 22, 536, 823.
Crewe-Pitt, 1392.
Cribbs, 147.
Croesus, 589, 1075*.
Croft, 1257, 1258.
Cross, King's, 780.
crude, 1393.
crusader, 1153.
Crust, 1574.
Cue, 1008.
cunt, 83, 148, 149.
Cupid, 1392.
Cuttack, 1603.

Cyr, St., 1055.
Cyril, 590.
cyst, 395.
czars, 396.

DAGMAR, 824.
Dago, 1267.
Daisy, 1394.
Dakota, 33, 1061.
Dale, 1009, 1070.
Dalkeith, 384, 782, 825.
Dallas, 150, 284, 530, 826, 1234, 1259, 1260.
Dalrymple, 1631, 1702.
Dame, Notre, 1203.
damn her, 921.
Dan, 690, 1395.
Dante Rossetti, 736.
Daphne, 1270.
Daphnis, 19.
Dare, Dolly, 1703.
Darjeeling, 285, 762, 1261.
Das Vizes, 155.
Datchet, 1396.
daughter, 397, 591.
Dave, 463.
Davey, Miss, 1408.
David I. Walsh, 522.
Deal, 654, 691.
Dean, 542.
Dean Howells, 707.
Debussy, 1276.
Debwar, 1020.
Decatur, 398, 1664.
Decca, 1480.
December, 1206, 1604.
Dee, 23, 60, 286, 755, 803, 827, 1090, 1154.

Deel, 654, 691.
De Fauw, 24.
Delaney, 1409.
Delft, 1262.
Delhi, 692, 922, 1186, 1541.
Del Norte, 25.
Delray, 464.
deluded, 288.
Demeter, 432.
De Peyster, 1087.
Derna, 1010.
Derry, 1674.
desired, 26.
Des Moines, 151, 1011.
detective, 152.
Detroit, 153.
De Vaughan, 957.
Devizes, 155, 828.
Devon, 543.
DeVue, Mrs., 594.
Dexter, 693.
d'hôtel, maître, 50.
Di Basle, 1336.
Dick, 303, 901*, 1155, 1263, 1387, 1398.
Dick, Screwy (Dismal, Moby), 1155.
Dicks, 1300.
D'If, 475.
Dijon, 265*.
dime, five-and-, 925.
Dinah, 139.
Dinwiddie, 1157.
diocese, 565, 1657.
Dirkin, 1318.
d'Isère, 176.
Dismal Dick, 1155.
Diss, 23*.

diversions, 337.
Divinity, 829, 923.
Djim, El, 593.
Doane, Tom, 1103.
Dockery, 80, 1514.
Doe, 287.
Dolly Dare, 1703.
Dolmossal, 166.
Dolores, 1012.
Domingo, 636.
Doncaster, 989.
dong, 157, 1013.
Dorchester, 1088.
Doric, 258.
Dorothy Lamour, 1025.
Dorse, 605.
Dorset, 694.
D-O-S-E, 1090*.
do't, 369.
Dot, 786.
Dottie, 695.
Douglas McDougal, 1294.
Dover, 27, 830.
Doves, Miss, 1264.
Dowd, 1158.
Downditch, 1096.
Dragoon, 975.
Dreikoningen, 1711.
Drew, 1511.
Drews, Miss, 696.
Drisquith, 1.
Drood, 1393.
Droop, 735.
Druid, 1265, 1410.
Drumrig, 289.
drunk, 1266.
Drury, 181.
Du Barry, 1411.
Dublin, 1089.

Dubois, 61.
Dubuque, 1575.
duck, 864.
Duff, 1159.
Dufferin, 1268.
Duluth, 290, 399, 416.
Du Maurier, Gerald, 302.
Dumfries, 28.
Dundee, 60, 291, 544, 595, 773, 1090, 1154.
Dunedin, 1412.
Dunellen, 1690.
Dunmore, 1695.
Dunn, 905.
Dunstan St. Just, 597.
Dupont, 1052.
Durand, 154, 846, 1287.
Duranty, 344.
Durkin, 1318.
Dutch Bols, 454.
Dutchman, 650.
Dyches, 1413.

EALING, 29, 697, 762*.
ease, 1679.
East Anglia, 1414.
East Arden, 379.
East Asia, 1418.
East Creek, 1152.
East Dockery, 1514.
East Lynne, 831.
East Wubley, 158.
Eau Claire, 314, 598, 599.
Eden, 126, 569.
Ederle, 832.
Edward, 1183*, 1710.
Ego, 1545.
Eileen, 994.

Einstein, 1415.
Eisteddfod, 315.
El Djim, 593.
elective, 152.
Eliot, T. S., 939*, 951*.
Elizabeth Arden, 379.
Elizabeth Barrett, 1240.
Elize, 1254.
Ellen, 188.
Ellery Queen, 1518.
Elmer, 517.
El Rocque, 202.
Eltham, 545.
emporium, 1269.
Eno, 1605.
Ensil, 242.
enthusiasm, 159.
Enus, 1571.
Epping-on-Tyne, 1014.
Epstein, 836.
Equador, 160.
equation, 1415.
Ermintrude, 159, 973.
erotism, 1253.
Errol Flynn, 1607.
ersatz, 1284, 1714.
Erskine, 1015.
Eskimo, 400, 1417, 1499.
Esther, 1087.
Estrekko (Estretto), 465.
et cetera, 1431.
Eton, 30.
Eurasia, 1418.
Eureka, 901.
Eustachian, 1718.
Eva, 1160.
Ewing, 1161, 1665.

Excusador, 698.
Exe, 222.
Exeter, 31, 432.

FAIR, 1270.
Fair, Warnesby, 1674.
fallacies, 1317.
Falls, Great, 1531.
Falls, Niagara, 1130, 1202, 1398*.
Falls, Sioux, 1398*.
fanatic, 1419.
Farben, I. G., 1052.
farces, 699.
Far Rockaway, 1162, 1514.
fashion, 32.
Fashoda, 1061, 1371.
Father John, 531.
Fauw, De, 24.
Faversham, 1254.
F.B.I., 884.
fellation, 1220.
fellatrix, 292.
Felusta, 908.
Fetters, 1271.
fiddle, 293.
Fife, 37, 466, 790, 835, 1091, 1334.
Fife, Misfortunes of, 835.
Figgle, O', 499.
finish, 168.
Finnegan, 924.
Fisherwood, 269.
Fisk, 950, 1092, 1204.
Fismes, 700.
Fitch, Abercrombie &, 1245.
Fitts, 775.

Fitz, Mc-, 775.
Fitz-Bluing, 294.
FitzGerald, 1204*.
five-and-ten, 925.
Flaccus, 711.
Flats, Tortilla, 656.
flea, 1576.
Fleam, 774.
Fletcher, 295, 1420.
Fletcherizer, 1213.
Fletcher's Castoria, 668.
Flo, 379, 926.
flock, 600.
Flood, the, 273.
Floozie, Fleur de, 1460.
Florence, 601, 833.
Florida, 160.
Fluff, 379*.
fly, Spanish, 1541.
Flynn, 5, 34, 831, 863, 1607.
Foerster, 1163.
Fogg, 602.
Folies Bergère, 161.
foot, 162.
Ford, 1137*.
Foreign Legation, 1349.
Foreign Legion, 497.
Forster, 1163.
Forsytte, 1338.
Fort Franza, 178.
Fort Tryon, 572*.
Fort Tunney, 1016.
Fort Worth, 789.
Forum, 711.
four, ninety-, 496.
Fox, 546, 1421.
frail, 1070.

France, 35, 326, 335, 548, 701, 703, 834, 927, 952, 1119, 1398, 1675.
Franchot Tone, 438.
François, 61.
Frank, 1093.
Frankie & Johnny, 937.
Franklin, 1604.
Frank Sinatra, 740.
Franz, 1720.
Franza, Fort, 178.
Fraser, 1095.
fraught, 1164.
Frazer, 1095.
Frazier, Brenda, 1418.
Fred, 36, 1155.
French Louisiana, 409.
Freud, 296, 478, 980, 1317, 1414.
friar, 552.
friars, 1658.
frigidity, 1622.
Frisco, 1165.
Fritz, 775.
Frome, 467.
Front, the, 509.
Frost, 163.
Ft.: see Fort.
fuck-all, 169.
futter, 468.
Fyfe, 37, 466, 790, 835, 1091, 1334.
Fyfe, Misfortunes of, 835.

GABLE, CLARK, 908*, 1043.
Gaelic, 320.
Gail, 1070.
Galactic Patrol, 358, 359.

Galbreathe, 782.
Gale, 1070.
Galeazzo Ciano, 723.
Galena, 1606.
Galsworthy, 349.
Gambetta, 1094.
Gandhi, 603.
Ganges, 1541.
Garber, Jan, 426.
Garden of Eden, 126, 569.
Gary, 1422.
Gasted, 298.
Gates, 1132.
Gauguin, 1443.
Gaul, 169, 928.
Gaza, 1095.
Gedunk, 1266.
geminarum, 156.
Gene, 469.
Geneva, 604, 1160, 1704.
George Bernard Shaw, 1620.
Geraldine, 994, 1017.
Gerald Du Maurier, 302.
Gerald the Warrior, 302.
Ghandi, 603.
Ghat, 702.
Ghent, 164, 165, 313, 1591.
Gibbons, 807*.
Gibraltar, 299, 549.
Gilbert & Sullivan, 742.
Giles (St.), 561, 1683.
gingery, 300.
girl, 301.
Gissing, 1423.
Gladstone, 521.
Gladys Cooper, 457.
Glantz, 703.
Glasgow, 470, 516.

Glass, 195, 1581.
Glenchasm, 1166.
Glend, 1424.
Glengarridge, 776, 867.
Glengozzle, 166.
Gloria, 302.
Gloria, Sanctus &, 558.
Gloucester, 40, 303.
Gluck, 471, 864.
G-men, 1599.
gnu, 502, 1654.
God, 278, 299, 566, 1374.
God damn her, 921.
Goditch, 1096.
Godiva, 1160.
God Save the King, 195*.
God Save the Queen, 720, 740.
Goetz, 1376.
Goff, 1705.
Gomorrah, 1653.
Gone With the Wind, 714, 985.
Good Hope, 188, 304, 561.
Goody, 42.
Gore, Ormesby-, 99*.
Gorgon, 525.
Goring, 1272.
Gorse, 605.
Gosham, 1167.
Goshen, 305.
Gould, 1098.
gown, 43, 1425.
Grable, 1644.
Grace, 401, 1273, 1632.
Grace, Havre de, 473.
Gracie Allen, 648, 1682*.
Grail, 1070.
Gramercy Park, 1345.

INDEX

Granada, 41*.
grandfather's balls, 1426.
Grandhomme, 1168.
Grant, 72.
Grass, High, 473.
Grasty, 472.
Great Bay, 1313.
Great Falls, 1531.
Greece, 236, 402.
Greeks, 337*, 351.
Green, 539, 720.
Green, Wood, 720.
Greene, Belle, 1002*.
Greenwich, 167.
Greet, 1206.
Grenada, 41*.
Grenadier Guards, 1427.
Gretel, 865.
Grew, Minister, 1645.
Grimby, 866.
Grimes, 306.
Grimmon, 1428.
Grimsby, 866.
Grinnig, 62*.
Grishkin, 951.
Groningen, 1711.
Groom, 56.
Grosham, 1167.
Grott, 786.
Grotton, 918, 1099.
Grotz, 1284.
grouch, 47.
Grundy, 1293.
Guantanamo, 582.
Guards, Grenadier, 1427.
Guzen, Van, 64.

HABIT, 929.
Hadley, 1100.
Haile Selassie, 1185*, 1488.
Haitian, 930.
Haki, 1429.
Hal the Bluff, 433*.
Hale, 1070.
Hall, 169, 191, 211, 638, 931, 1169, 1398*.
Hall, Trinity, 169.
Ham, 1430.
Hamburg, 665.
Hancock, 202.
Handel, 1276*, 1680.
hand-letterer, 1431.
handsome, 339, 1577.
Hankow, 1059.
Hanks, 48.
Hannah, 403, 1432.
hansom, 339. -
Harbor, Sag, 426.
Hardon, 379.
Harper's Bazaar, 1531.
Harris, Frank, 1627.
Harrison, 1494.
Harrot, 886.
Harrow, 170, 1274.
Harry, 171, 303, 1433.
Harvard, 355, 593, 911.
Harwich, 776, 867, 1275.
Hasdrubabel, 263.
Hasiampa, 452.
Hassid, Al, 1170.
Hatch, 307, 1276.
Havana, 1171, 1277, 1346.
Haven, New, 625.
Havre, Le, 458*.
Havre de Grace, 473.
Hawaii, 1680.

Hay, Le, 914.
Haydn, 745.
Hazelhurst, 686.
Hearst, 1018.
Heather, 172.
Heaven, 543, 712.
Heiress, Sterilized, 1172.
Helen, 188, 616, 1690.
helicopter, 868.
Hell's Kitchen, 363.
Henry the porter, 637.
Hensel, 242.
Hentz, 1434.
her, damn, 921.
here, 606.
Here's To It, 367.
Herman, 1060, 1101, 1435.
hernia, 1180.
Herschel, 1436.
Hessians, 520.
Hester, 1087.
Hestion, 173.
Hetrick, 932.
Heuser, Ann, 807.
Hewitt, Anne Cooper, 1172.
Hibernia, 1228.
Hichen, 1102.
hickory, 1560.
Hicks, 404, 1300, 1437.
High Grass, 473.
Hilda, 308, 1140.
Hill, Wohl's, 662.
Himavat, Mt., 607.
Hindu, 310, 1141.
Hitchin, 1102.
Hitler, Adolf, 1475, 1714.
Hitz, 775.
Hix, Theora, 404.

Hoare, Lady Maud, 99*.
Hobb, 1136.
Hobby, Col. Oveta, 414.
Hoboken, 498, 869, 1152, 1690.
Hoke, 704.
hole, 346, 933.
Hole, Wood's, 663.
Holyoke, 705.
Hong Kong, 49, 174, 1019, 1181, 1438, 1439.
Hooton, 249*.
Hoover, 1357*.
Hope, Good, 188, 304, 561.
Hopper, 1578.
Horatio, 405.
Horn, Cape, 188, 917.
horse, 605.
Horsett, 1338.
Horsham, 973.
hot, 870.
hôtel, maître d', 50.
Hotten, 1099.
Hottentot, 73.
Houdini, 899.
Howell, 474, 706.
Howells, 707.
Hub, 954*.
Hudson's Bay, 1313.
Hugh, 54.
Hughes, 51.
human nature, 368.
humours, 871.
Hunt, 175, 608, 1278.
Hunterian chancre, 1116.
Husing, 1347.
Huxham, 52.
Hyde, 709, 1182.

INDEX

I Am, 265, 510*.
Iberia, 564.
Ibu Plantation, 1661.
Iceland, 1287.
Ickes, 33.
Id, 1545.
If, Château d', 475.
I. G. Farben, 1052.
Ignatius, 532, 561*, 1440.
Ike, 1324, 1620.
Ilder, 308.
immoral, 311.
in, 1607.
Indian Maid, 939.
Indians, 1216.
inertia, 336.
Inge, 53.
injurious, 1279.
In Mobile, 1567.
Insane, Charles the, 1183.
inspect me, 1108.
interred, 709.
Ionic, 258.
Iowa, 708*, 777, 1441.
Iphigenia, 471.
Ipswich, 1, 1097.
Ipswith, 1.
Iraq, 202.
is, suppose, 1122.
Isaac Cox, 394.
Isère, d', 176.
Isherwood, 269.
Isis, 406.
Istanbul: *see* Stamboul.
it, 1611.
it, do, 369.
itch, 609.
It's Only Human Nature, 368.

Jack, 1, 32*, 469, 1167.
Jacques, 87, 528*, 787.
jade, 1280.
Jaipur, 297, 1020, 1667.
James (St.), 1529.
Jane, 9, 237, 1442.
Jan Garber, 426.
Japan, 119, 198, 1443, 1450.
Jean, 1706.
Jeanie, 244*.
Jeeter, 432.
Jeffers, 605*.
Jehovah, 278.
Jello, 553.
Jenny Wren, 925.
Jess, 477.
Jessary, 550.
Jesus, 523, 909, 934, 989, 1081, 1508, 1707.
Jesus H. Christ, 989.
Jew, 54, 177, 502, 503, 1319.
Jew beau, 778.
Jim, 29, 610, 1348.
Jimmie, 516, 1057*.
Joan, 102.
Joan Bennett, 1021.
Joan Crawford, 1028*.
Jo-anne, 1332.
Jock, 202, 787, 1184.
jockey, 1103.
Jodhpur, 297, 1020, 1667.
Joe, 416, 1021, 1724.
Joe Louis, 486.
John, Brother, 645.
John, Father, 531.
Johnny, Frankie &, 937.
John O'Rourke, 330*.
John's (St.), 637.

Johore, 270, 312.
joie de vivre, 1704.
Jonathan Edward, 1183*.
Jones, 1694.
Joppa, 1578.
Jossyl, 166.
joys, 1451.
Juana, Sor, 1659.
Juana, Tia, 757.
Judah, 1185.
Juliet, 93.
Juncal, 579.
Junction, Nottingham, 1314.
Junction, Winchester, 570.
June, 975.
Juneau, 582.
Jung, 478, 1317*.
junk, 1266.
Jupiter, 653, 1700.
Just, St., 597, 795.

KABOSCHEM, 1167.
Kabul, 431.
Kadoches, 479.
Kalamazoo, 502, 611, 630.
Kansas, 178, 557.
Kant, 1452.
Karnak, 480.
Kashmir, 1085.
Kay, 55.
Keats, 951.
Keefe, 551.
Keith, 407, 782, 1453.
Kelly, 481, 922, 1186.
Kenmare, 1044.
Kensale, 242.
Kensington, 677*.

Kent, 179, 313, 779, 1022, 1380, 1591, 1646.
Kentucky, 180, 482, 872.
Kerr, 1454.
Kew, 502, 536, 1455.
Kewry, 181.
Key West, 387.
Khartoum, 56, 1187, 1456.
Khayyam, Omar, 875*.
Khief, 551.
kid, 489, 490.
Kiev, 551.
Kilbryde, 709.
Kildare, 314, 599, 873, 1281.
Kilgore, 1695.
Kilkenny, 1023, 1104.
Kilkyre, 552.
Kilmer, Joyce, 1469.
kilts, 1596.
Kimble, 182.
Kincaid, 1282.
King, 1457, 1596*.
Kingdom of Heaven, 543.
King Kong, 613.
King Montezuma, 620.
Kings, 553.
King's Cross, 780.
Kinsey, 483.
Kippur, Yom, 1283.
Kitchen, Hell's, 363.
Kitts, St., 427, 775, 891.
Klare, 314.
Klee, 1090.
Klepper, 1105.
Klotz, 1284.
Knair, 599.
Knight, 876.
Knoll, Oak, 1579.

Knott, 786.
Knox, 1458.
Knut, 1142*.
Kong, Hong: see Hong Kong.
Kong, King, 613.
Koo, Wellington, 1188.
Krafft-Ebing, 1414.
Krapp, Van, 1106.
Kroll, 1579.
Krupp, 1459.
Kumsong, 1738.
kunt, 58, 914, 1379.
Kuntz, Betty-Jane, 311*.
Kurd, 1638.
Kutki, 1285.

L. A., 464.
ladder, 1473.
Ladore, 1351.
LaFarge, Mamie, 1024.
Lahore, 183, 238, 1020, 1189, 1721.
laid, 1460.
Lake, 614.
Lake Cooter, 1553.
Lamas, 1461.
Lamour, Dorothy, 1025.
Lamson, 339.
Lancaster, 989.
Lancelot, 1623.
Landing, Sweden, 434.
Landsdowne, 1190.
Lanny, 1722.
lap, 1286.
La Paloma, 207.
Lapland, 1287.
La Plata, 710.

La Platte, 1356.
La Roe, 1417.
lass, 1026, 1462.
Lautrec, Toulouse-, 1446.
Lavery, 658.
lay, 57, 1448.
Lea, 60, 1107.
Leaf, 782.
Leander, 640.
Lear, 1463.
leather, 1288.
Leda, 653.
LeDux, 1027.
Lee, 58, 60, 773, 1090, 1107, 1464.
Lee, Duchess of, 755.
leeches, 1465, 1715.
Leeds, 185, 555, 1289.
Leef, 782.
Lees, 1290.
Legation, Foreign, 101, 1349.
Legman, 781.
Le Havre, 458*.
Le Hay, 914.
Lehr, 59.
Leicester, 18, 874, 1087.
Leigh, 23, 60.
Leith, 782.
Lent, 1063.
Leo, 92.
Leon, 1466.
Lesbian, 342.
Lester, 18, 874, 1087.
LeSueur, 1028.
letterer, hand-, 1431.
Levant, 72.
Leven, Loch, 712.
Lewellyn 188, 616.

Lewis, Sinclair, 1608.
liber, 711.
Liberia, 484, 563, 1291.
libido, 1545.
Lichen, 1102.
Lido, 6*.
light, red, 1029.
lighterman, 485.
Lily, 184.
Limerick, 186.
Limoges, 1467.
Lincoln, 187, 1530.
Link, 408.
Linz, 62.
Liszt, 1276*, 1292.
Livy, 687.
Liz, 875.
Lizes, 828.
Llamas, 1461.
Llanfairpwllgwyngyll, 315.
Llewellyn, 188, 616.
Llouth, 935.
Loch Leven, 712.
Locke, 202.
Lockett, 1191.
London, 604, 1196.
long-rooted, 713.
long-standing, 1317*.
Loring, 1272.
Lorraine, 348.
Lothario, 75.
Lou, 39.
Louis, Joe, 486.
Louis XIV, 276, 390, 433.
Louise, 28, 1192, 1468.
Louisiana, 409.
Louth, 935.
Louvies, 1609.
lovers, 937.

Luck, 410.
Lucknow, 1470.
Lu-Ellen, 188.
lugger, 487.
Lundy, 1293.
Luntz, 316.
Lupescu, Magda, 1471.
Lynch, 189.
Lynches, Ashton-on-, 267.
Lynd, 714.
Lynn, 5, 34, 190, 1127.
Lynne, East, 831.
Lyster, 7.

MABLE, 317, 523, 783, 1030, 1055.
Mac, 411.
Mac-, Mc-, M':
McBride, 709, 715, 1633.
McCall, 191.
McCall's, 1531.
McClellan, 188.
McDougal, 318, 1294.
MacDowell, 1730.
McEwen, 1295.
McFail, 1070.
McFargle, 412.
MacFarr, 1472.
McFee, 716.
McFitz, 775.
McFuss, 1479.
McGee, 595, 1035, 1712.
McGill, 1296, 1668.
McGoffin, 319.
McGoon, 975.
M'Gurk, 1297.
McGuzzum, 64.
MacKameter, 194.

MacKay, 1298.
McKnight, 876.
McLean, 720, 1325.
McLellan, 188.
McLennin, 413.
McMeanus, 193, 1571.
McNabs, 1096.
MacNair, 314, 599.
McNamiter, 194.
McNeff, 1580.
MacPhail, 1070.
McPherson, 320.
McPherson, Aimée, 1174.
McPugh, 65.
McTavish, 617.
Machias, 473, 717.
Mack, 192.
madder, rose-, 1473.
Madras, 123, 195, 488, 1193, 1299, 1581.
Madrid, 196, 321, 489, 719, 938, 1031.
Mae, 1304.
Mae West, 160.
MAG 94 : 496.
Magdalen, 829.
Magda Lupescu, 1471.
Magee, 1712.
Magellan, Straits of, 188, 1690.
Maggie, 893.
Mahatma (Himavat), 607.
Mahatma Gandhi, 603.
Mahony, 652*, 1723.
mahout, 514.
Maid, Indian, 939.
Maience, 322, 1475.
Maine, 197, 237, 708*, 942, 1301.

Maître d'hôtel, 50.
Malacca, 1194.
Malay, 914, 943.
Malcolm, 718.
Malley, 208, 1682.
Malones, 1476.
Maloney, 652*, 1723.
Malta, 549.
Maltese, 618.
man, 1582.
Manchukuo, 198.
mandarin, 619.
Mandel, 1302.
Manet, 1444.
Manhasset, 1713.
Man in the Moon, 338, 734.
Marcel, 725.
March, 95.
Margo, 1276*.
Marin, 224.
Marine, 469, 720, 784.
Mark, 1634.
Marseilles, 785, 943, 1032, 1070, 1075.
Martin, 721.
Martinez, 224.
Marx, 959.
Mary, 677.
Mary, Virgin, 877, 999.
Mary Contrary, 393.
Masochist Queen, 1706.
mass, 1195.
Mass., 556, 1583.
masses, 722.
Masses, New, 884.
Master, 989.
Mat, 913.
Matthias, 717.

Maud, 66, 414.
Maud Hoare, 99*.
Maurier, Gerald du, 302.
Mauritius, 1691.
Mawr, Bryn, 183, 1447, 1573.
Maxine, 1303, 1477.
May, 67, 689, 914, 944, 954, 1304, 1478.
May, Cape, 914.
May, Queen of the, 1081.
May Day, 1510.
Mayence, 322, 1475.
Mazur, 1034.
Mc: see Mac.
me, 1614.
me, inspect, 1108.
Mecca, 1480.
Medes & Persians, 337.
Medina, 198.
Meek, 415.
Meggs, 1036.
Melanesia, 1660.
Melrose, 1309.
membrum virile, 1505.
Memphis, Tenn., 925.
Merkin, 1318.
Messiah, 1680.
Met, the, 1013.
metonymy, 1513.
metropolis, 1305.
Mexico, 708*.
M'Gurk, 1297.
Michigan, 1109.
Mickey, 1037.
mien, 1196.
Mike, 1620.
Milano, 723.
Miletus, 1306.

Mill, Old, 662.
Milpitas, 945.
Min, 34.
mind, 491.
miner, 1481.
Minneapolis, 68.
Minnehaha, 587.
Minnesota, 416, 1061.
Minsk, 32*.
Minsky's, 1589.
miscarriage, 1616.
miss, 946, 1154, 1307, 1482.
Mississippi, 1038.
Missouri, 1039, 1197.
Mobile, 1308, 1483, 1567.
Moby Dick, 1155.
modesta, 1485.
Mohave, 463.
Moines, Des, 151, 1011.
Moldavia, 1486.
Moline, 1487.
Molly, 69, 976.
Molucca, 1110.
Mombassa, 1488.
monk, 557, 1266*.
Monsanto, 1052.
Montclair, 314, 598.
Montebello, 1489.
Montezuma, 620.
Montmartre, 1681.
Montpasse, 1581.
Montrose, 1255, 1309.
Moon, 975.
Moon, Man in the, 338, 734.
Moon, Woman in the, 323.
Moore, 1040.
Morel, 1490.
Morgan, 199, 523, 1002.

Morgan, J. Pierpont, 1002.
Moritz (St.), 1491.
Morris, 760.
Morse, 605.
Mose, 324.
Moses, 278*, 1122.
Mosul, 166.
Mott, 621, 786, 1534.
mountain, 325.
Mount Himavat, 607.
Mount Shasta, 1698.
Mount Tamalpais, 717.
Mozart, 202*.
Mt.: *see* Mount.
much, 70.
Muir, 724.
Muldoon, 56.
Munda, 1660.
Munich, 200, 1198, 1311.
Murray, 1492.
Mussolini, 948, 1185.
mustard, 71.
myopic, 1493.
Myrtle, 622, 878, 929, 949.
Myrtle & Rose, 1309.

NAHANT, 72, 1495.
Nain, 879.
name, 1494.
namin', 880.
Nance, 326, 492, 1111, 1199.
Nant, 1495.
Nantasket, 493.
Nantucket, 212, 417, 419, 494, 623, 1496, 1669.
Naragansett, 1497, 1647.
Nashville, Tenn., 925.

Nat, 913.
Natal, 73, 74.
Natchez, 201, 1200.
nation, 521, 1349*, 1610.
nativity, 204.
Nazi, 1004, 1714.
near here, 606.
Neep, 624.
Nelly, 935, 1186, 1498.
Nelson, 32*.
Nepal, 130.
Nero, 836.
Nestor, 327.
neuter, 328.
Nevermore, 625.
Newcastle, 329, 725.
Newcombe, 1624.
Newfoundland, 888.
New Haven, 625.
New Lots, 1284.
New Masses, 884.
Newminster Court, 626.
Newt, 1142.
New York, 330, 845, 881, 947, 1201, 1312, 1690.
Niagara Falls, 1130, 1202, 1404*.
Nice, 627.
Nick, 726.
Nigeria, 1291.
night, 495.
Nile, 804, 909.
ninety-four (94), 496.
Nixon, 727.
nobilio, Spanish, 1112.
Nod, Cape, 586.
Nome, 1041, 1499.
Nordic, 1488.
Norte, Del, 25.

500   INDEX

North Carolina, 1234.
Northumbrian, 1265.
North Pole 1313*.
Norton, 205.
Norway, 1042, 1113, 1313, 1724.
Norwegian, 497.
Nor'wester, 1087.
nose, 1043.
Nostradamus, 549*.
Notre Dame, 1203.
Nottingham, 788.
Nottingham Junction, 570, 1314.
Novorossisk, 950, 1204.
nowhere, 314.
Nubian prince, 632.
Nucket, 494.
Numero Uno, 582.
nurse, 1315.
Nuys, Van, 903.

OAK KNOLL, 1579.
Oakum, 498.
oasis, 1500.
ocean, 1501.
O'Clare, 332.
O'Connor, 1114.
O'Dare, 1044.
O'Day, Molly, 1502.
Oden, 269.
Odessa, 1047, 1725.
O'Dole, 1513.
O'Doole, 206, 1098.
Oedipus Rex, 88.
Oedipus Smith, 1699.
Office, War, 1065.
O'Figgle, 499.

Ohio, 728.
Oklahoma, 207.
Old King Cole, 933.
Old Mill, 662.
old school tie, 572.
O'Malley, 208, 1682.
Omar Khayyam, 875*.
Omsk, 356.
once, 1503.
O'Neill, 1504.
Ontario, 75.
Oram, 951.
Orange, Duke of, 1316.
O'Reilly, 1505.
Orel, 1490.
Oriel, 1506.
Ormesby-Gore, 99*.
O'Rourke, 330*, 628.
Osset, 209.
Ostend, 76, 77, 882, 1578.
Oswego, 500, 1267.
Oudh, 883.
outside, 210.
Overholt, Old, 807*.
oversexed, 501.
Over There, 1563.
own it, 1611.
Oxford, 658.
oyster, 1726.

PABST, 807.
Packard, 135.
Paduce, 430.
pagoda, 1371.
Pajoder, 1061.
palaces, 1317.
Palau, 1686.
Palestine, 569.

INDEX

Pali, 976.
Pallas Athena, 808.
Paloma, La, 207.
Pamela, 334.
Papa, 580.
Papapoulos, 1305.
papoose, 430.
Paree, 595.
Paris, 1076, 1627.
Paris green, 1118.
Parisian, 333, 1507.
Park, 642.
Parker House roll, 1579, 1716.
Parma, 78.
Parr, 1472.
Parridge, 776.
Parsee, 388*.
Passamaquoddy, 889.
passes, 884.
Passover, 1680.
past, 357*.
pastor, 420.
Pat, 672, 913.
Pat, Father, 1356*.
Pater, 130*.
patio, 386, 1649.
Pau, 334, 1205.
Paul, 169, 211, 638.
Paul, St., 130, 169, 579, 638, 737, 979.
Paul the Apostle, 166, 1323.
Paul's, St., 1344, 1530, 1531.
Pawtucket, 212, 417, 623, 1496.
Peaches, 1715.
Pearl, 1425*.
Pearse, 954.

Peek, 1152.
Peels, 629.
Peet, Roger, 1206.
Pekin, 619.
Pekinese, 1119.
Pell, 421.
Peloponnesus, 1508.
penis, 213.
Penrang, 1509.
pens, 214.
Penzance, 335, 952, 953, 1510.
Peoria, 302*, 558.
Perce, 954.
Perch, 533.
Perkin, 1207, 1318.
Perse, 954.
Persia, 336.
Persians, 337.
Perth, 215, 789, 885.
Peru, 79, 138, 502, 536, 630, 770, 886, 1008, 1045, 1319, 1511, 1650, 1654, 1727, 1728.
Pete, 735, 1286, 1320.
Peter, 955, 1633.
Peter Abelard, 1203.
Peter of Orange, 1316.
petition, 1512.
Peyster, De, 1087.
Ph.D., 65*, 911.
Phidias, 1584.
Phyfe, 790, 835.
Phyllis, 887.
picture-palaces, 1317.
Pierre's, 302*.
Pigmay, 1246.
Piltdown, 631.
Pimlico, 1059.

Pinner, 729.
Pinole, 504, 1513.
Pipers, Cameron, 763.
Pish, 216.
piss, 730.
Pitlochry, 80, 1514.
Pits, 217, 775.
Pitt, Crewe-, 1392.
Pittochery, 80, 1514.
Pitts, 217, 775.
Pittwood, 732.
Placentia, 888.
Plain Jane, 237*.
plains, 633.
Plantation, Ibu, 1661.
Plata, La, 710, 740.
plumber, 60.
Po, 218.
Podunk, 1266.
poet, 422.
Pole, 1579.
Pole, North, 1313*.
Pompeii, 1046.
Poole, 431, 559, 1098.
Pooree, 595.
Pope, the, 544, 561, 1512.
Poppopoulos, 1305.
Porcellian, 1208.
pornography, 956.
Porson, 972.
Port Chester, 1087.
Porter (Mrs.), 939, 1337.
Portland cement, 1380.
portrayed, 1585.
Port Said, 1321.
Portugal, 631*.
Post, 423.
Pott, 1533.
Potts, 1284*.

Pratt, 1356*, 1672.
preach, 1209.
preferred, 1670.
Prentice, 81.
Preston, 505, 1322.
pretty-ass, 1515.
Priam, 875*.
Price, 1517.
prick, 82.
pride, 506.
prince, 632.
Priscilla, 424.
proclivity, 204.
Professor, 1047.
proportions, 973.
prostrate, 1323.
protoplasm, 425.
Provence, 1635, 1636.
prude, 507.
Prue, 1650.
pruritus, 124.
Prynne, 219.
Psyche, 220, 1324.
Pullman, 1647.
pump, 1729.
Puno, 582.
Purdbright, 731.
Purdue, 84, 503, 536, 630, 770.
Purkin, 1318.
push-push, 519.
Putnam, 1210.
Puttenham, 1210.
Pyongyang, 1738.

QUADROON, 734.
Quaker, 128.
quay, 85.

INDEX

Quebec, 350.
Queen, 469, 1586.
Queen, Ellery, 1518.
Queen, Masochist, 1706.
Queen of the May, 1081.
Queenshall, 931.
queer, 86.
queers, 1519.
Quirt, 1375.
'Quoddie, 889.

RABELAISIAN, 1415.
Racine, 720, 1325, 1520.
Rackstraw, 1327.
Radclyffe, 910.
Rafe, 974.
Rains, 633.
raisins, 1716.
Ramnugger, 508.
Randall, 634, 1115, 1302, 1328, 1521, 1684.
Randalls, 1048.
Rangoon, 56, 221, 338, 576, 734, 791, 975, 1187, 1522.
ranker, 1116.
Ransom, 339.
Rantoul, 431.
Rapp, 1717.
Rasputin, 396.
Rattray, 1304.
Ravel, 1544.
Rawls, 1211.
Rayloe, 1523.
Reading, 1117.
Redge, 1212.
red light, 1029.
Redwing, 939.
Regina, 560, 1524.

Reilly, 505.
Reims: *see* Rheims.
Rennes, 1049.
Reno, 890, 1050, 1605.
rescue, 1471.
Reverend, 1525.
Rex, 222.
Rex, Oedipus, 88.
Rey, Del, 464.
Rhea, 1114.
Rheba, 982.
Rheims, 87, 792, 1329.
Rhine, 925*.
Rhoda, 1061, 1371.
Rhode Isle, 89.
Rhodes, 635, 1696.
Rhodesia, 1057.
Rhône, 1051.
Rhyll, 90.
Ribbarridge, 776.
Rice, 1517, 1526.
Richard of Limerick, 186.
Rick, 186, 1387.
Riddle, 223.
ridebat, 418.
rigor mortis, 1692.
Riley, 1505.
Ringer, 91.
Rio, 92.
Riskin, 793.
Ritz, 775, 1213.
River, Tom's, 1589.
roar, 47*.
Robb, 1214.
Robles, 1215.
Rock, 202.
Rockaway, Far, 1162, 1514.
Rocque, 202, 639.
Roger the Lodger, 278.

Roger Peet, 1206.
Roman candle, 1521.
Romans, 711.
Rome, 340, 1330, 1685.
Romeo, 93.
Roop, 735.
Roosevelt, 32*, 1604.
Roque, 202, 639.
Rose, 1102, 1255, 1309, 1331, 1340, 1527.
rose-madder, 1473.
Rossetti, 736.
rostrum, 1612.
roué, 1053.
Rouen, 658.
Roumania, 1471.
Roup, 735.
Rover, 76, 577.
Rowell, 706, 1730.
Roy, Little, 528.
Royal, 1732.
Royal Marine, 720.
Royce, 794.
Roylem, 1341.
Roylette, 1731.
Rue de Rennes, 1049.
rule, 1216, 1342.
Rumania, 1471.
Rummy, 1343.
runt, 509.
Runyan, 1697.
Russa, Staraya, 1060.
Russell, Jane, 136*.
Russell, Lillian, 1645*.
Ruth, 341, 399.

SAAR, 1054.
sad, 342.

Sag Harbor, 426.
said, 347, 1528, 1655.
Said, Port, 1321.
Saint (St.):
St. Beese, 28.
St. Clair, 599.
St. Claridge, 776.
St. Cyr, 1055.
St. Domingo, 636.
St. Gail, 1070.
St. Gall, 169.
St. Giles, 561, 1683.
St. James, 1529.
St. John's, 637.
St. Just, 597, 795.
St. Kitts, 427, 775, 891.
St. Louis, 93.
St. Louis woman, 925*.
St. Moritz, 1491.
St. Paul, 130, 169, 579, 638, 737, 931, 979, 1169, 1398*.
St. Paul's, 1344, 1530, 1531.
St. Roque, 639.
St. Thomas, 1532.
St. Trap, 1090*.
St. Vitus dance, 1199.
Saki, 978.
Salamanca, 1074, 1098.
Salem, 1056.
Salinas, 224.
Salique, Boulevard, 1339.
Sally, 208, 976, 1682.
Sam, 64.
Samantha, 64.
Samarkand, 1287.
Samoa, 183, 892, 977.
Samson, 339.

INDEX

San Bruno, 582.
Sanders, 339*.
San Domingo, 636.
Sandow, 339*.
Santa Fe, 1246.
Santander, 640.
Santa Sofia, 552.
Sappho, 402.
Sarasota, 33.
Sark, 642, 1345.
Sarong, Sarah, 1637.
Saskatchewan, 1739.
Savannah, 1346.
Saviour, The, 1374, 1486.
Savory, 658.
say, 428, 1118.
scape-goat, 655.
Schenectady, 1613.
Schlitz, 807.
Schmitt, 643, 738.
Schmoosing, 1347.
Schneider, 644.
Schnossel, 166.
Schreiber, 1733.
Schwartz, 225.
Scone, 102.
Scott, 621, 1533.
Scott, Barbara Ann, 229.
screw, 645.
Screwy Dick, 1155.
Scringapatam, 796.
sea, 1120.
seaman, 343.
Seattle, 230, 231, 646, 647.
Seine, 237.
Selassie, Haile, 1185*, 1488.
Semantha, 64.
Sensitive Plant, 72.
Seoul, 1738.
Seringapatam, 796.
session, 1687.
sex, 648.
sexorium, 1269.
Shakespeare, 742.
Shalott, 786, 1534, 1689.
Shamokin, 1535.
shanty, 344.
Sharkey, 978.
Shasta, Mount, 1698.
Shaw, G. B., 1620.
Shea, 94.
Sheba, 982.
Sheen, Fulton J., 547.
Sheik, 919.
Shell, 1052.
Sherry's, 302*.
shit, 893.
Shittlecock, 232.
shocked, 562.
Shore, Bay, 809.
Shores, 1073.
Shorty, 1121.
Shriver, 1733.
Shroud, 1158.
Shrovetide, 345.
Siam, 95, 455, 510, 875*.
Siamese twins, 1648.
Siberia, 563, 564.
Sid, 1545.
Sidney, 350.
Siegel, 650, 1671.
Silesia, 1057.
Simms, 565.
Simon, 894.
Simoniz Kleener, 1606.
Simple Simon, 894.
Simpson, 339.
Sinatra, Frank, 740.

Sinclair Lewis, 1608.
sinned, 985.
Sioux, 1058.
Sioux Falls, 1398*.
siren, 1536.
Sirenis, 1571.
Sirocco, 1537.
Sissions, 566.
sister, 96.
Skat, 1614.
Skimms, 565.
Skinner, 97, 233, 729.
Skymms, 565.
Slade, Miss, 603*.
slavery, 658.
Sloan, 102.
Slough, 1059.
Smith, 1538.
Smith, Joseph, 961.
Smith, Oedipus, 1699.
Sneed, 507*.
Snodgrass, 1539.
Snood, 507.
Snook, 404.
Snyder, 55, 895.
Sochipper, 528*.
Sodom, 569.
Sofia, 552, 896.
Soho, 429.
soixante-neuf, 433.
Sol, 130*.
Solomons, 1657.
solon, 1615.
son, 739.
son-of-a-bitch, 8.
sons-a-bitches, 752.
sore, 99.
Sor Juana, 1659.
soul, 346.

South, 935.
Southampton, 658.
South Bend, 234, 1578.
Southbridge, 658.
South Carolina, 139, 141, 235.
South Greece, 236.
South Minneapolis, 68.
Soy, 266.
Spain, 100, 237, 348, 513, 649, 725*, 1540.
Spanish fly, 1541.
Spanish nobilio, 1112.
Sparta, 740.
spasm, 1348.
spermatozoa, 983, 984.
Spiegel, 650, 1671.
Spitzbergen, 897.
Split, 753.
Spode, 235.
Spokane, 240.
sport, 1542.
Spratt, 1672.
Springer, 1217.
Springs, 1638.
Spruce, 430, 515.
Spurgeon, 897.
St. : *see* Saint.
stallionate, 1639.
Stamboul, 241, 431, 476, 1218, 1219, 1550, 1734.
stammer, 1223.
Stanbul: *see* Stamboul.
Stanley, 458*.
Staraya Russa, 1060.
Starkey, 978.
Starr, 1543.
Stars and Stripes, 708*
states, 1132.

station, 101, 1220, 1349.
Stave, 898.
Steinbeck, John, 656, 658*, 1236.
Stekel, 981.
sterile, 986.
Sterilized Heiress, 1172.
Steuben, 235, 348.
Stokes, 814.
Stone, 102.
Stone, Van, 904.
Storm Troopers, 1004.
Stormy Weather, 195.
Strain, 237.
Straits of Magellan, 188, 1690.
Strand, 1374.
Strauss, 651.
Stravinsky, 740*. 1347.
Stream, 1248.
Streator, 432.
Strensall, 242, 844.
strewed, 1587.
struck, 38, 1221.
stuff, 433.
Sturgeon, 897.
stutter, 1222, 1350.
Sue, 536, 1688.
Suez Canal, 74*.
suite, 349.
Sukker Barrage, 1616.
Summit, 1617.
sun, 103.
suppose is, 1122.
Surat, 672.
Surrey, 1492.
Susie, 159.
Susquehanna, 1351.
Susy, 159.

Sutter, 468.
Sutton, 652.
Svoboda, 1061.
swan, 653.
Sweden Landing, 434.
Sweeney, 244, 899.
Sweenies, 244.
sweet, 435.
swell, 1544.
Swoboda, 1061.
Syd, 1545.
Sydney, 350.
Symes, 306*.
Syms, 565.

T., Y., 363.
Tacoma, 754.
Tagore, 183, 245, 1062.
Tahiti, 1224.
Tamalpais, Mount, 717.
Tanjore, 1020.
Tantivy, 1123.
Taos, 900.
tapeworm, 516.
tart, 1684.
Tartar, 279.
Tashkent, 1063.
Tassafaronga, 1662.
Tat, 913, 1356.
Taylor, 436.
tea, 755, 1588.
Teal, 654, 1561*.
Teddy, 1613*.
Tees, 28.
Tell, William, 748.
ten, five-and-, 925.
Ten Brink, 104.
Tenn., 925.

Tennessee, 1108.
tennis, 1064, 1229, 1554.
Terminus, 1124.
Texas, 1352, 1615.
Thayer, 1735.
Theocritus, 600.
There, Over, 1563.
They a' do't, 369.
thighs, 246.
thing, young, 105.
think, 437.
third, 1183*.
Thistlehurst, 686.
Thomas, St., 1532.
Thorpes, 517.
Thrace, 518, 936, 1353.
Thrale, 1070, 1546.
Threadle, 1147.
throat, 655.
Throstle, 166.
Thun, 338.
Thwart, 205*.
Thyme, 1354.
Tia Juana, 757.
Tiber, 711.
Tiberius, 1649.
Tibet, 351, 1673.
Tiffan, 247.
Tinz, 62.
Tip, 913.
Tiss, 117.
Titian, 1473.
Titius, 352.
Tobias, 423, 717.
Tobruk, 248.
toes, 1225.
Toilem, 1341.
Toledo, 353.
Tom, 303, 739, 1226, 1469.

Tomahawk Bluff, 131.
Tommy the Tough, 439.
Tom's River, 1589.
Tone, Franchot, 438.
Tong, 209.
Toni, 1723.
tonight, 106.
Tony, 592.
tool, 1342.
Tooting, 249.
Topeka, 901.
Torbay, 464.
toreador, 160*.
Toronto, 108.
Torquay, 464.
Torres, 760.
Tortilla Flats, 656.
Totten, 797.
Tottenham, 788, 1210, 1590.
Tough, Tommy the, 439.
Toulouse, 51, 250, 641, 1355.
Toulouse-Lautrec, 1446.
Touraine, 354.
Tours, 109.
Transvaal, 115.
Trap, St., 1090*.
Trasket, 251.
Traviata, La, 744.
Treadle, 1147.
treasure, 355.
Treat, 146, 1547, 1592.
tree, 802, 1356.
tree, apple, 111.
tree, chestnut, 1356.
tree, coconut, 519.
Trees, 1469.
Treet, 146, 567, 1547.

Trent, 313, 520, 1591.
Trete, 146, 567, 1592.
trigger, 252.
Tring, 1227.
Trinity, 829, 877, 923.
Trinity Hall, 169.
Tripper, Tommy, 528*.
Triton, 456.
Trock, 202.
Troon, 338.
Troy, 440.
Truman, Harry, 1466*.
Tryon, Fort, 572.
tsars, 396.
tubulator, 63.
Tuck, 1154.
Tucker, 441, 442, 916, 1232, 1548.
Tucket, 1496.
Tulagi, 1658.
Tulane, 1549.
Tunney, 253, 1016.
Tupper, 98, 735.
Tupps, 657.
Turk, 388, 521, 1297, 1550, 1679.
Turkey, 1551.
Turkish cadet, 351.
Turks, 351.
Tush, 254.
Twain, Mark, 1634, 1651, 1652.
Tweak, 255.
Tweed, 798.
Twickenham, 116.
Twin Falls, 1531.
twins, 1648.
Twiss, 117, 758.
Twistwith, 1, 1071.

Twitchin, 1102.
two, 536.
Twyss, 117, 758.
Tyburnia, 1180, 1228.
Tyne, 1354.
Tyne, Epping-on-, 1014.
Tyre, 728, 902.
Tyrone, 1552.

UG, 1708.
Uganda, 799.
Ukraine, 237.
Ulsterman, 1146.
Umsk, 356.
undressed, 572.
Uno, Numero, 582.
unsavoury, 658.
us, write, 124.
U.S.O., 1021.
Utah, 328, 1553.
Uttoxeter, 1125.

VAN BUREN, 659.
Vancouver, 1357.
Vanderbilt - Forsytte, 1338.
Van Gogh, 1193*, 1448.
Van Guzen, 64.
Van Nuys, 903.
Van Stone, 904.
Varden, 379.
Vassar, 910, 1279, 1397.
vast, 357.
Vaughan, 917, 957.
Veach, 1358.
vendor, 256.
Vendre, 1572*.
Venerio, Mons, 75.

INDEX

Venice, 1064, 1229, 1554,
Venus, 193, 358, 523, 808, 904, 1266, 1267, 1377, 1385, 1537*, 1571, 1699, 1700.
Verdes, Cape, 680.
Verdun, 905.
vermin, 359.
Vermont, 568.
verumque, 239.
veteramus, 554.
vexed, 501.
Vi, 1593.
Vic, King, 1685.
Vicar's, 1590.
vice, 1359.
Victor, 660, 1685.
Viking, 118, 1113.
village blacksmith, 1356.
Vinsizes, 155, 828.
Violet, 906.
Virgin, The, 265, 560.
Virgin Mary, 877, 923*, 999.
Virginia reeling, 1595.
Virginny, 257.
Visalia, 1640.
Vistula, 1618.
Vitalis, 150.
Vizes, Das, 155.
Vladivostok, 202.
Vogue, 1531*.
Von Blecks, 1555.
Vue, De, 594.

WAC, 1360.
Wadham, 443, 569.
Wagnerian, 1142*.
Waldorf-Astoria, 302.
Wales, 388*, 761, 785.
Walljasper, 1361.
Walsh, David I., 522.
Wamsutter, 1141*.
Wanamee, 1619.
Wantage, 987.
war, 119.
Ware, 685, 1556.
Wark, 360.
Warnesby Fair, 1674.
War Office, 1065.
Warrior, Gerald the, 302.
Warsaw, 1066, 1620.
Warwick, 258.
Waste, 1594.
Watts, 1284*.
Waugh, 24.
Wave, 1360.
Waverly, 658.
weep, 1230.
Wellington Koo, 1188.
Wemyss, 792.
wench, 361.
Wenzel, 242.
West, 387.
West, Key, 387.
West Creek, 1152.
Weston, 505, 1322.
Westphalia, 1368.
whanger, 259.
Wheeling, 120, 762, 1231, 1595.
whippersnapper, 1557.
White, 362, 1232, see also Wight.
Whitehall, 579.
Whitely, 1396.
White Man, 1216.

whore, 1067, 1068, 1126, 1558, 1721.
why, 1559.
Whyte, 362, 1232.
Wick, 1069.
widdershins, 1648.
Wight, 121, 988.
Wilde, 909.
Wilde, Oscar, 499.
William Tell, 748
Willie, 184, 661.
Willys, 887.
Wilma, 907.
Wilts, 1596.
Winchester, 1087.
Winchester Junction, 570.
Winsocket, 1362.
Wiscosset, 694.
Wise, 1736.
wit, 1597.
withershins, 1648.
Wohl's Hill, 662.
Wohunt, 260.
Woking, 1152.
Wokingham, 444, 445.
Wokingham Creek, 1152.
Wong, 1019.
wood, 571, 1560.
Wood Green 720.
Woods Hole, 663.
Wooster, 908, 1675.
Worcester, 908, 1675.
worker, the, 957.
Wrangle, 261.
Wren, Jenny, 925
Wright, 121, 988.
write us, 124.
Wrossil, 166.
Wubley, East, 158.

Wusih, 1641.
Wylde, 909.
Wylie, Philip, 1505*.
Wynn, 5, 1084, 1127.

X, 222*.
Xavier, 1374.

YAHODA, 1371.
Yale, 125, 1070, 1363, 1546, 1561.
Yap, 1128.
Yarrow, 1737.
Yars, 396.
Yatchio, 386.
Yates, 1132.
Yemen, 800.
Yom Kippur, 1283
Yorick, 258.
York, 262, 664, 881, 1026, 1312, see also New York.
you, 573.
Young, Brigham, 328.
young thing, 105, 363.
Ypres, 763.
Y.T., 363.
Yuno, 582.

ZAANDAM, 364
Zeiss, 1131.
zeppelin, 259.
Zerubbabel, 263.
Zerubbabub, 264.
zest, 572.
Zeus, 1355.
zoo, 665.
Zuck, 365.
Zug, 275.